MODELS OF MENTAL ILLNESS

MODELS OF MENTAL ILLNESS

Systems and Theories of Abnormal Psychology

By

THADDEUS E. WECKOWICZ
M.B., Ch.B., Ph.D.

Department of Psychology
Department of Psychiatry
Center for Advanced Study in Theoretical Psychology
University of Alberta
Edmonton, Alberta, Canada

CHARLES C THOMAS · PUBLISHER
Springfield · Illinois · U.S.A.

Published and Distributed Throughout the World by
CHARLES C THOMAS · PUBLISHER
2600 South First Street
Springfield, Illinois 62717

This book is protected by copyright. No part of it may be reproduced in any manner without written permission from the publisher.

© *1984 by* CHARLES C THOMAS · PUBLISHER

ISBN 0-398-04998-X

Library of Congress Catalog Card Number: 84-7

With THOMAS BOOKS *careful attention is given to all details of manufacturing and design. It is the Publisher's desire to present books that are satisfactory as to their physical qualities and artistic possibilities and appropriate for their particular use.* THOMAS BOOKS *will be true to those laws of quality that assure a good name and good will.*

Printed in the United States of America
SC-R-3

Library of Congress Cataloging in Publication Data
Weckowicz, Thaddeus E.
  Models of mental illness.

  Bibliography: p.
  Includes index.
  1. Psychology, Pathological—Philosophy. 2. Mental health—Philosophy. I. Title. [DNLM: 1. Mental disorders. 2. Psychotherapy. 3. Psychological theory. 4. Models, Psychological. WM 100 W387m]
RC437.5.W43   1984   616.89   84-7
ISBN 0-398-04998-x

In memory of my parents
Zofia and Waclaw Weckowicz

PREFACE

This is a book on systems and theories of abnormal psychology. It is intended for senior undergraduate and junior graduate students in clinical psychology, as well as for psychiatric residents, other mental health professionals, and interested laymen. It systematically presents various approaches to mental illness and mental health from the perspectives of different disciplines. The book attempts to lay bare the philosophical presuppositions underlying diverse theories of abnormality, and the concept of man implied by each of them. It definitely does not attempt to review the experimental and clinical literature. Instead, it is concerned with the conceptual issues. The book offers a general framework for various, often conflicting, approaches to the subject, and attempts to clarify some of the controversies without presuming to settle them.

ACKNOWLEDGMENTS

The author thanks the following individuals and publishers for permission to reproduce materials as indicated. Baillière Tindall Ltd., (London) for the quotation on p. 50 reprinted from E. Kraepelin, *Lectures on clinical psychiatry*, London: Baillière & Cox, 1913, p. 1. Oxford University Press (New York) for Figures 3 and 4 in Chapter 3 reproduced from J. R. Cooper, F. E. Bloom, & R. H. Roth, *The biochemical basis of neuropharmacology*, 3rd edition, 1978, Figure 6-13, p. 146, Dopamine and norepinephrine metabolism; Figure 8-2, p. 199, Metabolic pathways available for the synthesis and metabolism of serotonin, respectively. Simon & Schuster, Inc., (New York) for quotations on pp. 106, 107, reprinted from S. Freud, *A general introduction to psychoanalysis*, New York: Washington Square Press, 1967, pp. 377-378 and 459, and 21-22, respectively. Macmillan Publishing Co. Inc., (New York) for the quotation on p. 168 reprinted from K. Merton, *Social theory and social structure*, 1968, p. 185. Holt, Rinehart and Winston (New York) for the quotation on p. 177 reprinted from M. Opler's Urbanization, psychological disorders and the heritage of social psychiatry, in S. C. Plog & R. B. Edgerton (Eds.), *Changing perspectives in mental illness*, 1969, p. 102. The quotations on p. 197 are reprinted from *The sane society* by Erich Fromm. Copyright © 1955 by Erich Fromm. Reprinted by permission of Holt, Rinehart and Winston, Publishers. Plenum Publishing Corp., for the quotation on p. 212 reprinted from M. Andolfi, *Family therapy: An interactional approach*, 1979, p. 2. Family Process, Inc., (New York) for Figure 5, Chapter 5, reproduced from D. H. Olson, D. H. Sprenkle, & C. S. Russell, Circumplex model of marital and family systems: 1. Cohesion and adaptability dimensions, family types, and clinical applications, *Family Process*, 1979, 18, p. 17, Figure 1. Sixteen possible types of marital and family systems derived from the circumplex model. The Williams & Wilkins Co., (Baltimore) for Table 1, Chapter 5, reproduced from C. Madaness & J. Haley, Dimensions of family therapy, *Journal of Nervous and Mental Diseases*, 1977, 165, p. 92, Table 1, Comparison of different approaches to family therapy according to various dimensions. Van Nostrand Reinhold for the quotations on p. 285 reprinted from A. Maslow, 02Towards psychology of being, 1962, p. 12 and 14-15. Mrs. C. Dabrowski for the quotation on p. 302 from C. Dabrowski, *Psychoneurosis is not an illness*, Gryf Press, 1972, p. 1. Harper & Row (New York) for the quotation on p. 308 reprinted from T. Szasz, *The myth of mental illness: Foundation of a theory of personal conduct*, New York: Hoeber-Harper, 1961, p. 296. Harper & Row (New York) for the quotation on pp. 313-314 reprinted from A. Boisen, *The exploration of the inner world*, 1936, pp. 367-368.

The Center for Advanced Study in Theoretical Psychology, at the University of Alberta, under the leadership of Professor J. R. Royce, with its interdisciplinary seminars, provided the necessary intellectual climate which made the undertaking of this book possible. The preliminary draft of the book has been presented at Center seminars during the 1982, spring and summer terms. The author is grateful to the participants of the seminar: Drs. Joseph R. Royce, William W. Rozeboom, William J. Baker, Richard Jung, Alexander Matejko, Charles Bourassa, Herman Tennessen, Leendert Mos, Karl Pfeifer, Kellogg V. Wilson, Harry Garfinkle, and Mr. Frederick Bell, for their constructive criticism and discussion of the text. The author owes special gratitude to Dr. Leendert Mos, the Acting Director of the Center, and to the author's wife, Dr. Helen Liebel-Weckowicz for reading critically the whole text, pointing to possible errors and ambiguities, and suggesting improvements. Also Dr. Mos, by putting the technical facilities of the Center at the author's disposal, expedited in many ways the preparation of the manuscript. The author's wife Helen helped with some German source material.

Finally, the author offers special thanks to Mrs. Frances Rowe, who intrepidly typed and retyped several versions of the manuscript, and to Mrs. Evelyn Murison for preparing the bibliography and rendering secretarial help. Without their assistance this book would not have been possible.

T. Weckowicz
Edmonton, Alberta

CONTENTS

	Page
Preface	vii

Chapter
1. Introduction:
    The Basic Issues in the Field of Mental Health ... 3
    Introductory Remarks ... 3
    Models in Sciences and in Professions ... 5
    The Outstanding Philosophical Issues
      in the Field of Mental Health ... 9
    Professional Conflicts in the Field of Mental Health ... 19
    Contents of the Book ... 21
2. Concept of Normality ... 22
    Introduction ... 22
    Different Concepts of Normality ... 23
    Various Meanings of Psychiatric Diagnosis ... 39
3. Medical Models ... 48
    Introduction ... 48
    Disease and Constitution in General Medicine ... 50
    Disease Model in Psychiatry ... 57
    Constitutional Model in Psychiatry ... 82
    Other Models ... 86
    The Role of Medical Doctor in Modern Society ... 89
4. Psychological Models ... 92
    Introduction ... 92
    Psychodynamic Models ... 104
    Developmental Models ... 121
    Behaviouristic Models ... 127
    Cognitive Models ... 145
5. Sociocultural Models ... 166

	Introduction	166
	The Macrosocial Models of Mental Illness	181
	The Microsocial Models of Mental Illness	206
6.	Philosophical–Moral Models	245
	Introduction	245
	Hermeneutic-Linguistic Models	246
	Phenomenological-Existentialist Models	258
	Humanistic Models	282
	Moral-Legal Models	307
7.	Epilogue: Whither Psychiatry, Monism or Pluralism?	319
	Comparison of the Models	321
	Towards a Perspectivist View of Mental Illness	330

References 343
Name Index 375
Subject Index 385

MODELS OF MENTAL ILLNESS

Chapter 1

INTRODUCTION: THE BASIC ISSUES IN THE FIELD OF MENTAL HEALTH

INTRODUCTORY REMARKS

There is no doubt that at the present moment psychiatry and clinical psychology are in a state of crisis. The whole field of mental health is in a state of flux and turmoil. The basic presuppositions are questioned, and the roles played by different professions dealing with mental health are being redefined. One generation ago the field of mental health was recognized as belonging to medicine, although even then two approaches, the organic and the psychodynamic, were competing with one another. Mental pathology, similar to somatic pathology, was regarded as a product of the disordered functioning of a biological organism. It was understood in terms of the conceptual categories of the medical science—an applied natural science. The explanations offered were naturalistic and biological. In the framework of biology and medicine, man is conceived as an organism, a complex, deterministic, physiochemical system developed by the vicissitudes of evolution. Even Sigmund Freud, who offered a genuinely psychological explanation of the psychoneuroses and other psychopathological conditions, stayed largely within the general framework of medicine and biology and believed that the ultimate explanations would be physiological (Freud, 1957d). He also stressed the fact that mental events, like physical events, were strictly determined. In the early stages of his work, psychotherapy was regarded by Freud as a medical procedure to be applied by a physician, the agent, to a patient, the passive object. Later on, when his psychoanalytical technique had been developed, the patient's role became relatively more active and the physician's more passive. By that time Freud had accepted non-medically qualified lay-analysts and played down the medical approach.

The medical model has its merits. The development of the concept of insanity as an illness, to be regarded as a medical problem, was the great achievement of the eighteenth century, the Age of Enlightenment and Rationalism. Chains and other physical restraints were removed from mental patients by Phillippe Pinel, the great French humanist-physician. As a result the stigma, moral condemnation, and prejudice associated with insanity were markedly reduced. However, the application of the medical model to the explanation and treatment of psychological abnormalities has not been as successful as its application to the understanding and treatment of somatic diseases. Psychiatry has lagged behind the other medical specialties such as internal medicine and surgery where, by now, there has grown a body of well established scientific knowledge and techniques. In these medical specialties there exists a universally accepted paradigm for scientific investigation and for therapeutic procedures. Psychiatry is still a preparadigmatic discipline, groping for objective criteria by which to validate its knowledge claims. Even more importantly, it does not possess an objectively established theoretical framework. Consequently, psychiatric diagnoses are notoriously unreliable. There is a multitude of schools of psychotherapy each conceiving the process and goals of psychotherapy differently and each using completely different conceptual frameworks and languages. To complicate the matter even further, the field of mental health has become multidisciplinary. New professionals, such as clinical psychologists and psychiatric social workers, have entered the field. Their training is in behavioural and social sciences rather than in biology and medicine. Psychoanalysis and other dynamic schools of psychiatry, although originally conceived as an extension of the medical model, implicitly questioned many underlying assumptions of this model. In spite of the underpinnings of Freud's mechanistic metapsychology, psychoanalysis, which produced cure by bringing about insight into the analysand's motivations and by explicating the meanings of his symbolic productions, did not fit exactly into the mould of medical model. The sociocultural universe with its matrix of symbols and meanings has become increasingly relevant to an understanding of so-called "mental illness." The inadequacy of a purely biological frame of reference has led to questioning the assumptions underlying the traditional medical model. This model has been challenged and with it the scientific presuppositions of psychiatry. Various models have been offered as a replacement for it (Becker, 1964); however, numerous debates between the advocates of these seem to have generated more heat than light (Kessler, 1969).

The following themes can be discerned in current criticisms of the medical model: (a) The medical model, as applied in the form of labeling of social deviance by psychiatrists, interferes with the basic human rights of individuals; it tends to turn the person, who is a free agent, into an object. (b) The medical model, by postulating some hypothetical entities such as putative mental diseases, offers a false explanation of behavioural abnormalities. These abnormalities, which have resulted from faulty conditioning and learning, should be rectified by reconditioning and retraining in the hands of practitioners with a background in psychology rather than in medicine. (c) Psychological abnormalities are produced by faulty interpersonal relations and communications and thus are outside the scope of the traditional medical model dealing with discrete organisms. (d) The conflicts, anxieties, and mental preoccupations of so-called psychoneurotics are real, legitimate, and stem from the human predicament. They are not caused by disease.

The purpose of this book is to provide a conceptual clarification of the underlying assumptions of various models of mental illness that have been explicitly or implicitly offered by different authorities. Further, an attempt is made to classify the existing models into conceptual categories. The book is not, however, concerned with substantive theories or empirical findings but rather concentrates on metatheoretical issues. Substantive theories will be presented only as illustrations of specific points, for the purpose of conceptual clarification and not as an exhaustive review of the existing theories in psychopathology.

MODELS IN SCIENCES AND IN PROFESSIONS

Since the title of this book is *Models of Mental Illness*, it may be worthwhile before proceeding any further to discuss the concept of "model." The Oxford Dictionary gives the following three broad areas of meaning of the word: (1) representation of structure;

(2) type of design or plan; and (3) an object of imitation. In recent decades the term model has become fashionable, appearing in various contexts. It has been used quite extensively in scientific writings and particularly in connection with scientific theory construction. When discussing models in the context of science Kaplan (1964) stresses their analogical role isomorphic in certain essential features and aspects with the real world that they represent. Usually, certain structural and relational properties of the investigated aspect of reality are represented by a simplified analogue especially constructed for this purpose. However, a model is only analogous and not identical with the system it depicts. At times the isomorphism is quite precise, at others it does not amount to more than a metaphor. Models are used in certain limited areas of experimental psychology, as exemplified by mathematical models of learning, psychophysical functions, decision theory applied to signal detection, and by cybernetic models of information processing and behaviour control systems operating in the human brain. As well, a few theoretical models have been proposed to explain some narrow aspects of abnormal behaviour. However, this book will not be concerned with models in the narrow and precise sense as used in science. Rather, it will be concerned with models in the sense of broad conceptual perspectives on mental diseases and on the frameworks of therapy. The focus will be on the metaphors used and the concepts of man implied by various theoreticians.

When references are made in the field of mental health to medical and psychological models the meaning of the word is obviously not the same as in the sciences. What then is the meaning of this word when it is used in the present connection? In reference to the context of the current discussions of mental health and disease the word model refers sometimes to an object for imitation, sometimes to a paradigm case, and at other times to both at the same time. In the medical model, as applied to mental illness, the object for imitation is a physician or surgeon investigating the causes of physical illnesses and successfully treating the latter. In the psychological model of mental illness the object for imitation may be an animal learning psychologist successfully controlling the behaviour of a rat in a Skinner box by the schedules of reinforcement or a computer scientist writing and debugging computer programs to process information efficiently. In psychoanalytical psychiatry, the model may imply a paradigm case, for instance that of hysteria in the case of Anna O. treated by Breuer and Freud (Breuer & Freud, 1957). Also, in psychoanalysis certain metaphors have been used to help understand the observed phenomena in cases under treatment. One metaphor is that of a hydraulic system, with faucets and valves holding a steady pressure and regulating it by safety valves. Another metaphor invokes the image of a theatre stage with a drama enacted by three main actors: ego, superego, and id. At times the word model, in the context of mental health, implies the frameworks of certain basic sciences, e.g., biochemistry, neurophysiology, experimental psychology, sociology, or cultural anthropology.

The field of mental health is an applied field concerned not only with theoretical knowledge but also primarily with practice. Attempts are made to change the state and to influence the behavior of individuals or of whole communities in certain directions by means of therapeutic intervention, reeducation, intellectual enlightenment, or moral exhortations. In contrast to pure science, mental health is a field of practical goals and endeavours. In this context one can talk about models as blueprints for action. Such models would rationalize the successive steps in applied procedures and in decision making, in accordance with the precepts of operational research and praxiology (Kotarbinski, 1965). However, in order to be able to do that, there has to be a general agreement upon the goals to be achieved, which in turn reflect certain ultimate values. The latter usually have no generally accepted validity by the practitioners in the field of mental health, the clients, and the public. When there is no agreement as to goals and ultimate values the problem ceases to be that of models for the efficient practical action and blueprints for solving certain practical problems. Instead, it becomes a matter of different ethical codes, of different definitions of good life, and of different views on the nature of man. The debated issues are very often ethical and moral, far removed from those of theoretical understanding and of designs for practical actions with which models in science are concerned. Thus, the interests in the field of mental health go much deeper than those with which the blueprints of behaviour engineering are dealing. They frequently are concerned with ends rather than means. However, the underlying ethical and philosophical beliefs and conflicts are often not made explicit and are glossed over. The implicit moral and philosophical assumptions behind the beliefs in question belong, in many cases, to the unexamined metaphysical *Weltanschauung* (the world view) of members of a certain culture at a certain historical epoch. To make things even more complicated, in modern Western culture we have more than one implicit view of ethics, nature of man, and purpose of life. These views are aspects of competing ideologies of our changing society that usually remain unexplicated. For historical reasons different professions, such as medicine, social work, and clinical psychology, have frequently adopted somewhat different implicit value systems and philosophical perspectives. These circumstances have led to conflicts resulting in the development of different models of mental illness adhered to by different professionals. Theory and practice in the field of mental health are therefore concerned not only with the scientific issues but also with the ethical, moral, legal, philosophical, and religious ones. Consequently, frames of reference are sometimes advocated for dealing with the problem of mental illness that are different from those of biological, behavioural, and social sciences. These often reject the naturalistic scientific approach. Again, the designation of model may well be used in this context.

Any human enterprise, such as science, art, politics, or technology, is rooted in certain philosophical presuppositions about the interests, the purposes, and the values of man interacting with the world (Habermas, 1972). Psychiatry, clinical psychology, and medicine are not exceptions. It is often said that medicine is science and art—both an applied biological science and the art of healing. With the progress in scientific technology medicine is becoming less an art and more an applied science. Predictions are made that before long x-rays and the E.K.G. will be diagnosed by computers. Laboratory results will be fed into a computer that will make the diagnosis and prescribe the treatment. Somatic medicine is about to become a branch of technology based on biochemistry, physiology, serology, pharmacology, and other biological sciences. Psychiatry and clinical psychology are not moving in the same direction in spite of the assertions of some of the practitioners in the field. Some of these practitioners look for a panacea of a tranquilizing pill that will straighten the crooked molecules underlying the crooked thoughts of mental patients. Other practitioners believe that behaviour modification techniques will produce a technological breakthrough in the treatment of mental patients. These beliefs are viewed by many critics of the field with scepticism and cause alarm in those who value human freedom and dignity. Not only the possibility of mental health technology is questioned but also its value.

THE OUTSTANDING PHILOSOPHICAL ISSUES IN THE FIELD OF MENTAL HEALTH

Contemporary discussions and polemics about mental health point to some underlying philosophical issues that have been debated by philosophers for centuries. These are: (1) body-mind relationship; (b) determinism versus indeterminism of human behaviour and the related problem of free will and moral responsibility; (c) the question of value-free science, particularly as applied to man and to society; (d) mental health and morality; and (e) autonomy of the individual versus his conformity to the society.

It is obvious that the protagonists in various debates concerning the subject of mental health, e.g., the applicability of naturalistic-scientific medical model or appropriateness of various forms of behaviour engineering, take sides on these perennial basic philosophical issues concerning the nature of man and of society. The problems are often dismissed by followers of the positivistic tradition as pseudoproblems that stem from an outdated metaphysics. It is a moot point whether they can be resolved by a rational argument, dissolved, or swept under the carpet. However, these issues of ethics and ultimate values lie at the bottom of the theoretical controversies in the field of mental health at the present moment. They lie also behind many conflicts pitting one mental health profession against another. The controversial views in question are expressions of implicit, unexamined, gut-felt metaphysical beliefs of their proponents. No attempt will be made here to resolve these perennial philosophical issues; however, their importance will be shown for an understanding and explication of various models of mental illness.

Body–Mind Relationships

When we examine the first issue, the body-mind relationship, we can see that it is at the root of two basic orientations to the problem of mental illness (Kessler, 1969). The question that has been debated by the proponents of these two orientations for almost two hundred years in psychiatry is, "Is the cause of mental illness in the mind or in the body?" The organic psychiatrists, as for example Emil Kraepelin the father of the systematic psychiatry, have assumed that the causal nexus of abnormal symptoms and disordered behaviour is in the physiology or, according to more recent views, the biochemistry of the brain and therefore of the body. Whatever traditional metaphysical position with regard to mind-body relationship is taken by the organic psychiatrist in his more philosophical moments— whether dualistic interactionism, parallelism, or monistic double-aspect and identity theory—one cannot escape the impression that so-called mental phenomena and mental symptoms are regarded by him as epiphenomena. This position implies that the conscious experiences and mental symptoms are caused by some physicochemical event in the brain but that they do not cause anything. They are, to use a loose metaphor, like the smoke produced by fire and are only signs of something more real that underlies and causes them. These mental phenomena may be subjectively very real as far as the patient is concerned and produce immense suffering and distress, yet they are regarded by the organically oriented psychiatrist as being somewhat unreal and imaginary. They are viewed as meaningless in themselves and only as signs, or implicit signs, of some disordered physicochemical events in the brain. It appears that the only reality the organically minded scientist-physician takes seriously is the reality of physical space-time, electrons, other subatomic particles, and the electromotive forces produced by them. The feelings of distress, the moods, the obsessions, the delusions are considered by him to be figments of the disordered imagination of mental patients. They are epiphenomena, produced by a disordered brain.

On the other hand, the psychoanalysts and other psychodynamically oriented clinicians take psychological phenomena to be meaningful in their own right. The causal nexus of psychological abnormalities is in the psyche, in the desires, motives, and conflicts, whether conscious or unconscious. Mental symptoms are *not* epiphenomena caused by physicochemical events, but they also are not causing anything themselves. Rather they are produced by psychological causes, conscious or unconscious, that in addition can produce physiological and structural bodily changes. The fantasies, delusions, obsessions, and dreams of a patient are taken seriously. They can be understood in their own right because they possess intrinsic meanings. The products of the patient's mind make sense since they can be understood in the context of his experiential history, particularly when the existing gaps are bridged by unconscious psychological events reconstructed in the course of psychotherapy. Beliefs and thoughts that on first sight appear bizarre and incomprehensible, both to those who come into contact with the patient and the patient, become understandable and make sense when allowance is made for unconscious motivations, repressed memories, and unconscious conflicts.

The patient's feelings, emotions, sufferings, beliefs, compulsions, delusions, and hallucinations have meaning, similar to the psychological experiences of so-called normal individuals. Psychologically minded psychiatrists take seriously, in their own right, the inner experiences of patients as causes of the latter's mental illness. Moreover, in insight psychotherapy the cure is brought about by identifying psychological causes and by making the patient conscious of his unconscious motives, conflicts, and fantasies.

There is a third possible view of the causal nexus of mental illness, according to which the causes of the latter are neither in the physicochemical events of the brain nor in the psyche but rather are in the sequences of environmental events. This view is implied by behaviour modification therapists who follow the teachings of B. F. Skinner. They believe that normal and abnormal behaviour is caused by the contingencies of environmental events on the organism's actions or by the conjunctions of the former. Finally, a fourth possibility can be briefly mentioned. The causal nexus of mental illness may be located in interpersonal interactions or, more precisely, in interpersonal communications. The proponents of this view have been influenced by the symbolic interactionism theory in sociology. According to this position human mind and personality are the emergents of interpersonal communication processes. This topic will be discussed in greater detail in Chapter 5, which deals with the sociocultural models of mental illness.

Determinism versus Indeterminism

The second philosophical controversy is that of determinism versus indeterminism of human behaviour. Closely connected with it is the problem of free will and moral responsibility. The rejection of determinism is at the core of the contemporary criticism of the medical model of mental illness (Becker, 1964) and of behaviour modification therapy (Breger & McGaugh, 1965). According to the humanistic psychologists of the Third Force and the existentialist philosophers and psychiatrists, human beings possess free will and this is the essence of their humanness. That mental patients are human beings, capable of exercising free will, of making free choices, and of being morally responsible for their actions is a point of view particularly stressed by Thomas Szasz (1961a), Hobart Mowrer (1961), and William Glasser (1975).

The medical model, and generally the scientific model, emphasizes biological, psychological, and sociocultural determinism. It holds that a combination of hereditary and environmental causes determines human behaviour. Human beings are made what they are by their nature and nurture—by the genes and the environment. According to this way of thinking, a medical doctor, as a biological engineer, or a behavioural or social scientist, as a behavioural or a social engineer, can discover the causes underlying the abnormal behaviour of a patient. Consequently, by skillful engineering techniques they can alter the course of events with a view of controlling the patient's behaviour. The underlying metaphysical assumption of these practitioners is that of determinism,* even if it is in its weaker probabilistic form. It is regarded as a precondition of scientific ap-

---

*Determinism has to be distinguished on one hand from indeterminism, and on the other from fatalism. According to the doctrine of determinism all events have causes and by altering the causes one can influence the course of events. Fatalism assumes that events are predestined and that no manipulation of causes could alter their course. While science rejects fatalism with the latter's pessimistic outlook, it accepts determinism as the *sine qua non* condition for predictability and controlability of natural events. The scientific outlook is thus quite optimistic. Some prescientific views of insanity were fatalistic, leading to an emotionally negative and pessimistic attitude.

proach and of behavioural engineering. In contrast, humanistic psychologists and existentialist philosophers denounce the traditional scientific approach to human behaviour because it transforms subjects into objects and thus negates the essential character and the dignity of man.

Freud has taken an intermediate position. He may be said to have postulated a psychological determinism, which contrasted with the physical determinism accepted by organic psychiatrists. At the same time, he has denied the existence of psychological indeterminism of the sort asserted by libertarians—the proponents of free will doctrine. However, there is a deeper issue involved in psychological determinism presupposed by psychoanalysis. At issue is the status of conscious mental events, as against the unconscious ones, in relation to the thesis of determinism. One could ask whether acts that are decided freely after conscious considerations of all the relevant facts and arguments are still psychologically determined. We can answer this question, following Spinoza, in the affirmative, or else we can claim that causal explanation is not appropriate in this case. Some contemporary philosophers, particularly those influenced by the Oxford ordinary language school of philosophy (Taylor, 1964, 1966; Peters, 1958), have questioned the appropriateness of talking about causes when explaining human acts in terms of goal directed motives. Instead, they have offered explanations of human acts in terms of reasons and rules. This issue may have lost some of its importance with the advent of the computer and the cybernetic revolution, where the distinction between reasons and rules on the one hand and causes on the other has become blurred. With regard to the unconscious motives one could argue that the proferred explanations should also be in terms of reasons rather than causes. However, the psychodynamic explanation in terms of unconscious drives, motives, and conflicts in contrast to conscious ones has many causal, deterministic features. This statement can be supported by the following clinical observations. Patients often say that they cannot help behaving in certain ways, that they are controlled by compulsions or irrational fears, and that they are severely restricted in their free choices. They do not understand why they are doing certain things that cause distress and anguish. The patients are puzzled by the constraints on their freedom. The processes occurring in insight psychotherapy may be construed as freeing the patients from having their behaviour controlled by unconscious causes, and as rendering them capable of making free choices in terms of reasons and rules. As a result clients are no longer slaves of their passions and obsessions but rather rational free agents choosing freely their acts in the light of reason. Thus the process of psychoanalysis may be regarded as one that frees man from the bondage of unconscious irrational forces and enhances his rationality. Man becomes morally responsible for his acts. "Where id was, there shall ego be," said Freud (1964). This interpretation places him and psychoanalysis close to humanistic psychology, and it is compatible with libertarian-indeterminist position in philosophy. However, the validity of this interpretation may be questioned in view of the fact that, according to Freud, it is doubtful whether man can ever become completely free from the influence of the unconscious irrational forces. In some of his writings Freud is quite pessimistic with regard to this possibility (Freud, 1955b, 1961b). Be that as it may, the controversy of determinism as against free will and moral responsibility remains one of the central issues in the field of mental health.

Value-free Social Science

The third issue concerns the place of moral values in the field of mental health. It is a part of a much broader issue pertaining to the possibility and validity of value-free science in general and of value-free human and social sciences in particular.

As is well-known, David Hume in the *Treatise of Human Nature* (1896) said that he could not see how propositions containing "ought" terms could be derived from those containing "is" terms. This position has become one of the canons of the empiricist-positivistic tradition in science. According to this view science should be value-free. Philosophers and scientists who have made an attempt to establish the existence of objective values empirically have been accused of committing "naturalistic fallacy." The place of values in the scientific enterprise has become a particularly urgent problem in applied sciences. Applied science, whether physical, biological, or social, aims at bringing about some desirable ends; otherwise it would not be pursued. It generally has been assumed by positivistically-minded applied scientists that the values to be realized in their fields are determined by psychological or social choices that are outside the empirico-logical framework of science. The values are emoted, intuited, or arrived by a social consensus and taken for granted before the applied scientist sets about implementing them in his research. His investigations and resulting techniques of control are only the best means (instrumental values) to attain the desired ends (ultimate values). There is a possibility, in principle, of consensus with regard to the instrumental values; however, such a consensus is less likely with regard to the ultimate values. Although it is often presumed to exist, the latter consensus vanishes when the underlying assumptions are made explicit exposing certain unanswered questions of ethics and social philosophy. These are some of the questions that could be raised: If the aim of applied social science is to enhance human well-being and happiness, can the good or happiness of society or majority be put ahead of the good and happiness of the individual or minority? What is happiness? Can it be equated with good and right? Can happiness be equated with pleasure? As a result of these unanswered questions, applied social scientists have found it more difficult than their colleagues in physical sciences to adopt a detached attitude towards the ultimate values or to take them for granted. In addition, the two world wars, the mass extermination camps, and the nuclear bomb shattered the nineteenth century illusions about rationality, enlightenment, and progress. These events have indicated that science may be used for evil as well as for good purposes and that scientific discoveries may lead to the annihilation of mankind. Consequently, the problem of values facing any social scientist is of paramount importance when the subject of investigation is man. Such a scientist finds it difficult to separate facts from values. His research may have profound social consequences and may change his value system.

It is difficult to separate the notions of mental health and mental disease, putatively scientific concepts, from the value concepts of happiness and unhappiness or that of well-being of the individual. The same philosophical questions that have been asked in the context of human and social sciences also may be raised in the discussion of the problems of mental health and mental disease. Can mental health be equated with mental well-being? Is the latter associated with a maximum pleasure over the whole life span? Is pleasure to be equated with happiness? Is the absence of mental anguish and suffering a sufficient condition for mental well-being? Is well-being of the individual to be equated with the well-being of the society? Are there other important values implied by positive mental health in addition to pleasure and happiness? These are some of the questions that, indeed, have been asked. The fact that different ultimate values are implied by the concept of mental health as put forward by different theoreticians—Freudian psychoanalysts, Jungian analytical psychologists, behaviour therapists, humanistic psychologists, or organic psychiatrists—indicates that there is no agreement about these values. For example, it is argued by some humanistic psychologists that ultimate values concerning man and his society can be discovered by scientific inquiry, which will result in the establishment of "humanistic ethics" based on the universal needs of man. These psychologists link positive mental health with the realization of humanistic ethics and values. However, there is no general agreement on the universal needs of man apart from his basic organic needs. However, even if there should be such an agreement, deriving values from universally existing human needs could be construed as the naturalistic fallacy.

Mental Health and Morality

The concepts of mental health and mental disease are also entangled with openly moral and legal problems. The following is often asked in connection with the subject of legal responsibility. Is it possible to separate mental illness and, more generally, mental abnormality from crime, moral badness, depravity, and sin? This is the perennial issue of mad versus bad (Margolis, 1966) and is closely related to the question of free will and moral accountability. It is one of the most difficult problems that has baffled legal minds. Depending on the definition of the social situation, or social context, the same behaviour may be explained in morally and legally neutral, scientific terms of cause and effect or in terms of intentional acts. The first type of explanation attributes behaviour to physiological events occurring in the brain or to conditioning, the second to free choices of a legally responsible person. Those psychiatrists, psychologists, and social scientists who tend to look upon crime and social deviance as a disease, use the first type of explanation. Others who, like T. Szasz

(1961a), reject the naturalistic scientific type of explanation view all deviant behaviour in moral and legal terms. The most widely accepted position maintains that in the "disease of mind" state the freedom of deliberate choices or the freedom of will is constrained. The person acts under duress or constraint and is not responsible for his acts. Therefore, these acts are described in pathological instead of moral terms. According to this view, curing a disease of the mind is equivalent to freeing a person from a bondage and of restoring his capacity for making free choices.

Autonomy versus Conformity

The fourth issue, concerning the goals of mental health and the nature of mental illness, is that of autonomy of the individual versus his conformity to the society. According to some psychologists, so-called good adjustment, as exemplified by the citizens of Walden Two (Skinner, 1948a) or the "token economy" treatment in mental hospitals, consists of toeing the line and conforming to the norms of society. When mental abnormality is equated with social deviance, mental health becomes equal to social conformity. Man's mental health and happiness, according to this position, depend on his unquestioning acceptance of and obedience to social norms, while kicking the traces and rocking the boat leads to alienation from the community and maladjustment. It is easy to see that the conformity version of mental health is based on a homeostatic model of man and society with its presupposed goal of equilibration. The proponents of this version also assume that man is malleable and that he is moulded by his society into a shape common to all its members. This process is required for the maintenance of social equilibrium. Accordingly, the main dynamic force shaping human growth is that of socialization. Any disturbance of this process leads to social and psychological perturbations, which are often described (labelled) in terms of mental illness. On this view psychotherapy, or any therapy directed at psychiatric patients, is based on a method of socialization or resocialization of deviant and, at times, recalcitrant individuals.

A different view is adopted by humanistic psychologists. They emphasize the self-actualization process, the development of unique personality, and the achievement of personal autonomy. Unique personality and individuality are regarded as the highest ethical values. The Renaissance man is the ideal. On this view, the individual is in danger of being crushed by the society. Mindless conformity, according to humanistic psychologists, leads to denial of inner worth and prevents man from becoming self-actualized. Therefore, conformity leads to the profound dissatisfaction, unhappiness, and malfunctioning that are often defined in our society as mental illness. The conceptual model of human nature and of society underlying the theories put forward by humanistic psychologists is not based on the idea of homeostasis but rather on that of a growing, developing, open system (von Bertalanffy, 1968).

The issue of conformity versus autonomy crops up in various forms in the writings of different authors. Some take a middle position between the advocacy of complete conformism and that of complete autonomy. Thus, Freud in one version of his theory, accepts a homeostatic model and looks at psychotherapy as a technique to facilitate the adjustment of the individual to the society, which would allow better control of his antisocial sexual and aggressive impulses. At the same time, Freud, in his book on *Civilization and its discontents* (Freud, 1961b), is very pessimistic regarding the success of socialization processes. He doubts whether man can be completely moulded by social forces and perceives an irreducible tension between man's antisocial urges and these forces. Erich Fromm (1955) takes a more optimistic view. He believes that while man's growth can be stifled by a certain type of society and culture it is possible to design a humanistic (communitarian) society in which man will be able to attain self-actualization, realize his individual values, and satisfy his creative urges. The issue of social conformity versus autonomy and freedom of the individual is concerned with making the choice between the rights of mental patients and the rights of the society. It is also crucial for defining the role of the psychiatrist and in deciding whether he is the agent of the patient or of the state. An extreme position is taken by Thomas Szasz (1961a, 1965a, 1970), who defends the legal rights of mental patients to be social deviants. Different models of mental illness take differing positions with regard to the issue of social conformity versus individual autonomy.

PROFESSIONAL CONFLICTS IN THE FIELD OF MENTAL HEALTH

Another dimension along which models of mental illness can be compared has less to do with perennial philosophical issues and more with the sociology of the mental health professions. The various professions in the field, e.g., psychiatry, clinical psychology, and social work, have had different historical developments. They have followed unique traditions, have attained different social status, and possess distinct social attitudes and values. Psychiatry is the oldest and best established of the three. It is a specialty within the field of medicine. The latter together with law and ministry are the traditional professions, with a long history of well established sapiential authority and well defined social functions. Training for the medical profession, which for more than a hundred years took place in an academic setting, is still based to a great extent on the principle of apprenticeship. It relies on preceptorship, on following and imitating hospital teachers, whose authority, clinical acumen, and judgement are not to be doubted (Becker, Geer, Hughes, & Strauss, 1961; Merton, Reader, & Kendall, 1957). In spite of the distinctly empirical foundation of the medical sciences, this type of training tends to produce a somewhat authoritarian structure within the profession. It encourages an appeal to authority as a means of validating knowledge claims with regard to diagnosis and therapy. The client is referred to as a patient. The latter term denotes passivity and has an object character. Affixing these characteristics, in turn, tends to produce a benevolent paternalistic attitude in the doctor towards the patients, which can be described as the doctor knows best attitude. The mental hospitals run by psychiatrists, with auxiliary professionals in subordinate positions, tend to be highly stratified social structures conducive to an authoritarian ethos. Mental patients are at the bottom of the social ladder.

The basic sciences in medical training are biological sciences. A medical student who may become a future psychiatrist is usually taught these sciences in a manner that encourages a mechanistic bias and implies the Cartesian metaphysics. The latter postulates a body-mind dualism, with the body regarded basically as a thermodynamic machine that utilizes chemical energy. These biases produce a tendency in the members of the medical profession to perceive themselves as body engineers or body mechanics. Consequently, medically-trained psychiatrists tend to use a medical model borrowed from somatic medicine when trying to explain and to treat psychological disturbances. The explanations tend to be in terms of physicochemical events in the brain. The role of experiential and social factors is played down. As a result, the patient whose mind is sick because of a putative disease process in the brain tends to be regarded as an object, to be managed for his own good, but very often against his wishes.

On the other hand, the relative newcomers to the field of mental health, clinical psychologists and social workers, receive their basic training in behavioural and social sciences. In this training the biological factors in human behaviour are played down and the importance of individual experiences and the social environment is emphasized. The significance of authority in validating knowledge claims is minimized, and instead, the importance of experimental research is stressed. The ethos of the clinical psychology and social work professions is less authoritarian than that of medical profession. The client is recognized as a unique individual, a person, to a greater extent than in the case of a medical, or particularly a psychiatric, hospital patient.

The varied educational background and the conflicting social attitudes of the professionals in the field of mental health account for their tendency to single out different aspects of mental diseases and to take dissimilar approaches to treatment. Medically trained psychiatrists tend to emphasize biological factors such as heredity and to take more of a paternalistic doctor knows best attitude toward mental patients. The psychologists and psychiatric social workers, on the other hand, stress the unique experiences, interpersonal relations, and social environment as the causal factors of mental illness. These professionals are also more prepared than psychiatrists to regard their clients as unique individuals whose beliefs, wishes, and rights are to be respected. These differing educational backgrounds and varied ideological orientations of the mental health professions are important factors behind the diversity of mental illness models that have been proposed as explanatory schemata and blueprints for practice. The lines dividing the models offered by the different professions in the field of mental health are drawn even more sharply by the fact that they are struggling for power and dominance within the field. In our pluralistic society diverse pressure and interest groups, entrenched in professional guilds and trade unions, compete for power and influence with the newcomers trying to replace the establishment. As a result the ranks become closed, and each professional group tries to stress the uniqueness and superiority of its model to the exclusion of those advocated by the other professions. This state of affairs may lead to oversimplification of issues with polemics and rhetoric replacing cogent arguments.

CONTENTS OF THE BOOK

After a general introduction to the themes of the book in Chapter 1, Chapter 2 presents various ideas and concepts of normality and abnormality. Chapter 3 discusses the medical models (more than one medical model can be distinguished in the history of medicine). In Chapter 4, the major psychological models are reviewed. Chapter 5 deals with the sociocultural models. Philosophical-moral approaches to mental illness are presented in Chapter 6. Finally, in Chapter 7 the models are summarized and compared. General stock is taken of the problems that confront the theorist and the practitioner. Although no attempt at integration into a single all-embracing model is made, some metatheoretical remarks are made regarding the possible solution of the dilemma of diversity.

Chapter 2

CONCEPT OF NORMALITY

INTRODUCTION

The concept of normality, although intuitively understood by everybody, proves to be thorny when attempts at explication are made. It appears that different authorities imply different things when they talk about normality. One source of difficulty is that normality connotes both a factual (existential) judgement about the state of an organism and also a value judgement. While it is, in principle, not difficult to arrive at a consensus regarding factual judgements, it is much more difficult, if at all possible, to arrive at a consensus regarding value judgements. In the area of mental health, an additional difficulty is added by the fact that the concept of normality is implicitly embedded in the ideology and ethics of a given society at a particular historical period. This implies that the judgement of normality is relative to the context in which it is made. There have been several attempts to free the concept of normality from its cultural context in order to objectify it. Some efforts have also been made to make it value-free.

The concept of normality belongs to a complex of related concepts such as health and illness. It is also related to psychiatric diagnosis. The present chapter discusses the concept as well as the related concepts. An attempt is also made to explicate the meaning of psychiatric diagnosis. For a detailed discussion of normality, the reader is referred to the monograph by Offer and Sabshin (1966). In attempts to arrive at a value-free, objective concept of normality, four distinct strategies have been used. The first strategy is to replace the sociocultural context by the biological. The second is to take an actuarial point of view and equate normality with average characteristics in representative samples of a population. The third is to discover some transculturally and transtemporally human traits and base the concept of normality and mental health on them. The fourth strategy is to despair of ever defining the concept of normality and equate normality with an absence of illness. The last solution to the problem is accepted by most psychiatrists who subscribe to the traditional medical model of disease. This position can be restated: as long as a person does not express any complaints and as long as he does not manifest any symptoms of mental illness he is by definition normal. This dilemma confronts not only the concept of mental health, it also confronts the concept of physical health as well. It comes down to the question, Can the state of health be positively defined or only negatively as an absence of a disease? The World Health Organization defines health as, "a state of complete physical, mental and social well being and not merely the absence of disease and infirmity" (in Zubin, 1961). One may ask, What is meant by "complete well-being," and in what way does it differ from the idea of the "good life" and "perfect society," which philosophers have tried to define since the times of antiquity? To put it somewhat differently: In what way is it a medical problem instead of a philosophical one? Before this question can be answered, we have to review some of the meanings of the term normal or healthy.

DIFFERENT CONCEPTS OF NORMALITY

The following approaches to the definition of normality have been proposed in the literature at one time or another.

Normality as a statistical concept

The Belgian mathematician Adolph Quetelet (1796-1874) was the first to apply the Gaussian (bell-shaped) curve and Laplace's normal law of error to distribution of measurements obtained from human data, both biological and social (1842). In his *Essai de physique social* (*Essay on social physique*), 1835, Quetelet developed his theory of *l'homme moyen* (the average man). This theory postulated that the normal man (therefore, the ideal one) was the average man as defined by the mean or central tendency of the distribution of measurements of a trait in a given population. All deviations were due to smaller or greater errors of the creative processes of nature. The larger the error, the less frequently it occurred. However, more recent genetic theories (Dobzansky, 1962) indicate that variability, far from being a manifestation of errors of creative process, performs an extremely important role in the survival and evolution of the species. It assures the presence of a variety of genotypes ready to exploit a new ecological niche, thus assuring survival of species and leading to the evolution of new ones. Similarly, within the sociocultural context, deviance, the social equivalent of biological variability, leads to flexibility, change, and progress.

Independently from Quetelet's definition of the ideal man by the mathematical abstraction of the mean, his statistical method proved to be useful in biology, psychology, and sociology. Many distributions of biological, psychological, and sociological measures approach the normal Gaussian distribution when sufficiently large samples are used. Accepting the mean, or some other measure of central tendency as the definition of normal, has many advantages. It offers an objective, value-free criterion of normality, which moreover is one that can be arrived at empirically. Since the mean is an abstraction, some other central tendency measures, such as the mode (the most frequently encountered measure), may be conveniently used as the criterion of normality. Accordingly, the magnitude of certain characteristics occurring the most frequently in a given population may be regarded as being normal. Deviations in both directions from the central tendency are by statistical definition to a greater or lesser extent abnormal. The greater the deviation the greater the abnormality. However, since there is no discontinuity but rather a gradual transition from the mean to extreme deviations, cutoff points will have to be established. One method of establishing cutoff points is statistical and is provided by the measures of dispersion, such as the standard deviation or the variance. If a population is normally distributed, 68.2 percent of the population falls between one standard deviation above the mean and one standard deviation below the mean, and 95.4 percent of the population between two standard deviations above the mean and two standard deviations below the mean. If the latter criterion of the cutoff points is used close to 5 percent of the population will be considered abnormal and 95 percent normal. The 5 percent value coincides with the statistical convention for rejecting the null hypothesis that two samples came from the same population. Consequently, many psychologists accepted the two standard deviation cutoff point as separating the normal from the abnormal. For instance, mental deficiency is defined by an IQ more than two standard deviations below the mean. Different populations may vary in the amount of scatter. Some are scattered over a wide range, others cluster within a narrow range close to the central tendency. In the case of psychological traits relevant to normality and abnormality in some populations, wider ranges of behaviour variations will be within statistical bounds of normality (plus and minus two standard deviations) than in others. Thus, normality is relative to the variance or standard deviation of a given population as inferred by sampling procedures.

An alternative to the definition of the cutoff points by standard deviation is to consider cut-off points in each particular situation within which the variation of a physiological or behavioural characteristic is compatible with an adequate functioning. For instance in the case of mental deficiency a person with a certain low IQ may function quite adequately in a simple rural environment but function inadequately in a more complex urban environment requiring proficiency in such scholastic skills as reading, writing, and arithmetic. This relativistic approach was advocated by Ryle (1947). However, the definition of the range of variation compatible with adequate or normal functioning is fraught with ambiguities and difficulties. Adequate and inadequate are not either/or categories. One may be more or less adequate and the decision of where to place the cutoff point becomes quite arbitrary and has to be agreed upon. The adequacy may be considered as a lack of complaints from the individual or his associates. It, then, becomes a negative definition, similar to the definition of normality as an absence of disease.

There are further difficulties with the statistical approach to normality in addition to the arbitrariness of cutoff points between normality and abnormality. In many traits, such as human height or human aggressiveness, the average may be intuitively considered as normal and therefore desirable, while deviations in both directions, e.g., too much or too little aggressiveness or height, may be considered abnormal and therefore undesirable. However, there are other traits, such as intelligence, where it is counterintuitive to regard both mental deficiency and genius as both being abnormal, unless one accepts Quetelet's doctrine of the average man as an ideal. If Quetelet's doctrine is rejected, genius and mental deficiency, although both deviant, cannot be regarded in the same light. Another difficulty with the statistical concept of normality is the fact that more than one characteristic is used to describe human beings. Roger J. Williams (1956) points out that if 10 uncorrelated traits are used to describe a given population only 60 percent (0.95^{10}) of that population will have all the measurements within the range of two standard deviations above and two standard deviations below the mean. If, as more likely, 100 uncorrelated traits are used, only 0.59 percent (0.95^{100}) will have all their traits within normal limits. This is, of course, an exaggeration because most of the human traits are intercorrelated. However, it is obvious that one has to consider the profiles of traits and one has to decide how many traits deviating by more than two standard deviations are still compatible with a normal total profile. The multivariate analysis of variance, followed by profile analysis, could provide an approximate answer to this problem. Other multivariate methods, such as cluster analysis, may show that not only traits are correlated but also that people described by these traits form discontinuous clusters. This would indicate the existence of different populations with different means, profiles, and criteria of normality.

The statistical approach to normality does not provide a value-free criterion of normality because we still have to decide whether the mean magnitude of a trait is always desirable and which of the two extremes of distribution is more desirable than the other. If we define normality as the mean or mode of a distribution, we obtain a value-free, descriptive criterion of normality, but we completely miss its functional aspect.

Normality as a social norm

The concept of normality as a social norm applies only to mental health and does not, or perhaps only marginally, apply to physical health. The social norm theory bears certain similarity to the statistical theory of normality. However, it should not be confused with the latter. While the statistical theory represents an outside observer's view of the system, the social norm theory represents the point of view of the actors participating in the social system. It represents the perception of their own roles and their expectations concerning the role performance of others. Thus, the social norm theory is concerned with the beliefs of society members, which may or may not coincide with their objective modal behaviour (Parsons, 1967). In this context one has to distinguish the role performance norm as an ideal from the average performance that may be reasonably expected by the members of the society from themselves and from one another. In societies that place a high value on conformity, the average norm of behaviour becomes highly valued and regarded as an ideal. A deviation in either direction is avoided. The refusal of Hopi Indian children to compete (Klineberg, 1954) may serve as one example. According to the social norm theory of normality, behaviour deviating from what is believed to be a modal behaviour is regarded as abnormal, unnatural, morally reprehensible, and sometimes branded as sick.

The two approaches to normality discussed so far have defined normality in terms of an average. The next to be discussed are the functionalist approaches, which treat normality and health as ideals that are approximated by people only to a greater or lesser extent but never realized, or alternatively in a weaker form, as states of adequacy.

Normality as an ideal

Since the concept of ideal is value-loaded, it is worthwhile to discuss briefly the concept of value. Value is an object or a property that is judged to be good or desirable. It is the subject of propositions asserting not only facts but also the desirability of certain states of affairs. Whether the value judgement propositions can be reduced to factual ones has been a subject of lively debates among philosophers. Those who with Aristotle, the Stoics, and the Utilitarians believe that values exist objectively in the external world and can be discovered by an empirical inquiry and cognitive judgement are called cognitivists or naturalists. Those who, like Kant, believe that values are objective but are a property of the metaphysical order and can be discovered only intuitively are called intuitionists. Finally, philosophers like Hume who maintain that all the propositions referring to value express only desires or approvals believe in subjectivity of values. For example, Stevenson, a positivist, proposed an emotive theory of value according to which value judgements are nothing but expressions of emotions and exhortations (1944). These differences in the philosophical views on the nature of values have affected scientists. Thus, those influences by the positivistic philosophy insist on value-free science. The position taken by proponents of value-free social science and psychology is disputed by those scientists who follow philosophical traditions other than positivism.

Psychologists and social scientists who explicitly or implicitly espouse the Utilitarian or humanistic ethics claim that by an empirical enquiry into human nature (human behaviour or human personality) and into human society they are able to establish the objective values that will guide humanity in the direction of what human beings and their society ought to be. The members of the humanistic psychology movement and the proponents of positive mental health espouse this point of view. The Utilitarian (hedonistic) ethical assumptions are also implicit in Freud's writings, perhaps due to the fact that Freud as a young man was exposed to John Stuart Mill's philosophy (Ellenberger, 1970). While an ethical theory is obviously implied by the proponents of ideal positive mental health, a few remarks are necessary regarding physical health as an ideal. Can ideal physical health, even if not discovered in the empirical data, be constructed from them? If we take a functionalist point of view and describe an organism as a functioning system we may, with a degree of certainty, extrapolate what an ideal system should be. The case of a well, or a perfectly well, functioning system implies the same meaning of good as that of a good knife—good for a certain purpose such as cutting, resisting rust, and so on. It is a case of the instrumental sense of the word good, a case of an instrumental value (von Wright, 1963). Customarily, when we describe human social behaviour in terms of values, we usually are concerned with the realm of moral values; when we talk about a perfect or a good biological organism, or for that matter a perfect or a good machine, we are concerned with instrumental values. While, in a sense, moral values also can be instrumental (extrinsic) to some supreme intrinsic ethical value such as pleasure, happiness, excellence, human dignity, or self-actualization, they presuppose conscious human beings endowed with free will, making free choices and interacting with one another in a social context. To illustrate the difference between the meaning of good in the context of moral values and the meaning of good in the context of instrumental values, in a narrow sense, the following examples

may be used. A criminal who mugs and robs an old man is considered bad, morally bad (opposite to morally good). He is brought to justice and punished. Cancer or the bubonic plague bacterium are also bad; however, they are not bad in the moral sense but only bad in the instrumental sense. They are eradicated, but they are not brought to justice and are not morally condemned and punished.*
Instrumental values, in a narrow sense, help us realize a state that we consider desirable. This would apply to such systems as a well functioning car or a biological organism fit for survival.

The question can immediately be asked whether human behaviour, human personality, and human society also may be regarded as systems for which objective criteria of ideal functioning can be found free from moral considerations. If such criteria can be found, a hierarchy of instrumental values could be established to bring about the ideal state. Thus, discourse concerning human and social behaviour would be removed from the realm of moral values to that of instrumental values. Even if this were possible, an affirmative answer to this question would be far more difficult to obtain than in the case of a purely biological system. It is relatively easy to arrive at the consensus that the criterion for a biological system is its survival, its freedom from physiological malfunctioning, and its reproduction. Such a consensus is much more difficult to obtain with respect to human personality and human society. Very different utopias have been proposed by social philosophers throughout ages. What is heaven for some is hell for others. Philosophers writing on the subject of moral values and ethics have tried to define what the good life is or ought to be. However, there is no agreement on the subject. Is good life the maximization of pleasure? Is it the conformity to the norms of the society? Is it creative deviance? Or is it consciousness of the human condition and the enhancement of human dignity? These

---
*There is a possibility that, in addition to instrumental values, physical illness may be associated also with moral valuation. Thus, Sigerist (1932) points out that in classical antiquity physical illness was associated with shame because of a deviation on the part of the sick person from the ideal of bodily beauty and health. In the Judeo-Christian tradition, according to Sigerist, physical illness has tended to be associated with guilt and regarded as a punishment for sin. In contrast, it also could be associated with virtue, as a cross to be borne with patience. The Medieval view of pestilence is an example of disease regarded as a punishment for sin. The story of Job is an example of disease regarded as a virtue.

are but some of the considerations that must be taken into account when designing an ideal personality and an ideal society.

The conception of normality as an ideal assumes, similarly to the conception of normality as an average, a continuum between normality and abnormality. In contrast to the theory of normality as an average, this continuum does not stretch in two opposite directions from the central average but instead from extreme abnormality to ideal normality or from extreme pathology to perfect health. In case of mental health, situated near the pole of extreme pathology will be the most severe psychotic cases, farther towards the center will be less severe psychotic cases, and still farther will be psychoneurotic cases, followed by cases of slight maladjustment, which includes the majority of the population. Well adjusted and highly stable individuals will be placed on the continuum close to the pole of ideal normality, with self-actualizing and creative individuals occupying the position closest to this pole. The pole of ideal normality, since it is an ideal, will be unoccupied.

The theory of continuity represented by the concept of normality as an average and the concept of normality as an ideal has to be contrasted with discontinuity theory represented by the concept of normality as the absence of disease.

Different ideals of normality

When considering the concept of normality, or positive mental health, as an ideal we have to consider the context for which we are setting the ideal. To put it differently, we have to answer the question, An ideal for what? The following possibilities have to be considered: (a) an ideal for the biological species, (b) an ideal for humanity in its biological, social, and spiritual aspects, considered transculturally and, thus, free from cultural and historical relativism, (c) an ideal for a given culture, and finally (d) the ideal for a particular, unique, individual personality. All these ideals of normality have had their proponents. The ideal for biological species means an ideal hereditary constitution, a possible optimal combination of genes or an ideal genotype. It is difficult to know exactly what such a genotype may be like. It presumably should be free from metabolic deficiencies caused by lethal dominant and recessive genes. Such a genotype should be mainly heterozygotic, endowed with a maximum of vigor and adaptability. It would be capable of functioning in the widest possible range of environments. It would be a genotype with a maximum potential for the development of intelligence and creativity. It would also be a genotype with a hereditary potential for a stable and resilient temperament. We are immediately confronted, of course, with the nature versus nurture controversy. To what extent are characteristics inherited and to what extent are they acquired? A phenotype is a product of the interaction between the genotype and the environment. The latter needs for its ideal development certain optimal environmental factors such as proper climate, nutrition, population density, and the absence of pollution and parasites. In addition to these a social organism like man needs a social milieu. Thus, it is impossible to separate the physical and biological environmental factors from the cultural ones.

The next concept to be discussed is the ideal of mental health for man that transcends his biological nature and is concerned with his cultural and spiritual aspects. This ideal is associated with Humanistic and Existential philosophies. The humanists view man as possessing needs and aspirations invariant across cultures and historical epochs, the most important of which is the need to actualize his spiritual and creative potential. Many designs for ideal mental health proposed by humanistic psychologists such as Maslow (1954) or Fromm (1965) are inspired by Humanistic philosophy and ethics. They stress the autonomy of the individual and also his ability to relate to other people and uphold the values of his culture, but at the same time the ability to actualize himself and create new individual values. The blueprints of ideal positive mental health offered by psychoanalysts such as Kubie (1954) and Grinker (1963) differ somewhat in the emphasis from that of the Humanistic psychologists. The psychoanalysts emphasize, in their ideal of mental health, ego strength, freedom from repression, and successful sublimations. The ego analysts, such as Heinz Hartmann (1958), emphasize also the autonomy of the conflict-free sphere of ego and the self-actualization of an individual. Combining the humanistic and psychoanalytical points of view Marie Jahoda, in her book *Current Concepts of Positive Mental Health* (1959), summarizes the current blueprints for positive mental health under six headings: (1) a positive and accepting attitude of an individual towards his own self, (2) growth development and self-actualization, (3) an integration of psychological functions, (4) personal autonomy, (5) an undistorted perception of reality, and (6) a mastery of the environment.

In contrast to the humanistic psychologists, existentialists deny the reality of an invariant human nature or essence. According to them existence precedes essence (Sartre, 1956), and man continually creates his own nature. Therefore, they do not offer blueprints for positive mental health. However, the existentialists assert the dignity of man who faces the predicament of his existence. One can ask whether the blueprints and prescriptions for ideal mental health should come under the category of health and disease, a medical category, or under that of ethics and treated accordingly. Is a man who approaches the proposed ideal of positive mental health a moral and virtuous man or a healthy man? To put it differently, one can ask, Is it a design for good life or for health?

The next ideal of mental health to be considered is the ideal for a given culture or historical epoch. According to this approach, each culture has its own unique value system, cultural norms, and social role expectancies. The values of a culture find expression in its primary institutions such as child rearing and in secondary institutions such as mythology and art (Linton, 1956). The cultural values internalized through socialization are embodied in the basic personality structure (Kardiner, 1945). Presumably, the basic personality structure becomes the cultural ideal of a man who is perfectly adjusted and in harmony with his culture. However, the problem besetting this ideal of positive mental health is that of cultural relativism, which affects both the domains of ethics and of mental health. If ethical norms are defined as relative to a culture, there is no possibility of arriving at a code of ethics or legal system that would transcend the cultural boundaries. One could readily agree with cultural relativism as far as customs and perhaps sexual mores are concerned, but one intuitively draws the line when cultural relativism is applied to murder, plunder, and enslavement of one man by another. Generally, there is a tendency to look for the ethical invariances that are transcultural. In the domain of mental health the proponents of cultural relativism state that what is normal in one culture is abnormal in another. For example, according to Ruth Benedict (1934), the most extreme proponent of cultural relativism, a typical native of the Dobu island, considered normal by his compatriots, would be diagnosed a paranoid schizophrenic in the Western culture. This position is generally rejected, as there is good evidence that grossly psychotic individuals are recognized in all cultures although the expression of symptoms may be culturally moulded. However it is more difficult to arrive at a cross-culturally accepted ideal of positive mental health. Normality as a cultural ideal is almost indistinguishable from normality as the social norm. The difference is that the social norm view of normality takes as its model the behaviour of the average member of the culture, while the cultural ideal takes as its model the behaviour of its hero.

The last concept to be considered is normality as an ideal for a particular, unique individual. While the previous concepts of normality as an ideal can be described as nomothetic, the present concept is idiographic. Each personality is unique, the result of unique heredity and life history. What is normal and healthy for one personality may be abnormal and pathological for another. Carl Rogers (1963) in his client-centred, nondirected counselling comes closest to endorsing this idiographic point of view. According to Rogers, since each personality is characterized by a unique pattern of adjustment and growth, the psychotherapist has no preconceived ideas of what the normality or the state of mental health for a particular client should be. There is a great similarity between the humanistic and the individualistic concepts of normality. The difference is in the emphasis. While the humanistic concept emphasizes humanness in general, the individualistic concept emphasizes the unique individual. The process of self-actualization and individuation is important for both, since individuality is one of the attributes of being human.

So far, we have discussed various frames of reference of the concept of normality as an ideal. Presently, we shall discuss two basic conceptualizations of normality as an ideal that are applicable to all the frames of reference. These two conceptualizations are (1) ideal normality as a static or stable state, a state of being, and (2) ideal normality as a process, a state of constant change or growth, a state of becoming. This is the issue of being versus becoming ideals of normality. One conceptualization opts for the metaphysics of *Parmenides* and assigns a high value to stability. The other conceptualization opts for the metaphysics of *Heraclitus* and assigns high value to change, *panta rhei*. In the framework of systems theory, these conceptualizations are in terms of closed (steady-state) and open systems.

The ideal of normality as a static state has had a long history in medicine. The Hippocratic-Galenian tradition equated the state of health with an equilibrium and harmony of body constituents and functions. Many systems of ethics in antiquity, such as the *Nicomachean Ethics* of Aristotle, stressed the golden mean: balance and harmony. In modern times the idea of balance and stability found its expression in the concept of homeostasis. According to this conceptualization, a system of negative feedback mechanisms maintains a steady state in face of a changing environment. A thermostat is an example of such a system. When the temperature increases above a certain point, the fuel supply is cut off (negative feedback); when it drops below a certain point the fuel supply is opened (negative feedback). When the temperature remains within the prescribed narrow range, the two feedback mechanisms are idle. Homeostatic mechanisms play an important role in physiological systems. The body temperature is maintained at a constant level. The blood acidity and blood constituents are maintained at constant levels by complex homeostatic mechanisms.

The success the concept of homeostasis had in physiology inspired psychologists to apply it to their own discipline. Hull (1952) and Miller (1959) based their drive reduction theory of motivation on the concept of homeostasis. According to this theory, a state of need such as hunger for food or a need to escape a noxious stimulus produces a state of general drive that energizes and activates the organism. When the need is satisfied, the drive will be reduced, and a state of balance and tranquility will be regained. This theory became very influential, partly because of the prestige of Clark Hull and his rigorous formulation of this theory. Parallels have been drawn between it and the theory of motivation implied in Freud's theory (Dollard & Miller, 1950). According to Freud a drive emanating from the id produces a state of tension that seeks a discharge. When it is discharged, a state of balance and tranquility is regained by the organism. Thus, the idea of "adjustment," developed in both Functionalist psychology and Freudian psychodynamic psychology, presupposes a state of inner equilibrium combined with an equilibrium between the organism and its environment. Equilibrium, balance, stability, and adjustment became value-loaded, honorific words. According to the stable state conceptualization, ideal normality is equated with a state of equilibrium, stability, and adjustment. The optimal state for an organism is that of inertia and inactivity at the lowest level of negative entropy compatible with life. The organism only reacts to external and internal changes causing a disturbance of the equilibrium, it does not initiate any actions spontaneously.

This concept of the living organism was very congenial to the S-R (stimulus-response) behaviouristic psychology that dominated the American scene in the first half of this century. It regarded an organism as a reflex machine and viewed man as a robot (von Bertalanffy, 1967). In the past twenty years the drive reduction and homeostasis theory of motivation has been criticized both by experimental and by clinical psychologists as well as by biologists (von Bertalanffy, 1966). Living organisms display curiosity, playful behaviour, and need novel stimuli. In addition they grow and evolve into more complex forms. Human beings read thrillers, ride roller coasters, climb mountains, and indulge in artistic creativity. Homeostasis, although important in maintaining an integrity of the organism, fails to explain all biological, psychological, and societal phenomena. As a result of these criticisms, the ideal of normality as a process of continuous growth has been increasing in popularity in recent years. According to this idea, human personality is in a constant state of growth or of becoming (Allport, 1955). An arrest of psychological development spells stagnation and even regression. All goals are really fictitious, and as soon as they are attained man sets new goals. Thus, normality and health are equated with constant growth and development.

This conceptualization of health and normality finds support in an extended version of open systems theory. According to this theory, living organisms are open systems that not only maintain a steady state in the face of a changing environment but also grow in complexity, thus attaining a less probable state and increasing negative entropy. This principle applies both to ontogeny and phylogeny, to the evolution of ever more complex (higher) species as well as to the development of more complex (higher) cultural forms. An important attribute of human life in its biological and societal aspects is a constant progress and change. The theoreticians who value progress, development, growth, and creativity equate these processes with normality, mental health, and well-being. They believe that a good adjustment and inner equilibrium are not sufficient to account for positive mental health. Briefly, the ideal normality and positive mental health is equated by them with maximization of negative entropy.

Normality as the absence of illness

The last concept of normality to be discussed is normality as the absence of illness. This is a negative concept of mental health. Since it is noncontroversial and appears to be value-free, this concept has many adherents, particularly among psychiatrists who follow the medical model of disease. If there are no manifestations of mental disease a person is regarded as normal and healthy. As the medical concept of disease will be analyzed in the following chapter, it suffices to say here that this theory is really far from being noncontroversial. The disease concept implies a state that is qualitatively different from the state of health or normality. This presupposition has been questioned in the field of somatic medicine; certainly it is even more problematic in the field of mental health.

We have already shown that when disease is reified it becomes regarded as an ontological entity with a resulting quest for the essence of a given disease. Disease conceived as an entity entails a discontinuity between disease and health, or between abnormality and normality, and also between one disease and another. If disease means only a label for a disordered biological system, this system can be characterized by certain parameters. The deviation of values beyond certain critical points on these parameters indicates faulty functioning. If we know the parameters of a physiological system or behavioural pattern, we may attempt, in principle, to define normality and disease quantitatively. Moreover, a simplistic unifactorial view of disease causation has been replaced by a multifactorial view. Consequently, we may as well abandon the concept of disease entities entirely and, instead, talk about physiological and behavioural disorders. It appears that we are dealing with complex biological and ecological systems that are in equilibrium. A change beyond certain values of the parameters of these systems will upset the equilibrium and produce clinically manifest diseases. Reacting to the blurring of the distinctions between health and disease in modern physical medicine, Williams and Siegel (1961) have suggested that a new branch of medical science be established. They call this new branch propetology (leaning towards). It is concerned with the tendencies towards pathology. If this suggestion is generally accepted, the continuity point of view will supersede that of discontinuity in the field of physical medicine. Conceived in the terms of the system theory, disease model implies continuity between health and disease rather than discontinuity. This was already suggested by Claude Bernard (1961), although in different words, more than one hundred years ago.

However, in physical medicine the disease model is generally accepted and sufficient for practical purposes. When the traditional disease model is applied to the field of physical health, it is, for all practical purposes, possible to draw the line between disease and normality, even while making allowances for gray areas. It is much more difficult to do so in the field of mental health. In epidemiological studies of this field that use the disease concept, the prevalence of normality in a given population may be established by calculating the prevalence and incidence rates of diseases. The prevalence rate refers to the proportion of the population (often calculated as number of cases per 100,000 population) diagnosed in a given period of time (e.g., one year) as suffering from a disease. The incidence rate refers to the proportion of the population who have contracted the disease in a given period of time (the new cases). From these rates the morbidity risk rates for a disease can be calculated for a given population or a group in the population. By calculating these rates for all diseases we can, in principle, calculate the proportion of the population who are sick or who will develop a sickness at some time during their life and, thus, draw a line between normal and abnormal.

There are two methods of calculating these rates. The first method is to conduct a census of mental hospital populations, which can be extended to the patients attending psychiatric outpatient facilities and the offices of private psychiatrists and of clinical psychologists. The reported figures depend on the presence of psychiatric facilities and hospital admission policies, which can vary a great deal. The second method is an epidemological survey of representative samples of populations. The figures obtained from the surveys of representative samples of the general population estimate the prevalence of mental illness or abnormality at much higher rates than those obtained by the first method. The figures vary from 80 percent in the Manhattan study (Srole et al., 1962) to 9.3 percent (Pasamanick et al., 1964) and depend on the adopted criteria of mental illness. A recent review of epidemiological studies of mental illness prevalence in the United States estimates the rate at between 15 percent and 25 percent (Dohrenwend, Dohrenwend, Gould, Link, Neugebauer, & Wunsch-Hitzig, 1980). It can be seen from these examples that the estimates of normality and abnormality based on prevalence of mental illness and maladjustment vary considerably, indicating that there is no agreement on the criteria.

An important issue in making a distinction between normality and abnormality is that of continuity versus discontinuity. According to the continuity view mental illness and health constitute one continuum: starting with normality, followed by mild psychoneuroses, the severe psychoneuroses, the mild psychoses, and ending with the most severe psychoses. This is the point of view of the psychoanalytical school of thought and in particular of those of its members who believe that there is only "one mental illness" (Menninger, 1963). Other authorities postulate more than one dimension to describe psychopathology. Thus, Eysenck (1961) postulates two independent, orthogonal dimensions: neuroticism and psychoticism. Each person occupies a point determined by these two dimensions. The traditional medical point of view on the other hand is that of discontinuity. Disease entities such as schizophrenia, depression, and obsessional-compulsive neurosis are qualitatively different from one another, and they are all qualitatively different from the state of normality or mental health. Although there may be a dimension of general pathology or severity of illness (Endicott, Spitzer, Fleiss, & Cohen, 1976), diseases are considered discontinuous and independent from one another. For instance, the same patient at the same time may be suffering from both schizophrenia and obsessional-compulsive neurosis or hysteria.

VARIOUS MEANINGS OF PSYCHIATRIC DIAGNOSIS

In the remainder of this chapter a brief analysis is offered of the various meanings of psychiatric diagnosis. The main concern of the present discussion is with the intensional rather than the extensional aspects of the concept. Regarding the extensional aspects, it suffices to say that a respectable level of diagnostic reliability can be attained when the diagnosticians agree on and are trained in the use of specific criteria. Thus, in a recent study of sixty-eight newly admitted psychiatric patients in the New York State Psychiatric Institute, the interjudge reliability was 0.88 (Spitzer, 1975). However, when there is no strict agreement on the criteria the interjudge reliability is low as indicated by the differences in the diagnosis of the same patients by American and British psychiatrists (Cooper, Kendell, Gurland, Sharpe, Copeland, & Simon, 1972). The diagnosis, or ostensive definition of a behaviour as mental illness, depends to a great extent on the social conventions and the context. Whether a person is declared sane or insane depends on the circumstances, as has been shown by Rosenhan (1973).

The intensional meaning of psychiatric diagnosis depends on the degree of the theoretical commitment of the diagnostician and on his purpose.

Diagnosis as a convention

This diagnosis implies a minimum of theoretical commitment. The purpose of such a conventional diagnosis is to enable clinicians and researchers to communicate with one another. The examples of this type of diagnostic procedures are such schemas as *The American Psychiatric Association Diagnostic and Statistical Manual of Mental Disorders* (DSM-III, 1980) or *Research Diagnostic Criteria* (RDC) (Feighner, Robins, Guze, Woodruff, Winokur, & Munoz, 1972), which aim at a standardization of diagnoses and an improvement of the communication among clinicians and research workers.

Diagnosis of a syndrome

This type of diagnosis[*] makes only a weak theoretical commitment, although stronger than in the case of diagnosis as a convention. It implies a low level of inductive generalization. It claims that, *in general*, certain symptoms tend to occur together because there is a correlation among these symptoms. For instance, thought disorder, hallucination, social withdrawal, and flatness of affect tend to occur together. The syndrome diagnosis takes cross-sectional viewpoint: certain symptoms tend to occur together at certain points of time; they are intercorrelated.

Diagnosis as prognosis

This type of diagnosis makes a somewhat stronger theoretical commitment than the previous one. It predicts from the presence of certain signs and symptoms and from the history of their development in the patient the further course of events. It predicts symptoms that will appear in the future and the ultimate outcome of the patient's illness. This type of diagnosis takes a longitudinal point of view. It predicts from the past history and the present state the future outcome. Diagnosis as prognosis, therefore, postulates low power inductive laws (limited generalization laws). The operational meaning of Emil Kraepelin's diagnostic procedures exemplifies this type of diagnosis. Notwithstanding the surplus meaning Kraepelin attached to his nosological categories, from the operationalist point of view, he was only claiming that certain patients had poor prognoses and other patients good prognoses. The patients whom he labelled on the basis of their symptoms and past history as *dementia praecox* had a poor prognosis and were going to deteriorate. The patients whom he labelled manic-depressives had

---

[*]For the benefit of the nonmedical reader the distinction between symptom, sign, syndrome, and disease is spelled out. Symptom is a circumscribed pathological subjective experience such as pain, discomfort, or hallucination. Sign is a circumscribed objective, morphological, functional physiological or behavioural abnormality. Syndrome is a cluster of symptoms and signs occurring together. It may be produced by different, usually unknown, etiological factors or pathological mechanisms. Disease is a nosological entity in which in addition to a specific syndrome there is a typical natural history of the onset, course, and outcome. It is produced by specific etiological factors and pathological mechanisms.

a good prognosis regarding the present illness but were likely to develop a relapse.

Diagnosis of a disease

This diagnosis implies the strongest theoretical commitment. It means that operationally defined variables are firmly embedded in a *nomological* network of theoretical concepts, with high power of general explanatory validity (Hempel, 1961). To put it differently a proper concept of disease implies a valid theory that explains it. It means that causes and mechanisms behind the data of observation are known, that relationships are understood, and that predictions can be made with a high degree of probability. Very few psychiatric conditions satisfy these requirements (see Chapter 3).

The remaining two types of psychiatric diagnosis cannot be easily placed on the continuum of theoretical commitment.

Diagnosis as a decision

The first to be discussed in this category is diagnosis as a decision. A decision regarding the patient is an important aspect of most diagnostic processes. A psychiatric diagnosis entails usually some decision regarding the disposal and treatment of the patient. For instance, when a patient is diagnosed as schizophrenic or psychotic, he is usually committed into a mental hospital and is put on large doses of tranquilizers. On the other hand if a patient is diagnosed as an immature personality, he is recommended for psychotherapy. Hollingshead and Redlich (1958) have found that patients belonging to the low socioeconomic classes tend to be diagnosed schizophrenic, to be committed to mental institutions, and to receive physical therapy. They also found that patients belonging to the high and the middle social classes tend to be diagnosed as psychoneurotic or personality disorders and treated by psychoanalysis. It may very well happen that two patients displaying the same symptoms, depending on their social background and economic circumstances, may be assigned different diagnoses to justify different decisions regarding their disposal. Thus, the diagnosis may be a justification for the disposal and therapeutic decisions, which are made not only on the clinical grounds but also on the social and economic grounds. The meaning of diagnosis therefore may lie in the decisions made about the patients. These decisions may be such as to commit a patient to a mental hospital or not commit him, to charge him with a crime or not to charge him, to treat him with E.C.T., phenothiazines, lithium, or psychotherapy or not treat him, and so on. All these administrative and therapeutic decisions are justified and backed by the diagnostic labels.

The psychiatric diagnostician, therefore, is a decision maker. Moreover, he must make forced decisions. He cannot postpone his decisions and withhold his judgement in the way a scientist can do when evidence is insufficient. In recent years we have seen the development of decision theory that offers formal mathematical models of rational decision making. Since human decision making approximates these models, a brief scrutiny of them may be useful to see how they can apply to the psychiatric decision making and diagnosis. The first model is the application of Bayes' theorem, originally proposed by Rev. Bayes, an English eighteenth century mathematician. According to this theorem

$$p(A/B) = \frac{p(B/A) \cdot p(A)}{p(B/A) \cdot p(A) + p(B/\overline{A}) \cdot p(\overline{A})} \qquad (1)$$

(See the text for the explanation of the symbols.)

An example from a recent controversy stirred up by Rosenhan's study (1973) on being sane in insane places will illustrate the application of this theorem to psychiatric diagnosis. Rosenhan arranged for twelve confederates to present themselves at twelve different mental hospitals and to complain that they had been hearing voices. On the basis of this complaint, eleven out of twelve pseudopatients were admitted to mental hospitals with the diagnosis of schizophrenia. In his paper, Rosenhan used these results to argue that psychiatric diagnosis is unreliable and leads often to an incarceration of sane people in mental hospitals. Rosenhan's article provoked a lively polemic. Davis (1976), in his rebuttal of Rosenhan's argument, contended that the psychiatrists were quite justified in their decision of making diagnosis of schizophrenia on the basis of auditory hallucinations. To support his argument Davis, following Meehl and Rosen (1955), used the Bayes theorem. According to this theorem $p(A/B)$ is the conditional probability of schizophrenia (A) in the presence of hallucinations (B), p(B/A) is the conditional probability of hallucinations in the presence of schizophrenia, p(A) the probability of schizophrenia (the base rate, or a priori probability), p(B/$\overline{A}$) is the conditional probability of hallucinations in the absence of schizophrenia, p($\overline{A}$) the probability of absence of schizophrenia, and p(B) the overall probability of hallucinations. The theorem may be rewritten in the form

$$p(A/B) = \frac{p(A) \cdot p(B/A)}{p(B)} \qquad (2)$$

From these two equations Davis derives an inequality:

$$\frac{p(A)}{p(\overline{A})} > \frac{p(B/\overline{A})}{p(B/A)} \quad \text{given } p(A/B) > p(\overline{A}/B). \qquad (3)$$

This inequality implies that the diagnosis of schizophrenia in the presence of hallucinations is more often right than wrong (i.e., its probability exceeds 0.50) if, and only if, the ratio of the base rate of schizophrenia to the base rate of nonschizophrenia is greater than the ratio of the rate of hallucinations in the absence of schizophrenia to the rate of hallucinations in the presence of schizophrenia. According to Davis, the rate of hallucinations in schizophrenia is estimated at 35 percent (p = 0.35) and the rate of hallucinations in other psychiatric patients at 10 percent (p = 0.10) (Zigler & Philips, 1961). Davis estimates further, on the basis of reported statistics, that 72.4 percent (p = 0.72) psychiatric patients presenting themselves in state mental hospitals are, when chronic brain syndrome is excluded, eventually diagnosed as schizophrenics. Therefore

$$\frac{0.72}{0.28} > \frac{0.10}{0.35} \text{ or } 2.57 > 0.29$$

This inequality strongly supports the decision of using the presence of hallucinations as a criterion for schizophrenia. From the equation (1) it can be calculated that the presence of hallucinations in patients presenting themselves in a mental hospital increases the probability of the diagnosis of schizophrenia to p = 0.90. This example does not necessarily indicate that all the assumptions underlying Davis's argument are true, but it illustrates the application of the Bayesian theorem to the psychiatric decision making.

The second mathematical model of decision making as applied to psychiatric diagnosis is the signal detection model, mainly used in psychophysics (Swets, Tanner, & Birdsall, 1961; Coombs, Dawes, & Tversky, 1970). Suppose that a psychiatrist is trying to decide whether to take seriously a patient's suicidal threats, diagnosing him as a depressive, admitting him to the hospital, and putting him under close observation. There is always a possibility that the patient is only acting out, putting on a histrionic display and that he will never carry out his threats. Further, let us assume that there are certain signs and symptoms that indicate with a greater or lesser degree of probability that the patient, in actual fact, will make a serious suicidal attempt. These indications of suicidal risk may be thought to form a continuum from the zero level of risk to an almost complete certainty that a patient will try to commit suicide. Let us call this continuum the index of suicidal risk. If the psychiatrist decides on a cutoff point (decision criterion) at a certain level of the suicidal risk index, he will admit patients with a higher index than the cut-off point and will not admit patients with a lower one. He will also probably diagnose the latter patients as neurotic and psychopathic rather than as depressives. Among the admitted patients there will always be some who are acutely suicidal and who will make suicidal attempts, fortunately thwarted because the patients are under constant observation. These patients, in the signal detection terminology, will be "hits." In the admitted group there also will be patients who will not make suicidal attempts and will be found to be just hysterics. These patients will be false alarms. Among the patients who have not been admitted will be those who will commit suicide, or make a serious suicidal attempt (misses), and those who will prove not to be really suicidal (correct rejections). Moving the cutoff point (decision criterion) to a lower level of the suicidal risk index will increase not only the number of hits but also the number of false alarms. It will decrease the number of misses as well as the number of correct rejections. Moving the cutoff point (decision criterion) to a higher level of the suicidal risk index will have the opposite effect. It will increase the number of correct rejections and will decrease the number of hits. It will decrease the number of false alarms and will increase the number of misses.

In setting the cutoff point for considering the suicidal risk as serious and therefore diagnosing depression our psychiatrist may be motivated by two considerations. If he considers that preventing suicide, at any cost, is the most important consideration, he will set the cutoff point at a low level of the suicidal risk index, so as to maximize the number of hits and minimize the number of misses. On the other hand if he attaches a great importance to human rights he will be reluctant to deprive patients of their freedom by committing them to a mental hospital. He will try to minimize the number of false alarms and maximize the number of correct rejections. As a result, he will tend to set the cutoff point at a higher level of the suicidal risk index. These relationships are illustrated by Figure 1. The signal detection model presupposes the existence of two independent populations: the genuinely suicidal patients and the pseudosuicidal patients. On the average, the genuinely suicidal patients will score higher on the suicidal risk index than the pseudosuicidal patients. However, there will be a considerable overlap. This model has two important parameters: B (decision criterion), which expresses the response bias, in our case the psychiatrist's diagnostic bias, and d', the cut-off point that produces the best discrimination between the genuinely suicidal and the pseudosuicidal patients. For our discussion only the parameter B, the diagnostic bias, is important, since calculating the d' parameter would involve systematically changing the payoff matrix of hits, misses, false alarms, and correct rejections. Such experimental changing of the payoff matrix would not be acceptable on ethical grounds.

Other mathematical models of decision making using utility functions have been proposed (Coombs, Dawes, & Tversky, 1970). Some of them could be applied to psychiatric decision making.

Diagnosing as labelling

The next type of diagnosis to be considered is diagnosis as labelling and stigmatizing. This aspect of psychiatric diagnosis is emphasized by Scheff (1966, 1975) and by Szasz (1961b). According to this view, the purpose of psychiatric diagnosis is to stigmatize and label social deviants. Psychiatric diagnosis implies negative valuation and rejection. Charles Stevenson, in his *Ethics and Language* (1944), calls this type of labelling a persuasive definition, the purpose of which is to convey a negative valuation rather than objective

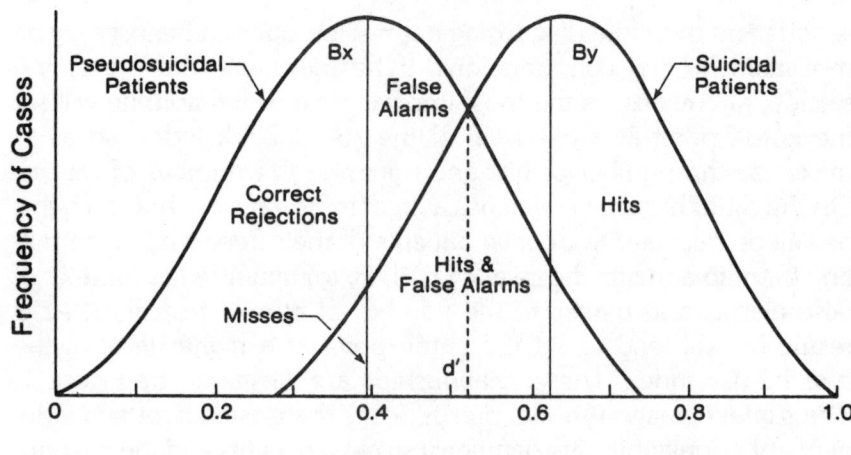

Bx — Cut-off point (decision criterion) biased towards prevention of suicide.

By — Cut-off point (decision criterion) biased towards preservation of civil rights.

d' — Cut-off point for the best discrimination.

Note: "Hits", "False Alarms", "Misses" and "Correct Rejections" apply when Bx is used as the cut-off point.

Figure 1. Signal detection as related to suicidal risk.

information. If you call somebody a psychotic, a schizophrenic, a psychopath, or a sociopath, these labels have the same negative emotive connotations as that which is conveyed by such epithets as madman, criminal, crook, hippy, and so on. They are similar to such designations as communist, radical, or fascist, which have definitely negative emotive connotations in our society. This topic will be discussed further in Chapter 5.

Scheff (1966) also stresses the fact the psychiatrist, by virtue of his medical training, is quite ready to make Type 2 statistical error—to diagnose the patient as having a disease, when he is actually healthy, rather than to make Type 1 statistical error—to diagnose a patient as healthy when he is actually suffering from a disease. This strategy, which is justified in some areas of somatic medicine where diseases are quite determined, in psychiatric patients leads to unnecessary social stigmatization. The medical and psychiatric strategy is in contrast to the practice of jurists who lean backward not to make Type 1 error—to find an innocent man guilty. In case of doubt they prefer a guilty man to go free rather than an innocent man be convicted.

Nomothetic versus idiographic diagnosis

Finally, all diagnoses can be divided into mainly (1) nomothetic in their intent and mainly (2) idiographic. The nomothetic type of diagnosis pigeonholes patients into certain general diagnostic categories that imply some general scientific laws. The traditional medical disease model entails this type of diagnosis. The idiographic diagnosis considers each patient as a unique individual and tries to arrive at his description and assessment in the particular context of the biological, psychological, and social factors influencing the patient. Psychodynamic psychiatrists, the Rogerian psychotherapists, and the Meyerian biopsychiatrists are predominantly idiographic in their diagnostic procedures.

To conclude, the concept of normality and the process of psychiatric diagnosis confront us with a much greater complexity than could be gathered from a cursory examination.

Chapter 3

MEDICAL MODELS

INTRODUCTION

The decision whether a model or a theory of mental illness should be considered medical or nonmedical depends on the choice of the criteria. One possible criterion lies in the actual approach to mental illness, i.e., the therapeutic practice of the members of the medical profession. Thus, in America psychoanalysts are usually also psychiatrists and therefore medically trained. Indeed, in the popular mind psychoanalysis is closely identified with psychiatry. On the other hand, it is also possible to look at the theoretical framework of the medical sciences and consider as medical only the models of mental illness that can be accommodated in this framework. Since psychoanalysis cannot be easily accommodated within the ambit of the basic biological sciences, now taught to medical students as constituting the foundation of clinical medicine, it should not be considered a medical theory. It will be discussed, therefore, together with other psychological approaches in the next chapter.

In the present discussion, medical models are identified with somatic or organic approaches to mental illness. This position may be criticized because it artificially divides man into body and mind. It can be said that a physician always treats the whole man. This criticism is certainly justified. However, owing to the pervasive influence of the Cartesian metaphysics of body-mind dualism and due to the influence of mechanistic materialism on the medical sciences during the nineteenth century, the split into body and mind has become a reality in medical thinking. Medicine has claimed as its domain the body of man leaving his mind to philosophy and to what used to be called moral sciences. Anatomy, physiology, and later on biochemistry became the basic sciences of medicine. The human body, including the human brain, came to be regarded as an exceedingly complex machine to be explained by chemical and physical processes. The psychological approach to man was regarded as being outside the domain of medicine and, when smuggled into it, was regarded with suspicion as nonscientific and smacking of quackery. When, at the end of the nineteenth century experimental psychology was established as a biological science separate from philosophy, it was not established in the medical faculties but rather in the faculties of philosophy and humanities, even though its most important founders, Gustav T. Fechner, Wilhelm Wundt, and William James, were all medically qualified. During the lifetime of its founder, psychoanalysis, particularly in Europe, was outside the mainstream of academic psychiatry, which tended to be somatic in its orientation. It was only after the second world war and only in America that psychoanalysis came to dominate psychiatry. Consequently, only models of mental illness conceived within the framework of anatomy, physiology, biochemistry, and pathology can reasonably be regarded as medical.

It is true that the organically oriented psychiatrists have been interested in mental phenomena. They have offered excellent descriptions of psychopathological phenomena, which because of an absence of physical signs have served as diagnostic criteria for various mental illnesses. However, in the scheme of somatic psychiatry the psychopathological phenomena have no intrinsic meaning of their own; they are only manifestations of disease processes in the brain. Although the organic psychiatrist often has rejected materialistic philosophy and has not regarded his own thoughts and imagery or those of normal people as epiphenomena, he has taken a materialistic position when confronted with mental patients. In such a situation he has regarded inner experiences and utterances of his patients as a product of pathological processes in the brain. The causation has tended to be regarded as unidirectional: from the disordered physiological events to abnormal mental phenomena and not vice versa. Only more recently and under the influence of psychodynamic theories has the possibility of a reversal of the direction of the causes been entertained with the rise of psychosomatic medicine.

The traditional attitude of the organic psychiatrists can be illustrated by the words of Emil Kraepelin, the father of modern organic psychiatry. In his *Lectures on Clinical Psychiatry* (1913) he opens the first lecture with the following statement:

> Gentlemen, the subject of the following lectures will be scientific psychiatry, which, as its name implies, is that of the treatment of mental diseases. It is true, in the strictest terms we cannot speak of the mind as becoming diseased, whether we regard it as a separate entity or as a sum total of subjective experience. And, indeed, from the medical point of view, it is the disturbance of the *physical foundations* of mental life which should occupy most of our attention.... But, the incidence (manifestations) of such diseases are generally seen in the sphere of psychical events, a department with which the art of medicine has dealt very little as yet.

This statement indicates that for Kraepelin mental illnesses were diseases of the brain and that abnormal psychological phenomena were only symptoms of these diseases. In the history of medicine one can distinguish two models: that of disease and that of constitution. The disease model has tended to stress a discontinuity between health and disease, while the constitutional model has emphasized a continuity between the two. Owing to the revolutionary discovery that bacteria cause many diseases the disease model has come to dominate medicine and for a while eclipsed almost completely the constitutional model.

DISEASE AND CONSTITUTION IN GENERAL MEDICINE

Before these two models are discussed in the context of psychiatry, it is worthwhile to survey the scene of general medicine and to discuss briefly the evolution of the concept of disease from the middle of the nineteenth century to the present time. This step will clarify, in the light of modern biology, both the concept of disease and the concept of constitution. It has to be stressed at the outset that the division between disease and constitution is arbitrary and may not reflect actual reality. Nevertheless, it is deeply ingrained in medical thinking about pathology.

Disease Model

Dorland's *American Illustrated Medical Dictionary* defines disease as, "a definite morbid process having a characteristic train of symptoms.

It may affect the whole body or any of its parts; its cause, pathology and prognosis may be known or unknown" (in Selye, 1956). What does this definition imply? It implies that disease is an altered state of the organism that constitutes a break from its natural state and development. It also suggests that disease is an extrinsic development that is alien to the organism. There is an etiological factor or factors that at a certain point in the life history of the organism start a pathological process affecting a certain organ, a system, or the whole organism. This pathological process manifests itself in a malfunctioning of bodily organs during a certain period of time. It causes cellular changes, which can be established at the postmortem. It manifests in physiological and biochemical derangements, causing characteristic signs and symptoms of the particular disease. Further, it is an ongoing process that has a more or less definite beginning, a typical natural history, and a certain prognosis: death, recovery, or chronic invalidism. Ideally, the etiology as well as the mechanisms behind the pathological process are well understood in terms of biochemistry and molecular biology. It has to be admitted that even in somatic medicine, with the exception of acute infectious diseases, very few diseases approach these requirements.

The great discoveries of bacteriology in the second half of the nineteenth century revolutionized medical thinking at the time and firmly established the disease model. They also gave rise to the simplistic notion that specific bacteria cause specific diseases. The causal relation was codified by Koch's famous postulates (Susser, 1973). However, as more facts became known, this simplistic notion had to be abandoned and was replaced by one of multifactorial causation. In infectious diseases, as in any other diseases, one deals always not only with a pathogenic agent affecting the organism but also with the organism's reaction to the pathogenic agent. Very often the reaction of the organism is more damaging than the effect of the pathogen. In a sense, disease is a reaction to rather than an effect of noxious forces (Wolf, 1968). This fact is particularly important in autoimmune processes, characterizing later stages of some infectious diseases such as syphilis, tuberculosis, and leprosy. Other diseases such as multiple sclerosis and allergic encephalomyelitis are suspected to be autoimmune. These diseases are usually chronic and run a recurrent course. Other conditions in which the relation between the pathogenic organism and the host organism is not clear are the slow virus diseases such as human subacute encephalitis and the Kuru disease. A rare presenile dementia, the Creutzfeldt-Jakob disease, has recently been found to be caused by a slow virus. Other presenile dementias such as the more common Pick's disease are suspected also to be so caused.

The traditional disease model implies an extrinsic agent invading the organism and causing a disease process. "An ugly visitor falling upon hapless victims by chance" (Menninger, 1963). This condition is the best satisfied by infectious diseases that are caused by bacteria and viruses. However, the books on pathology describe other types of diseases that do not fit the picture so well but that come near enough to fit the disease model rather than the constitutional model. There are extrinsic factors other than bacteria and viruses (said to cause diseases): toxins, dietary deficiencies, and traumas. Toxins may cause acute illness with delirium and mental confusion. An acute mental illness associated with poisoning by exogenous toxins was described by Karl Bonhoeffer as "exogenous toxic psychosis" (exogenous reaction type). Other toxins, such as air pollutants, heavy metal ions (e.g., mercury), and pesticides may cause chronic poisoning. Nutritional deficiencies, for example, lack of proteins, vitamins, and certain essential minerals, can cause diseases.

The diseases due to intrinsic factors are malignant tumours (neoplasms) and hereditary or congenital metabolic abnormalities. In malignancies, such as cancer, at a certain point of an organism's life history a cell or a group of cells starts behaving as an alien entity competing for nourishment with normal cells and destroying tissues and organs. There is, therefore, a similarity between diseases caused by malignant tumours and diseases caused by bacteria and viruses.

The position of hereditary metabolic errors is less clear. These conditions are definitely produced by endogenous inherited factors. However, the hereditary metabolic abnormalities are regarded by the medical profession as diseases discontinuous with the state of health. The inborn metabolic errors may be divided into those caused by an inheritance of single pathogenic genes and those caused by chromosomal abnormalities. The first are due to recessive or dominant abnormal genes and involve usually an absence or abnormality of one enzyme. The second are due to chromosomal abnormalities produced by noxious extrinsic factors during myosis of the germ cells or during early phases of gestation. They involve more extensive enzymatic abnormalities.

It is customary in genetics to distinguish two modes of inheritance. The first mode is associated with single genes of major effect. The second is polygenic. In the first mode traits are inherited according to the Mendelian laws, while in the second the polygenic inheritance traits are continuously distributed in the population. Such characteristics as intelligence, height, and inherited personality traits are polygenically determined. Their continuous distributions usually follow the Gaussian curve. In addition to the monogenic and the polygenic there is also the genetic heterogeneity mode of inheritance in which a trait is determined by a combination of a small number of specific genes. Although distinction is rather arbitrary, it makes sense to consider the metabolic errors and other pathological traits of the organism, produced by inheritance of a single gene of major effect, as belonging to the disease model category. In contrast, the conditions associated with continuously distributed traits, which are inherited polygenetically, fit better the constitutional model.

Following this distinction, the familial mental subnormality, representing the lower end of normal distribution of intelligence, belongs to the second model, while the special syndromes of subnormality, such as Phenylketonuria (PKU), belong to the first. Phenylketonuria (phenylpyruvic idiocy) is an inborn metabolic abnormality, inherited by a single autosomal gene. The abnormality is caused by an absence of the enzyme, phenylalanine hydroxylase, which converts the amino acid phenylalanine into another amino acid, tyrosine. A metabolic block is produced. Since phenylalanine is not metabolized it tends to accumulate in the body. Eventually, the accumulation of phenylpyruvic acid and other abnormal metabolites of phenylalanine cause damage to the nervous system, associated with mental subnormality, by interfering with the metabolism of the amino acid tryptophan. Since phenylalanine is not essential for the metabolism of the organism and can be replaced entirely by tyrosine, a precursor of dopamine and noradrenaline, the damage to the nervous system and mental retardation can be prevented by a phenylalanine free diet. Phenylpyruvic acid is excreted in urine, and may be detected about four weeks after birth by a simple urine test, using 10 percent ferric chloride. Phenylketonuria, which is easily diagnosed and prevented by relatively simple therapeutic measures, has been discussed in detail for two reasons. First, it shows that a single gene-determined metabolic error affects only one small aspect of the functioning of the organism, and when it is remedied the organism is restored to normality. The condition may be regarded as extrinsic to the totality of the organismic functions, and therefore it fits the disease rather than the constitutional model. Second, phenylketonuria has become a model disease for biochemical studies of schizophrenia and other endogenous psychoses. This is due to the fact that phenylketonuria is caused by an abnormality in the early stages of the metabolic sequence leading to the production of catecholamines, important neurotransmitters of the brain. Abnormalities of catecholamines and other biogenic amines have been suspected to be the etiological factors in schizophrenia and manic-depressive psychosis.

Most of the metabolic errors are produced by recessive genes (Huntington's chorea, caused by a single dominant gene, is an exception). These genes express themselves in the phenotypes only in the homozygotic form (the two alleles are the recessive genes). They do not express themselves in the heterozygotic form. Because of this, recessive genes responsible for metabolic error can survive for a long time in a population. However, when they express themselves they are removed from circulation, because the affected individual usually does not reproduce. They are replaced by mutations, caused by such environmental accidental factors as radiation and certain chemical agents. Since the rate of mutations is rather low, diseases produced by an inherited metabolic error are rare.

The expression of dominant or recessive genes of major effect may be suppressed by other genes of the genome. This is described as gene penetrance. Because of the differences in penetrance, the inheritance of the traits determined by single genes of major effect may not exactly follow the Mendelian laws. The effect of the total genome on the individual gene is expressed in the phenotype as an interaction between the hereditary disease and the total constitution of the organism.

The interaction between disease and constitution perhaps warrants the recognition of another model, the diathesis-stress model, in addition to the disease and the constitutional models. The expression of a characteristic due to a metabolic error may be modified not only by the penetrance of the determining gene but also by the environmental factors. A mild metabolic disorder may not seriously affect an organism in a protected environment but may cause a breakdown in adjustment when the organism is exposed to general or specific stress.

The disease model presupposed the existence of discrete entities, the disease categories. A nosology that carves nature at the joints is an ideal to be aimed at. However, with many gaps in the existing knowledge, it is possible to propose different taxonomic systems. They may be based on clinical syndromes by which diseases manifest themselves, they may be based on the etiological factors, or they may be based on the histopathological changes found at the postmortem. The existing taxonomies in medicine are usually based on a mixture of the three. Also, the disease categories may be broad or narrow. Some clinicians look for specific, i.e., particular disease entities, while others prefer to use broader categories, stressing the communalities of certain pathological processes and the reactions of the organism to them. Into such broad categories are grouped inflammations, malignancies, collagen diseases, or stress diseases. Finally, one can ask whether there are any common properties of sickness as such, irrespective of the particular specific pathologies. Such a one disease theory was proposed by Hans Selye (1956) as the general adaptation syndrome (GAS). The latter is a general physiological reaction to noxious agents and stress, regulated by endocrinal mechanisms and influenced by psychological factors (Selye, 1978). Many common diseases may be largely due to errors of adaptation to stress rather than to damage by noxious agents.

Other investigators, without going as far as Selye and without postulating only one disease, recognized the importance of life stress as a cause of certain diseases. Harold Wolf (1968), in his book *Stress and Disease*, stated that, "since stress is a dynamic state within an organism in response to a demand for adaptation, and since life itself entails constant adaptations, living creatures are continually in a state of more or of less stress" (Wolf, 1968). Stress is conceived as both physical and psychological. Since living involves the constant exposure to stress, causing wear and tear of the organism, disease appears to be coterminous with life. More recently, Holroyd (1979) has reformulated the role of stress in the causation of diseases in terms of the transactions between the individual and the environment. The physiological reaction to stress depends on the behavioural coping mechanisms. If the individual has psychological resources that allow him to cope with a stress situation the physiological reaction does not exceed the normal bounds. However, a failure to cope adequately with the demands of the environment may cause a physiological disregulation harmful to the organism.

Constitutional Model

The development of the new science of endocrinology, early in the twentieth century, revived interest in constitutional model. Hormones became the modern version of the humors of the Hippocratic-Galenian medical system. In particular, this interest was revived in the twenties and the thirties of the present century by the work of G. Draper (Draper, Dupertius, & Caughey, 1944), who was concerned with the relation of the human constitution to various somatic diseases. Constitution may be defined as that aggregate of hereditary characteristics, influenced to a greater or lesser extent by the environment, which determines the individual's total anatomical, physiological, biochemical, and psychological makeup. From the genetic point of view it may be regarded as the genome of the individual's cells, the totality of his polygenically inherited traits. The actual phenotype is always a product of the interaction of the genotype and the environment. Individual differences in the presence of a homogeneous environment indicate that they are due to hereditary factors. The presence of individual differences in a genetically homogeneous sample, as in the case of identical twins, indicates that these differences are determined by the heterogeneity of the environment. By using certain statistical techniques it is possible to establish the proportion of the variance of a given characteristic, which is determined by heredity. This is the basis of the concept of heritability of traits.

Because many protagonists of the constitutional model based their human typologies on anthropometric data, the concept of constitution has become strongly associated with that of physique. This is unfortunate. The physique is only one possible criterion for typology. Although it is obviously genetically determined, it may be more modifiable by such environmental factors as diet and exercise than it was believed to be by the early proponents of the constitutional point of view. Some disappointing results of the early attempts to relate disease, character, and temperament to the human physique as determined by somatotyping could have stemmed from a wrong choice of the criterion for constitutional typology. Ideally, the criterion for such a typology should be the genetic map of the *karyotype* (chromosomes) of the human cell. This ideal has been attained in the fruit fly (*Drosophila*), but it is far off as far as human beings are concerned. In the meantime, certain biochemical and serological characteristics may provide a better criterion than physique for human typology. With regard to human pathology, acute infections fit the disease model the best, the heredodegenerative diseases fall between the disease and the constitutional models, and the degenerative processes due to aging such as arteriosclerosis could best be described as processes associated with the variations of the human constitution rather than diseases. After this digression into general pathology and human biology we return to the disease and constitutional models in their application to the problem of mental illness.

DISEASE MODEL IN PSYCHIATRY

Nosology

The contemporary disease model of psychiatry has its roots in the system of psychiatry created by Emil Kraepelin (1855-1926). Since Wilhelm Griesinger (1817-1868) there was a trend in psychiatry to attribute psychoses to brain diseases and to pay attention to the form of mental disorders rather than to their contents. The discoveries in bacteriology and pathology and the desire to emulate the natural sciences model drew the attention of the psychiatrists away from individual patients to disease entities. Patients tended to be regarded as only reflecting the disease processes. Kraepelin was a careful observer who was not satisfied with a cross-sectional description of his patients but also conducted longitudinal studies of them. He was interested in the natural history of the diseases and their eventual outcome. He attempted to relate clinical syndromes to pathological changes in the brain and other laboratory findings, including those obtained by the methods of experimental psychology—Kraepelin collaborated for a time with Wilhelm Wundt in Leipzig. There were some mental diseases such as general paralysis of the insane or senile dementia that easily could be attributed to anatomo-pathological changes in the brain. Others, in which insanity appeared to be equally profound, were more difficult to connect with such changes. However, since many diseases such as tuberculosis, Bright's disease, or Syndenham's chorea had been originally described only on the basis of clinical observations, Kraepelin decided to follow the same course, hoping that the future research would reveal the pathological changes in the brain. On the basis of longitudinal observation of the patients who did not show gross pathological changes in the brain, he came to a conclusion that they suffered from two distinct disease entities. The first disease started early in life, soon after puberty. It was characterized by bizarre symptoms such as thought disorders and hallucinations, but more than by anything else it was characterized by profound apathy and loss of interest in the environment. This disease had a downhill course ending in a complete dementia and almost never in a recovery. The other disease started usually somewhat later in life, was characterized by pronounced affective disorder, either melancholia or mania. The course of this disease was recurrent, its attacks alternated with periods of health. Moreover, very often melancholia and mania alternated with one another. The first disease was called by Kraepelin *dementia praecox*, the second, manic-depressive psychosis.

Kraepelin was a great systematizer. He was concerned with designing a taxonomy that would provide categories reflecting naturally occurring diseases classified according to their etiology. He also wanted to find out whether certain syndromes were proper nosological categories or only subvarieties of diseases. His famous textbook of psychiatry went through nine editions (1883-1927). Kraepelin's approach towards mental illness went beyond pure theorizing. He believed that mental hospitals should be modeled after general hospitals. Mental patients should be treated exactly in the same way as patients suffering from physical illnesses. Like other patients, mental patients should be kept in bed. Kraepelin was intent on casting mental patients in the sick role. To use the distinction drawn by Siegler and Osmond (1974), Kraepelin changed the social role of mental patients from impaired into sick.

While hysteria became the main concern of early psychotherapists, for mental hospital psychiatrists dementia praecox came to occupy the central focus of attention. In unambiguously organic psychoses, even of the incurable ones, pathology was understood. Those who could not be cured tended to die quickly. Patients suffering from dementia praecox, or as it was renamed by Bleuler, schizophrenia, tended to live a normal span of life and filled up mental hospitals. Moreover, they presented a mystery of a profound mental derangement and alienation without obvious morbid pathology of the brain. Consequently, schizophrenia became the number one problem in the field of mental health presenting a challenge both to the researcher and the clinician. In the past seventy years or so a tremendous amount of effort has been expended to find out on the one hand the organic causes of dementia praecox and on the other to delineate the boundaries of the disease. As has been stated previously, one of the problems confronting the nosographer is the problem of the breadth of the taxonomic categories. Kraepelin tended to broaden the categories that had been used by his predecessors. For instance, he included certain syndromes described earlier in a broader category of dementia praecox. Some of his successors and contemporaries broadened further the category of dementia praecox. Others considered the category of dementia praecox too broad and tried to split it into narrower nosological entities, which they considered as true diseases.

Since it soon became obvious that dementia praecox could occur later in life and did not always lead to dementia, Eugene Bleuler (1857-1939), a Swiss contemporary of Kraepelin, offered in his 1911 book, *Dementia Praecox or the Group of Schizophrenias* (1950), a new interpretation of the concept of dementia praecox. Instead of focusing on the history and the prognosis of the disease, Bleuler turned his attention to the clinical symptoms. He chose as his criterion for the diagnosis of schizophrenia, the new name he gave to dementia praecox, the presence of fundamental symptoms—the combination of symptoms that distinguished this disease from other mental diseases. The fundamental symptoms, which occurred together only in schizophrenia and not in other diseases, were disorder of associations, disorder of affect, and ambivalence. The other symptoms were accessory; they could be present or absent.

Another distinction made by him was between the primary and secondary symptoms. The primary symptoms, i.e., disorder of associations (looseness of association), affective changes, stereotypy, and vasomotor disorders, were caused by organic disease processes in the brain. The secondary symptoms, which included delusions and hallucinations, resulted from a reaction of the patient's personality to the organic disease process. An analogy could be drawn to the dream state. The fact that dream thoughts were illogical, disorganized, and out of touch with reality was due to a low level of physiological functioning of the brain—the brain was idling. On the other hand, the contents of dreams was determined by the previous experiences of the dreamer. The schizophrenic thinking was autistic and complex determined, while the normal thinking was reality determined. Because mental life of the patient was fragmented into primitive emotional complexes, Bleuler changed the name from dementia praecox to schizophrenia—split personality. He also subdivided it into simple, catatonic, hebephrenic, and paranoid schizophrenias. In addition to changing the name, he broadened the diagnostic category to include cases with an onset later in life and cases that recovered. As the title of his book indicates, he did not think of schizophrenia as a unitary disease but rather as a group of diseases, displaying a similar symptomatology. Further, in addition to the organic brain disease processes he recognized the importance of the psychologically determined contents of the morbid experiences. Thus, he recognized the distinction made subsequently in the German psychiatry (Birnbaum, 1923) between the organic pathogenic factors, determined by the disease process, and the psychological pathoplastic factors, determined by the personality development.

In spite of Bleuler's contributions, the differences of the opinion as to how broad the concept of schizophrenia should be has not ceased to cause trouble for the researchers and the clinicians. It appears that psychiatrists belonging to different schools and practicing in different parts of the world vary in the scope of the diagnostic category that they call schizophrenia. For example, the concept of schizophrenia, as used in America, is broader than that used in Europe. This state of affairs leads to a confusion in communication and to contradictory research results. While Bleuler broadened the concept of schizophrenia, the German neurological school of psychiatry tried to break it down to narrower categories, each representing a disease associated with a lesion localized in a specific part of the brain. The neurological psychiatrists, representing the brain localization research tradition of the nineteenth century, were very impressed by the fact that the specific neurological symptoms could be related to the specific neurological lesions. The locus of the lesion causing a loss of a function came to be regarded as the center for this function.

The neurological school of psychiatry in Austria and Germany, represented by such men as C. Westphal, T. Meynert, C. Wernicke, and more recently K. Kleist, espoused the strict localization of the brain functions point of view. Its most important representative, K. Kleist, distinguished altogether twenty-five different varieties of schizophrenia, some typical and some atypical (Fish, 1962). The atypical schizophrenias had a strong familial association. He considered the twenty-five varieties of schizophrenia as distinct heredodegenerative diseases, each associated with a putative degenerative lesion at the specific site of the brain. Since there was no evidence for such putative lesions, Kleist's theory was called by his critics "Kleist's mythology of the brain." K. Leonhard, a follower of Kleist, although continuing the tradition of the neurological school of psychiatry, has been less concerned with associating specific narrow disease entities with the specifically localized lesions in the brain and instead has tried to link them with the specific pathogenic genes. He has distinguished systematic and nonsystematic schizophrenia, corresponding to Kleist's typical and atypical schizophrenias. Altogether, he distinguished nineteen different varieties of schizophrenia, sixteen systematic and three nonsystematic, each representing a different disease (Fish, 1962).

The problem of the breadth of diagnostic categories, and by implication of disease entities, has preoccupied not only researchers working with schizophrenia patients but it also has concerned those who have been investigating manic-depressive psychosis. Particularly the clinically common condition of depression has caused trouble. The term depression has been sometimes used to describe the mood of the patient and at other times as a nosological entity. The first may be regarded as a symptom or manifestation of the second. The question has often been asked whether it is possible to distinguish normal, but perhaps excessive, changes of mood from disturbances of mood caused by a disease process. Kurt Schneider (1920) believed that it was possible and distinguished the reactive from the endogenous depression. This distinction has not been generally accepted. According to "one disease" theory of depression, the basic etiological factor in all depression is the same—a somatic disease process, probably due to the disturbance in biogenic amine metabolism. Variations in the clinical picture are due to the fact that depression is a spectrum disease in which the same etiological factor may be modified in its expression by the various constitutional and secondary psychological mechanisms. In addition, the severity of the disease processes may be responsible for the spectrum extending from a mild psychoneurotic depression at one end to a florid psychotic depression at the other end. Briefly, according to the one disease view of depression, the pathogenic disease-causing factor is the same, and the differences in the clinical pictures are due to the variety in pathoplastic factors. This view of depression was endorsed, among others, by Lewis (1938), Kendell (1968), and Post (1972). The proponents of the two depression theory, endogenous and reactive, base their arguments on the differences in the symptomatology and the response to treatment. They claim that these differences exist even when the variation in the severity is accounted for. This view is represented in addition to Schneider (1959) by Mendels and Cochrane (1968), Pollitt (1960), and Kiloh and Garside (1963). The distinction has also been confirmed by the numerical taxonomy (cluster analysis) technique (Pilowsky, Levine, & Bolton, 1969).

A similar distinction was made in schizophrenia. Patients were divided into reactive and process schizophrenics (Kantor, Wallner, & Winder, 1953). The distinction has a somewhat different meaning in Europe from that in America. In Europe it connotes a differentiation into a schizophrenia caused by organic brain disease and a schizophrenia-like reaction to an environmental stress. The distinction is equivalent to that between endogenous and reactive depressions. In America the distinction is based on the premorbid personality adjustment.

In addition to the distinction of depression into reactive and endogenous, other categories of depression have been proposed. Kraepelin, in a later edition of his textbook, distinguished involutional melancholia from manic-depressive psychosis. However, there is no agreement among authorities on this point. Some consider involutional melancholia as a distinct nosological entity, some as an attack of manic-depressive psychosis occurring late in life. Lately, the involutional melancholia category has been abandoned. More recently, Perris (1966) has introduced the distinction, originally suggested by Leonhard (1957/1979), into bipolar and unipolar depressions. These two varieties of endogenous depression are considered two different illnesses. The first is characterized by alternating attacks of depression and mania—the true circular psychosis. The second is characterized by recurrent attacks of depression. In addition these two types of depression differ in symptomatology and in the genetic determinants. It has been shown that in bipolar depression, the onset is earlier, the episodes are shorter and more frequent than in unipolar depression, and the genetic loading is higher in bipolars than in unipolars. Finally, while unipolar depression occurs more frequently in women, bipolar depression is more evenly distributed between the sexes (Lehmann, 1977). The two depressions are caused by different genes according to the proponents of the unipolar-bipolar distinction.

Van Praag (1974, 1977), and Maas, Fawcett, and Dekirmenjian (1972) have tried to base the classification of depression on the differences in metabolism of biogenic amines. The classification of depression was recently reviewed by Lehmann (1977). He distinguishes endogenous (vital) depression, which is divided into unipolar and bipolar (manic-depressive), and exogenous depression, which is divided into somatogenic (secondary to a somatic systemic disease or an external toxin) and psychogenic. The latter is subdivided into reactive (e.g., a reaction to a bereavement or a disappointment in love) and neurotic (a personality characterized by a proneness to mild depression and anxiety). It is quite clear that there is even less agreement on the taxonomy of the manic-depressive psychosis than that of schizophrenia. The title of a recent review by Kendell (1976) is rather ominous: "The classification of depression: A review of contemporary confusion." To confound further the taxonomy of mental diseases, many cases display both the characteristics of schizophrenia and manic-depressive psychosis. They are diagnosed as schizo-affective disorders. The existing taxonomy is far from being able to carve nature at the joints.

Since the last edition of Kraepelin's textbook in 1927, several modifications have been proposed of his original nosological classification. The latest comprehensive classification of mental disorders is that offered by the DSM-III (*Diagnostic Statistical Manual of Mental Disorders*, 3rd ed.), published in 1980 by the American Psychiatric Association. This latest classificatory system may be described as a retreat from the disease model that was promulgated by the Kraepelinian nosology. The approach taken by the DSM-III is frankly only descriptive and atheoretical, aimed at maximizing the diagnostic reliability and descriptive specificity. The purpose of the new classificatory schema is to improve the communication among clinicians and researchers by means of specific and operationalized descriptive categories. Following the formulation proposed by Blashfield and Draguns (1976), the DSM-III stresses the use of its classification as a basis of communication, as a key to scientific literature, and as a means of precise description. It is noncommital as to the uses of its classificatory schema for prediction and theory construction.

To improve the diagnostic interjudge and test-retest reliability, it uses conjunctive rather than disjunctive categories delineating narrow syndromes, which are carefully operationally defined. About one hundred and ninety syndromes are listed. They are grouped in larger categories that form a hierarchy. This feature of the classification provides a decision tree that allows one to arrive at the diagnosis by progressive choices between two alternatives at a time. Thus, if a reliable description is entered, the making of final diagnosis may be left to a computer (Spitzer, Endicott, & Diagno, 1968). The DSM-III does not assume that the delineated syndromes represent nosological disease categories. There is no assumption that mental disorders are discrete entities, qualitatively different from one another and from the state of normality. Thus, the classificatory schema is neutral on the continuity versus discontinuity issue.

The classificatory system proposed by the DSM-III is multi-axial. There are five diagnostic axes: Axis I is concerned with the diagnosis of clinical syndromes, Axis II deals with personality disorders and developmental abnormalities, Axis III with physical disorders and conditions, Axis IV is concerned with the severity of psychological stresses, and Axis V with adaptive functioning during the past year. The two last axes use seven-point rating scales to assess the severity of psychological stresses and the adequacy of psychological functioning. While Axis I classifies mental disorders, which are described as pattern of symptoms, Axis II classifies individuals. According to the DSM-III classificatory schema each patient is diagnosed on the five axes. Thus, the approach to diagnosis is multidimensional. The classificatory system is much more complex than the one offered by Kraepelin. In contrast to the Kraepelinian schema, it is purely descriptive and does not make assumptions about disease entities causing the symptoms.

So far, this discussion has dealt with attempts to narrow down the scope of diagnostic categories in search for unambiguous disease entities. It is also, of course, possible to broaden the categories and to end up with only one, all embracing mental disease. In his book *The Vital Balance* (1963), Karl Menninger develops an argument that there is only one mental disease and that the variations in the symptoms are due to the degree of its severity. Since his theory, although couched in medical terms, is definitely psychological it will be briefly discussed together with other psychological models in the next chapter. In "one disease" theory the severity of the illness is identified with regression.

The disease model of mental illness, from the time it was recast in its modern form by Kraepelin at the turn of the century, has been beset with the problem of the proper size of the diagnostic units that would correspond to real diseases existing in nature. The proposed breadth of taxonomic categories has varied between very narrow homogeneous entities on the one extreme and the theory of only "one disease" at the other. The difficulty in making the proper choice is caused by the existence of a great many cases, as for instance schizo-affective disorders, that do not fit the existing basic categories but fall in between them. This leads to loose definitions and to vague boundaries of disease entities.

A solution to the vagueness of the diagnostic categories is to apply statistical methods in an attempt to establish an objective classification. The use of factor analysis is a misguided attempt to achieve this purpose. Factor analysis does not establish discrete categories but rather only continuous dimensions of a domain. Therefore, it does not fit conceptually the disease model but is admirably suitable for use in the constitutional model. A more suitable statistical technique to be used in the disease model framework is numerical taxonomy (cluster analysis) (Everitt, 1974; Fleiss & Zubin, 1969). This method, in contrast to factor analysis, establishes in a population clusters of individuals having the same characteristics. So far, only a few studies used this technique to establish nosological categories (Pilowski et al., 1969; Wing & Nixon, 1975).

One difficulty in relating clinical syndromes to their organic causes is the fact that there may not be a one-to-one relationship. In the discussion of the spectrum theory of depression, it was pointed out that somewhat different, pathoplastically modified clinical syndromes may have the same pathogenic etiology. The opposite also may be possible. Somewhat different pathogenic processes may produce the same clinical picture. Different infections and other pathological conditions may produce fever and cachexia.

Etiology

The disease model presupposes the existence of organic disease processes. Since the turn of the century, a tremendous amount of effort has been expended to discover the organic causes of the so-called functional psychoses. In psychiatric classifications a customary distinction is made between symptomatic psychoses caused by known organic brain diseases and functional or endogenous psychoses. In the first case, even when the etiology is unknown there are obvious histopathological changes in the brain or gross biochemical changes in the bodily fluids. In acute conditions, due to an infection or a toxic state there is delirium, confusion, and clouding of consciousness. In chronic states due to a chronic infection, degeneration, or neoplasm, when the pathology is diffuse affecting evenly the whole brain, there is a dementia. It is characterized by impairment of memory, reasoning powers, and personality deterioration. If a chronic lesion is localized in a part of the brain, depending on location the patient may display symptoms that are similar to those occurring in functional psychoses. In contrast to organic (symptomatic) psychoses, no gross structural pathology has been found in functional psychoses.

Researchers are confronted with a mystery of a gross psychological disorder and a brain that is normal in its appearance. As a result, the term functional psychosis has been coined. What could be the meaning of this term? If one takes an extreme dualistic position, it could mean that the brain is healthy but that there is a disease of the soul or mind. This position was abandoned in the middle of the nineteenth century with the passing of the *Psychotiker* (psychological) school of German psychiatry. The second meaning of functional disorder may be illustrated by an analogy with the computer. There are two basic languages in the computer technology. The first is the input language with which the computer software is concerned. The second language is the machine language used by the computer hardware. It is possible to cause a breakdown in the functioning of the computer by feeding to it a wrong program, written in a software language. It is also possible to cause a breakdown by tinkering with the electronic circuitry of the computer. Following this analogy psychologists are concerned with the software language, the information input into the brain, and neurophysiologists with the machine language and the hardware of the brain. If a functional disorder means a disorder caused by a faulty information input such as faulty conditioning or habit formation, it is not in the domain of the medical models but rather in the domain of psychological ones.

The third meaning of the term functional disorder could be the presence of an organic abnormality that has not yet been detected. This is the position taken by the organically minded psychiatrists, who look for the somatic causes of schizophrenia and manic-depressive psychosis. The fact that a lesion cannot be discerned under the microscope does not mean that it is not there. The group of poisons called cholinesterase inhibitors, which includes some of the deadly nerve gases, can produce profound psychological disorders and even death, without apparent lesions of the brain. Biochemical lesions may not easily, if at all, be detected under the microscope.

In order to base the disease model of mental illness on solid ground it is important to establish the organic causes and pathological mechanisms that are responsible for the symptoms. Otherwise there is a danger of circularity. It is the danger of defining schizophrenia as a disease manifesting itself by disorder of thought, perception, and affect and then diagnosing schizophrenia when all or some of these symptoms are present. As yet there is no possibility of using some objective criteria for diagnosis such as postmortem pathological findings or laboratory reports—the usual procedures in medicine. In this situation, schizophrenia could become a metaphysical essence, hidden behind the observed symptoms.

Bacteriological-Serological Approach

It is outside the scope of this book to review the immense literature on biological research of schizophrenia and manic-depressive psychosis. Only some main themes and ideas will be reviewed. The discovery of the cause of general paralysis of the insane (GPI) at the turn of the century had a tremendous impact on the organically oriented psychiatrists. A disease that for more than a century had been a mystery and that had been attributed to a variety of causes from head injury to disappointment in love was found to be caused by syphilitic infection. The fact that not very long after the discovery of its cause a cure was found in the form of malarial treatment kindled high hopes that the cause of schizophrenia and other psychoses will soon be discovered. Julius von Wagner-Jauregg, the discoverer of the malarial treatment, has been the only psychiatrist to receive the Nobel prize. Quite naturally, the attention of many researchers turned to microorganisms as a possible cause of schizophrenia and manic-depressive psychosis. The bacterial theory fitted the disease model very well. Moreover, the discovery that some chronic inflammatory states, such as GPI, occurring a long time after the actual infection, were not caused so much by the bacteria themselves but by the autoimmune processes explained the lack of an obvious connection between schizophrenia and an infection. All sorts of bacteria were suspected as pathogens of schizophrenia. It was linked to syphilis (Marie & Toporkoff, 1929), tuberculosis (Baruk, Bidermann, & Albane, 1932), influenza, and other acute infections (Menninger, 1926). Rosenow (1955) suspected a specific strain of streptococci to be the pathogenic agent in schizophrenia. A focal infection as a cause of schizophrenia was proffered by H. Cotton (1923). As a result, many schizophrenic patients had their teeth extracted, sections of the bowel resected, and the uteri removed. V. M. Buscaino (1929) maintained that schizophrenia was caused by a toxin containing indol, produced by the intestinal bacterial flora and absorbed by the body. This early literature has been reviewed by Nolan Lewis (1936).

In recent years, although the bacterial or autoimmune theory has been overshadowed by the metabolic error theory, it has not been by any means abandoned. It has been suggested that schizophrenia is an autoimmune disease, because it runs a recurrent course similar to that of many known autoimmune diseases. In addition, the presence of autoantibodies reactive to the patient's tissues and generally of antibodies destroying brain tissue has been found in the serum of schizophrenia patients (Witz, Anavi, & Weisenbeck, 1977; Heath, 1970). The level of brain reactive immunoglobulins has been reported to fluctuate with severity of the schizophrenic illness (Arnkraut, Solomon, Allowsmith, & McLellan, 1973). A suggestion also has been made that schizophrenia and depression are slow virus diseases. Psychotic depressives and to a lesser extent schizophrenics have been found to have complement fixing antibodies against herpes simplex virus (Rimon & Halonen, 1977; Torrey & Paterson, 1973). There is a difficulty inherent in these bacterial and autoimmunological theories. In autoimmune and slow virus diseases there is a breakdown of the nervous tissues, destruction of the neurons, or demyelination of the nerve fibres. None of these occurs in schizophrenia or manic-depressive psychosis.

Biochemical Approach

The metabolic error theory was first proposed by J. J. Moreau de Tours (1845) who drew a parallel between hashish intoxication and insanity. B. A. Morel (1860) suggested a possibility that insanity was caused by an endotoxin. Kraepelin believed that dementia praecox was caused by an endotoxin resulting from a metabolic error. R. Gjessing (1938) described abnormalities of nitrogen metabolism in a small subvariety of schizophrenia called periodic catatonia. Buscaino, as has been mentioned before, suggested that schizophrenia was caused by a toxic indol compound, produced by intestinal bacteria. This toxin was absorbed into the bloodstream, failed to be detoxified by the liver, and could adversely affect its metabolism. The interest in the endotoxin theory was revived by a seminal paper of H. Osmond and J. Smythies (1952). These authors drew attention to a similarity between the structural formula of adrenaline, a neurohormone, and that of mescaline, a hallucinogenic drug. They also suggested that the mental state produced by mescaline intoxication may be more like the mental state in schizophrenia than that occurring in deliria caused by other toxic substances. Stoll (1947) described lysergic acid diethylamide (LSD_{25}), which in minute quantities of less than 100 micrograms produced a psychotic-like reaction. Since then, other hallucinogenic substances have been described. All of them contain either a phenol or an indol ring with several methyl ($-CH_3$) groups attached to it. A psychosis-like state, produced by hallucinogenic drugs, was called model psychosis and replaced for a while GPI as the model of schizophrenia.

The hallucinogenic endotoxin theory of schizophrenia gave rise to a lively controversy in the fifties. The claim that psychopathological states induced by hallucinogenic drugs were similar to schizophrenia was disputed by many authorities. It was said that the states induced by hallucinogenic substances were more like the exogenous toxic psychosis, originally described by Bonhoeffer, than schizophrenia. Also, no convincing and unambiguous proof was produced for the presence of a hallucinogenic substance in the bodies of schizophrenic patients. However, the controversy gave an impetus to biochemical research into the metabolism of the phenol and indol ring containing substances occurring naturally in the human body. Joseph Axelrod (1966, 1971) mapped out the metabolic pathways of catecholamines, dopamine, and noradrenaline, the derivatives of tyrosine. For this achievement Axelrod was awarded the Nobel prize. Others (Barachas & Usdin, 1973; Chase & Murphy, 1973) have investigated the metabolism of tryptophan, an indol ring containing amino acid and its derivative serotonin (5-hydroxytryptamine). The three biogenic amines: dopamine, noradrenaline, and serotonin have been found to be synaptic transmitter substances in certain neuronal systems of the brain. These systems have been mapped out by the technique of fluorescent histochemistry (Olson, Nystrom, & Seiger, 1973). The nigro-striatal (a part of basal ganglia-complex) and the meso-limbic pathways are the two dopaminergic systems. The neurons of the nigro-striatal system originate in the zona compacta of the substantia nigra in the midbrain and project into the caudate nucleus of the striatum. A deficiency of dopamine in the nigro-striatal synapses causes Parkinson's disease (Hornykewicz, 1976) and perhaps is related to retarded depression (Bunney, Janowsky, Goodwin, Davis, Brodie, Murphy, & Chase, 1969). The neurons of the mesolimbic dopaminergic system originate in midbrain ventral tegmental area in a close proximity of the substantia nigra and project to nucleus accumbens and olfactory tubercles, which are both parts of the limbic system. A dysfunction of the dopaminergic meso-limbic system has been implicated in pathogenesis of schizophrenia. The neurons of the noradrenergic system are found in the reticular system of the pons and the medulla oblongata. One pathway projects from the locus coeruleus of the pons, via the dorsal bundle to the cerebral cortex, the cerebellar cortex, and the hippocampus. It controls rapid eye movement sleep (Jouvet, 1969). The neurotransmitter deficiency in this system may be related to hallucinations. The other projection is from other reticular nuclei of the pons via the medial forebrain bundle to hypothalamus and limbic system including amygdala. It is related to motivation and mood regulation. Its deficiency may cause anhedonia implicated both in vital depression and in schizophrenia. The serotonergic system is diffuse and is less well delineated than the other two systems. One projection is from the raphé nuclei of the midline of the brain stem to several brain areas, including the hypothalamus, amygdala, forebrain, and the cerebral cortex. This system has been linked with the control of the slow wave sleep (Jouvet, 1969). Its deficiency may be responsible for insomnia occurring in depression.

There are also synaptic transmitter substances, such as gamma-amino-buturic acid (GABA), which are inhibitory. GABA is the major inhibitory neurotransmitter producing both pre- and postsynaptic inhibition in the central nervous system. Its deficiency in the striatum is suspected to be the cause of Huntington's chorea. Diazepam (Valium®) and other benzodiazepines, which are used as anxiolytic (antianxiety) and anticonvulsant drugs, have been found to sensitize GABA receptors in the brain and potentiate the inhibitory action of this neurotransmitter (Braestrup & Nielsen, 1980). Thus, there is a possibility that a deficiency of the GABA system in certain parts of the brain, such as the limbic system, may cause a state of chronic anxiety. One also may speculate about the existence of an endogenous anxiolytic neurohormone, yet to be discovered, that has the same GABA receptor priming properties that characterize benzodiazepines.

Recently a group of peptides has been described with the properties of neurotransmitters (Hughes, Smith, Kosterlitz, Fothergill, Morgan, & Morris, 1975). These peptides occur in two forms: enkephalins and endorphins. They react with the synaptic receptors that specifically bind opiate drugs such as morphine and heroin. The central nervous system areas concerned with pain perception, such as medial thalamic nuclei, trigeminal nerve nucleus, and substantia gelatinosa of the spinal cord, are the sites where these receptors are found. Enkephalins and endorphins may be related to the gating mechanism of pain perception (Melzack, 1973) and may inhibit pain perception. They also may regulate mood.

The aromatic amino acids (phenylalanine, tyrosine, and tryptophan) are metabolized into the biogenic amines by enzyme controlled chemical processes of hydroxylation and decarboxylation. Phenylalanine is hydroxylated into tyrosine, the tyrosine is further hydroxylated into dopa, which in its turn is decarboxylated into dopamine. The latter by hydroxylation is in its turn converted into noradrenaline. Dopamine and noradrenaline are synaptic transmitters, stored in a bound form in the vesicles of the presynaptic nerve terminals. When the neuron discharges the synaptic transmitter is released into the synaptic cleft and triggers off the receptors at the postsynaptic surface of the second neuron. The neurotransmitter does not remain attached to the receptors but is, in part, reabsorbed by the presynaptic nerve terminal. In part, it is metabolized into a methylated form by the enzyme catechol-O-methyl-transferase (COMT), present in the cytoplasm of the presynaptic terminal and in the synaptic cleft. Dopamine is partially converted into 3-methoxytryptamine and noradrenaline into normetaadrenaline. The portion of the neurotransmitter substance absorbed back into the presynaptic neuron is partially reconverted into the bound form and partly deaminated by the enzyme monoamine oxidase (MAO) inside the neuron in the mitochondria. There are two forms of MAO: types A and B. Different types of MAO are associated with different neuronal systems: type A with noradrenergic and dopaminergic, while the B with serotonergic system. To make a long story short, dopamine and noradrenaline are by the appropriate enzymes subjected to transmethylation, deamination, and aldehyde dehydrogenation. Dopamine is metabolized into homovanilic acid (HVA) and 3-methoxy-

4-hydroxy-phenylethanol (MOPET), noradrenaline into vanilylmandelic acid (VMA) and 3-methoxy-4-hydroxy-phenethylenglycol (MHPG). These metabolic end products are excreted by the body. VMA is predominantly the metabolic end product of noradrenaline from parts of the body outside the central nervous system, while MHPG is the end product of the brain noradrenaline. Tryptophan is hydroxylated and then decarboxylated into serotonin (5-hydroxytryptamine), which is deaminated by MAO into 5-hydroxyindoleacetic acid (5-HIAA) before being excreted by the body. These metabolic processes are presented in Figures 2, 3, and 4.

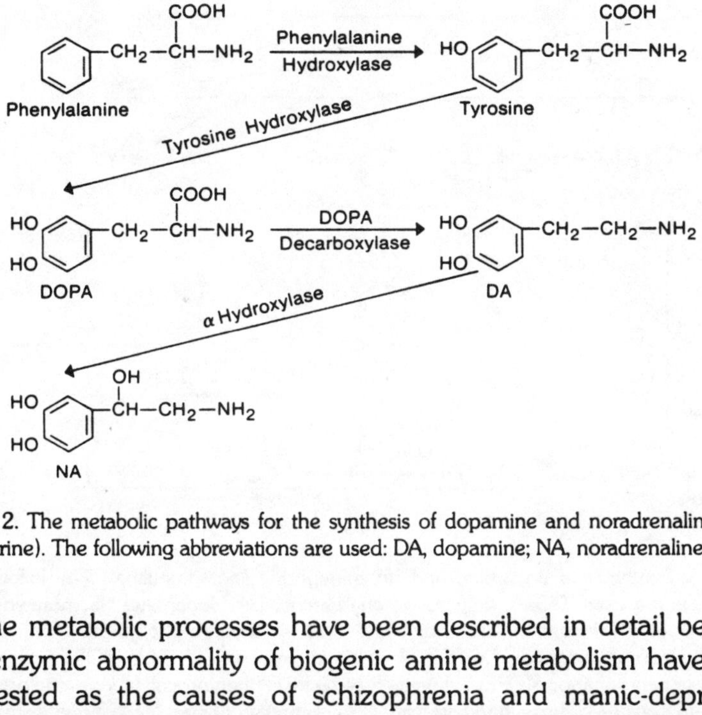

Figure 2. The metabolic pathways for the synthesis of dopamine and noradrenaline (norepinephrine). The following abbreviations are used: DA, dopamine; NA, noradrenaline.

The metabolic processes have been described in detail because the enzymic abnormality of biogenic amine metabolism have been suggested as the causes of schizophrenia and manic-depressive psychosis. Moreover, the end products of the metabolism of the three biogenic amines present in urine and the cerebrospinal fluid have provided the clues for identifying the particular amines that might be causally implicated in various clinical conditions. This could serve as a basis for the disease classification (Deleon-Jones, Maas, Dekirmenjian, & Sanchez, 1975).

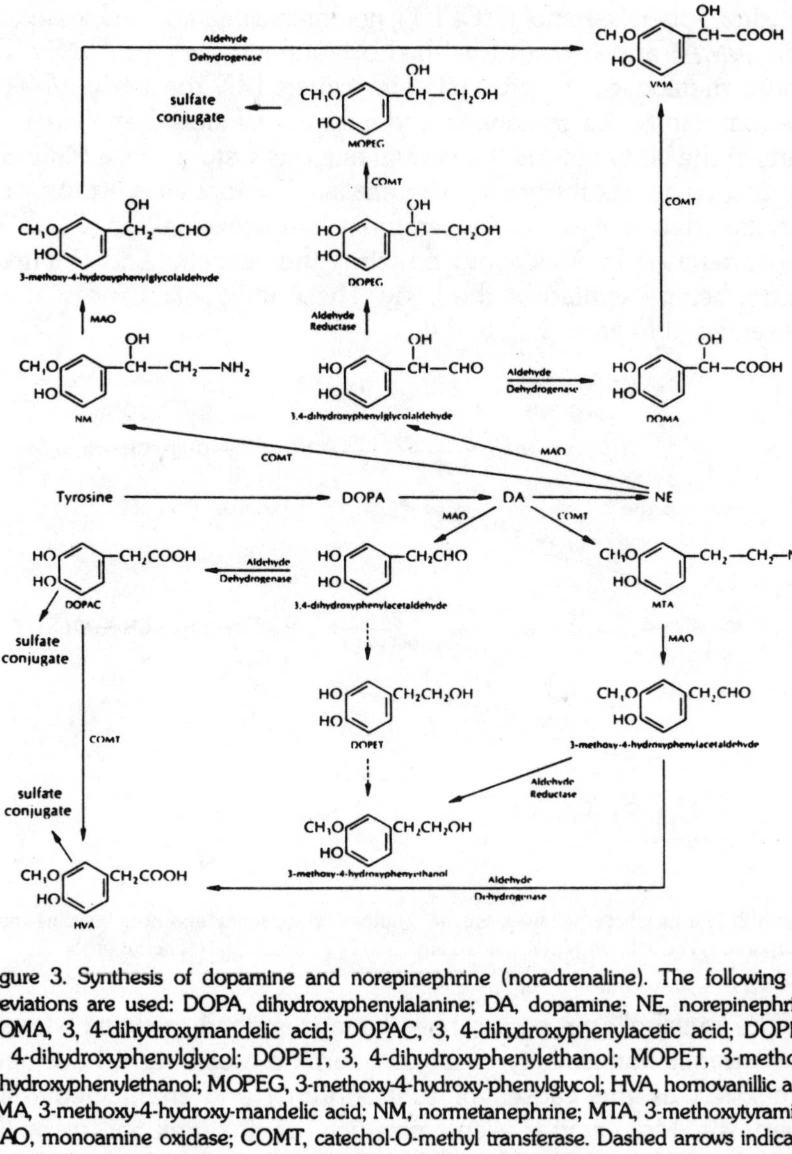

Figure 3. Synthesis of dopamine and norepinephrine (noradrenaline). The following abbreviations are used: DOPA, dihydroxyphenylalanine; DA, dopamine; NE, norepinephrine; DOMA, 3, 4-dihydroxymandelic acid; DOPAC, 3, 4-dihydroxyphenylacetic acid; DOPEG, 3, 4-dihydroxyphenylglycol; DOPET, 3, 4-dihydroxyphenylethanol; MOPET, 3-methoxy-4-hydroxyphenylethanol; MOPEG, 3-methoxy-4-hydroxy-phenylglycol; HVA, homovanillic acid; VMA, 3-methoxy-4-hydroxy-mandelic acid; NM, normetanephrine; MTA, 3-methoxytyramine; MAO, monoamine oxidase; COMT, catechol-O-methyl transferase. Dashed arrows indicated steps that have not been firmly established. By permission of Oxford University Press, reproduced from Cooper, Bloom, & Roth, 1978, pp. 146-147.

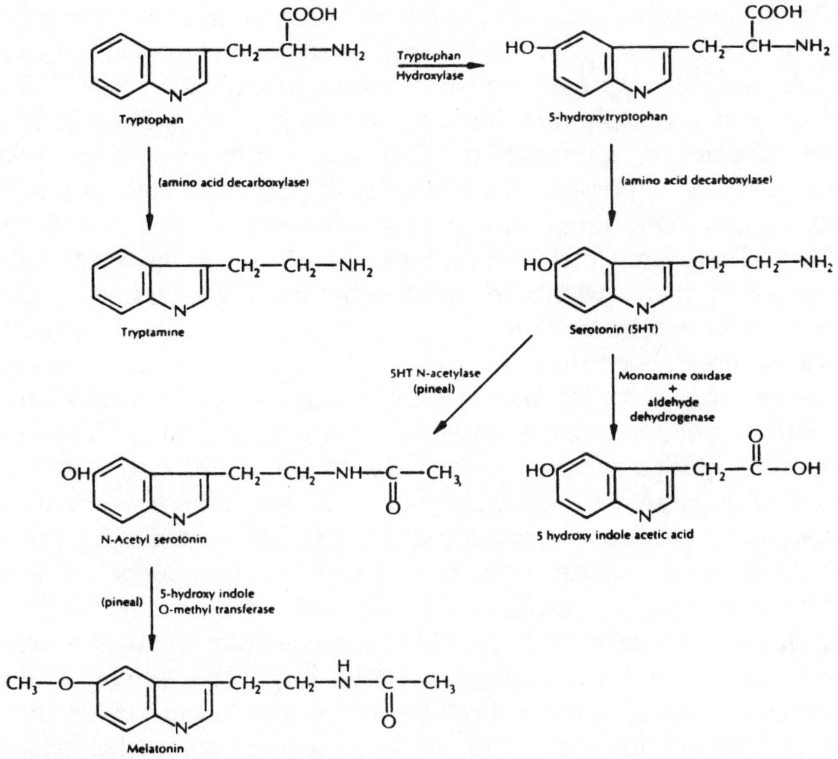

Figure 4. The metabolic pathways available for the synthesis and metabolism of serotonin. By permission of Oxford University Press, reproduced from Cooper, Bloom, & Roth, 1978, p. 199.

The biochemical theories of functional psychoses may be divided into two groups. The first group assumes that there is a novel toxic substance produced by an error in the metabolism of biogenic amines. The theories belonging to the second group deny the existence of a novel toxic substance, instead they attribute the causation of schizophrenia and manic-depressive psychoses to an imbalance of biogenic amines. In different conditions there is a deficiency or an excess of certain biogenic amines. Both groups of theories maintain that there are genetically determined enzymatic abnormalities that cause errors in the metabolism of biogenic amines. The theories in the fifties and the sixties, and those predominantly concerned with schizophrenia, postulated the existence of a novel toxic substance. More recent theories, and those mainly concerned with manic-depressive psychosis, subscribe to the view that the causal factor in functional psychoses is a deficiency or an imbalance of the biogenic amines.

An early theory postulating a toxic substance was the adrenochrome theory of schizophrenia (Hoffer, Osmond, & Smythies, 1954). Adrenochrome, a product of adrenaline oxidation in vitro, was suggested as a possible candidate for the hypothesized toxic substance causing schizophrenic disease. However, since the results of Axelrod's research into the metabolism of catecholamines cast doubt on the in vivo existence of adrenochrome, the attention of the workers turned in another direction. Axelrod had shown that both adrenaline and noradrenaline were metabolized by transmethylation, the process controlled by the COMT enzyme. Since most of the hallucinogenic substances contain a phenyl or indol ring with several methoxy groups attached to it, Harley-Mason, Laird, and Smythies (1958) suggested a possibility that in schizophrenics a chemical compound similar to mescaline is produced by an excessive transmethylation of adrenaline or noradrenaline. It was suggested that this hypothetical compound was dimethoxyphenylethylamine (DMPE). It differed from normally occurring normetaadrenaline by the presence of a second methoxy group. DMPE has been identified as the compound found in urine of schizophrenics, producing a characteristic pink spot on the paper chromatograph (Bourdillon, Clarke, Ridges, Sheppard, Harper, & Leslie, 1965). However DPME taken orally or injected did not produce psychological changes in volunteers (Friedhoff & Hollister, 1966). In addition further studies failed to confirm the presence of DPME in urine of schizophrenics and linked it to dietary factors (Perry, Hansen, & Macintyre, 1964).

However, there is other evidence of an abnormality in the transmethylation processes in schizophrenia patients. Methionine, an amino acid, is a methyl group donor and as S-adenosylmethionine is the cofactor of the COMT enzyme in the transmethylation reactions. It was found to cause exacerbation of schizophrenic symptoms when administered together with a MAO inhibitor (Pollin, Cardon, & Kety, 1961). Also, a higher incidence of schizophrenia than in general population was reported among the relatives of patients suffering from homocystinuria, an inborn error of methionine metabolism associated with mental deficiency (Carson, Cusworth, Dent, Field, Neill, & Westall, 1963). The transmethylation hypothesis suggested that a possible causal factor in schizophrenia was a metabolic block. An absence or deficiency of an enzyme caused an accumulation of catecholamine metabolites. The backlog of the metabolites could cause a damage of the nervous system directly, or the metabolites could be converted by the process of transmethylation to substances that could cause such damage. Other errors of catecholamines also have been suggested. Stein and Wise (1971) put forward a theory that schizophrenics converted dopamine into toxic 6-hydroxydopamine. This compound destroyed the synapses of the neurons of the "reward system" of the brain. When 6-hydroxydopamine was administered into the ventricles of rats it decreased the self-stimulation behaviour. Stein and Wise believed that anhedonia, an inability to appreciate rewards, was an important feature of schizophrenia.

Errors of the tryptophan metabolism also have been considered as possible causes of schizophrenia. McIsaac (1961) suggested that the pineal gland hormone, melatonin, was chemically similar to the hallucinogenic compound harmine, which contains an indol ring. Melatonin is normally synthetized in the body from serotonin. McIsaack suggested that in schizophrenics serotonin is converted into a substance similar to harmine instead of melatonin. An excessive melanin pigmentation in schizophrenics, which may be due to a deficiency of melatonin, a melanin synthesis regulating hormone, is in keeping with the theory. Finally, Beckett (1973) has reported the presence in the human serum of an enzyme that converted serotonin into N,N-dimethyltryptamine (bufotenine), a hallucinogenic compound. A lack of the enzyme in the body that normally destroys this compound could be the cause of schizophrenia.

The more recent theories, particularly those concerned with manic-depressive psychosis, stressed an imbalance of the biogenic amines rather than the presence of an abnormal toxic metabolite. A hypothesis has already been mentioned that attributes the cause of schizophrenia to an abnormality of the dopaminergic meso-lymbic system synapses (Bunney & Aghajanian, 1975). There is either an overproduction of dopamine or, more likely, an abnormal sensitivity of the postsynaptic receptors producing overactivity of the meso-lymbic system. The abnormal sensitivity of the postsynaptic receptors could be due to a deficient postsynaptic inhibition, to the absence of an enzyme that normally destroys excessive quantities of dopamine at the receptor sites, or, which is the most likely, to an abnormally high number of these receptors. Schizophrenic patients improve when treated with phenothiazines and haloperidol, drugs that block dopaminergic synapses. Because these drugs block also the dopaminergic synapses of the nigrostriatal system, they produce as a side effect Parkinsonism (a state similar to that occurring in Parkinson's disease). Amphetamine, which increases the amount of dopamine at the meso-lymbic synapse, may produce schizophrenia-like psychosis in humans and behavioural stereotypy, a state similar to catatonia, in animals. In addition to abnormalities and deficiencies in the biogenic amine neurotransmitters, abnormalities in the polypeptide neurotransmitters and synaptic modulators have recently been suggested as the cause of schizophrenia.

Manic-depressive psychosis has been related to a deficiency, excess, or imbalance of the biogenic amines noradrenaline, serotonin, and dopamine. Depression, particularly the depressed mood, has been attributed to a noradrenaline deficiency in the diencephalic reward system (Schildkrout, 1965; Stein, 1966). Anhedonia, an inability to experience pleasure, is one of the main symptoms of vital depression. A deficiency in the functioning of the brain reward centers, discovered by Olds and Milner (1954) in animals, offered a plausible physiological explanation of the depressive illness. A serotonin (5-hydroxytryptamine) deficiency has been proposed as another possible cause of depression (Coppen, 1972; Laplin & Oxenkrug, 1969). Finally, a deficiency in dopamine has been suggested as a factor in retarded depression, accounting for psychomotor retardation occurring in this condition (Bunney et al., 1969).

Manic symptoms have been attributed to an excess or imbalance in the biogenic amines. Antidepressants such as tricyclic drugs and the MAO inhibitors increase the amount of the available biogenic amine neurotransmitters at the synapses. The tricyclic drugs accomplish it by retarding the re-uptake of the neurotransmitter into the presynaptic nerve ending. The MAO inhibitors suppress the activity of MAO. An overdose of these drugs may precipitate mania in depressed patients. Reserpine, a tranquilizer, converts the bound neurotransmitters into the unbound and thus makes them vulnerable to the destruction by MAO. Reserpine depletes the store of the biogenic amines in the brain of experimental animals and produces in them a state bearing some resemblance to that of retarded depression in humans. Finally, reserpine produces depression in man. Since all three biogenic amines are similarly affected by antidepressant drugs and reserpine, a lot of ingenuity has been put into the attempt to find out which one is implicated in manic-depressive psychosis. The fact that the final products of the metabolic breakdown of the three biogenic amines excreted in the urine are different (VMA and MHPG in noradrenaline, 5-HIAA in serotonin, and HVA and MOPET in dopamine) has provided useful leads. However, the results of these investigations have been inconclusive. Because chemical analysis of urine is not very reliable and because it is important to separate the biogenic amine metabolites in the central nervous system from those in the rest of the body, an analysis of the cerebrospinal fluid (CSF) has provided a better method than urinalysis. In addition to the concentration, a turnover rate of the metabolites can also be measured. Thus, the CSF level of MHPG could give a clue as to the amount of noradrenaline in the brain. The levels of HVA and 5-HIAA could provide such clues as to the amounts of respectively dopamine and serotonin. Since the quantities are very small and in a constant flux, the method that uses probenecid, a drug that blocks the membrane transport, has been used to increase the quantities of the biogenic metabolites in the CSF (Van Praag, Flentge, Korf, Dols, & Schut, 1973; Van Praag, 1977). The results indicate that there are subgroups of depressive patients showing an evidence of deficiency of different biogenic amines (Van Praag, 1974, 1977). To complicate the issues further, an electrolytic imbalance at the nerve membrane has been described in depression (Shaw, 1966). Lithium salt treatment, effective in mania and in bipolar depression, probably restores the electrolytic balance.

The search for the specific biochemical lesions, localized in the different neuronal systems, and determined by the unique pathogenic genes of major effect suggests a shift towards a neo-Kleistian position. It aims at discovering the specific biochemical causes of different types of depression and schizophrenia. This development leads to splitting of the existing Kraepelinian categories and delineating narrower, homogeneous disease entities produced by specific enzymatic abnormalities. The fact that the two brain hemispheres have somewhat different structure and subserve somewhat different functions suggests further possibilities for differential pathology (Dimond & Beaumont, 1974). The neuronal systems associated with the specific neurotransmitters may subserve somewhat different functions in the two hemispheres. There is some evidence that schizophrenia may be associated with an impairment in the functioning of the dominant hemisphere while manic-depressive psychosis is associated with such an impairment in the nondominant hemisphere (Flor-Henry, 1974). Furthermore, diffuse organic brain lesions usually result in dementias, while the localized ones, particularly those in the temporal lobe and the limbic system, may produce florid psychotic symptoms. These are often indistinguishable from those of functional psychoses.

Genetic Approach

There is no doubt that there is a strong hereditary component in both schizophrenia and manic-depressive psychosis. The concordance rate in monozygotic twins is much higher than in fraternal twins (e.g., Kallmann, 1946). The figures vary from study to study, but with the exception of one study by Tienari (1968) they all show the same trend (Rosenthal, 1971). The high concordance rate for identical twins is obtained, even if they are reared apart. The adaptive studies indicate that children tend to be concordant for schizophrenia with their biological rather than with their foster parents. Studies of manic-depressive psychosis point in the same direction (Rosenthal, 1970). If schizophrenia and manic-depressive psychosis were to fit the disease model, they had to be produced by single genes of major effect, causing defects in specific enzymes, and had to be inherited according to the Mendelian laws. However, the inheritance of either condition does not follow these laws. There are marked deviations from the expected Mendelian ratios in the heredity of functional psychoses. These deviations are explained by the presence of other genes or environmental factors such as stress that modify the penetrance of the pathogenic gene of major effect. Unfortunately when this argument is used any inheritance patterns can be explained as due to a single dominant or recessive gene. Also, relatively high rates of schizophrenia and manic-depressive psychosis in general population (1% and 0.7% respectively) argue against the monogenic theory. Heredo-degenerative diseases that usually are caused by a pathogenic recessive gene are rare. Because the affected subjects tend not to reproduce, the genes are removed from the gene pool and are replenished only by mutation. However, the rate of mutation is quite low: 1 in 200,000 or 1 in 300,000. One way out of these difficulties that is consistent with the neo-Kleistian position is to assume, together with Elenmeyer-Kimling and Paradowski (1966), that schizophrenia and manic-depressive psychosis are not single genetic entities but rather heterogenous groups of genotypes. These collections of genotypes manifest themselves as single phenotypes of schizophrenia or manic-depressive psychosis. Each genotype has a low frequency rate, yet together they produce frequency rates in keeping with that of schizophrenia and manic-depressive psychosis. In a similar vein, Rosenthal (1970, 1973) has proposed a genetic heterogeneity theory of schizophrenia transmission. According to this theory, schizophrenia is produced by certain combinations of a small number of specific genes at more than one locus. Different combinations of genes produce overlapping but somewhat different patterns of symptoms. Thus, there is a schizophrenia spectrum of genetically related disorders that differ in severity and, to a degree, in symptomatology.

The disease model of mental illness is in many ways very attractive. It holds a promise that for each specific disease will be found a specific remedy in the form of a drug or drugs. If mental illness is caused by a metabolic error, a drug can be found to rectify it or to counteract its effects. Phenothiazines and other major tranquilizers have revolutionized the treatment of schizophrenia and have reduced drastically the mental hospital population. Tricyclic drugs, monoamine oxidaze inhibitors, and lithium carbonate have been found quite effective in the treatment of manic-depressive psychosis and other depressions. These developments during the past twenty-five years have enhanced the prominence of the disease model in psychiatry, as did the bacteriological discoveries one century earlier in general medicine. However, while this model has been found to be useful in explanation of functional psychoses, it is less so when applied to psychoneuroses. The latter conditions tend to be explained in constitutional and psychological terms.

CONSTITUTIONAL MODEL IN PSYCHIATRY

The constitutional model assumes a biological continuity between normality and abnormality and regards diseases as the extremes of normal variation. From the genetic point of view, the constitutional model is polygenic: the constitution is determined by the totality of genes (genome) of an individual. The inborn characteristics so determined present continuous normal distributions. Since genotype is a scientific abstraction, one is always dealing with phenotypes, which are products of the interaction between heredity and the environment. Consequently, the concept of constitution is really dealing with an evolving organism. While ecology is concerned with the environmental factors affecting the life history of the organism, constitution is concerned with its heredity, its inborn *Anlage*. The main focus of psychiatry is the personality of the developing organism. Hence, the constitutional model in the context of psychiatry deals with the hereditary aspects of personality development. The latter has to be viewed as being always the product of the interaction of the heredity and the environment. While the German psychiatric tradition has tended to stress heredity, and therefore the constitution in the personality development (Schneider, 1958), the American tradition has stressed the environment. Therefore, the latter tradition has been preoccupied with the life history of the individual. Both approaches, the constitutional and the psychological, regard mental diseases as extreme ends of the normal distribution, of certain characteristics of physique and personality, or combinations of such characteristics.

The concept of constitution has become associated with that of physique because many researchers used it as the criterion for establishing the constitutional types or dimensions. As has already been mentioned, physique is only one aspect of constitution, and it may not be its best criterion. Originally, constitution was described in terms of discrete types. This was at the time when the dimensional thinking in biological sciences was not generally adopted or clearly understood. The types referred to ideal types, presupposed by the extremes of continuous distributions. The constitutional approach is holistic. It does not separate body from mind to the same extent as does the disease model. Both mind and body are aspects of a single organism. Nor does this approach dismember the whole human organism into its parts and organs. For example, it does not concentrate on the brain in a search of the seat of the disease processes.

The best known system of constitutional psychiatry was developed in the twenties and the thirties by Ernst Kretschmer (1925). His system was anticipated by similar systems proposed by Rostan, by De Giovani, by Viola, and by Beneke (Kallmann, 1953) and was in the broad tradition of the Hippocratic-Galenian system of medicine. Kretschmer described three main types of physique: pyknic, leptosomic (asthenic), and athletic. In addition, he described a minor type, called dysplastic. The physical types were conceived by him as ideal types and not as discrete taxonomic categories. Therefore the bulk of population presented mixtures, or amalgams, of types in different proportions. The term ideal types referred to extremes of the variation of the physique in the population; thus, Kretschmer's types were really dimensions. Certain patterns of psychological traits described by him as character and temperament were associated with types of physique. Schizoid character was associated with the leptosomic, the athletic, and the dysplastic physiques. Cyclothymic character was associated with the pyknic physique. He believed that physique, character, temperament, and different kinds of mental illness were the expressions of the same biological constitution (*Formkreise*). Their association was correlational rather than causal.

The leptosomic physical type was described as lanky, long, narrow, and angular, with long spidery legs and arms, a long neck, and a receding chin. It was reminiscent of Don Quixote, the hero of the well-known novel by Cervantes. Not only physique but also the leptosome's character was also Quixotic. The athletic type had heavy bones, powerful muscles, broad shoulders, and narrow hips. He was reminiscent of the superman of the children's comics. He was cold, aggressive, and ruthless. The pyknic type was rotund, chubby, and pot-bellied, with a short neck and a round head, a moon-like face, short arms and legs, and stubby fingers. He was reminiscent of Don Quixote's faithful servant, Sancho Panza. He was jolly, warm, practical, good humoured, and good natured and possessed all the earthy qualities of Sancho. The less frequent dysplastic type showed bodily proportions that were out of balance. This type was associated with gross endocrine disorders.

Each constitutional type was associated with a certain inborn temperament, described in terms of the sensitivity of the nervous system, mood-colouring, psychic tempo, and psychomotor speed. These basic psychobiological characteristics produced under the environmental influences a variety of character types. The schizoid character was associated with three clusters of traits: (1) asocial, quiet, reticent, eccentric, (2) timid, shy, delicate, oversensitive, nervous, excitable, fond of nature and books, and (3) well-behaved, consistent, dull, stupid, docile, good-hearted. The affective reaction of the schizoid character type varied between the extremes of the psychaesthetic scale, from excessive reaction to insufficient reaction, or from excitement to apathy. The three clusters of traits associated with the cyclothymic character were (1) sociable, good-hearted, friendly, cosy, (2) cheerful, humorous, lively, hot tempered, and (3) quiet, soft, serious minded. The affective reaction of the cyclothymic character fluctuated between the extremes of the diathetic scale from depression (sadness) to elation. Schizophrenia and manic-depressive psychoses were the extremes respectively of the schizoid and of the cyclothymic characters. These psychoses could also be brought about as a result of reactions of the schizoid and the cyclothymic characters to stress situations. Kretschmer's theory was a continuity theory. Normality merged through the schizoid character with schizophrenia and through the cyclothymic character with manic-depressive psychosis. He believed that the endocrines were the most important constitutional factors responsible for the varieties of physique and temperament, including psychotic breakdowns. This can be illustrated by the following quotation: "To back up the secretional approach comes the following empirical material from the region of the *endogenous psychoses as the extreme exaggeration of the normal types of temperament*" (Kretschmer, 1925; italics added).

Kretschmer described human physique and character in terms of types and not in terms of dimensions, although he thought that most people presented mixtures of types. Such a formulation of the theory was fraught with the possibility of a conceptual confusion. William H. Sheldon (1940, 1942) proposed a similar theory to that of Kretschmer that was, however, conceptualized explicitly in terms of dimensions. Sheldon differentiated three basic dimensions of human physique: endomorphy, mesomorphy, and ectomorphy. These dimensions expressed the relative strength of the development in each individual of the three original embryonic layers (endoderm, mesoderm, and ectoderm) from which all the tissues were derived. Endomorphy was associated with the development of the digestive system, a derivative of the endoderm. Mesomorphy denoted the degree of development of the muscle and bone structures, derived from the mesoderm. Finally, ectomorphy expressed the degree of development of the sensory organs and the nervous system, both ectodermal structures.

There is a similarity between the predominantly endomorphic somatotype and Kretschmer's pyknic type, between the predominantly mesomorphic somatotype and the latter's athletic type, and finally between the ectomorph and Kretschmer's leptosome. Each individual somatotype, however, was rated independently, from 1 to 7, on the three basic components. In addition, somatotyping involved assessments of the degree of dysplasia (disproportion of the bodily parts) and the degree of gynandromorphy (the degree of bisexual characteristics). The three basic dimensions of physique were associated with three basic personality dimensions. Endomorphy was associated with visceratonia, which was characterized by the love of comfort, relaxation, and sociability. Mesomorphy was associated with somatotonia, characterized by the love of vigorous exercise and self-expression. Finally, ectomorphy was associated with cerebrotonia, characterized by an excessive sensitivity to the environment and inhibition. Sheldon was mainly concerned with personality theory rather than with abnormal psychology. However, he did carry out some somatotyping of mental patients. He reported that hebephrenic and catatonic schizophrenics showed a high degree of dysplasia and gynandromorphy. They scored high on ectomorphy and low on mesomorphy. Paranoid schizophrenics were high on mesomorphy. Manic-depressives were high on endomorphy and mesomorphy. The subsequent research on the relation of physique to personality and to mental illness has proved to be disappointing. The high correlations reported by Kretschmer and Sheldon between physique on the one hand and the personality and mental illness on the other have not been confirmed. However, since physique is only one of the possible aspects of human constitution, the disappointing results of the somatotyping approach do not completely discredit the constitutional model. The choice of a better criterion for the determination of the constitution than that provided by the assessment of physique and anthropometry may put the constitutional model on a better footing.

The constitutional model is associated with the polygenic mode of inheritance. The individual's physical constitution, biological makeup, and psychological temperament are determined by his whole genotype, the totality of his genes, or genome. A cut-off point on the continuous distribution separates individuals considered normal from those considered abnormal.

OTHER MODELS

The Bipartite (Combined Disease-Constitutional) Model*

So far, theories have been discussed that could be characterized as either fitting the disease model or the constitutional model. However, there has been an attempt to combine these two models in one psychiatric system. The credit for this attempt goes to the group of German psychiatrists known as the Heidelberg school. This group included Karl Jaspers, a psychiatrist philosopher, H. W. Grühle, W. Mayer-Gross, and Kurt Schneider.† Karl Jaspers, in his *General Psychopathology* (1963), distinguished psychopathological symptoms that could be meaningfully connected with the psychological past history of the patient from those that could not be so connected. The first could be understood in the sense of German *Verstehen Psychologie*,‡ in terms of the patient's total personality, his motivational system, his values, and his past life experiences. The second could not be so understood. These symptoms constituted a clear break with the psychological past of the patient, and they were meaningless within this context. The first group of symptoms

---

*The term bipartite is borrowed from E. Boring (1957). The latter describes Oswald Kulpe's combined "act" and "content" psychology as "bipartite."

†Kurt Schneider spent most of the professional life not in Heidelberg but in Munich. However, in his theoretical orientation he was a member of the Heidelberg school and moved to Heidelberg after the second world war.

‡The concept of *Verstehen* (understanding) and of *Erklarung* (explanation) together with the types of explanation will be discussed in detail in Chapter 6.

was a manifestation of the personality development, while the second was a manifestation of a disease process. They could be phenomenologically described, but they could not be comprehended (*Verstehen*). Jaspers was not clear about the meaning of the disease processes in functional psychoses. He did not commit himself to the view that they were organic diseases of the brain. Kurt Schneider, (1958, 1959) is much clearer on this score. He divided the whole field of psychopathology into two domains. The first domain encompassed disease processes due either to manifest brain pathology or, as in the case of functional (endogenous) psychoses, to putative brain pathology. The second domain covered personality development and was subdivided into abnormal reactions and psychopathic personalities. Abnormal reactions were excessive reactions to stress situations brought about by such events as bereavements, disappointments, or threats. Examples of abnormal reactions were reactive depression and battle exhaustion. Psychopathic personalities mainly were due to hereditary constitutional factors and, to a lesser extent, to individual experiences that caused extreme deviation of the individual from the norm of the population. In the German psychiatric tradition, psychopathy (pathological personality) is a value-free biological concept, which has nothing to do with immorality and law breaking. It designates individuals who deviate markedly from the mean magnitude of a normally distributed trait. Deviations on some traits have more social importance than deviations on others. Since there are continuous variations in the magnitude of individual reactions to a stress situation and in the magnitudes of the personality traits, there is a continuity among the phenomenon described under the heading of personality developments. Normality merges by imperceptible steps with abnormality. In contrast, there is a discontinuity between the disease processes and the state of normality. Also pathological symptoms occurring in disease processes cannot be understood (*Verstehen*) in the context of personality development. Abnormalities occurring in personality developments, although according to Schneider mainly constitutionally determined, have a psychological meaning in this context. The examples of primary delusions and overvalued ideas will explain the difference. Primary delusions occur completely out of the blue; they cannot be explained by personality dynamics. Overvalued ideas can be understood as exaggerations of normal ideas or as products of adjustive personality mechanisms. Primary delusions occur in disease processes, overvalued ideas in personality developments. A remarkable feature of the Schneiderian system was the absence of the category of psychoneurosis. Cases usually described as psychoneuroses fell under the categories of either abnormal reactions or psychopathic personalities. They were regarded by him as constitutionally determined. Schneider, thus, found in his system room for both the disease and the constitutional models.

The Diathesis-Stress Model

Abnormal reactions to stress situations, described by Schneider, can be subsumed under the diathesis-stress model. This model envisages an interaction of hereditary predisposition, determined either monogenically or polygenetically, with environmental factors such as general or specific stress. It can be illustrated by Meehl's diathesis-stress theory of schizophrenia (Meehl, 1962). According to this theory, potential schizophrenics are born with a neurological defect (*schizotaxia*) causing cognitive slippage and malfunctioning of the brain's reward system. These, in turn, result in a blurring of messages passing through the brain's information channels and in anhedonia. An individual with such an inborn defect when exposed to an unfavourable family environment early in life develops a shy and antisocial personality (*schizotypy*). Later in life when subjected to an environmental stress, such an individual will develop schizophrenia. A somewhat similar theory of schizophrenia was proposed by Zubin and Spring (1977). It envisages schizophrenia as a multicausally determined condition in which a genetically determined brain dysfunction causes a decompensation of adjustment in the presence of stress. The brain dysfunction produces only vulnerability to, and is a necessary, but not sufficient cause of schizophrenia. Another illustration is provided by the polygene threshold model of schizophrenia inheritance proposed by Gottesman and Shields (1967). This model assumes that all people are distributed along a continuum of inherited liability for schizophrenia. On this continuum there is a threshold point above which individuals become phenotypically schizophrenic. Its location is relative to the degree of environmental stress, to the required performance, and to the social tolerance of deviance.

Finally there was the psychobiological theory of Adolf Meyer (1957), now of only historical importance, in which the disease and constitution concepts were replaced by broad psychobiological reactions (*ergasias*) of the total organism to environmental stress.

THE ROLE OF THE MEDICAL DOCTOR IN MODERN SOCIETY

To conclude the present chapter on medical models, a few remarks are appropriate regarding the role of the medical doctor in our society. Siegler and Osmond, in their book *Models of Madness and Models of Medicine* (1974), distinguish three basic occupational roles of medical practitioners: that of the medical scientist, that of the public health expert and an administrator, and that of the clinician-therapist.

The role of the clinician-therapist is of special interest in the present context. He enters into dyadic relations with his patients. The patient-doctor relationship has been institutionalized as a very special one, similar to that between confessor and penitent or between lawyer and client. It has been enshrined in the code of medical ethics, which can be traced back to Hippocrates and probably further back to the Aesculapian priests of ancient Greece. The clinical medical role is reciprocal to that of the "sick role" described by Talcott Parsons (1972). According to Parsons the sick role in our society exempts the subject from his normal social responsibilities, obliges him to seek medical help, and binds him to cooperate in the treatment so that he gets well as soon as possible. An important aspect of the sick role is freedom from responsibility for being sick. Thus the patient-doctor relationship involves two complementary roles: the sick role and the therapist role. The doctor-patient relationship, as it exists in our society, can be further analyzed into two basic types of relations, combined in various proportions and in varying degree of emphasis. The first type is the relation between an expert offering a professional advice and a client seeking the advice. In our society, if a person has a problem, such as a leaking roof, a malfunctioning car, or a legal or financial problem he may seek an expert's advice. An expert, who is usually licenced or recognized as such, is expected, for a fee, to give his honest advice to the best of his knowledge. It is up to the advisee to accept or disregard the offered advice. The authority of the expert may be described as sapiential (T. T. Paterson, in Siegler & Osmond, 1974). Some aspects of doctor-patient relationship can be characterized as that between an expert and a client.

The second type of relation is that between a guardian and a ward. The guardian acts *in loco parentis*. He exercises an authority over his ward in the best of the latter's interests. He makes the decisions affecting the well-being of the ward, even against the latter's will. This is justified by the belief that the guardian knows better than the ward what is in the best interests of the latter. Any act of deception, even in the best interest of the patient, casts the relation between a doctor and his patient into one between a guardian and his ward. This includes such therapeutic maneuvers as prescribing placebos, using suggestions, and hiding the seriousness of prognosis from the patient. The doctor's authority stemming from the guardian-ward aspect of doctor-patient relationship may be described as "Aesculapian." This changes slightly the meaning given originally to the designation by T. T. Paterson (in Siegler & Osmond, 1974) and relates it to the deceptions practiced in the Aesculapian temples of the Ancient Greece. In the field of mental illness, the guardian-ward aspect of the doctor-patient relationship has been more prominent than in the field of somatic medicine. The psychiatrist has very often been acting as a guardian of the patient on behalf of the state. The latter has often been completely or partially deprived of his civil rights and put in the position of a child vis à vis its parents. Treatment in the past has often involved deception such as suggestion, prescribing placebos, or withholding information from the patient. In addition, a strict control has been exercised over the latter's behavior. A variant of the guardian-ward type of relationship is that obtaining between a faith healer or shaman and his patient. In this case there may be no conscious deception, unless it is self-deception. Both parties are genuinely convinced about the efficacy of the therapeutic method, although it may lack a scientific validity. The positive therapeutic results are brought about by suggestion or autosuggestion. The charisma and the Aesculapian authority of the healer is an important ingredient of therapeutic relationship.

Medical Models

In recent years both in the field of somatic medicine and psychiatry the guardian-ward aspect of the doctor-patient relationship has been played down and the expert-client aspect emphasized. The patient is informed about his prognosis even when this involves telling him that he is suffering from a terminal illness. The nature of treatment is discussed with him and deception is avoided. Doctors are prepared to admit the limitations of their knowledge. The traditional dictum "doctor knows best" is being abandoned. The stress is on equality, honesty, and openness of the relationship.

Addendum

After this book had gone to press a review of brain dysfunctions in schizophrenia was published by L. J. Seidman (Schizophrenia and brain dysfunction: An integration of recent neurodiagnostic findings, *Psychological Bulletin*, 1983, *94*, 195-238). This review presents recent evidence based, among others, on CAT (computerized axial tomography) and PETT (positron-emission transaxial tomography), novel x-ray techniques, which indicate the presence of nonspecific anatomic brain damage in 20 percent to 35 percent of schizophrenic patients. This occurrence is particularly common in chronic, process schizophrenics. Thus, in addition to the bacteriological, biochemical, and genetic approaches to the etiology of schizophrenia, there can be discerned a neuroanatomical one.

Chapter 4

PSYCHOLOGICAL MODELS

INTRODUCTION

St. Augustine once said that he understood what time was until he was asked to define it. The same may be said about the descriptive term psychological. This is not the place to discuss in detail the profound philosophical issues of the nature of mind, the body-mind relationship, and the psychological explanation. However, some of these issues need to be mentioned, because different psychological models of mental illness make different tacit philosophical assumptions regarding the human mind. In his well-known book, *The Concept of Mind* (1949), Gilbert Ryle states that the accepted metaphysical position, which he attributes to Descartes, conceives of two kinds of substances: the material and the mental. This assumption leads to a homunculus theory of "a ghost in the machine" as the conceptualization of mind and body, with the resulting blind alley of solipsism and the mystery of mind-body interaction. Moreover, conceptual categories such as causes, spatial locations, and forces, borrowed from the Newtonian physics and applicable to the description of material objects, are applied to mental entities, thus leading to a category mistake. Ryle rejects any concept of mind conceived of as an entity situated behind the face, in the brain, consisting of ghostly images, ghostly thrusts, and other ghostly mechanisms, and serving as an explanation of observed behaviour. Instead, taking cues from the ordinary language usage, Ryle proposes that physical and mental are two kinds of descriptions of human behaviour. These descriptions do not contradict but rather complement one another and serve different purposes. They answer different kinds of questions. When we observe a chess player moving a chess piece or a soldier saluting the flag we can describe these events in terms of physical laws—in terms of the physiological happenings in the brain, nerves, and muscles or in terms of certain rules, such as the rules of the chess game or army regulations. In short, we can describe in terms of purposes and intentions. Whether a description in terms of reasons, rules, purposes, and intentions can, without loss of meaning, be reduced to one in physicalistic terms is an important philosophical question. The attempts to answer this question gave rise to lively controversies both in philosophy and psychology.

The theme of different types of explanation of human conduct was further developed by R. S. Peters in his readable little book, *The Concept of Motivation* (1958). Peters distinguished three types of explanation of human behaviour: the his reason explanations, the causal explanations, and the end-state explanations. The first type of explanation refers to rule following acts carried out for certain reasons. For instance, Jones crosses the street and enters a cigar store where he buys some pipe tobacco. The reason for this act was his intent to buy some pipe tobacco, which is quite understandable because Jones is a pipe smoker. Moreover, Jones follows certain rules such as waiting his turn to make the purchase, addressing the store clerk politely, and paying the requested amount of money. Jones's behaviour is understood in terms of the logic of situation (Popper, 1945). The causal explanation of behaviour may address itself to two different types of questions. One can inquire into the bodily mechanisms such as nerve impulses and muscular contractions, which are necessary conditions for Jones's behaviour, but not sufficient to explain its meaning, or one may inquire into its psychological causes.

There is a brand of behaviourism called logical behaviourism that has tried to reduce the meaning of sentences describing human behaviour to sentences describing physical movements of the body. This extreme position is, however, usually rejected. A standard position in ordinary language philosophy maintains that human behaviour can be described in two different frameworks, It can be described as a series of intentional acts motivated by reasons and entailing intelligent decisions, free choices, and valuations. It also can be described as a concatenation of physical movements, produced by causes, and explained in accordance with the principles of physics and physiology. Some behaviours, such as signing a cheque, can be described, depending on the question asked, in either of the two frameworks. Others, such as falling or having an epileptic seizure, can be described only in the framework of physical movements. They are not acts and have no intentional meaning.

This rather extreme position limits the concept of cause to physical causes where an exchange of physical energy occurs. According to this view, only the physiological explanation of behaviour is in terms of causes; the psychological explanation is always in terms of reasons and intentions. On this account, talking about psychological causes does not make sense. The less extreme position embraces a weaker conception of causality, more in keeping with David Hume's view, and accepts a regular conjunction as sufficient to define causality. On this view, it makes sense to talk about psychological causes. Peters takes this second position. According to him the second type of questions with which the causal explanation of behaviour is concerned are questions about psychological causes. They take the form of asking "what made a man behave in a strange way" or "what possessed him to do that." This explanation deals with cases of irresistible impulse, compulsion, or extreme emotional disturbance, when a person is driven to behave in a certain way by, as it were, an external force. The distinguishing characteristic of acts, for which the explanation by reasons is suitable, from the type of behaviour for which the explanation by psychological causes is suitable, is that in the first case, the person is an active agent who initiates free acts while, in the second case, the person is a passive victim to whom something happens. The psychological models of mental illness are an example of the second case where the explanation by psychological causes is applicable. Confronted with a bizarre and deviant behaviour, particularly when it is out of keeping with the previous behaviour of the person, we ask "What caused him to behave in this way" or "What possessed him" and are satisfied when a psychiatrist answers "because he is insane" or "because he suffers from schizophrenia." Another type of situation where causal explanation is applicable is the situation having to do with an acquisition of habit or learning in general. We explain a certain habit or a certain skill of the individual by quoting his past history and his exposure to those situations in which he could practice his skill or acquire a certain habit.

The third type of explanation of behaviour proposed by Peters is the end-state explanation. This is a high-level explanation to a very general type of question such as "why men eat" or "why men have sex." The answer is "to live" or "to procreate." The explanations of behaviour by invoking a pleasure principle or avoidance of unpleasure or attaining of reward belong in this category. The need satisfaction or drive reduction explanations used often in psychology belong to this category, as does the explanation that uses the model of homeostasis. The end-state explanation has to be distinguished from the explanation made by his reason. Both are teleological explanations; however, the subjective (his) reason of a person may be different from the objective (the) reason explanations. Thus, Jones's (*his*) reason why he enters a café and orders a cup of coffee and a sandwich is his desire to have a bite and not a need to replenish calories, although the latter may be *the* reason. When organisms are conceived of in terms of functioning systems a teleological end-state explanation makes sense. However, there is always a danger that this explanation may be vacuous, such as the explanation of a certain behaviour because it is rewarding when rewarding is not defined independently from the behaviour in question. From these various types of explanations of behaviour, one has to distinguish the attempts at justification as when pleas and excuses are made for certain behaviours. In this logical mode, stress is on apportioning responsibility, blame, or praise for a certain behaviour rather than an intellectual understanding of it. The explanations of human behaviour and its disorders offered by various psychological models is a mixture of the types of explanation of behaviour described by Peters.

Scientific psychology, which at one time in Germany was designated as *Erklärung Psychologie,* uses, by and large, causal and end-state types of explanation. The psychology of understanding (*Verstehen Psychologie*) uses the act and "his" reason type of explanation. In practice these two types of explanations are not easy to distinguish from one another, and their applicability depends on the frame of reference. Scientific psychologists do not talk about causes, they talk about independent and dependent variables. They aim at showing that when other conditions are unchanged, a change in the independent variable is sufficient condition for a change in the dependent variable. This type of explanation is causal, in the weak sense of causal. Psychologists in their attempt at being objective regard their subjects as passive objects to be manipulated by the experimental procedures. So even behaviours that have all the characteristics of acts are regarded within the experimental framework as caused by the manipulation of certain experimental procedures. Within the context of the psychology of understanding and of everyday life, beliefs are regarded as reasons for certain behaviour. On the other hand, in experimental social psychology they are regarded as causes. This is exemplified by the attribution theory research (Shaver, 1975; Weiner, 1972), where beliefs are manipulated to produce certain behavioural effects.

The frameworks used in experimental psychology often are mixtures of the causal and act types of explanation. With the notable exception of Guthrie (1952) and a few other early workers, behaviouristic psychologists describe behaviour on the level of acts rather than on that of muscular movements. Behaviour with which psychologists are concerned is usually described as that of the whole organism and as goal directed. However, it also means more than that. Body temperature regulation is carried out by the whole organism and is goal directed—to maintain the constant body temperature—however, body temperature regulation is regarded as a physiological phenomenon rather than a psychological or behavioural one. The behavior, of interest to behaviouristic psychologists, is one that is usually accompanied by such conscious experiences as intentions, decisions, setting goals, and checking the results of actions, although some behaviour episodes may be automatic. So even at the height of the behaviouristic tide in the thirties and forties, it was tacitly assumed that conscious episodes accompanied and were inseparably intertwined with the behaviour studied by psychologists, although they were not the subject of their study.

Behaviorists offer molar rather than molecular descriptions of behaviour. They are concerned with acts that result, for instance, in the bar being pressed independently of whether the rat does it with the left or the right forepaw or with its mouth.* The number of ways the rat can press the bar is very large. The effect of the bar being pressed is rewarded. Moreover, the rat emits the bar pressing

---

*To put it differently, behaviourists are interested in the function of the responses and not in their topography. However, it is only but a short step from the description in terms of the function to that of the "meaning of the responses."

spontaneously unless it is under control of a stimulus. However, the experimental psychologist is not concerned with the rat's reasons for pressing the bar, nor with the rat's intentions. He is concerned with the rate of bar pressing, which he is influencing with schedules of reinforcement. The first is the dependent variable, the second independent variable. The same method with appropriate modifications is also used with human beings. The type of explanation offered is a hybrid of the three types of logical explanations proposed by philosophers. They are purposeful acts that are, however, caused by experimental manipulations of independent variables. Moreover, the efficacy of the causes such as stimulus or reward is defined not only by the physical properties but also by the responsiveness to them of the experimental subject, as it were, to their meaning for him.

Another example of a hybrid explanation is the one used in dynamic psychology (depth psychology). In his *Psychopathology of Everyday Life,* Freud (1960) claims that the concept of unconsciousness offered a psychological explanation for certain occurrences such as memory lapses, slips of tongue, dreams, and psychopathological symptoms, which previously were explained on the basis of physiology of the brain. This feature of psychoanalytical theory has come to be called psychological determinism. This implies that all psychological events are determined and they do not happen by chance or spontaneously. However, psychological events may be determined but not necessarily psychologically determined. When one takes the epiphenomenological position, which was popular in scientific circles at the end of the nineteenth century, one assumes that all psychological (conscious) occurrences and states are determined by physiological states of the brain but not vice-versa. Freud's contribution was to show that psychological phenomena that appeared to be meaningless and, therefore explained in purely physiological terms had their hidden meanings, intents, purposes, and reasons. They result from unconscious motives and wishes. If one limits causal and deterministic explanations to the realm of physics and physiology, Freud's discovery that apparently meaningless conscious occurrences had hidden meanings restricted rather than extended the scope of psychological phenomena to be deterministically explained. By introducing the notions of unconscious motives, wishes, and defences Freud implied that many behavioural episodes that were regarded previously as occurring automatically were really acts carried out for certain reasons and with certain intentions. The following quotation from Freud may serve as an illustration. "You will also recognize the two important analogies with the symptomatic act we analyzed; mainly, the discovery of the sense or intention behind the symptom and the relation of it to something in the given situation which is unconscious" (1967).

The self was, as it were, split. The right hand did not know what the left hand was doing. From the point of view of consciousness the particular abnormal behaviour was caused by what appeared to be an alien force. The subject was driven to behave in a certain way. The behaviour happened to him, but it was not initiated by him, he was a passive subject. Yet, from the point of view of the unconscious, abnormal behaviour was an act carried out for a certain reason. Because free, deliberate, and rational acts are associated with fully conscious behaviour, while the unconscious behaviour has the hallmarks of being blind, automatic, and rigidly determined, it makes sense even in a philosophical context to regard unconscious motives and wishes as causes of rather than reasons for behaviour. However, these unconscious motives when they become conscious—when the analysant acquires an insight into his motives—presumably cease to be causes and become reasons. The analysant may indulge in the irrational behaviour if he freely chooses to do so. Peters refers to the psychodynamic type of explanation as quasi-causal.

There are many other ambiguities associated with psychological models of mental illness, apart from the type of explanation offered. These ambiguities stem from philosophical presupposition of the psychological theories on which the models are based.

It is customary to talk about two kinds of psychology, one referred to rather loosely as phenomenological and the other as behavioristic. Phenomenological psychology is concerned with consciousness, with subjective, private events and states of the mind. Behaviouristic psychology is concerned with objectively and publicly observed behaviour. In its radical form behaviourism denies the existence of private subjective consciousness and reduces the whole mental life to the physical, publicly observed movements and to physiological events in the brain. The more commonly accepted methodological behaviorism does not deny the reality of consciousness but rather maintains that scientific psychology can be concerned only with publicly observable, repeatable, and measurable events. The mentalistic, introspectionist psychology, which sometimes erroneously is called phenomenological, is a phenomenalist psychology. It assumes consciousness to be localized in the brain and regards sense data and feelings as the stuff of which the mind is made. Contents of consciousness are private and inferred only by analogy from the external signs and verbal reports. This theory of consciousness is the one criticized by Gilbert Ryle as a category mistake and an improper use of language. It has also been criticized in the philosophical phenomenology of Edmund Husserl (1962) and more recently by Merleau-Ponty (1963). The latter, which can be described as phenomenological psychology proper, does not separate behaviour as being external and physical from consciousness as being internal and mental. They interpenetrate one another and can be described as a manner of existing or as the structure of behaviour. The whole behaviour cannot be reduced into its constituent physical movements. It forms a gestalt-like temporal structure. There are three forms of structure of behaviour: the lowest form is the syncratic structure, in which response is bound to stimulus; the higher form is the removable structure, in which a gestalt-type organization of the perceptual field is in a dialectic relationship with a gestalt-type organization of the response of the total organism; and the highest form of behaviour structure is the symbolic form, characteristic of human beings. In this form the reacting organism by intentional acts converts the physical environment into symbol systems. In phenomenological psychology proper, consciousness is not inside the head but rather in the relationships of man-in-his-world, although of course physiological events in the brain are necessary, but not sufficient, conditions for the existence of consciousness. This topic will be discussed further in Chapter 6.

Apart from the issue of private consciousness and public behaviour, there are other theoretical issues that are reflected in various psychological models of mental illness. One such issue is that of peripheralism versus centralism in behaviouristic psychology. The issue concerns the location of physical equivalents of such psychological phenomena as thinking and feeling. Are they covert muscular and glandular responses, or are they physiological events in the brain with no peripheral counterpart? Another issue is that of the presence or absence of psychological hypothetical concepts and intervening variables.

The black box doctrine, advocated most forcibly by B. F. Skinner (1953) and his followers, maintains that psychologists are concerned only with observable external behaviour and with such environmental events as stimuli, reinforcements, and their contingencies on the subject's responses. They reject mentalistic concepts such as subjective experiences or hypothetical constructs as mythical and redundant for the science of behaviour. They leave the interior of the black box to neurophysiologists. In this respect their position is similar to that of Ryle: they deny the existence of the ghost in the machine, inside the head, either in the form of subjective sense data and mental acts or in the form of various hypothetical constructs, such as ego and superego of psychoanalysts or even habits and excitatory potentials of other behaviouristic schools. The recent resurgence of mentalism associated with the rise of cognitive psychology has tended to put the ghost back into the machine, in the guise of cognitive maps, cognitive structures, belief structures, schemas, channels of communication, and information storage. The advances in computer technology and the artificial intelligence research have been particularly responsible for the rise of cognitive psychology and for the return of the ghost.

Computers use basically two languages: the programme language and the machine language. The programme language or languages give general instructions for certain information processing operations to be carried out. They are translated by the computer compiler into the machine language for detailed execution of the instructions. Thus, there is the molar and the molecular level of the computer operations. The molecular level can be compared to the neurophysiological level of neurons and synapses of the brain. The molar level at which the programme language is operating represents a higher level of organization and integration of the countless molecular processes, controlled by the machine language. It may be that the new ghost in the machine of the cognitive psychologists may represent a molar, high-level organization of molecular, neuronal, and synaptic physiological brain events. The new ghost in the machine behaves something like a computer programme. Whether the computer programme metaphor contributes to a better understanding of the ontology of the human mind will be shown by further scientific research and philosophical enquiry. Perhaps a future research utilizing several computers in interaction will produce even a better model of the human mind.

Another issue of importance for psychological models of mental illness has arisen in the context of developmental psychology. This is the issue of nativism versus empiricism and the related concept of epigenesis. The question is asked to what extent personality traits, cognitive aptitudes, and even conceptual categories are inherited or acquired through experience. The empiricist tradition takes the Lockean view of the human mind and regards it as a passive *tabula rasa* (a clean slate) on which impressions of the external world are registered. The nativist tradition follows Descartes, Leibnitz, and Kant and believes that mind actively moulds experience through its innate ideas and a priori conceptual categories.

Recently there has been a retreat from empiricism to nativism mainly due to the influence of the work of ethologists and of psycholinguists. Ethologists, in contrast to early behaviourists such as Watson (1930), believe that emotional patterns and even cognitive categories are to a great extent inherited. In their claims for nativism they found an ally in Noam Chomsky (1957), a linguist, whose theories have had a tremendous impact on psycholinguistics and on cognitive psychology in general. Chomsky believes that basic linguistic competence and deep language structures are inherited and not learned and are only actualized in the particular language one acquires. The notion of deep cognitive (competence) structures that are inborn (preformism) or evolve in a dialectic interaction with the environment (epigenesis) is shared by many psychologists and social scientists. This point of view is called structuralism. Apart from Chomsky, important structuralists are Jean Piaget (1971), who represents the epigenetic version of Structuralism or as he calls it the constructivist version of structuralism, and Levi-Strauss (1963), who views the structures of cultural symbols as a reflection of the inborn structures of the human mind. Gestalt psychology represented an early version of Structuralism. There is a facet of Freudian theory, particularly in its later version, that can be classified as structuralist and epigenetic. Various structures, such as ego, id, and superego, and mechanisms are postulated to account for the observed behaviour. Moreover, these structures are believed to develop epigenetically. An inborn *Anlage* interacts with the environment producing a succession of stages of mental development. The epigenetic point of view, which postulates stages of development, differs from that of behaviouristic psychology, which regards the growth of mind as a quantitative accumulation of habits. According to the latter, the learning laws are the same from birth to old age.

Grossly oversimplifying, the following models of mind can be discerned in the welter of contemporary psychological theorizing. The first model of mind is mind as an energy system. This is represented by early psychoanalytical theory, particularly by its dynamic and economic versions. It is also represented by ethologists (Tinbergen, 1951) and by drive reduction theorists. In this model, the stress is on the concept of motivation, conceived as drive. Common to the theories that regard mind as an energy system are the ideas of homeostasis and closed system. The metaphor of energy is often used by motivation theorists who view drives, instincts, and needs as types of forces. The second model is the functionalist model of mind. The organism through acquired S-R responses or through operations on the environment manages to stay alive and adjust itself to the environment. The Thorndykian and Skinnerian approaches to learning and the adaptive model of the psychoanalytical theory come under this heading. The third model regards mind as an information processing system. This is the model of mind subscribed to by cognitive psychologists and also to some extent by the ego psychologists. Since an acquisition of information entails maximization of negative entropy and complexity, this model of mind assumes mind to be an open system. The fourth model of mind, closely related to the previous one, is the structuralist model, as represented by Piaget, Chomsky, Levi-Strauss, and the structural-developmental version of the psychoanalytical theory. This model assumes the presence of innate structures or potentialities to develop such structures. These structures are not directly experienced or observed; rather, they are inferred from the organization of cognitive processes and behaviour and also from the regularity and orderliness of development. The development proceeds through well defined stages. There are two versions of the structuralist developmental model. In the preformist version, the structures exist in potential form at birth and only actualize themselves in the maturational-developmental process. In the epigenetic version, the structures develop in a dialectic interaction with the environment. The final outcome is not completely determined at birth but also depends on the environmental factors. Using closed and open systems designations only as metaphors, it could be said that the preformist version of structuralism has characteristics associated with a closed system, and the epigenetic version has characteristics associated with an open system (von Bertalanffy, 1968). The fifth model is of greater importance in sociology than in psychology. It is the interactionist or the communication model of mind. This model assumed that the human mind emerges from interactionist, transactional, and communicative processes between individuals. Theories based on it will be discussed in Chapter 5. Among the theories to be discussed in the present chapter the interpersonal psychiatry of Harry Stack Sullivan represents an application of the interactionist model.

The five models of mind described so far are models that have evolved within the framework of scientific psychology. However, there are other models of mind implied by humanistic, phenomenological, and existentialist psychologies. They will be dealt with in Chapter 6. The psychological models of mental illness to be discussed do not exactly follow the scheme of the five models of mind that has been presented above. In addition to a purely conceptual analysis, certain historical traditions and professional affiliations have to be taken into consideration when delineating models of mental illness. However, there is a considerable overlap between the proposed models of mind and the proposed models of mental illness. Thus the behaviouristic model of mental illness presupposes the functional model of mind, and the cognitive model of mental illness presupposes the information processing model of mind. Psychoanalytical theory causes some problems because it has many facets that have been described as the topographical, dynamic, economic, structural, developmental, and adaptive models. However, it has a sufficient degree of coherence to be treated as a distinct model of mental illness.

Psychological models, in contradistinction to medical models, assume that the causes of mental illness are psychological, although the interpretation of this term varies with different models. The psychiatric symptoms have psychological meaning, and they are related to past experience of the patient. They have *suis generis* intrinsic meaning: they are psychological (behavioural) effects of psychological (behavioural) causes.

All the psychological models can be divided into three main groups: the psychodynamic, the behaviouristic, and the cognitive. In addition, one could distinguish the developmental model, which constitutes an important aspect of most psychodynamic theories but which also has wider connotations and covers several important theories outside the psychodynamic tradition.

PSYCHODYNAMIC MODELS

The roots of all psychodynamic models are in Freudian psychoanalysis, although there are important antecedents such as Mesmerism, the hypnotic treatment carried out by Jean-Martin Charcot and by Hyppolite Bernheim, the work of Morton Prince (1906) with multiple personalities, and the work of Pierre Janet (1889). The common features of these psychodynamic approaches is the belief that man is activated by unconscious and irrational motives and conflicts and that consciousness and rationality constitute only surface beneath which there is an abyss from which well-up primordial animal-like impulses, some destructive and some creative. According to this tradition, man's precarious rationality teeters on the brink of collapse always in danger of being engulfed by dark forces of irrationality.

The psychodynamic models stress the irrational in man. What is meant by the unconscious varies from one psychodynamic theory to another. At least four different concepts of the unconscious can be distinguished. The first is one that can be described as co-consciousness. Consciousness, because of a weakness of its integrative power or because of an induced hypnotic condition, becomes dissociated into two or more separate consciousnesses—the co-consciousnesses. These may be unaware of each other, or the awareness may be one-sided. One co-consciousness may be aware of the other while the other may be not aware of the first. Some co-consciousnesses may be more primitive than others, but there is no basic qualitative difference between them. This concept of the unconscious was held by Morton Prince and Pierre Janet. A somewhat similar phenomenon to that of co-consciousness is the common case of double meaning or of an ambiguous figure. An individual may be aware that a certain message has a double meaning or he may be aware of only the one meaning. Ambiguous figures and pictures provide a common example of alternating states of awareness or frames of experience.

Another conception of the unconscious is the field of awareness that is outside the focus of attention. The total psyche may be compared to a dark room and consciousness to a light spot produced by a light beam. There will be some objects in the focus of the beam that are sharply discerned, those in the periphery of the light spot that are only dimly discerned, and those in the darkness that cannot be discerned at all. The dark area outside the area illuminated by the light beam is the domain of the unconscious. This view of the unconscious was held by William James (1950) and it corresponds to the Freudian concept of the preconscious. Jean Paul Sartre's nonreflexive consciousness also belongs to this category (Sartre, 1956).

The third conception of the unconscious, that of Sigmund Freud (1953a) equates it with the domain of the mind where psychological processes are qualitatively different from those occurring in consciousness and can only indirectly manifest themselves in such conditions as dreams and psychotic phenomena. There is a barrier between the unconscious and the preconscious. The unconscious, which is qualitatively different, may be regarded as a seat of primitive impulses and images. It does not follow the laws of logic and is not governed by the principle of reality but rather by the principle of pleasure. Thus, it may be regarded as the source of disruptive and pathological forces. On the other hand, it also may be regarded as a fountainhead of creative life forces to which man can turn to be rejuvenated and, indeed, reborn. This latter view of the unconscious was held, in particular, by Carl Gustav Jung (1953). Jung believed that beyond the individual unconsciousness was a collective unconscious containing inborn structures of the mind called "archetypes." The structuralist point of view maintains that there are unconscious structures that perform important psychological functions.

Finally, the existence of the unconscious may be denied. On this view, the unconscious is a sort of make-believe. A person intentionally deceives himself that he is unconscious of certain things or happenings. However, deep down he is really aware of them but does not want to admit it to himself because he wants to deceive himself. Wilhelm Stekel (1927) and Alfred Adler (1963) held this view of the unconscious.

In the psychodynamic models, the psychological causes of abnormal behaviour are unconscious. The treatment consists of an uncovering, insight-producing psychotherapy. This type of therapy bears similarity to a Socratic self-examination and an explication of one's motives. Self-knowledge is therapeutic. The analysand acquires an insight into certain facts about himself, the knowledge of which he, in a sense, possessed before. The therapist does not impart this knowledge to the analysand. He only acts as a catalyst expediting the process of self-illumination.

In insight psychotherapy, the patient perceives at a certain point the meaning of his symptoms, all their connection with other symptoms, and certain events in the patient's life history. This insight into the meaning of the symptoms has to be not only on the intellectual level but also on an emotional one. Thus, the knowledge acquired by self-examination has an existential dimension in addition to the purely intellectual one. The treatment deals with psychological reality, which is as important as physical reality. To quote Freud (1967) with regard to the products of mind:

> They have indeed also a kind of reality; it is a fact that the patient has created these phantasies and for the neurosis this fact is hardly less important than the other—if he had really experienced what they contain. In contrast to material reality these phantasies possess psychical reality, and we gradually come to understand that in the *world of neurosis psychical reality* is the determining factor.

The patient has to overcome his resistance to achieve insight. Freud (1967) states:

> The labour of overcoming the resistances is the essential achievement of the analytical treatment; the patient has to accomplish it and the physician makes it possible for him to do this by suggestions which are in the nature of an *education*. It has been truly said therefore, that psychoanalytic treatment is a kind of re-education.

A frequent criticism of psychoanalytical therapy and other insight therapies, particularly from the behaviourist quarters, is the contention that talk therapy does not do anything to the patient. This criticism can be answered by stating that man is a symbolic animal and that symbols and words exert a tremendous power over his fate. In *A General Introduction to Psychoanalysis*, Freud (1967) remarks:

> The patient's unenlightened relatives—people of a kind to be impressed only by something visible and tangible, preferably by the sort of 'action' that may be seen at a cinema—never omit to express their doubts of how mere talk can possibly cure anybody... Words and magic were in the beginning one and the same thing and even to-day words retain much of their magical power. By words one of us can give to another the greatest happiness or bring about utter despair; by words the teacher imparts his knowledge to the student; by words the orator sweeps his audience with him and determines its judgments and decisions. Words call forth emotions and are universally the means by which we influence our fellow-creatures. Therefore let us not despise the use of words in psychotherapy and let us be content if we may overhear the words which pass between the analyst and the patient.

Thus, Freud quite early realized the importance of symbolic processes in the control of man's behaviour and their role in consciousness. He believed that when preconscious processes become linked with the mnemonic system of linguistic symbols, the system presently called semantic memory, the scope of consciousness is considerably expanded (Gedo & Goldberg, 1973). This theme of the importance of symbolic processes has recently been further developed by M. Edelson (1971), R. Schafer (1976), and Lacan (1966).

There are wide variations in the actual psychotherapies used by different dynamic schools. In some the role of the therapist is more active than in others. The previous remarks about the patient acquiring an insight on his own is particularly appropriate to classical psychoanalysis in which the analyst plays a passive role, serving only as a screen for the analysand's projections of his inner objects—the important figures from his past. Analysis is mainly concerned with the analysand's transference neurosis. In other psychodynamic schools the role of the psychotherapist is often more active.

Depending on the extent to which dynamic processes are internalized, and also depending on the extent to which importance is attached to the developmental processes in childhood, the psychodynamic models may be subdivided into (1) intrapersonal-developmental,

(2) interpersonal-developmental, and (3) interpersonal-situational models. These will be discussed below.

The Intrapersonal-Developmental Psychodynamic Model

The Classical Freudian Theory

The Freudian psychoanalytical theory may serve as an illustration of the intrapersonal-developmental model of mental illness. In the present discussion attention will focus on the psychoanalytical theory as it applies to mental illness rather than to personality and social issues. However, it is not easy to separate these three aspects of psychoanalytical theory from one another. Rapaport and Gill (1959) and Rapaport (1960) have distinguished the specific and the general theory of psychoanalysis. The specific theory is concerned with clinical applications of psychoanalysis and is close to empirical data. The general theory is more abstract and is concerned with the underlying metapsychological assumptions. From the metapsychological point of view it is possible to distinguish in Freud's theory four conceptual models: the dynamic, economic, developmental, and adaptational. The first is concerned with the conflict of unconscious forces. The second deals with the vicissitudes of sexual drive energy (libido), which tends towards an even distribution so as to maximize positive entropy. The third model focuses on orthogenic, psychosexual development during which the child progresses through orderly stages. Finally, the fourth model deals with the equilibrium between the inner drives and the demands of reality (Gill, 1963).

The dynamic model exists in two varieties: the earlier topographical and the later structural. According to the topographical model the mind is like a container, filled with mental stuff, subdivided into three areas: the conscious, the preconscious, and the unconscious. A repression barrier separates the unconscious from the preconscious. This barrier acts as a censor, keeping the contents of the unconscious from entering the preconscious. Only in dreams or in lapses of attention, when the censorship is relaxed, can unconscious impulses and wishes enter the preconscious in disguised form. The psychological processes in the unconscious are called primary. They are not bound by the time and space realities or by logic but governed by the pleasure principle. The unconscious impulses demand immediate discharge and the unconscious wishes demand immediate gratification.

Later, the topographical model was set aside in favor of a structural or tripartite model. The three regions of mind (the conscious, the preconscious, and the unconscious) were replaced by three structures: ego, id, and superego (Freud, 1961a). These hypothetical constructs are analogous to mechanisms, performing different functions that are never directly observed but only inferred from the contents of consciousness. The id was the source of libidinal and aggressive drives that could also energize and be used by the other two structures. The drives are characterized in terms of their source, impetus, aim, and object. The source refers to the erotogenic zone from which the drive originates. The impetus refers to the amount of energy utilized by the drive and measured as *cathexis*. The aim denotes the type of consummatory activity associated with the discharge of the drive, and the object denotes the target of the drive. Drives emanating from the id, which is controlled by the pleasure principle, demand an immediate discharge and gratification. These drives are checked by the ego, which operates in accordance with the reality principle. As a result there is a delay in drive gratification that allows for socially acceptable means of drive discharge. The ego finds a compromise between the reality principle, the demands of the superego, and the demands of the id. In performing its task, the ego uses suppression and neutralization of libidinal cathexes and also defence mechanisms that distort the perception of reality. Some ego defences such as projection, introjection, and withdrawal are associated with early, immature phases of the psychosexual development; other defences such as sublimation, rationalization, and repression are associated with more mature stages of the development. The third apparatus of the mind—the superego—develops as a result of the resolution of the Oedipal phase of the psychosexual development and arises from identification with the parent of the same sex. The superego is the source of moral standards of behaviour and can be identified with the Christian concept of conscience. These three parts of the mind, id, ego, and superego, are in constant conflict using libidinal and aggressive forces to check one another.

The developmental model of psychoanalysis is an epigenetic one. The successful completion of each developmental stage depends on the history of development at earlier stages. The psychosexual stages, which cover the first five or six years, are oral, anal, urethral, and phallic. The phallic phase is associated with the Oedipal object choice. The child in the Oedipal phase of psychosexual development is sexually attracted by the parent of the opposite sex and feels threatened (castration fears in the case of boys) by the parent of the same sex. The Oedipal stage is resolved by the renunciation of the Oedipal object and by an identification with the parent of the same sex. The resolution of the Oedipal phase is followed by the period latency, which lasts until puberty. Each stage is characterized by different sources, aims, and objects of libido gratification. Because of difficulties in resolving conflicts associated with various psychosexual stages, a fixation may occur at any one or more of the stages, which creates a vulnerability of the individual for future neurotic or psychotic symptoms. A situation of stress, particularly when it has some symbolic hidden meaning for the individual, may cause regression to the stage of psychosexual development at which the fixation occurred and precipitate a full-blown neurotic or psychotic breakdown.

Since the death of Freud in 1939, some important theoretical developments have occurred that have modified the picture presented so far—notably the ego psychology proposed by Heinz Hartmann (1958) and the work of Heinz Kohut (1971) on self-concept and self-identity. Hartmann has pointed out that the ego possesses inborn capacities that mature spontaneously to achieve personality integration and cognitive and behavioural competence. These are outside the area of neurotic conflicts. Hartmann's reformulation has brought psychoanalytical theory closer to the self-actualization theories of personality proposed by Maslow (1954) and Rogers (1965). The weakness of the ego, whether inborn or due to developmental circumstances, has become an important explanatory concept in the etiology of mental illness and particularly that of schizophrenia.

Kohut has been concerned with the Freudian concept of narcissism. Freud (1957b) dealt with narcissism in an early paper in which he described primary and secondary narcissism and two types of neurosis: the narcissistic and the transference neuroses. In early infancy, the libido is turned on oneself. This is the stage of the primary narcissism. It is followed by turning libido to external (anaclitic) objects—the persons who take care of the infant's needs, usually the mother.

Secondary narcissism occurs when later in life libido is withdrawn from the external objects and reinvested in the self. In the presence of primitive ego defences it may lead to schizophrenic breakdown—a narcissistic neurosis. However, Freud never dealt with the problem of self-development. While Melanie Klein (1949) and Ronald Fairburn (1954) dealt with this problem in terms of introjected objects, Kohut has taken one step further and conceptualized development of the self in terms of reciprocal relations to the other. He indicated that this complex process involves several stages before a constant and stable self-concept is achieved. The latter is maintained by continual narcissistic investments. Further, he has drawn attention to neurotic anxiety, which does not stem from a conflict with an infantile object but rather from a fear of self-disintegration and annihilation. Thus, Kohut has brought psychoanalysis close to existential psychiatry.

According to Freudian theory psychiatric symptoms are of similar nature as dream productions and slips of the tongue. To quote Freud: "Neurotic symptoms then, just like errors and dreams, have their meaning and, like these, are related to the life of the person in whom they appear" (1967). Neurotic symptoms result from unconscious conflicts between ego, superego, and id. They take a form of a compromise between the conflicting drives and are shaped by the ego defences. When repression and sublimation fail there is a return of the repressed in a disguised form of mental or somatic symptoms. There is a regression to earlier stages of psychosexual development. More primitive ego defences such as projection, introjection, isolation, undoing, and acting out, which are maladaptive and self-defeating, are utilized by the ego. Roughly, the extent of regression determines the severity of psychiatric symptoms. Thus, a slight degree of regression produces mild neurotic symptoms, a more profound regression causes more severe neurotic syndromes, and finally an extreme regression is associated with psychotic breakdowns such as schizophrenia or manic depressive psychosis. However, all symptoms are overdetermined and may express simultaneously unconscious conflicts at different levels of psychosexual development, both genital and pregenital. The same symptom may be determined by conflicts at the genital and pregenital levels. There is a continuity between mental health and mental disease and also between psychoneurosis and psychosis. To quote Freud, "neuroses and psychoses are not separated by a hard and fast line, any more than health and neurosis" (quoted by Gedo & Goldberg, 1973). Gedo and Goldberg (1973) offered a multidimensional model of regression as a truer picture of clinical reality rather than as a simple unidimensional one. Following Anna Freud (1965) they postulated the presence of several lines of development, such as the development of a sense of reality, typical situations of danger, object relations, narcissism, typical defences, and so on. Regression may proceed along these developmental lines to different degrees, thus producing a complex multilevelness of symptomatology. Moreover, psychological functions typical for different levels of psychosexual development have a potential for independent maturation and attainment of autonomy. Depending on the level of regression and the autonomy of the psychological functions, different clinical pictures obtain and different metapsychological models are applicable.

In what follows, a brief outline will be given of the psychoanalytic interpretation of psychopathology and various clinical syndromes.* In conversion hysteria there is a transformation or conversion of psychical excitation into somatic symptoms such as functional paralysis, anesthesia, chronic pain, and blindness. The psychical overexcitation is a result of a failure of repression of libidinal impulses. The pathogenic conflict is at the level of the Oedipal phase of psychosexual development with a regression occurring to this phase. In phobia, also called anxiety hysteria, anxiety associated with certain specific situations serves as a danger signal for ego that it may be overwhelmed by drive impulses. The feared external objects and situations represent symbolically an unconscious internal object and memories of situations related to conflict at the Oedipal stage. The unconscious conflict in obsessional-compulsive neurosis occurs at the anal-sadistic level of psychosexual development and is about passing or withholding feces, which unconsciously are regarded as a precious object. The neurosis is characterized by persisting urgent irrational thoughts or impulses to perform certain actions, felt by the patient as completely alien to his nature. Attempts at supression cause anxiety that is only relieved by yielding to the compulsion. These thoughts and actions

---

*Only a brief outline of this topic can be presented here. The interested reader is referred to Fenichel (1945) for further details.

have a peculiarity of being voluntary and involuntary at the same time. The ego defences used are that of isolation and undoing. The first separates affect from ideas; the second cancels the forbidden thoughts and acts. When ego defences are successful, the resulting clinical picture is that of an obsessional or anal personality rather than of obsessional-compulsive neurosis. The anal personality is characterized by the traits of orderliness, cleanliness, frugality, and parsimony due to the defense mechanism of reaction formation. In psychosomatic disorders (organ neuroses) repressed affect equivalents cause functional disorders of various organs leading eventually to organic pathological changes.

Psychoanalysis has also offered psychopathological explanations of psychopathic personalities and sexual perversion. A few examples will now be given. Impulse-ridden characters use acting out as a defence against their unconscious conflicts. Homosexuality, depending on the type, is caused either by an abnormal Oedipal identification with the parent of the opposite sex or, in pedophiliacs, by fixating on sex objects identified with the self as a child. Fetishism, which is a sexual attraction to nongenital parts of a woman's body or to articles of her clothing, is an attempt to deny unconsciously her lack of penis and to allay the subject's castration anxiety. Paranoid delusions are explained by the presence of latent homosexuality, which is warded off by the defences of reaction formation or projection. The unconscious proposition "I love him" becomes by means of reaction formation "I hate him" that, in turn, by means of projection becomes "he hates me." This distorted proposition becomes a paranoid delusion of persecution.

In an important paper, *Mourning and Melancholia*, Freud (1957c) compared melancholia (depression) with a normal state of mourning. In the latter state an external object has been lost, which causes pain and anguish. In melancholia an internal object that had been incorporated in the ego is lost. As a result the patient experiences impoverishing of one's ego and a profound feeling of worthlessness. The patient expresses ideas of guilt and self-depreciation. Because of the ambivalence of feelings towards the internal object, the ego feels responsible for the object loss. The internal object that was lost from the ego is unconsciously viewed as cruel, sadistic, and revengeful. As a result, aggression is turned against oneself, giving rise to acute guilt feelings and suicidal tendencies. In mania there is a denial of the internal object and flight into reality. The vicissitudes of introjection and expulsion of the internal object contributed to the development of the concept of super-ego and to the structural, tripartite model of psychoanalysis.

Schizophrenia was regarded by Freudians as a manifestation of secondary narcissism and profound regression to the earliest infantile stages of psychosexual development when ego was extremely weak or had not yet been formed. As a result, primitive mechanisms of defence are used, the sense reality is faulty, and thought is prelogical and has magical properties. Thinking is similar to that which occurs in dreams. In the beginning of psychosis there is a withdrawal of libido from the external world and reinvestment of it back into the patient's body and his psychological processes (secondary narcissism). This leads to delusions of cosmic catastrophe bringing about the end of the world, as well as to hypochondriacal-somatic delusions and distortions of the bodily image. This phase is followed by the phase of restitution of the world. A phantasy world is created, populated by internal objects that have been projected onto the real world. The line dividing the inner and outer reality disappears. This externalized world, an animistic world of phantasy, is ruled by magic instead of the reality principle. The ego defence mechanisms that are being used are the primitive ones of projection, introjection, identification, and withdrawal. In recent years, psychoanalytical theories of schizophrenia have placed greater stress on a failure of the synthetic and autonomous functions of the ego. Further, the inability in these patients to form an adequate self-concept, distinct from that of the other, has been attributed to disorders of secondary narcissism.

To conclude this section, a few remarks are appropriate with regard to Freud's views on society. A common criticism by social scientists and the neo-Freudians levelled at classical psychoanalysis is that Freud was using a biological concept of man instead of regarding man as a product of his society. He regarded the socialization and acculturation of children, leading to a renunciation of instinct, to be the cause of neurotic conflicts (Freud, 1961b). The young organism had to adjust to a social reality and to use ego defences to control the gratification of biological impulses with a resulting frustration. Thus, socialization was regarded as a compromise between the demands of the biological drives and the reality represented by society. Civilized man, like the neurotic, was a victim of unconscious conflicts that he had to keep under control by using defences. Civilization could therefore be regarded as a collective neurosis. This conclusion led Freud to a pessimistic view of man's future. He predicted a mass discontent that would lead to bloody wars and revolutions. Not all psychoanalysts share Freud's pessimistic view of the inevitable conflict between man and his society. According to the ego psychologists (Hartmann, 1958) the ego possesses synthetic and autonomous functions that are outside the ego-id conflict area. Therefore human beings have a potential for being integrated into society independently of the necessity of warding off id impulses by ego defences. Alfred Adler and neo-Freudians regard man as basically a social creature. To these theorists we now turn.

The Theory of Alfred Adler

The theories of Alfred Adler (1963, 1964) and Karen Horney (1950) offer other examples of the intrapersonal dynamic model of mental illness. They differ in important respects from that of classical psychoanalysis. Both of them emphasize the role of society in shaping the psychodynamics of the individual. They also emphasize the holistic aspect of human personality and reject Freud's tripartite model of ego, id, and superego, replacing it by a concept of dynamic self.

According to Adler, man is a purposeful system with the goal of self-realization and social survival. He has a dominant need to perceive himself as an integrated unit purposefully striving to achieve individually determined goals. He attempts to achieve superiority in order to overcome the complex of inferiority that is the result of helplessness experienced as a small child. Each individual establishes for himself goals and organizes his experiences and motives into a personal life-style. He creates fictitious ideals, which have nevertheless a subjective reality for him. In his theorizing about life-style and fictitious ideals, Adler was influenced by Idealistic Positivism—the philosophy of the as if of Hans Vaihinger (1911). According to this Austrian philosopher, absolute truths and ideal norms of human conduct do not exist, rather man creates them as fictions important for individual and social survival. Life-style according to Adler is the individual's unique adaptation to his social milieu that contributes to social integration but at the same time allows for individual autonomy and gives meaning and significance to his life. Individual development is not biologically and socially determined but rather self-determined. The individual along his life path freely chooses the goals he wants to pursue. In this respect Adler's theory is indistinguishable from that of humanistic and existentialist psychologists. Adler's concept of life-style bears a great similarity to the *project* of the existentialists. The regnant human motif is will to power—the drive to dominate the others, which, however, is tempered by social feeling—a need to belong, to be integrated into society, and to serve useful social purposes. Otherwise, the untamed will to power causes conflict between man and society leading to his isolation and neurotic maladjustment. Psychoneuroses are caused by childhood experiences of neglect or overprotection, resulting in a negative self-image of weakness and helplessness, as well as a negative image of society as rejecting and hostile. Attempts at compensation produce various neurotic syndromes, which are misguided adaptations of the total personality. The unique family constellation and the child's ordinal position are of greater importance in shaping early experiences than the Oedipus complex. However, ultimately the inner psychological world is the individual's own creation rather than a product of external causes.

Adler rejects diagnostic labels and looks at each case as a unique individual attempt at adjustment. In their attempts to integrate their life-style and to enhance their self-concepts the individual patients are using such mechanisms as "conquest through weakness"—a flight into simulated physical illness in order to control other people. Adler has described certain life-styles such as the ruling, the getting, and the avoiding as maladjustive. However, each patient creates, in the context of individual development and subjective experience, a unique constellation of symptoms, a unique gestalt.

The Theory of Karen Horney

The theories of Karen Horney, which are more recent, were influenced by contributions from sociology and anthropology to a greater extent than the theories of Adler. It has been pointed out by anthropologists and historians of medicine that neurotic symptoms and syndromes vary from culture to culture and epoch to epoch and so do family constellations and conflicts associated with them. Consequently, the interest has shifted from the biological to the sociological determinants of psychoneurosis.

Influenced by these developments, Karen Horney has rejected the biological theory of libido, of the Oedipus complex, and of psychosexual stages. Instead, she has stressed the importance of cultural factors and interpersonal relations for the dynamics of personal development. The individual is seen as constantly interacting with his social milieu. Although Horney regarded the self as unitary, she distinguished three aspects of it: the actual self—the sum total of the individual's experiences, the real self—the integrative agent, bringing about a state of harmonious wholeness, and the idealized self— incorporating unrealistic neurotic goals. A person can become alienated from the actual self or from the real self. In the first type of alienation there is a denial of personal feelings and a failure of self-perception. In the second there is a failure to actualize the personality potential for growth and creativity. According to Horney, the sources of neuroses are (1) distorted parent-child relationship, (2) distorted relations between the self and others, and (3) a discrepancy between the potential of achievement and the actual, neurotically stunted growth of the individual. Early childhood experiences were considered to play a crucial role in the genesis of psychoneurosis. The conflicts resulting from inconsistent parental attitudes, from parental overstrictness, rejection, or overprotectiveness, produced general neurotic reactions in children that were characterized as (1) moving toward—a clinging dependence, (2) moving away— withdrawal to solitude and privacy, and finally (3) moving against—an attitude of general hostility.

Neurotic conflicts manifest themselves as a feeling of anxiety, and certain pathological character traits developed to cope with it. However, the central inner conflict is that of self-hatred leading to an alienation from the self and creation of a pseudoself. The sense of genuine identity is lost and is replaced by a false identity. This can lead to depersonalization and a distortion of bodily image. More often, it leads to adopting contrived roles in social interactions. The therapy aims at removal of distorting and stifling influences of the past so as to allow for the individual growth and self-actualization.

It can be seen that there is a great similarity between the theories of Adler and Horney and the theories of the humanistic and existentialist psychologists such as Carl Rogers, Abraham Maslow, and Rollo May. There is also a similarity between these two perspectives and the more recent developments within classical psychoanalysis such as the ego psychology of Heinz Hartmann.

Interpersonal Developmental Psychodynamic Model

The interpersonal psychiatry of Harry Stack Sullivan

In contrast to the previously discussed psychodynamic theories, which stressed the internalized past interpersonal relations, the interpersonal psychiatry of Sullivan (1953) stresses the presently existing ones. For him, the self and personality exists only in the context of interpersonal relations. The self is a mirror reflecting the attitudes of the significant others. To put it differently, self is a social phenomenon, and the unit of analysis is not an individual patient but rather an interacting dyad or a group. Thus, Sullivan has followed the lead of such sociologists as G. H. Cooley (1966) and, in particular, George Herbert Mead (1972). Consequently, he has abandoned the biological framework of classical psychoanalysis for the sociological one of interpersonal transactions. He defines psychiatry as the study of interpersonal relations conducted by the psychiatrist as a participant observer. His unit of study is an interpersonal relation. Since man is by nature social, in addition to the basic biological needs, he has needs for social recognition (need for satisfaction) and acceptance by others (need for security). If these needs are not satisfied, man feels insecure, has low self-esteem, and experiences anxiety. The latter is an important force that can cause personality disintegration, but it also motivates man to achieve. To cope with anxiety the individual develops in his childhood a self-system of dynamisms. The early relation between the child and his mother, or the mothering one, plays an important role in this process. If this relationship is satisfactory, he develops feelings of security and trust in the external world and people, which are the prerequisites for high self-esteem and self-respect. On the other hand, an unhappy relationship inducing anxiety results in a low self-esteem and self-respect. The attitudes of the mothering one are reflected in the child's self-perceptions as good me, bad me, or not me. The bad me and not me self-perceptions tend to be repressed by the dynamisms of the self-system. However, in the process, the growth of the latter may be warped and result in a psychoneurosis.

Sullivan distinguishes three stages in the emotional and cognitive development of personality: the protaxic, parataxic, and syntaxic. The protaxic stage is characterized by the lack of distinction between the self and the external world, by absence of time perspective, and by magical thinking. The parataxic stage is characterized by a lack of real understanding of causality and by seeking the explanation of external events by apparent temporal connections. Finally, the syntaxic stage of the mature personality is characterized by logical consensually validated thinking and is a product of maturity and successful socialization. There is a similarity between these three developmental stages and the sensory-motor, concrete operational, and formal operational stages proposed by Jean Piaget. Emotional security and self-esteem are needed by the child for successful navigation through these stages of cognitive development. Unsatisfactory interpersonal relationships can arrest the development at the protaxic and parataxic stages or cause a regression to them. The periods of infancy, childhood, preadolescence, and adolescence involve different types of interpersonal relationships. These relationships are more important than infantile sex drive for shaping personality.

Neuroses and psychoses are not regarded as diseases but rather are personality developments warped by unsatisfactory interpersonal relations. Even schizophrenia is not very far from the normal process of living. Thus, according to Sullivan, mental illness is continuous with normality. In psychoneuroses, certain tendencies are dissociated because they are anxiety inducing and are substituted for by neurotic symptoms. In schizophrenia, dissociated tendencies become conscious and cause a state of overwhelming anxiety threatening self-disintegration. There is a state of panic followed by catatonic withdrawal. Subsequently, the individual attempts to reconstruct his experienced world, which is psychotic and alien, but less threatening than the world of normal experience.

Sullivan was particularly interested in schizophrenia, the causation of which he conceived of in purely psychological terms. In contrast to Freud, Sullivan believed that schizophrenia was amenable to psychoanalytical therapy. In psychotherapy, Sullivan regarded patient-therapist relations as genuine ones and not just the transference shadows of the original child-parent relations. In this respect, Sullivan's technique comes closer to the practice of humanistic psychologists and existentialists than to classic psychoanalysis.

Interpersonal Situational Dynamic Model

Gestalt therapy of Frederick Perls

This therapy (Perls, 1969; Perls, Hefferline, & Goodman, 1951) may serve as an example of the interpersonal situational model. In his formulations, Perls was influenced by ideas of gestalt psychology, by Kurt Lewin's psychological field theory, and particularly by the organismic neurology of Kurt Goldstein. Perls describes his system of psychotherapy as belonging to humanistic psychology. However, there are certain features of his theory that are undoubtedly psychodynamic. Perls postulated the existence of personality layers superimposed on one another like onion skins. The most superficial layer is the cliche layer, which is concerned with social conventions. Underneath it is the layer of personality concerned with playing stereotyped, inauthentic roles. Still deeper is the impasse layer characterized by phobic attitudes and attempts to avoid the experience of nothingness and emptiness. Underneath it is the implosive layer, which is characterized by a fear of death and an impasse of opposing forces. At this level, the individual is overcome by existential anxiety. Finally, still deeper is the explosive layer. When this layer is reached the individual overcomes his stereotyped social roles and becomes an authentic person, capable of experiencing and expressing genuine emotions. The true self is revealed.

Gestalt therapy is not concerned with the individual's past or with causal explanations. It is concerned with the individual's present experience as he relates to others in a concrete, interpersonal context. Intellectual explanations and verbalizations are discouraged; instead, spontaneous emotional experiences and nonverbal communications are emphasized. The past is not held responsible for illness and psychological difficulties. Although the presence of certain defensive layers of personality are proposed, the underlying conflicts are existential rather than seen as stemming from former traumatic child-parent interactions. Thus, gestalt therapy can be characterized as being both psychodynamic and existential.

DEVELOPMENTAL MODELS

Most of the psychodynamic theories are, at the same time, developmental theories of mental illness. However, the developmental model can be conceptually separated from the psychodynamic, and indeed, developmental theories stemming from academic psychology have made independent contributions to the understanding of abnormal behaviour. The ontogenetic and phylogenetic theories of psychological development are complemented by the theories of the hierarchical organization of the nervous system.

The orthogenic developmental model asserts that the course of ontogeny is lawful and follows an orderly sequence. There is a directionality in the development that, however, can be reversed, leading to a regression to earlier phases of development. The stages of development form an orderly sequence from the immaturity pole at one end to the maturity pole at the other. There is a hidden assumption of valuation in the immaturity-maturity polarity. Mature behavior is considered to be higher, more advanced, and more adaptive to the physical and social milieu than immature behaviour. However, immature biological and psychological functions sometimes serve a useful purpose as in the case of healing of tissues, involving dedifferentiation of cells, and as in the case of mental creativity where there is a "regression of mental functioning in the service of the ego" (Kris, 1952).

According to the developmental model, psychopathology is caused by a regression to a lower level of psychosexual, cognitive, and emotional development—the more extensive the regression the more profound the psychopathology. Thus, mild maladjustment and psychoneurosis is caused by a regression to more recent developmental stages, while psychosis is caused by a regression to an archaic infantile level. The development may be unidimensional or multidimensional.

While the psychoanalytical theories have dealt mainly with the emotional development of children and psychopathological regression, other developmental theories have dealt with cognitive development and with the formal aspects of the orthogenic psychological development. The former is illustrated by Jean Piaget's theory, the latter by Heinz Werner's theory of orthogenesis.

The contribution of Jean Piaget

Jean Piaget (1954) is mainly interested in the cognitive development of normal children. This is part of his more general interest in genetic epistemology. He is concerned with the question of how knowledge of the external world develops in children and also, more broadly, in society at large. As his starting point he takes the two basic biological functions of assimilation and accommodation as the fundamentals of organismic adaptation to the environment. The interplay of these two functions produces sensory-motor schemas that the infant internalizes and uses in his transactions with the environment. On this basis, the infant builds his image of the world and of external reality. This development progresses through the following orthogenic stages: the sensory-motor, the preoperational, the concrete operational, and the formal operational. Of primary interest to abnormal psychology is the process of decentering that goes on during the child's development. The cognitive attitude in early childhood is characterized by egocentricity, an inability to take on other person's point of view or to form an objective notion of time and space—the universe centers on the child. The period of infancy is characterized by an inability to separate the external and internal realities.

Although Piaget is mainly concerned with cognitive development, there are obvious implications for a child's emotional, social, interpersonal, and moral development (Piaget, 1965). As the child progresses from earlier to later stages, he becomes more capable of sharing experiences with other people, of adjusting to the social group, and at the same time he attains moral autonomy based on cooperation and reciprocity. It can be recognized that these characteristics are those regarded by psychodynamically oriented psychiatrists as distinguishing mentally healthy, well-adjusted, mature individuals as against egocentric psychoneurotics and autistic psychotics. There is a great similarity between Piaget's theory of development and particularly that of Harry Stack Sullivan. The latter also stressed the progression from prelogical thinking and egocentric attitude of a young child or a psychotic patient to logical, consensually validated thinking and socialized attitude of an adult or a normal person. Since schizophrenic patients show disorder of logical thinking and impaired concept formation, attempts have been made to apply Piaget's theoretical formulations to the investigation of schizophrenic cognitive processes. These attempts so far have met only with limited success (e.g., Cameron, 1938). There are also formal similarities between Piaget's structuralism and the structural model of psychoanalysis. Both presuppose that the human mind possesses a potential for certain mental organizations that are actualized in the spiral of interactions between the organism and the environment. This epigenetic point of view assumes that more recent and advanced organizations are built on the foundations of the earlier and more primitive ones. In Piaget's theory, they are identified as cognitive structures mapping the world and operating on it. In the structural psychoanalytical model, they constitute the ego mechanisms delaying drive gratification so that its expression can occur in a socially acceptable manner.

Erik Erikson's epigenetic theory of personality development

Erik Erikson (1963) proposed an epigenetic theory of ego development. He believes that there are eight stages of ego development, each characterized by a typical conflict confronting the individual. Different cultures phrase these conflicts somewhat differently and require somewhat different solutions. The progress from one stage of ego development to the next depends on successful solution of the conflict typical for this stage. The first stage is characterized by the conflict of basic trust versus basic mistrust, between cravings for sameness and for novelty. It is concerned with a sense of continuity of important persons ministering to the needs of the infant. The next stage of ego development is that of autonomy versus shame and doubt. During this stage the infant strives to attain bowel control, but these attempts may lead to shame and doubt. The third stage is of initiative versus guilt. Phantasies of aggression against the parent of the same sex lead to feelings of guilt. The following stage of industry versus inferiority coincides with the beginning of schooling or performance of other chores and leads to an experience of feelings of inferiority. The next stage, associated with puberty, is characterized by a conflict of identity versus role confusion. The changing status from child to adult leads to doubts about the identity and the sex role. The stage that follows is characterized by the conflict of intimacy versus isolation. It centers around the problem of establishing permanent relations with a partner of the opposite sex without losing personal autonomy. The seventh stage is characterized by the conflict of generativity versus stagnation and centers round the problems of procreation and creativity. The last stage, associated with middle age, is characterized by the conflict of ego integrity versus despair. It is concerned with the existential problem of life meaning and with developing a life-style expressing the values of one's culture. It has to be noted that Erikson applies the theory of epigenetic development beyond childhood and adolescence to cover the whole life span.

Epigenesis presupposes an interaction between the developing organism and the environment. Thus, maturational readiness is always complemented by learning processes. The proper sequence of experience fitting maturational readiness leads to an orderly progression through the developmental stages. In contrast, preformism attributes development solely to maturation. Those psychopathologists who stress only organic factors in maturation and in regression implicitly subscribe to the preformist point of view.

Henri Ey's Jacksonian model of psychopathology

Hughlings Jackson, in his Croonian Lectures (1932), suggested that the nervous system is hierarchically organized with the more mature level of integration inhibiting the less mature levels. When a pathological process causes dissolution of the higher integration level, a lower one is released resulting in a regression and primitivization of mental life. The latter, if sufficiently profound and global, results in a psychotic breakdown.

Henry Ey (1969) has elaborated the Jacksonian theory into the organo-dynamic system of psychiatry. To begin with, he deals with the crucial problem for any system of psychiatry, the body-mind relationship. He rejects both Cartesian dualism and the double aspect theory. Instead, he proposes a dialectic or dynamic process that is instrumental in the evolutionary passage from the organic infrastructure to the psychic superstructure. Through the phylogenetic and ontogenetic development of infrastructure, a more complex psychic superstructure is produced that dialectically interacts and controls the infrastructure. The laws governing the organization of the superstructure are different from those of the organization of the infrastructure. The psychic superstructure evolves in the direction of enhancing its psychological features at the expense of purely physiological ones. When a partial dissolution of the dynamically organized psychic superstructure occurs, as a result of pathological processes in the neuronal organic infrastructure, there is a lowering of the mental level of functioning and, sometimes, a complete regression to the purely physiological level.

According to Ey, mental illness is a manifestation of the disorganization of the psyche and sometimes of its complete disintegration. He equates the Freudian unconscious and the *automatisme psychologique* of Pierre Janet with low and primitive levels of psychological organization. Consciousness represents the highest level of psychic integration. "The conscious mind is that aspect of psychic life which organizes all that has been experienced into a kind of representative awareness" (Ey, 1969). It binds the past to the present and projects the latter into the future, reflects back on its contents, and also gives structure to reality. In psychosis there is an unstructuring of reality. Ey divides mental disorders into acute and chronic. The acute ones are caused by disorders of consciousness. In milder forms, they manifest themselves as manic-depressive psychoses. A more profound dissolution of consciousness produces hallucinatory deliria, dreamlike, oneroid, and confusional states. The chronic mental disorders are by-products of the pathology of personality development. In milder forms they manifest themselves as neuroses, in more severe forms as chronic delusions and chronic schizophrenia. In the most severe form they produce dementias. Although Ey accepts psychological factors such as learning in psychotic development, he believes that the dissolution of psychic organization and its regression to a lower level is caused by organic pathology. However, this does not detract from the phenomenological reality of psychopathological symptoms.

Heinz Werner's theory of orthogenesis.

The most general formal principles of development have been formulated by Heinz Werner (1948, 1957) in his theory of orthogenesis. According to orthogenic principles, development progresses from a state of relative globality and lack of differentiation to a state of increasing differentiation, articulation, and hierarchic integration. In regression, the direction of change is reversed and is from high differentiation to relative globality. This orthogenic principle applies to the development of embryos, growth and maturation of organisms, evolution of species, psychological development, and to the progress from primitive to highly complex cultures. In pathology, particularly brain pathology, there is a regression from highly differentiated to more global and primitive functioning. However, the products of development and regression although displaying certain formal similarities are by no means identical. There are important differences as well as similarities. Thus, a child, a primitive man, and a schizophrenic are not the same, although their cognitive processes bear some formal resemblance. According to Werner development progresses (1) from the syncretic to the discrete, (2) from the diffuse to the articulated, (3) from the indefinite to the definite, (4) from the rigid to the flexible, and (5) from the labile to the stable. There is a similarity between these polarities and the polarities distinguishing the primary and secondary processes in Freud's theory.

Werner was interested in abnormal psychology and conducted some research on perceptual and cognitive processes of schizophrenics. He showed that there were many primitive features present in schizophrenic perception and thinking. Thus he conceptualized schizophrenia as a regressive process with the severity of schizophrenia related to the depth of regression. Werner only described schizophrenic processes without expressing any views as to their causation.

The developmental model summary

All the developmental theories, whether stemming from the psychoanalytical or the experimental tradition, show certain common features. Cognitively mediated, voluntary, fully conscious processes appear later in life and dominate the purely sensimotor, impulsive, reflex type of behaviour (Baldwin, 1967). Also, the here and now egocentric orientation is replaced by a more objective temporal and spatial perspective. The developmental model of mental illness has been very influential in American psychiatry and in the mental health movement. Karl Menninger's theory of one mental disease (Menninger, 1963) is an illustration of it. According to Menninger there is only one mental disease, which varies in severity. The severity depends on the degree of regression to immature levels of psychosocial development. The extreme level of regression is incompatible with the adjustive processes necessary for life and, hence, leads to death. To state the claims of this model in a somewhat exaggerated form: superior mental health is equated with maturity and mental illness with immaturity. Mental disease is a regression from maturity to immaturity, while recovery is a progression from a regressed state of immaturity to that of maturity. The developmental model, perhaps with the exception of Ey's theory, is a continuity model without a clear dividing line between mental health and disease and between neurosis and psychosis. However, there are some discontinuities between the developmental stages.

BEHAVIOURISTIC MODELS

The behaviouristic model of mental illness has come into prominence only relatively recently, although behaviourism was launched by J. B. Watson seventy years ago (Watson, 1913). For years, behaviourism was confined to the experimental psychology laboratory and animal research. After the second world war, behaviouristic ideas were adopted by a group of clinical psychologists who vigourously challenged the dominant psychodynamic model and offered an alternative in the form of behaviour therapy. The proponents of behaviour therapy identify it with the psychological model, which they contrast with both the somatic and psychodynamic perspectives, regarded as exemplifying the medical model (Ullmann & Krasner, 1965).

Some therapeutic practices, which pass under the name of behaviour therapy, have, particularly in recent years, exceeded the framework of strict behaviourism (Locke, 1971). The behaviouristic model not only is concerned with the practice of behaviour therapy but it also serves as a foundation for some explanatory theories of psychosis and neurosis.

The history of behaviourism, its theoretical foundations, its metaphysical assumptions, and its varieties are discussed elsewhere (Weckowicz & Liebel-Weckowicz, 1982). It suffices to say that there are nine, three primary and six secondary, characteristics of behaviourism, which are given different prominence by its proponents. These are elementarism (atomism), associationism, hedonism, scientific objectivity, reductionistic materialism, environmentalism, peripheralism, pragmatism, and a generality of laws of behaviour. The present discussion of behaviouristic contributions includes also those stemming from Pavlovian theory. The specific behaviouristic models of mental illness vary a great deal in their properties depending on the specific theoretical assumptions. For example, the Skinnerians reject any central, unobserved entities or events as mythical and are concerned only with observable peripheral responses. Therefore, they describe mental illness in terms of maladjustive responses or operants. The Russian school of objective psychology has never subscribed to peripheralism and rejected the empty organism, or the black box, assumption. Consequently, Pavlov (1941) and his followers offered a model of mental illness that is based on hypothetical brain processes such as central excitation, supramarginal inhibition, and induction. The followers of Clark Hull (1943, 1952), Miller (Dollard & Miller, 1950), Mowrer (1950), and Spence (Spence & Taylor, 1953) have taken an intermediate position. Their models eschew explicit physiologizing and use such hypothetical constructs as drive, usually described as anxiety, habit strength, reactive inhibition, and generalization gradient. All these theoretical concepts are used by behaviour therapists in a rather unsystematic way, which contributes to the conceptual confusion. Three types of behaviouristic models of mental illness may be distinguished: (1) Pavlovian, or the classical conditioning model, (2) Hullian, or the S-R model, and (3) Skinnerian, or the operant conditioning model. They differ primarily in the paradigms of learning and in the stress on the peripheralist or centralist explanations. These models now will be briefly described.

The Pavlovian classical conditioning model

In the final years of his work, Pavlov (1941) became interested in the problem of mental illness. He tried to explain various mental diseases such as schizophrenia and hysteria in terms of cortical physiological abnormalities manifested by conditioned reflexes. The Pavlovian model is based on the paradigm of classical (respondent) conditioning, which is explained by the processes taking place inside the central nervous system. Its constructs (excitation, inhibition, and stability) are states and properties of these processes, displayed by different individuals to varying degrees. In some the excitatory processes predominate, in others the inhibitory. Also, in some individuals cerebral processes are stable and in others labile. Depending on these characteristics, individuals differ in their responses to conflict and stress. Those with a predominance of unstable excitation respond with excitement and aggression. Those in whom unstable inhibition predominates react with immobility, anxiety, and depression. A more severe stress produces paradoxical or even ultraparadoxical states leading to withdrawal and catalepsy. In paradoxical states, conditioned reflexes are abnormal, strong stimuli produce weak responses, or even inhibition, and vice versa. Pavlov believes that schizophrenia is caused by abnormal inhibitory processes, characteristic of paradoxical states. The latter are responsible for such schizophrenic symptoms as apathy, negativism, stereotypy, and catatonic stupor.

The classical conditioning paradigm is the basis of aversion conditioning and counterconditioning, otherwise known as the reciprocal inhibition (Wolpe, 1958) and desensitization in behaviour therapy. In aversive conditioning, certain stimuli, such as the smell of alcohol in treatment of alcoholics or photographs of nude males in treatment of homosexuals, are presented together with noxious stimuli. These noxious stimuli, such as injections of apomorphine or application of electric shock, produce vomiting or pain. The smell of alcohol or nude photographs become associated with such aversive reactions as nausea and fear and are therefore avoided. In counterconditioning, an aversive reaction to an object, such as fear, is replaced by an incompatible reaction such as relaxation or a feeding response. In desensitization, a gradually increased exposure from indirect to direct fear producing stimuli causes extinction of fear reaction.

The Hullian S-R model

Some theories of mental illness and some behaviour therapies are based on the Hullian theory (Hull, 1943, 1952). Clark L. Hull (1884-1954) was the most important figure of the American Behaviourism. His hypothetico-deductive theory is also known as a drive reduction theory. It postulates certain hypothetical constructs that describe mediating processes between stimuli and responses. The four most important constructs are drive (D), habit strength ($_sH_r$), reactive inhibition (I_r), and conditioned inhibition ($_sI_r$). Unsatisfied bodily needs, such as hunger, thirst, or noxious stimuli, produce a generalized drive, which energizes behaviour. The drive can be reduced by a certain response, for example, finding and consuming food. A response to a stimulus if associated with drive reduction is reinforced and becomes a learned habit. Depending on the frequency of reinforcement habits differ in strength and form a hierarchy from strong to weak. A frequent repetition of response without reinforcement produces reactive inhibition that dissipates with rest. However, eventually it may be replaced by conditioned inhibition (habit not to respond). In its heyday, Hull's theory influenced some experimental psychologists who were also interested in abnormal psychology. The three most important ones were Neil Miller (Dollard & Miller, 1950), H. Mowrer (1950), and Shoben (1949). These authors tried to translate Freudian psychoanalytic theory into the language of Hullian S-R theory. Anxiety was equated with the generalized drive state (Spence & Taylor, 1953). Incipient verbal responses became response-produced stimuli that could control behaviour and were equated with consciousness. Psychoanalytical therapy was explained in terms of desensitization during which anxiety associated with external and somatic conditioned stimuli became attached to verbal responses and were extinguished. No attempt was made to create a new therapy based on learning theory, but orthodox Freudian theory was described in learning theory terms.

Sarnoff Mednick (1958) has proposed a theory of schizophrenia based on Hull's S-R model. He believes that due to a physiological defect schizophrenic patients have abnormally flat generalization gradients of learned responses. This condition is responsible for their thought disorder. According to Mednick anxiety in these patients is associated with the rise and further flattening of generalization gradients. Consequently stimuli that are only slightly similar to the original anxiety-producing stimuli become threatening. This has a snowballing effect of further increasing anxiety and generalization gradients. To cope with anxiety the patient learns to make responses that produce irrelevant stimuli completely unrelated to the original threatening ones. As a result, the anxiety level is reduced. Thus, the patient learns to produce irrelevant and bizarre associations. Finally, in the chronic stage irrelevant responses and thoughts predominate, keeping anxiety at a low level. Overt anxiety is at a minimum, but the patient displays autistic and bizarre ideation most of the time.

The therapeutic effect of negative practice in certain conditions such as ticks and stuttering is explained by Hullian reactive inhibition (I_r). This treatment, originally described by K. Dunlap (1932), has been extended further by Yates (1958) to phobic and obsessional conditions. In this therapy undesirable behaviour is voluntarily repeated producing an aversive increase of reactive inhibition. To avoid it, the subject learns not to perform the undesirable behaviour. This process is called conditioned inhibition ($_sI_r$). J. Wolpe (1958) also bases his therapy of reciprocal inhibition on the Hullian theory. However, the relation between the two is not very clear.

Operant conditioning: Skinnerian model

In recent years the Skinnerian behaviouristic model of mental illness has become very influential. It is peripheralistic and based on the operant conditioning paradigm. In contrast to other behaviouristic models, it rejects the existence of inner variables or causes. This model explains abnormal behaviour in terms of observable and measurable responses of the organism to reinforcements. Responses are measured by counting their frequency. To quote Skinner, "The study of behaviour, psychotic or otherwise, remains securely in the company of the natural sciences so long as we take as our subject matter the observable activity of the organism, as it moves about, stands still, seizes objects, pushes and pulls, makes sounds, gestures, and so on ... We also remain within the framework of the natural sciences in explaining these observations in terms of external forces and events which act upon the organism" (1956). He finds a similarity between postulating inner causes of behaviour and the animistic explanation presupposing spirits, essences, and other ghosts in the machine. The study of the inner process in the brain that mediate between the sensory input and behavioural output should be left to neurophysiologists. He even goes so far as to say, "it might have been better to dismiss the concept of mind (either conscious or unconscious) altogether as an explanatory fiction, which had not survived a crucial test" (1956). Thus, Skinnerians reject the notion of the mental apparatus of libido, unconscious conflicts, ego, defence mechanisms, and superego. Briefly, they reject the whole Freudian psychological machinery.

Skinnerians reject also such Hullian constructs as drive, habit strength, reactive inhibition, and even the clinical construct of anxiety. They find also the concept of personality redundant and mythical. Further, they reject nosological disease entities, such as schizophrenia or manic-depressive psychosis, unless they can be described precisely in terms of biochemical and neuropathological processes. In this case the brain pathological processes explain abnormalities of behaviour and the disease labels are redundant. On the whole, Skinnerians reject the biological definition of adaptation and normality (Buchwald & Young, 1969). The concept of adaptation is value-free to the extent that it is not associated with any intrinsic values but rather depends on the situation. For example, the social role of mental patients may be adopted because it offers such reinforcements as an excuse of failure (Krasner, 1969). Various psychiatric clinical syndromes such as schizophrenia, particularly in the chronic form, may be produced by shaping the behaviour of mental hospital patients to perform certain roles such as of nontroublesome mental patients. Certain types of behaviour such as apathy and social withdrawal and even thought disorder are reinforced by the nursing staff and psychiatric aides to produce quiet, resigned mental patients who will display schizophrenic symptoms on demand. The mental hospital psychiatric aide culture may be instrumental in creating various psychiatric syndromes (Ullmann, 1969). Shaping of behaviour also explains why psychiatric syndromes differ from culture to culture and from one period to another. Skinnerians are not concerned with the past history of patients but only with reinforcing contingencies of the present behaviour. They are interested only in behaviour control rather than in an understanding of it.

Skinnerians believe that abnormal behaviour is learned and is not intrinsically different from normal behaviour. This is stated succinctly by Ullmann and Krasner: "Maladaptive behaviours are learned behaviours, and the development and maintenance of a maladaptive behaviour is no different from the development and maintenance of any other behaviour. There is no discontinuity between desirable and undesirable modes of adjustment or between 'healthy' and 'sick' behaviour." They further state, "Maladaptive behaviour is behaviour that is considered inappropriate by those key people in a person's life who control reinforcers" (1965).

This view of mental illness goes even further than that usually associated with the theory of continuity. The latter theory denies the presence of qualitative differences between mental health and disease. However, it accepts the existence of quantitative differences. It postulates a dimension along which people can be placed from the extreme abnormality at one end to perfect adjustment at the other end. According to Ullmann and Krasner, normality or abnormality of behaviour depends on the particular social norms and the bearers of these norms who control reinforcements. "Definition of adjustment is not absolute but shifts from time to time and place to place" (Ullmann & Krasner, 1965). For example, it has been pointed out by Kingsley Davis (1938) that in America the concept of mental health and adjustment often implies the acceptance of the Protestant ethics with a stress on social values of democracy, egalitarianism, worldliness, asceticism, individualism, rationalism, and hard work. These are traditional American middle-class values, which are unintentionally imposed by psychotherapists on their patients (Rosenthal, 1955; Holzman, 1961). However, in an article in which he compares behaviour therapy to a social movement and the behaviour therapist to the leader of such a movement, Ullmann (1969) addresses the problem of the value system that should guide the behaviour therapist in his dealing with the clients and in his role as a potential social engineer. He states, "The limitations imposed on the behaviour therapist are essentially the limitations imposed on the citizen in general: not to violate the rules that make social living possible" (1969). It seems that the principle that guides the behaviour therapist in the shaping of behaviour of their clients is to maximize their positive reinforcements without depriving other people of their share. It resembles John Stuart Mill's dictum in his essay *On Liberty* (1945) that the freedom of one man ends where the slavery of another begins. However, as every economist knows, there is a scarcity of reinforcers. Perhaps the answer to this dilemma is the creation, through reforms, of a new society in the image of *Walden Two* (Skinner, 1948a).

In a similar vein, Krasner (1969) states that the therapist has to be aware of his value system and to make it explicit rather than to pretend that his activity is value-free. He is also quite clear on the point that when there is a conflict between the values of the client and the values of the society the therapist should side with the society. Since the latter is the major source of reinforcement for the individual and since his goals are primarily social, the therapist should act as an agent of the society for the benefit of the client. Does it mean then that the task of the behaviour modifier is to enforce social conformity and to stamp out social deviance? Not necessarily so. In his capacity as a social engineer, the behaviour modifier could bring about reforms of social institutions and perhaps of the society at large. However he should not do so by imposing his own values in the manner of the philosopher-king in Plato's *Republic* but in the manner of the leader of a social movement (Ullmann, 1969; Krasner, 1969). The latter, through a process of social interaction, tries to express and implement the evolving values of a group of people.

Krasner (1969) goes so far as to state that changing social institutions may be the most efficient way to modify individual behaviour. What kind of institutional reforms and what kind of society should be aimed at? The reforms should aim at maximizing the general level of positive reinforcement and at minimizing aversive, punitive measures in a free and open society (Krasner, 1969; Ullmann, 1969). Such a society presupposes man to be a free agent making free choices. Can the idea of freedom be reconciled with the environmental determinism of Skinnerian behaviourism? Skinner (1971) states in *Beyond Freedom and Dignity* that the concept of individual freedom may be an illusion and that it should be put to rest together with the idea of autonomous man. People revolt not against social controls as such; they revolt against aversive controls. When positive social reinforcements are used, people accept social controls unquestioningly and submit to them gladly. To put it differently, people can be conditioned to be happy with their lot. It is suggested that happy men make free choices that are expected of them by the society. Consequently, the aim of social reform is maximization of general level of positive reinforcement, which comes close to being a new version of Jeremy Bentham's felicific calculus. The Skinnerian version of freedom, which is based on positive reinforcement and is compatible with the complete environmental determinism, has been found to be lacking by many critics. They compare the Skinnerian man to a robot, responding to reinforcements, a puppet buffeted and pushed around by environmental forces (Chein, 1962; von Bertalanffy, 1967). Even Krasner perceives behaviour therapy as a social reinforcement machine (Krasner, 1962). His reply to the critics is that man is both a robot and a pilot in complementary roles. In the latter role he tries to discover the laws governing his behaviour to be able to follow them. Finally Krasner comments, "To investigate how human behaviour works is not to robotize man, but to humanize him" (1969).

It seems that his idea of freedom is reminiscent of Spinoza's idea. To be free is to know the laws determining one's behaviour. This also seems to be the message coming through the pages of Skinner's *Beyond Freedom and Dignity*. However, the majority of the Skinnerian behaviour therapists look upon themselves as technologists, leaving the realm of values and the definition of normality to social and moral philosophers.

Skinner distinguishes two types of conditioning: respondent conditioning, which is the classical Pavlovian conditioning, and operant conditioning. In respondent conditioning the response is elicited by a stimulus, the unconditioned stimulus. In operant conditioning the response is emitted spontaneously by the organism and brings about a change in the environment. It operates on the environment. Responses are emitted with certain frequencies, and they have certain probabilities of occurring. If they are reinforced, their probability increases. So frequencies of behaviour depend on contingencies of reinforcement. Reinforcers may be positive, for example, giving food, or negative, for example, removing a noxious stimulus. To avoid the circularity of the definition of reinforcement Premack (1959) has suggested that behaviour occurring at higher frequency is reinforcing for behaviour occurring at lower frequencies. Various schedules or contingencies or reinforcement may be used. Reinforcement may be continuous or partial. Partial reinforcement may be further divided into ratio and interval schedules. If reinforcement is given after a certain number of responses, it is a ratio reinforcement. If it follows the first response occurring after a certain time interval, it is an interval reinforcement. Ratio and interval reinforcements may be fixed or variable. In a fixed schedule, the reinforcement is given after a definite number of responses or after a definite time interval. Variable reinforcement is given on an average after so many trials or after an interval of certain average length. There are many more complex schedules of reinforcement in existence; however, they are primarily used in the laboratory. Stimuli such as light, the sound of a bell, or the presence of mother may signal that the operant (operant response) will be reinforced. The organism learns to discriminate the situation when reinforcement is available or not available. However, the stimulus that signals the availability of response, the discriminant, does not elicit the response, rather the response is emitted spontaneously by the organism. (This is an important difference between the Skinnerian operant conditioning and the S-R theory.)

The property of a stimulus to act as a discriminant generalizes from the original stimulus to other similar stimuli. In fact, the discriminant may become a secondary reinforcer. The organism learns to bring about the discriminant so that it may be reinforced when performing the operant. Thus operants may form a chain of responses. Each response is followed by a discriminant and the final response is followed by the primary reinforcer. A removal of a discriminant associated with reinforcement, time-out, is aversive. If two stimuli, one of which is a discriminant, have to be differentiated the process is helped by fading in or out one of the stimuli. Nonreinforced responses are simply extinguished. If the probability of the desired response is zero or very low, recourse may be taken to the shaping of behaviour. These responses are reinforced, which to some extent approximate the desired response. The latter can be approximated and eventually attained by gradual steps. Originally, Skinner believed that respondent conditioning was associated with involuntary, emotional responses, controlled by the autonomic nervous system, and operant conditioning, with voluntary responses controlled by the central nervous system and executed by the striated muscles. However, the recent research on biofeedback (Miller, 1969) has thrown considerable doubt on this distinction. Such responses as heart rate or blood pressure can be controlled by operant conditioning. Although the two paradigms of learning can be distinguished by laboratory procedures, actual learning has always had two aspects: the operant and the respondent.

An application of the Skinnerian model to psychopathology is a theory that attributes depression to low response-contingent reinforcement rates. Lewinsohn (1974) has proposed such a model of depression. The number and the range of reinforcing events are reduced. A low rate of reinforcement has a dysphoric effect, producing apathy, fatigue, and psychomotor retardation. This state may be brought about by a failure of the environment to supply reinforcements or by an inability of the depressed person to obtain them by appropriate behaviour. There is also present a secondary effect of social reinforcement of depressive symptoms by sympathy the subjects receive from their relatives, friends, and therapists. In a similar vein, Ullmann and Krassner (1975) attribute schizophrenic symptoms to social learning in the families of the patients. Normal behaviour is extinguished and a bizarre one is reinforced.

Behaviour Therapy

The past thirty years have seen the development of a new method of treatment that has challenged both traditional psychotherapy and somatic methods of treatment. It has originated in the psychological laboratory and constitutes a genuine contribution from experimental psychology to psychiatry. This method covers a great variety of techniques known as behaviour therapies. All of them are based on the principles of learning theory developed in animal laboratory research by experimental psychologists. In clinical situations, behavior therapists apply learning principles to modify maladjustive behaviour. Some of these techniques use classical (respondent) or operant conditioning and are unambiguously behaviouristic. Others involve modification of the patient's imagery and thoughts and can hardly be conceived of as behaviouristic (Beck, 1970; Locke, 1971).

Lately, many new techniques categorized as behaviour therapy have been introduced that are quite frankly cognitive (Ledwidge, 1978). All these techniques, based on principles of learning, aim at removing symptoms rather than at altering personality or treating disease. Eysenck (1959) has stated that there is no neurosis causing symptoms but merely the symptoms themselves, which are simply learned habits. Therefore, cure coincides with elimination of symptoms. Behaviour therapists deny that there is a neurosis or psychosis beneath the symptoms and doubt whether there is symptom substitution as claimed by psychoanalysts. The behaviourist motto is "cure the symptoms and you have eliminated the neurosis." Consequently, the behaviour therapist's approach is straightforward. He deals with definite complaints of patients such as fears of certain situations, tics, or obsessional thoughts, which are considered by him to be bad habits. His remedy for them is to use definite and explicit retraining procedures. There is no interpersonal emotional involvement between the therapist and the patient. Another feature of behaviour therapy is that, in contrast to psychoanalysis, it stresses concrete behaviour rather than verbal expressions of the patients. It plays down the symbolic or semantic level of behaviour and tries to bring about the cure by altering the concrete behaviour.

Although contemporary behaviour therapy originated in the early fifties, the idea of treating mental illness by reeducation is quite old and goes back to the moral treatment of the insane in the nineteenth century (Bockoven, 1963). Behaviour therapy was inaugurated by the pioneering work of Watson and his students on experimental phobia produced by conditioning in Little Albert and the treatment of a similar case by counterconditioning (Watson & Reyner, 1920; Jones, 1924). Modern behaviour therapy was launched by the work of Joseph Wolpe (1952) on experimental neurosis as learned behaviour, followed by the development of reciprocal inhibition therapy (Wolpe, 1958). At the same time, Eysenck (1952b) published an article in which he questioned the effectiveness of psychoanalysis, stating that the recovery rate of patients treated by psychoanalysis was not higher than that in untreated cases or treated by supportive therapy. He suggested that treatment of psychoneurosis should be based on the learning theory principles (Eysenck, 1959). Ayllon and his associates did the pioneering work on application of operant conditioning to behaviour modification of chronic schizophrenic patients in a mental hospital setting (Ayllon & Azrin, 1968; Ayllon & Michael, 1959).

Some behaviour therapy techniques will now be described. Systematic desensitization and assertive training have been developed by Wolpe (1958) as reciprocal inhibition (counterconditioning) techniques. In systematic desensitization a hierarchy of situations is established that produce anxiety reactions in the patient from very mild to very strong. The patient is also trained in progressive muscular relaxation using the technique described originally by Jacobson (1938). The patient while relaxing is told to imagine a situation that produces only slight anxiety reaction. If no fear is experienced, the patient is told to imagine a situation that produces somewhat stronger anxiety reaction and so on until the situation producing the strongest anxiety reaction is imagined without experiencing anxiety. Many studies have been carried out to find out whether muscular relaxation (reciprocal inhibition) is essential for the treatment of anxiety or whether just imagining progressively more threatening situations (desensitization) is sufficient. Modifications of this method are exemplified in the techniques of flooding and implosion (Stampfl & Levis, 1967). The patient is encouraged to imagine the situation that produces the most intensive anxiety and is the most threatening. He is encouraged to sweat it out till the extinction takes place. In assertive training the patient is given fictitious examples of people overcoming their timidity by asserting themselves, and the patient is then encouraged to assert himself in real life situations.

In aversive therapy based on classical conditioning (Franks, 1958) the stimulus that evokes attraction such as the smell of alcohol or a picture of an object of the same sex is paired with noxious stimuli such as nausea-producing apomorphine injections or painful electric shocks. A fear reaction is produced, and the patient avoids the object to which he was previously attracted. A modification of this method is the covert sensitization (Cautela, 1966). The patient is instructed to imagine an object that produces an undesirable attraction and at the same time to imagine a situation that produces a strong aversive reaction. In "thought stopping" the patient is instructed to think the undesirable morbid thought that crowds into his mind, for example, an obsessional thought. The therapist suddenly shouts "stop." The thought trend is interrupted by an unexpected stimulus. Next, the patient is instructed to say "stop" himself when the undesirable thought occurs. Negative practice involves the voluntary mass practice of an undesirable habit such as a tic, stuttering, or a compulsion, A reactive inhibition followed by the conditioned inhibition leads to the disappearance of the undesirable habit (Yates, 1958). A variant of this technique is stimulus satiation (Ayllon, 1963). The patient is encouraged to expose himself to an undesirable stimulus and to collect unnecessary objects (old newspapers and other junk) untill he becomes satiated with this activity and discontinues it.

Operant conditioning principles can be used to increase the frequency of certain responses by reinforcing them or to extinguish certain responses by not reinforcing them (Ayllon & Michael, 1959). A variation of this technique is "token economy" (Paul & Lentz, 1978; Rimm & Masters, 1979). The patient is rewarded for desirable behaviour by tokens, which he can exchange for cigarettes, candy, or special privileges (Ayllon & Azrin, 1968). A behaviour that occurs originally with zero frequency can be produced by shaping, by gradually approximating the desired response. Speech behaviour in mute catatonic schizophrenics has been produced by this technique (Isaacs, Thomas, & Goldiamond, 1960). Patients can be instructed in self-control (for example, stimulus control and self-rewarding). Thought stopping, previously mentioned, is an example of this technique. Another example is instructing a patient to indulge in self-rewarding activity such as lighting a cigarette or having an ice cream cone after a period of desirable activity such as studying (Ferster, Nurnberger, & Levitt, 1962). Finally, in modeling techniques the patient is presented with a model whom he imitates (Bandura & Walters, 1963). It is difficult to decide whether modeling, unless supported by contingent reinforcement, should be considered a behaviour therapy or a cognitive therapy.

Recently, a new technique of biofeedback has been developed (Budzynski & Stoyva, 1969). In this technique the patient is taught to control certain physiological functions such as heart rate, blood pressure, or EEG frequency, which usually are not under voluntary control, by providing him with a suitable feedback.

A few remarks are needed on the place of behaviour therapy among the other therapies. Kanfer and Phillips (1969) divide all psychotherapies into interaction therapy, instigation therapy, replication therapy, and intervention therapy. The interaction therapy is conventional, evocative therapy that is either insight producing (uncovering) or supportive. Krasner (1969) calls this type of therapy friendship therapy. In this type of therapy the stress is on idiosyncratic emotional relationship between the client and the therapist. The goal is the change of the total personality of the client. The other three types of therapy are behaviour therapies. In the instigation therapy specific suggestions are systematically used. The therapist assigns specific daily tasks to the client. The latter reports on his daily activities, and the therapist teaches the client the best means to modify his extratherapeutic environment and to apply learning techniques to his behaviour. The client learns to become his own therapist. In the replication therapy miniature situations are created in the therapy setting that replicate some critical segments of the client's life. The therapy setting is a model of a real life situation. Systematic desensitization of Wolpe is an example of replication therapy. Finally, the intervention therapy involves control of behaviour by operant techniques in real life situations. It can be carried out in an institutional setting where the client is under constant observation. The token economy is an example of an intervention therapy.

Krasner (1969) when considering the scope of therapeutic procedure distinguished three roles for the therapist. In the first role the therapist is a purveyor of friendship, who satisfied emotional needs of the client. This type of therapy covers conventional insight and supportive therapies. In the second role the therapist acts as a behaviour technologist who alters specific segments of the client's behaviour. The therapist who uses behaviour modification techniques does not get involved emotionally with the patients. He also remains neutral with regard to the value aspect of his professional activity. The client or his relatives present the therapist with a concrete problem of maladjustment, and he deals with it the best he can. In the third role the behaviour therapist acts as a social engineer. He makes explicit value judgements with regard to what behaviour in clients should be reinforced and also how the social institutions shaping the behaviour of clients ought to be changed. The social institution may be a mental hospital, a prison, or a school, or it may be the society at large. As has been mentioned before, most behaviour therapists, Wolpe and Eysenck may serve as examples, take social values involved in behaviour modification for granted and leave the realm of values to moral and social philosophers.

The Constitutional-Behaviouristic Model of Eysenck

Hans Jurgen Eysenck (1952a, 1967) has proposed a model of mental illness that has the unique properties of combining a constitutional psychology with the S-R behaviouristic psychology. Its framework is provided by the theory of personality and by experimental psychology rather than by psychiatry. According to Eysenck, individuals differ in the polygenetically determined physiological characteristics of the central nervous system. These differences occur along four independent dimensions: introversion-extraversion, neuroticism, psychoticism, and general intelligence. The first three dimensions describe temperamental differences among people and are important for understanding of mental illness. They are determined by the inherited biological constitution, which in interaction with the social environment produces personality traits. Personality is described in terms of continuous dimensions rather than in terms of discrete types. Psychopathology is associated with certain extremes of these dimensions. Eysenck's conclusions are based on the method of factor analysis. He uses criterion analysis and rotates factors so as to maximize differences among population groups predicted by the theory. In devising his battery of personality tests, Eysenck has taken a behaviouristic approach and has included several objective tests, which can be reliably scored. The first personality dimension is the bipolar factor of extraversion-introversion. Its hypothetical underlying constitutional, physiological property of the nervous system is the habitual level of cortical arousal controlled by the ascending reticular activating system. Introverts display habitually a high level of cortical arousal and extraverts a low level with most people falling in the middle. Differences in the level of the cortical arousal determine differences in conditionability and in the optimal level of novel stimulation sought by the organism. Extraverts acquire conditioned reflexes slowly and extinguish them quickly. They build up reactive inhibition fast. Consequently, they are slow learners and forget the learned material quickly.

Contemporary research in motivation (Hebb, 1955) has indicated that the organism seeks an optimal level of arousal and finds the level of novel stimulation input associated with it pleasant. Too little stimulation, which results in a low level of arousal, and too much stimulation, resulting in a high level of arousal, are aversive. Because of the habitual low level of cortical arousal, extraverts require a relatively high stimulus input to maintain the optimal level of arousal. The opposite holds for introverts. Moreover, a low level of stimulus input, which is aversive to an extravert, may be pleasant for an introvert, and a high level of stimulus input, which is pleasant to an extravert, may be aversive to an introvert.

From this physiological hypothesis, Eysenck makes predictions about personality traits and socialization processes of introverts and extraverts. Because introverts learn easily they are also socialized easily and may become even oversocialized. On the other hand, extraverts, who learn slowly and forget quickly, encounter difficulty in the socialization process and may be undersocialized. At the same time, extraverts, who require a high stimulus input to maintain the optimal level of arousal, constantly seek novel stimuli and excitement, while introverts tend to withdraw from contact with the external world. These predictions were tested and confirmed in several studies (Eysenck, 1963). The extravert tends to be outgoing, aggressive, active, in constant contact with the external world, but at the same time inconsiderate of other people. The introvert tends to withdraw, likes to be left alone, is interested in his inner world, and is timid in relations with other people.

The second dimension is that of neuroticism. In Eysenck's early studies, neurotic patients were found to score high on this dimension. The underlying hypothetical constitutional physiological property of the nervous system is the intensity of autonomic nervous system arousal controlled by the limbic system. Eysenck believes that cortical arousal and limbic system arousal are relatively independent of one another. The tendency to high limbic system arousal results in high autonomic nervous system reactivity, emotional instability, and anxiety. These characteristics tend to distinguish normal, stable persons from unstable neurotics.

For the third dimension, psychoticism, Eysenck does not offer a definite neurophysiological theory. However, he believes that this trait is biologically determined and inherited. It seems that individuals who score high on the psychoticism factor are vulnerable to developing psychosis under stress. In addition to borderline schizophrenics, prison inmates score high on this dimension. High psychoticism is characterized by aggressiveness, antisocial behaviour, egocentricity, suspiciousness, and an inability to relate to other people.

Eysenck's model is a hierarchical model. The lowest level of hierarchy is represented by S-R habits, which are learned according to the Hullian theory principles. At the intermediate level are the first order factor traits, and at the highest level are the second order factor traits of extraversion, neuroticism, psychoticism, and general intelligence. As one moves from the lowest to the highest level of hierarchy, learning becomes less important and the hereditary constitution more important. The second order traits may be construed as dimensions orthogonal to one another. They serve as Cartesian coordinates of a hypothetical space in which each individual is represented by a point. Pathology is associated with certain areas of this four dimensional space. Neurotics occupy the area of space situated near the positive pole of the neuroticism axis and are further subdivided into dysthymics and hysterics depending on their position in relation to the extraversion-introversion axis. Dysthymics are high on neuroticism and are near the introversion pole of the extraversion factor. They include obsessional-compulsives, neurotic depressives, phobics, and chronic anxiety states. Hysterics are high on neuroticism and are close to the extraversion pole. They include, in addition to hysterics, patients diagnosed as psychopathic personality. Finally, psychotics occupy the area of space situated near the positive pole of the psychoticism axis. Eysenck's system is a continuity theory. However, the dimensions of neuroticism and of psychoticism are independent and orthogonal to one another. Therefore, neurotics do not occupy the position in between normals and psychotics as they do in the psychoanalytical version of the continuity theory.

As far as the treatment of psychiatric patients is concerned, Eysenck is an advocate of behaviour therapy aimed at the eradication of faulty habits and their replacement with adjustive habits. Behaviour therapy may be aided by psychotropic drugs in order to deal with aspects of maladjustment determined by constitutional factors. Eysenck believes that a combination of behaviour therapy and drug administration should replace psychoanalytical therapy, which he considers ineffective.

COGNITIVE MODELS

During the past twenty years experimental psychology has been undergoing a Kuhnian revolution (Kuhn, 1962). Its whole paradigm has changed. The S-R behaviourism has been replaced by cognitive psychology. This change has affected the fields of learning, of perception, of motivation, and of personality. It also has affected abnormal and clinical psychology. The perspective has changed. Previously unacceptable theories have become scientifically respectable and are believed to hold great promise for the progress of psychology. Three factors have been influential in bringing about the transition from the S-R to the cognitive paradigm. The first factor has been the development of computer and servomechanism technology in association with the technique of programming as well as with the newly developed sciences of cybernetics, information, decision and automata theories, and finally the study of artificial intelligence.

The second factor has been the impact of structural linguistics and psycholinguistics as represented by the work of Chomsky (1968), Schank (1975), and Fodor (Fodor, Bever, & Garrett, 1974). The third factor has been a change of views on the nature of scientific enterprise as reflected by the current philosophy of science (Lakatos, 1970). Logical Positivism and Operationism have been abandoned and unobserved entities are accepted as epistemologically valid. The modern liberalized view of science assigns the same validity to theoretical constructs as to the data of observation. It does not separate the language of theory from that of data. The latter are believed to be influenced by the theoretical framework, with the implication that there is no immaculate observation. This demoted status of empirical data gives a wider latitude to ampliative inference and generalization. Science is not only concerned with predicting certain events but also with their understanding. In the field of psychology, this changing view of science has caused a shift of interest from publicly observable peripheral events, such as stimuli and responses, to unobservable, but inferred, mediating processes. Mediating processes, which were described in the days of introspective psychology in the phenomenalist terms, are presently described in terms of information processing, often using metaphors borrowed from the computer technology.

The domain of cognitive psychology is very broad covering many theories that, however, have certain features in common and make similar assumptions about the nature of man. All of them view man as a rational problem solver. In contrast, psychoanalysis sees man as irrational and driven by blind instinctive impulses, while behaviourism sees him as a reflex machine. The concept of man as a rational problem solver presupposes the existence of a complex information processing brain. The cognitive psychologist is concerned with the abstract aspects of information analysis and synthesis and with symbolic transformations, leaving the underlying neurological mechanisms to neurophysiologists. He has substituted the concept of information input and output for that of stimulus and response of behaviourism. According to him the behaviour of the organism is determined not by the external stimuli but by the internal representations of the environment (cognitive maps) and of the goal to be attained. These involve both the present information input and that stored in memory. The organism selectively attends to certain stimuli, encodes information in the short-term memory, classifies it in accordance with the preexisting categories, compares it with and evaluates it in relation to the preexisting cognitive structure, and stores it in the long-term memory. Further, the organism retrieves the required information from the long-term memory and formulates a plan of behaviour (Mahoney, 1974). Cognitive psychology focuses on the schemas and plans of behaviour rather than on discrete responses. To put it in everyday language, man behaves in accordance with the way he perceives and makes sense of a situation. He constructs his world from the incoming information and his past experience. Man's mental constructs, thoughts, ideas, expectations, and beliefs are important determinants of his behaviour. In the implied philosophical view of man, there has been a shift from the epistemology of naive realism to a representational one and a shift from associationism to rationalism. However, reason is not conceived as the Transcendental Reason of Idealistic philosophers from Plato to Kant and Hegel but rather as the one characteristic of electronic computers and sophisticated automata. It can be described in terms of the logic of algorithms and heuristics used in computer programs.

According to the assumptions of cognitive psychology, man is rational because he uses practical, if not formal, logic in solving his problems. He is trying to arrive at a coherent and self-consistent system of beliefs about his world and himself. This last aspect has been stressed in particular by some social psychologists such as Festinger (1962) and McGuire (1960) but recently has been questioned by some clinical psychologists (Mahoney, 1974). However, there is no doubt that man tends to relate his beliefs to one another and to fill the existing gaps in his knowledge by assumptions, so as to arrive at a relatively coherent picture of the world. Men and animals guide their behaviour by expectancies and by means-ends relationships. They try to confirm or disconfirm their expectancies. Thus, each man behaves like a scientist. He formulates certain hypotheses about his physical and social environment. He tests these hypotheses and either confirms or rejects them. However, sometimes a false hypothesis is not rejected in spite of the empirical evidence because it is firmly embedded in a system of beliefs. A disconfirmation of the hypothesis would lead to the collapse of a coherent world picture. A change of one belief may require a change of other beliefs. This sketchy presentation of cognitive theory provides a basis for understanding the cognitive model of mental illness. The idea that mental illness may be due to a disorder of reason is quite old and can be traced back to the eighteenth century (Kant, 1966a), as can be the therapy of correcting one's thoughts through reasoning, persuasion, and self-instruction (Coué, 1922; Bain, 1928; Carnegie, 1948). Coué instructed his patients to repeat "Day by day, in every way, I am getting better and better." This statement was supposed to influence the patient's belief about himself and his health. The belief in its turn was expected to influence the patient's behaviour. However, this approach was eclipsed by uncovering therapies based on psychodynamic theories, which stressed the irrationality of man.

The last twenty years have seen a rise of a definite cognitive model of mental illness. This development may be attributed to the impact of cognitive psychology and to a reaction against both psychodynamic and behaviouristic theories of mental illness. The theories of mental illness that come under the rubric of the cognitive model can be divided into two groups: those stressing mainly abnormalities of cognitive structure and those stressing mainly inefficient behavioural strategies. While the first group deals mainly with the information input, the second is mainly concerned with the behavioural output. However, both groups admit that in human behaviour, central mediating information processes are always involved.

Distorted Cognitive Structure Model
Kelly's theory of personal constructs

An example of cognitive structure model of mental illness is George Kelly's theory of personal constructs (Kelly, 1955). His pioneering work preceded other cognitive theories of mental illness by about twenty years. Kelly follows the philosophy of constructive alternativism, an offshoot of Dewey's Pragmatism, which maintains that there are various ways in which the world can be cognitively constructed. The cognitive construction that offers the best prediction is chosen and is discarded only when predictions based on it are no longer confirmed. Each man is his own scientist; he builds a system of cognitive constructs representing the physical and social worlds, derives hypotheses, and tests them by predicting future events. Kelly states the fundamental postulate of the theory as follows: "A person's processes are psychologically channelized by the way in which he anticipates events" (Kelly, 1955). Therefore, a person's behaviour can be predicted from his understanding of the physical and social world.

Such motivational concepts as drives, instincts, or needs are not necessary to explain human behaviour. Man is motivated to test his hypotheses about the world, so as to find it predictable and comprehensible. Although some constructs are shared by the members of a society, others, particularly those concerning interpersonal relations, are quite idiosyncratic. Personal constructs are dichotomies such as good versus bad, strong versus weak, and so on, into which people and social situations are categorized. The basic constructs are derived from interpersonal relations in early childhood. They can be measured by the *Role Construct Repertory Test* (Bannister, 1970). Personal constructs are organized into a hierarchical structure with regnant superordinate, and subordinate constructs. The regnant constructs are superordinate constructs, which perform the role of the executive program. They assign the subordinate constructs to exclusive categories. Constructs can be tightly or loosely organized. They can be dilated, having a wide application, or constricted, having a narrow application. Comprehensive constructs are those that have attained a high degree of dilation and that subsume a wide variety of events. A person tries to elaborate his construct system so as to encompass the greatest possible range of predictable events. However, a person can also become enmeshed in his construct system and be enslaved by his own ideas. Because constructs are implicatively related to one another a disconfirming experience may not be enough to invalidate a construct. Kelly explains mental illness in terms of disordered personal constructions. Mental illness is characterized by personal constructions that are used repeatedly in spite of consistent invalidation. The client's cognitive constructs fail to attain their purpose. Mental abnormality may be described as a faulty stance towards one's future. Extreme dilation and loosening of constructs may lead to an unpredictable personal world and to social withdrawal. Kelly identifies this condition with schizophrenia. Extremely constricted and tight constructs produce a rigid obsessional personality. A precipitous testing of hypotheses, a foreshortening of the C-P-C (circumspection, preemption, and control) cycle, leads to impulsive behaviour.

According to Kelly psychotherapy aims at a revised conceptualization of a person's whole course of life, at a restructuring of his personal constructs, and at changing his expectancies. It is a psychological process that changes the client's outlook on some aspect of life. In some respects the therapy is similar to that of Carl Roger's nondirective client centred counselling. However, sometimes more directive methods of treatment are used, such as "fixed-role" therapy in which the client is asked to write a role sketch or to play a certain role.

Rational-emotive therapy of Ellis

While Kelly's philosophical commitment is to Pragmatism, Albert Ellis (1970, 1973) is committed to Rationalism. Ellis has developed "rational-emotive therapy" (RET), the purpose of which is to treat irrational thinking. The rationalism of Albert Ellis takes its inspiration from the Stoic philosophy, in particular from the teaching of a late Stoic, Epictetus (50-138 AD). Epictetus believed that the world (macrocosm) was basically rational, as was its creation—man (microcosm). The duty of men was to follow the natural order of things and to accept the world and themselves. This conduct led to a state of *euthymia*, a spiritual peace and well-being. Men were not disturbed by events that happen to them but rather by their view of those events. Unhappiness was caused by irrational beliefs about oneself, other people, and the world.* Although, in contrast to the Stoics, Ellis does not believe in the rational design of the universe, he accepts the naturalistic ethics of the Stoics. His humanistic ethics are based on factual judgements and not on normative ones of shoulds and oughts. He values the most happiness, freedom, creativity, and the enlightened self-interest of each man. The basis of emotions are rational evaluative judgements rather than gut feelings. This view agrees with that of Magda Arnold (1960) and is supported by the work of Schachter and Singer (1962). The latter have shown that there are strong cognitive components in emotional reactions.

Rational-emotive therapy (RET) deals largely with beliefs, attitudes, and values rather than with the stimuli and responses. Its purpose is to provide the client with a better balance between his individualistic, self-seeking tendencies and his social duties. It uses the A-B-C method of viewing mental disturbance. "A" is the activating experience, "B" the belief about this experience, and "C" the upsetting emotional consequence. While other psychotherapies are concerned mainly with "A" and "C," rational-emotive therapy is concerned with "B." It tries to replace irrational beliefs by rational ones. If the client learns to perceive his difficulty or his losses more rationally, he is on the road to recovery. An attempt is made to make the client realize that although man is the measure of all things he is not perfect. There are no absolute criteria for human conduct. All criteria are relative to the context. The aim of RET is an alteration of beliefs rather than production of specific responses. RET is not concerned with analyzing the client's past but with his present beliefs. Ellis rejects the Freudian model, and he denies the existence of the unconscious. However, he admits that there is some similarity between RET and the Adlerian psychotherapy. In contrast to psychoanalysis, RET tends to be directive with a strong persuasive element.

---

*Similar ideas were put forward by Spinoza in the seventeenth century.

The client is engaged in quasiphilosophical discussions regarding his beliefs, his motives, and his values. He is also instructed in humanistic ethics. Ellis is quite sympathetic to the theories of the humanistic psychologists, but he is wary of the irrational attitudes and the antiscientific sentiments expressed by some of them. He believes that ethical humanism ought to go hand in hand with the scientific method. Science and technology do not dehumanize and alienate man as long as they remain means for human betterment and do not become sanctified as ends in themselves.

Cognitive theory of depression of Aaron Beck

Aaron Beck (1967, 1974), who began as a psychoanalyst, has come to the conclusion, as a result of his psychotherapeutic experience and research, that a disorder of cognition rather than that of affect is fundamental to depression. The depressed affect is secondary to a distorted perspective from which the depressed patient views himself, his world, and his future. The starting points of departure for Beck were certain psychoanalytical formulations. Freud, in his paper on *Mourning and Melancholia* (1957c), pointed out that although the states of mourning and melancholia were similar there were also some differences. In melancholia there was a devaluation and deprecation of the ego that does not occur in mourning. While some psychoanalysts conceived depression in terms of an identification with the lost object and in terms of turning aggression on oneself, others became interested in the self-devaluation and self-deprecation theme. Bibring (1953) focused on the loss of self-esteem, self-devaluation, and self-deprecation as the central psychological themes of depression. He believed that low self-esteem may be caused not only by a loss of the love object but also by frustrated aspirations. Similar views were held by Jacobson (1953) and Gaylin (1968). The latter has attributed low self-esteem in depressed patients to a crisis of self-confidence.

Beck has found that depressed patients are characterized by a loss of self esteem, self-deprecation, and a sense of being losers throughout their lives. They have a low self-regard and tend to unduly criticize and blame themselves for their failures. They suffer from a feeling of deprivation and a feeling of inability to cope with their duties and obligations. These feelings bring about a desire to escape and even to commit suicide. Beck has described a cognitive triad of depression consisting of a negative view of the world, a negative view of the self, and a negative view of the future. Depressed patients view the world as always thwarting, defeating, and frustrating them. Relatively trivial events are perceived as spelling personal disaster. Minor losses and misfortunes are exaggerated out of all proportion. Depressed patients tend to read insults, ridicule, or disparagement into the attitude of other people towards them. These patients feel that other people criticize and reject them. As a result, they become highly self-critical and tend to devalue themselves. Depressed patients very often set for themselves unrealistic goals, and when they fail to attain them they blame and deprecate themselves. They feel themselves to be inferior and much worse than other people. Depression is characterized by a pessimistic outlook. The patients have negative expectancies, view their future pessimistically, and always expect the worst to happen. They show a systematic error in interpretation of experience with a bias directed against themselves and make arbitrary inferences on insufficient evidence. Furthermore, there is a tendency to misconstrue perceived situations, so as to make them congruent with depressive themes, as well as to maximize the unfavourable events and minimize favourable ones. These cognitive biases are automatic and beyond voluntary control. Contrary to the conventional views of depression, Beck believes that depressive affect is not primary; it is secondary to cognitive judgements and evaluations. In this respect his views of affect are similar to that of Magda Arnold (1960).

According to Beck (1974), a depression-prone person, in the course of his life, becomes sensitized to personal losses and other unfavourable experiences. He is more likely than others to suffer childhood bereavement. His parents often set for him unrealistic, perfectionistic goals that he fails to attain. These traumatic experiences attune his cognitive apparatus to focus on untoward events and magnify their importance. This results in a snowball effect, with pessimistic expectancies becoming self-fulfilling prophecies. Eventually, the person comes to look at himself as a born loser. In this situation, any minor loss or disappointment may precipitate reactive depression.

As far as treatment is concerned, Beck (1970) uses a form of cognitive therapy. Arbitrary inferences, selective abstractions, and overgeneralizations are pointed out to the patient. An attempt is made to straighten his cognitive distortions. Further, patients are put through the performance of tasks of increasing difficulty. By succeeding on easier tasks the self-confidence of the patients is restored and they are ready to tackle more difficult ones. Eventually, these patients learn to face the future with confidence and optimism. Similar therapies for depression have been suggested by Burgess (1968) and by the Japanese *Morita* therapy (Kora, 1965).

Attribution theory

Similarly to many cognitive theories, attribution theory developed in the context of social psychology (Shaver, 1975; Kelly, 1972). It originated in the pioneering work of Fritz Heider (1958). According to attribution theory behaviour is influenced by the perception of its causes. Attributing different motives and causes to one's own behaviour and also to the behaviour of others influences differentially the course of one's behaviour. It is possible to attribute failure to the lack of skill or insufficient effort, both internal factors, or to the difficulty of the task or to plotting of enemies, both external factors. Fatigue, an inability to concentrate and think clearly, may be attributed to lack of sleep or to an incipient mental illness. The cure may be attributed by a patient to an insight and his control over his behaviour or to a pill. Feelings of arousal can be attributed to the side effects of a drug or to one's anger, fear, or amusement (Schachter & Singer, 1962). An abnormal behaviour may be attributed to a disease, a personality trait, or to situational factors, such as stress or harmful interpersonal interaction.

All these factors influence differently the perception of a person's own behaviour and of the behaviour of other people. In their turn, different perceptions cause different outcomes of behaviours. An example of attribution theory as applied to clinical psychology is the locus of control concept (Rotter, 1966). On the basis of experimental evidence Rotter suggested that people differ in the attribution of the locus of control of their behaviour. The externals attribute the causes of the outcomes of their behaviour to external environmental factors, such as task difficulty, chance, luck, or conspiracy by others. The internals attribute the outcome of their behaviour to such intra-organismic factors as ability, skill, effort, or fatigue. Some of these factors such as the task difficulty and skill are stable (fixed); others such as effort, luck, or fatigue are relatively variable (Weiner, Frieze, Kukla, Reed, Rest, & Rosenbaum, 1971). It is not certain whether the external versus internal locus of control is a permanent personality trait or is situationally induced (Mahoney, 1974). The empirical evidence suggests that internals can cope with life situations much better, show more initiative, and are more responsible than externals (Phares, 1973). Chronic mental patients, prison inmates, and mental defectives have been found to be externals. Abramovitz (1969) has found that college students who score high on a depression scale tend to be external in their placement of the locus of control.

Another application of attribution theory to clinical psychology is misattribution therapy. In misattribution therapy an artifice is used to change the perceived causality of behaviour or physiological reactions. An attempt is made to manipulate attribution (labelling) of clinical symptoms (Winett, 1970). Thus, snake phobia causes increased pulse rate when the client is confronted with the picture of a snake. By providing false feedback indicating to the client that his pulse rate goes down on repeated exposure of the picture, it is hoped that his phobia will be cured. He is no longer attributing the physiological manifestations of fear reactions to the picture of a snake and consequently ceases to be afraid of snakes. It seems that this technique works only when phobia is mild (Bandura, 1969).

Attempts have been made to prolong the effects of drug therapy by shifting their attribution from external (drug) to internal (personality) factors (Davison & Valius, 1969). The clinical phenomenon of arousal-induced arousal, such as fear of ones' fear or being depressed by one's depression, responsible for spiralling effects on the symptoms, also had been analyzed in terms of attribution theory. Deliberate self-induction of the feared state such as in the paradoxical induction technique of Frankl (1963) may break the vicious circle by changing the attribution of the feared state. The theory of attribution research is closely related to the research stemming from self-perception theory (Bem, 1967). According to this theory human beings infer their motives, attitudes, emotions, and other inner states from observing their own behaviour. Consequently, changing the behaviour of a person will change his self-perception, which would influence his further behaviour. Using reinforcement to change abnormal behaviour of a client will, through changed self-perception, eventuate in an intrinsically motivated behaviour, no longer dependent on external reinforcement.

Inefficient Behavioral Strategy Model

Learned helplessness depression model of Seligman

The learned helplessness model of depression proposed by Martin Seligman (1974, 1975) is similar to the attribution theory model. However, the stress in Seligman's model is on the behavioural output rather than on the cognitive structure. It originated in animal laboratory, and it is therefore confronted with the same difficulty as other animal models: namely, of relating experimentally produced abnormalities of animal behaviour to those of human psychopathology.

Working with dogs, Seligman and Maier (1967) have found that dogs subjected to inescapable electric shocks subsequently display an impairment of escape and avoidance learning in the shuttle box situation. They just lie down and "take" shocks. These findings have been extended to other animal species and to other noxious stimuli.* The learning difficulty occurs also when different noxious stimuli are used in the learning situation from those in the no escape, uncontrollable situation. Similar findings have been obtained in human beings. It seems that an individual subjected to uncontrollable events (noxious stimuli) learns that nothing will help him avoid noxious stimuli or solve a problem. He develops a generalized expectancy that behaviour outcome is uncontrollable, which reduces the motivation to respond. This state has been called learned helplessness by Seligman. Since the subject attributes the reception of noxious stimuli to uncontrollable external causes rather than to its own responses, learned helplessness may be explained in terms of the locus of control attribution theory (Miller & Seligman, 1975; Abramson, Seligman, & Teasdale, 1978). Learned helplessness in animals can be cured by forcing them to respond, as in the case of dogs dragged by leashes across the barrier of the shuttle box. Dogs can also be immunized against learned helplessness by exposing them to escape-avoidance

---

*There is a possibility that the "helpless" behaviour of animals after an exposure to unavoidable electric shocks may be caused directly by noradrenaline depletion in the brain rather than a result of learning (Weiss, Glazer, & Pohorecky, 1976).

learning before subjecting them to a no escape situation. Seligman believes that depression, particularly reactive depression, is a manifestation of learned helplessness. An individual learns to expect that no effort on his part is of any avail in avoiding stressful situations or attaining desirable goals. The outcome is independent of his responses. "He throws in the towel" and gives up and regards life as a "no win" situation. This expectation results in a pessimistic outlook, psychomotor retardation, and depressed mood.

The learned helplessness theory has found some confirmation in experiments carried out on subclinically depressed college students who showed similar behavioural deficits as individuals previously subjected to inescapable noxious stimuli or insoluble problems. Recently, Abramson, Seligman, and Teasdale (1978) have reformulated the learned helplessness model so as to bring it in line with the attribution theory. According to this reformulation, when a noncontingency between response and outcome is perceived subjects attribute their helplessness in the situation to a cause. The attributed cause can be perceived as internal or external, stable (fixed) or unstable (variable), global (applicable to every situation), or specific (applicable only to a particular situation). The particular attribution determines whether helplessness and failure are perceived to be persistent or momentary, to apply to broad or narrow range of situations, and whether it will lower self-esteem. The latter is lowered when failure is perceived as persistent, internally determined, and specific to the individual. When these ideas are applied to depression they explain its main features. Persistent low self-esteem and guilt feelings are explained by the attribution of failure to internal causes, which are global, chronic, and stable. The intensity of depression depends on the certainty of failure expectation and on the importance of the outcome. Thus, the type of depression may differ depending on the individual attribution style. According to the new formulation of the learned helplessness theory, depressives are internals rather than externals in their perception of the locus of control. On this account, the theory is now committed even more than before to the cognitive and mentalistic point of view. It has become a cognitive structure rather than response strategy theory.

Cognitive Theories Stemming From the Tradition of Behaviour Therapy

The inefficient behaviour strategy model of mental illness is further exemplified by some theories and practices developed within the tradition of behaviour therapy. These theories and psychotherapeutic practices have been reviewed by Mahoney (1974), Thoresen and Mahoney (1974), and Meichenbaum (1974), and they will not be reviewed in detail here. Behaviour therapy, although it originated within the framework of behaviourism, has been influenced in recent years by the cognitive revolution occurring in experimental psychology. Even in the heyday of behaviouristic peripheralism, some allowance was made for covert responses. Watson (1930) explained thinking by subvocal speech. Hull (1952) introduced the notion of fractional anticipatory goal responses. Osgood (1953) developed a theory of central mediation by hypothetical covert responses (r) and stimuli (s). Originally, these mediating mechanisms were conceived in peripheralistic terms and as such were assumed to be potentially observable. As time went by peripheralism was abandoned, and these mechanisms came to be regarded as hypothetical constructs located in the brain, or depending on preference, in the mind. However, the behaviouristic psychologists have conceived the structure of inner mediating events to be the same as that of overt behaviour. They describe these central events in terms of stimuli, responses, and reinforcements. Moreover, they assume that the principles of conditioning apply to both the overt and covert events. To put it differently, a ghostly reflex arc is believed to exist within the observed reflex arc. This postulate of the liberalized behaviouristic theory is called by Mahoney (1974) the continuity assumption.* The cognitive theory of learning has abandoned the continuity assumption, and to explain mediation it has borrowed constructs from information theory and computing science.

Cognitive models of behaviour modification may be divided into

---

*The "continuity" assumption between overt and covert learning principles has to be, of course, distinguished from the continuity hypothesis of mental health and mental illness. To avoid confusion, I use quotation marks when talking about "continuity" between overt and covert learning principles.

those that are based on the liberalized behaviouristic theory of learning and those based on cognitive and social theories of learning. The first conceptualizes behaviour therapy in terms of covert conditioning, the second in terms of cognitive learning. Strictly speaking, only the second group should be considered as applying cognitive model to mental illness. The first should be classified as behaviouristic.

Models based on liberalized behaviouristic theory (covert conditioning). In covert conditioning the antecedent event (stimulus), the behaviour (response), and the consequent event (reinforcement) may all be covert (Thoresen & Mahoney, 1974). Wolpe's systematic desensitization and his reciprocal inhibition techniques very often involve the use of a covert stimulus (covert antecedent). The client is asked to imagine certain fearful objects or scenes while he is relaxing. Since the imaginary stimuli are covert, this technique is an example of covert counterconditioning. In the thought stopping technique the client reproduces covertly a stop signal that disrupts a maladaptive rumination. In the coverant (covert operant) control of behaviour, a technique described by Homme (1965), the client is instructed to utter a covert aversive statement when confronted with a stimulus releasing an undesirable behaviour. This is followed by a second statement that releases a behaviour incompatible with the undesirable target behaviour and also serves as a reward. In this case, both the antecedent and consequent events are overt, but the behaviour is covert.

In the covert sensitization, a technique described by Cautela (1966), clients are instructed to imagine aversive stimuli when confronted with stimuli releasing undesirable behaviour. A vivid imagery producing strong aversive emotional reaction is encouraged, which interferes with the undesirable behaviour. This method has been used with varied success in the treatment of alcoholism, obesity, and sexual deviance. Cautela (1970) has also used the technique of covert reinforcement. In covert positive reinforcement, the client is trained to produce some pleasant, rewarding imagery, which is paired with an imagined desirable response. In covert negative reinforcement, a covert aversive image is terminated on the initiation of a desired response. In the covert extinction technique (Cautela, 1971) a feared object is imagined or an imaginary rehearsal of feared situation is carried out until the fear reaction is extinguished.

This technique is also sometimes described as implosion therapy or symbolic flooding and involves a covert response (behaviour).

In addition to the assumption of continuity between covert and overt learning, covert conditioning therapies make, according to Mahoney (1974), the automaticity assumption. This is an assumption that a reinforcing event contiguous with a response affects it without being produced by it. An illustration of the above is the superstitious behaviour in pigeons described by Skinner (1948b). An association by contiguity is assumed without necessary connections. Cognitive theory proper rejects the automaticity assumption. Instead, it postulates that only the consequences of goal directed behaviour are reinforcing and that the connection between the two has to be perceived by the organism as necessary to be effective. This argument about necessary connections can be extended further. It can be argued that the cognitive theory of learning proper assumes the existence of symbolic processes characterized by implicative rather than associative connections and by intentionalities between *significants* (symbols) and *significates* (objects represented by symbols). Briefly, meaning cannot be reduced to associations by contiguity but rather involves intentionalities and implicative relations.

Models based on cognitive and social learning theories. The second group of cognitive behaviour modification models has abandoned the premises of the S-R and Skinnerian behaviourism and adopted those of information processing, cognitive learning, and social learning theories (Bandura, 1977a). These behaviour modification techniques do not attempt to modify particular circumscribed responses; however, they do attempt to alter broad expectations of behavioural outcomes and their general strategies. The assumption of continuity between overt and covert learning has been abandoned. Learning is explained not by covert conditioned reflexes but, instead, by more complex, hierarchically organized symbolic and linguistic processes. This model embraces such behaviour therapy methods as self-instruction, coping skill training, instruction in problem solving, and modelling processes.

The approach of Albert Bandura and his associates (Bandura, 1969, 1977a, 1977b; Bandura & Walters, 1963) to behaviour modification has been particularly important in the context of cognitive theory. His social learning theory stresses the importance of modelling as a learning process. Learning by modelling occurs in higher animals, and it is even more important in human beings. According to Bandura, modelling cannot be explained on the basis of simple conditioning. It involves abstracting a cognitive blueprint from the behaviour of the model and the discovery of general rules to be followed. Subjects may combine various aspects of modelled behaviour from different models and create a new pattern. Bandura believes that expectancies are learned rather than stimulus-response connections. He stresses self-regulation by self-instruction, self-reinforcement, and self-evaluation. The subject is concerned with self-efficacy (Bandura, 1977b), his ability to perform coping behaviour, rather than with its outcome. The aim of cognitive therapy is to teach coping skills with a resultant high level of self-efficacy, rather than to teach particular adaptive responses. This technique induces confidence in the client so that he can cope with anxiety aroused by difficult situations. According to Bandura, "the value does not inhere in the behavior itself but rather in the positive and negative self-reactions it generates" (1977a). Self-evaluation with respect to others and one's own standards is therefore very important. The subject regulates his behaviour according to the effect it will have on self-evaluation. Finally, Bandura rejects the environmental determinism of behaviourism and instead postulates a reciprocal determinism of man-and-his-environment through the medium of his behaviour. Man's behaviour is shaped by the environment, but simultaneously the environment is shaped by man's behaviour. Since presumably the man-environment system is an open system, a dialectical spiral of interactions can be envisaged responsible for the creativity and innovativeness of behaviour.* Bandura's reciprocal determinism avoids the dilemma of an infinite regress, with which behaviour engineers are confronted when they try to explain the value choices guiding them in their behaviour engineering.

Many notions developed in the social theory of learning have

---

*The person-behaviour-environment system is an open system and is not based exclusively on negative feedback mechanisms. In the latter case, the end-state would be an equilibrium with no room for personal growth and creativity. The system of "reciprocal determinism," proposed by Bandura, must contain positive as well as negative feedbacks, and it must allow for a degree of permanent disequilibrium between the person and his environment to allow for a creative growth and innovation.

been applied to cognitive therapy. The general coping skill approach has been applied to treatment of phobias (Goldfried, 1971), to the anxiety management training (Suinn & Richardson, 1971), to the stress inoculation technique (Meichenbaum & Cameron, 1973a), and to interpersonal problem solving (Spivack & Shure, 1974). Overt and covert modelling have been used in the treatment of phobias (Kazdin, 1973). Two kinds of human models have been tried: the coping and the mastery models. The coping models display the same difficulties in beginning sessions as clients but gradually overcome them. The mastery models can tackle problems at once. It was found that clients identify themselves better with coping models.

A self-instruction technique has been developed by Meichenbaum (1974) and his students. It has originated in the work of Luria (1961) and Vygotsky (1962) on thought development in children. According to Luria, a child's behaviour is first controlled by the commands of adults and later the child controls his behaviour through audible self-talk, which eventually becomes subvocal and still later internalized as thought processes. Meichenbaum instructs subjects to control their behaviour by self-talk. He has been successful in training schizophrenic patients to control their thought processes by self-instructions (Meichenbaum & Cameron, 1973b). Meichenbaum (1971) has applied the method of self-instruction to impulsive children. These children display an impulsive behaviour characterized by extremely brief response latencies and a high frequency of errors. Self-instruction allows children to monitor and regulate their behaviour. Thorsen and Mahoney (1974) have discussed in detail various self-control methods.

Cognitive Reinterpretations of Psychoanalytical Theory

The same evolution in the direction of cognitive theory that has characterized behaviouristic psychology also can be discerned in the recent trends in psychoanalysis. It has particularly affected metapsychological theorizing. This development is reminiscent of an earlier one when, at the height of the popularity of behaviourism, attempts were made to equate psychoanalysis with the Hullian drive reduction version of behaviourism and translate the psychoanalytical concepts into the behaviouristic ones (Dollard & Miller, 1950).

The theory of ego defenses had some cognitive connotations,

which anticipated the current developments in psychoanalysis. It assumed that incoming information was distorted so as to make it congruent with the self-concept. Heinz Hartmann (1958) has developed further the idea of the ego as an information processor and an executor of behaviour. The ego psychologists have suggested that there is a conflict free zone of the ego concerned with the efficacy of behaviour. In recent years, the concept of ego strength has been emphasized in psychoanalytical theorizing.

Colby's computer model of psychoanalysis

The work of Kenneth Colby has brought psychoanalysis even closer to modern cognitive theory. In his book, *Energy and Structure in Psychoanalysis,* Colby (1955) offered an alternative metapsychology to that of the classical psychoanalysis. He proposed a cyclic-circular structural model as a replacement for the "tripartite" model of metapsychology.* The cyclic-circular model is much more complex than its tripartite counterpart and more in keeping with the modern cognitive and cybernetic theory. The basic unit of the system is not the cathexis but the concept-meaning (meantent).

The psychic apparatus is a complex information processing system concerned with information encoding, transfer, and storage. The sensor part of it gathers information from the external world and also monitors internal physiological processes. This information is enriched by the information stored in the long-term memory. The latter is divided into the proprial self-referring system and the systems concerned with the physical and social aspects of the environment. In passing through the memory systems, the concept-meanings, which originated in the sensor, are elaborated or attenuated. Finally, through the emittor the information may be transferred into the motor system and/or may enter the relinkor and be fed back into the sensor to modify the incoming messages. Thus, two processes are postulated. The initial process is unconscious and elaborates the cognitive import of the messages as they pass through the systems. The second-

---

*In proposing his cyclic-circular model of metapsychology, Colby takes a conventionalist (instrumentalist) position and does not make any ontological commitment to it. He definitely rejects any idea of isomorphism between his model and neurological structures or physiological processes.

ary process recirculates the finally integrated messages back to the receptors and is conscious. Consciousness, which is related to attention, monitors the incoming information and modifies its meaning. There is a similarity between Colby's cyclic-circular and Neisser's analysis through synthesis models (Neisser, 1967). Colby rejects the hydraulic model of classical psychoanalysis. He is not concerned with quantities and distribution of energy but only with patterning of energy in the form of pulsation. Different frequencies of pulsation encode the concept-meanings. Thus, Colby's cyclic-circular model is not an energy system but an information processing model.

While the cyclic-circular model is concerned with metapsychology and only indirectly with mental illness, Colby's later model of computer simulated paranoia is of more direct relevance. Colby (1975) has written a computer program that simulates the paranoid processes. In the discussion of the artificial paranoia, Colby has abandoned the physicalistic metaphor altogether. He is concerned with the analysis of the linguistic behaviour of paranoid patients, the underlying symbolic system of behaviour rules and intentions. Colby explains paranoid behaviour in terms of rules and reasons of a linguistic game rather than in terms of mechanical causes. He believes that there are three kinds of explanation of human action, which are easily confused. The first is in terms of physical causes and is appropriate for the physiological level. The second is in terms of reasons, rules, intentions, and beliefs. It applies to acts of a conscious person. The third type of explanation is in terms of unconscious reasons, referring to symbolic representations that are sealed off from reflection, deliberation, and free choices. These unconscious symbolic dynamisms, similarly to mechanical causes, are inaccessible to voluntary control. Man can be both a free agent utilizing his symbolic processes and a victim of these processes. A computer simulation model offers an interpretative explanation that makes intelligible the connections between the symbolic input, the intervening symbol-processing (an internal state), and the symbolic output.

Colby singles out the features of paranoid behaviour, following Tomkins' theory of paranoia (Tomkins, 1963): (1) suspiciousness, (2) self-reference, (3) hypersensitivity, (4) fearfulness, (5) hostility, and (6) rigidity. The latter author believes that in paranoid patients information processing is monopolized by a permanent state of vigilance attuned to maximize the detection of insult and to minimize the possibility of humiliation. Colby has also incorporated into his model of paranoia the theory of Swanson, Bohnert, and Smith (1970). These authors suggest paranoid patients protect their homeostatic equilibrium by attributing causes of its disturbance to external sources. The artificial paranoia computer program is based on the rules of verbal behaviour consistent with these theoretical formulations of paranoia.

Psycholinguistic Approaches to Psychoanalysis

The convergence of psychoanalysis with cognitive psychology may be further illustrated by Edelson's (1971) reinterpretation of psychoanalysis in terms of Ernst Cassirer's Symbolic Forms philosophy and Lacan's (1966) reinterpretation in terms of structural linguistics. The interest in the link between psychoanalysis and psycholinguistics is exemplified further by several recent publications in a volume edited by Spence (1976). These papers address themselves to the application of the modern psycholinguistic theory to psychoanalysis. The authors discuss the language and general semantic phenomena occurring in dreams, altered states of consciousness, and schizophrenia. Martindale, in his paper, suggests that the linguistic structures revealed in regressed states of consciousness are identical with the deep semantic structure of the basic, subjective lexicon characteristic of normal states of consciousness. Two papers by Freedman and Steingert are concerned with kinesic expression and language construction in various pathological states.

We have seen that there has occurred a convergence of the psychodynamic and behaviouristic models towards the cognitive model of mental illness. This shift towards the cognitive model implies a changing concept of man and a changing concept of mental illness. Man is conceived as a rational problem solver, using symbols and capable of self-determination. Mental illness is explained in terms of disorders of these capacities. Oversimplifying, it could be said that the cognitive model equates mental health (sanity) with rationality and mental illness (insanity) with irrationality. Rationality has a broader scope than one possessed by intelligence and cognitive abilities as measured by psychometric tests. In addition to the other two, its scope covers interpersonal relations and social functioning.

In contrast to uncovering psychoanalytical therapy and Rogerian counselling, cognitive psychotherapy is directive and didactic. The cognitive therapist plays an active role more congruent with that of a teacher than that of a traditional psychotherapist. Similar to the other psychological models of mental illness, the cognitive model is one of continuity between health (normality) and illness (abnormality). The same cognitive mechanisms and processes are operating in both cases.

Chapter 5
SOCIOCULTURAL MODELS

INTRODUCTION

Some Important Issues in Social Sciences

Sociologists and anthropologists take society and culture as their frame of reference. For them, an individual is only a link, or a point, in the social fabric. Sociocultural models of mental illness are based on this presupposition. The explanations of mental illness offered by social scientists vary a great deal and depend on the position they take on certain basic issues in social theory.

The first issue concerns the nature of social sciences. The sociologists who take the positivistic point of view believe that these sciences are not essentially different from physical sciences (Lundberg, 1939, 1961; Nagel, 1961). Their objective methodology is based on empirical hypothesis testing, on replicable observations and measurements. According to them the social sciences deal with value-free events that can be described in physicalistic terms. This approach is represented typically by behavioural sociology (Michaels & Green, 1979) and by Exchange Theory (Homans, 1950, 1967). Others believe that social sciences are not concerned with physical events but rather with shared meanings of social actors. Thus, there is a difference between a piece of paper flying because it is blown by the wind and a man fleeing from a pursuing angry mob (MacIver, 1937). In the second case we are not concerned with physical forces but rather with the experiences of fear and anger that give meaning to and define the social situation to the fleeing man and the pursuing mob.

The existentialist (Douglas & Johnson, 1977), phenomenological (Psathas, 1973), and humanistic (Hoult, 1979) sociologists are the most extreme representatives of this point of view, which is also shared by Peter Winch, an ordinary language philosopher. In his book, *The Idea of Social Science,* Winch (1958) points to the essentially different nature of the social sciences from that of the physical sciences. The explanations of the former are in terms of rules, reasons, intentions, and actions of language games (Wittgenstein, 1953) rather than in terms of deterministic causes. The positivistic and the humanistic points of view coincide with two opposing models of man, the mechanistic and the anthropomorphic (Harre & Secord, 1972). The first considers man an object passively responding to external forces, and the other views him as a free agent, creatively initiating actions. Max Weber (1947) takes a middle position and states that in sociology there are two kinds of enquiries. One is concerned with subjective meanings experienced by social actors and uses the method of understanding (*Verstehen*). The other is concerned with the regularities of collective actions and uses the method of explanation (*Erklärung*). The majority of sociologists lean also towards a middle position. They see social behaviour as determined by the social structure and assigned roles. Thus, they accept the objectivity of social phenomena without reducing them to physicalistic events.

The second issue that has divided social scientists is that of psychological reductionism. It is related to the question Thomas Hobbes asked in the seventeenth century. Can social order be explained by human nature? Many social philosophers, including Thomas Hobbes, Adam Smith, John Stuart Mill, Le Bon, and Sigmund Freud (1955a), have explained social phenomena in terms of individual psychology. Among modern social scientists, George Homans (1967) and behavioural sociologists represent this point of view and reduce collective behaviour to individual conditioning and mutual reinforcement. Others, such as Auguste Comte, Herbert Spencer, and Emile Durkheim, take an antireductionist stand and believe that society has a sui generis reality irreducible to psychological phenomena.

The third issue, closely related to the previous, is that of human nature in its relation to society. Three views on this subject can be distinguished. The first maintains that man is inherently antisocial, motivated by aggressive and sexual impulses, and that he is selfish and greedy. According to this view the basic determinants of behaviour are biological drives that are inhibited, suppressed, and channelized by society. This view is represented by Hobbes, by Freud (1961b), and by Durkheim (1951, 1964). The second view regards man as infinitely malleable by society. It plays down the biological determinants of human behaviour while stressing the social and the cultural. The social values and norms instilled during socialization become the mainsprings of motivation. A quotation from a classical paper, *Social Structure and Anomie,* by Robert Merton (1968) may serve as an illustration of this position. In his criticism of the Freudian position he states:

> With the more recent advancement of social science, this set of conceptions has undergone basic modifications. For one thing it no longer appears so obvious that man is set against society in an unceasing war between biological impulses and social restraint. The image of man as an untamed bundle of impulses begins to look more like a caricature than a portrait. For another, sociological perspectives have increasingly entered into the analysis of behaviour deviating from prescribed patterns of conduct.

Sociocultural determinism characterizes structuralist-functionalist theories in sociology and anthropology. In anthropology, the culture and personality school of thought, which in the early days was influenced by Freudian theory (Roheim, 1950), sees the basic personality types (Linton, 1945) with their specific conflict to be mirroring culture. The third view of human nature in relation to society is represented by the Humanistic sociologists and neo-Marxists who, in contrast to the structuralist-functionalists, put stress on social progress and reject value-free social science. This view attributes to man a potential for self-actualization, creative growth, and betterment, which is often frustrated by social conditions. Men in mutual interaction with society change society and in the process become changed themselves. Erich Fromm (1955), Herbert Marcuse (1964), and Jurgen Habermas (1971) exemplify this point of view.

The fourth issue debated in social sciences is that of cultural and historical relativism, which is closely related to the issue of social determinism. Is human nature invariant or does it depend on specific cultural and historical factors? Those who believe in pan-human norms, anchored in human biopsychological potentialities (Halmos, 1957), believe also that the ethical standards and the criteria of normality are universal for all men irrespective of culture and of historical epoch. On the other hand, the proponents of the cultural relativism maintain that what is regarded as immoral, deviant, and pathological in one culture may be considered moral and normal in another. Each culture has its specific values, norms, and ethics. Ruth Benedict (1959) was perhaps the most vocal member of this point of view. According to her a normal member of the Zuni tribe would be diagnosed as suffering from obsessional-compulsive neurosis by a Western psychiatrist. The typical behaviour of Dobu islanders would be adjudged as paranoid by the Western standards. A shaman hearing voices of spirits would be labelled a schizophrenic. The same would apply to St. Joan of Arc if she were transplanted from the Middle Ages to the modern Western world. Also a wicked witch of the Medieval period would nowadays be regarded as a mental patient. These examples will suffice. Cultural relativism is associated with the from within culture, *emic*, point of view. Social scientists who reject cultural relativism look for transcultural universals, invariants, and functional prerequisites (Parsons, 1951), making it possible to develop standards for evaluating different cultures. They adopt the from outside culture, *etic*, point of view.

The four issues dividing social scientists have affected also their thinking about mental illness. Those who accept without reservations sociocultural determinism tend to reject psychological reductionism. They see individual psychopathology as a manifestation of a warped social structure. Those who take the humanistic point of view think of mental illness in terms of a conflict between an individual and his society. The idea of cultural relativism has undermined the notions of biological causation of mental illness and of medical nosology. It has thrown a new light on the Freudian theory by drawing attention to the fact that family patterns vary a great deal in different cultures. For example, Malinowski (1953) has found that the Freudian explanations based on the Oedipal complex do not apply to the matrilineal and matrilocal Trobriand family where the authority figure for a boy is not the father but rather the maternal uncle, a member of his clan. The incest taboo is directed against sister-brother rather than against mother-son relationship. Some critics have gone even further and have doubted whether sex is the most important conflict in all cultures. For example, the Siriono Indians of Eastern Bolivia who constantly face the threat of starvation dream about food instead of sex. This preoccupation is reflected in their mythology (Holmberg, 1950). The *windigo* cannibalistic psychosis, to be discussed later, provides another example.

Recently, the notion of cultural relativism has been a subject of severe criticism. It has been pointed out that all cultures have the concept of madness, which describes behaviour occurring outside institutionalized, socially defined situations with shared meanings. Some recent studies of personality and transcultural psychiatric research have shown that the claims of the early personality and culture students, in particular that of Ruth Benedict, were exaggerated. Especially, her diagnoses of whole cultures as paranoid or megalomanic have been criticized as illfounded and as expressing ethnocentricity.

The Societal Definition of Mental Illness

The next two topics to be discussed are the definition of mental illness in its social context and the relation of mental illness and of illness in general to social deviance. Illness is both a biological and sociological phenomenon. An organism responds to sickness not only biologically but also psychologically by displaying an illness behaviour (Mechanic, 1966). This behaviour during illness may be described as the sick role, which may vary from culture to culture. Zborowski (1952) has described different responses to pain in patients of the Jewish, Italian, Irish, and Old American ethnic background, which he attributes to different patterns of mothering in these ethnic groups. Illness involves an incapacity of an actor to fulfill certain obligations of his roles and to perform some of his tasks (Parsons, 1951, 1972). Consequently, there is a breakdown in the functioning of the social system, causing the mechanisms of social control to be brought into operation. In this respect, illness in its social aspect is a form of deviance. However, it is a special kind of deviance that is legitimated by the society. The ill person enters the sick role, which entails certain privileges and duties. The incumbent of the sick role is exempted from normal social role responsibilities. He is absolved from blame for being ill. The causes of illness are beyond his control, but he is obliged to try to get well and seek the advice and help of a physician. Parsons considers every illness psychosomatic. However, he states that a predominantly somatic illness impairs the performance of specific tasks associated with certain roles, while a mental illness interferes with playing the roles themselves.

In Western culture illness is treated as a naturalistic phenomenon in contrast to crime and sin, which are concerned with values and mores and therefore treated in legal and moral terms. This does not apply to other cultures and epochs where the line is not so clearly drawn and illness is often regarded as a manifestation of sin and moral weakness. An example of the above is the Medieval conception of mental illness, which regarded it as either a demonical possession or a manifestation of witchcraft. Another important distinction between illness and crime concerns personal responsibility. In the pure case of illness, man is a hapless victim of something that befalls him. In contrast, in the legal-moral frame of reference, a criminal is the culprit responsible for a criminal act initiated by him. When the social-deterministic frame of reference is applied—the theory of action frame of reference—the criminal behaviour is believed to be caused by motivational system of the perpetrator, which is a product of his socialization. Thus, social control in the case of illness consists of treatment and in the case of crime consists, depending on the frame of reference, of punishment or reeducation. It is quite obvious that, in contrast to frankly somatic illness, functional mental illness lies in a gray area. It can be considered either as a disease befalling the patient or a self-motivated social deviance. There are other types of deviance, such as blindness, physical handicap, and stuttering (Lemert, 1951) that, although produced by causes beyond the victim's control, are associated with special social roles into which the victims are cast by the society. These conditions may be described as impaired. They are, in contrast to acute physical illness, associated with social disapproval and rejection. In this respect they are similar to mental illness.

When discussing the problem of social definition of mental illness or madness, the important question that arises is one concerning the criteria used by lay people in ascribing the status of a madman in contrast to that of a criminal or a sinner. The behaviour in both cases is deviant from social norms and violates the mores of the given society. In both cases it is disapproved. However, in the case of crime or sin the person is adjudged morally and legally responsible. In the case of madness the person who is brought under control is restrained, his behaviour is feared, but he is not morally condemned or legally held responsible. One explanation is that the man-in-the-street when confronted with a grossly deviant behaviour uses psychology of understanding (*Verstehen Psychologie* of Max Weber). He puts himself in the shoes of the violator of mores and empathically tries to understand his motivation, his intention, and his purpose. If he succeeds he condemns the deviant behaviour as immoral and criminal. On the other hand, if he fails to understand the motives he defines the behaviour as due to madness, either temporary or permanent. The latter designation depends on whether the locus of causality is placed in a particular situation or in the person who violates the mores. When transactions between an individual and the others break down and his behaviour is not understood, he is thought to be insane. A glass wall, as it were, separates a madman from his associates. He lives in his own private world. His behaviour can be seen, his speech can be heard, but they do not make sense to others. Labelling a deviant as a delinquent and morally condemning him or labelling him as queer, strange, and sick depends on the ability to understand his behaviour (Mechanic, 1962).

The Cummings (1956) have distinguished qualitative deviance, involving bizarre, inappropriate nonnormative behaviour, which is more likely to be labelled as mental illness by the general public, from quantitative deviance, closer to normal behaviour. Thomas Scheff (1966) describes incomprehensible behaviour as residue deviance. The recent sociological movement of Ethnomethodology (Garfinkel, 1967; Zimmerman, 1979) is concerned with understanding the rules emerging in social interaction by which common sense, social reality, and the validity of behaviour are established. On the basis of these rules, the status of insanity is ascribed in the context of everyday life. Jeff Coulter (1973) has analyzed the process of ascription of insanity. He found ascriptive practices context-bound and highly variable. However, insanity ascription is based on culturally furnished knowledge and beliefs and it follows specific types of reasoning and inference. For instance, in England the diagnosis of schizophrenia is based mainly on the presence of hallucinations, thought disorder—inability to play language games (Wittgenstein, 1953)—and delusions. Coulter points out that the diagnosis of insanity is made on the commonsense basis and that the scientific formulations of psychiatry and psychopathology are used only as the rationalizations of the decision. To quote him, "... psychopathology (is) understood as a theoretical enterprise that aims to rationalize the experience with insane members of a community in scientific terms" (1972).

All cultures have the concept of madness. However, the latter is not intrinsic to behaviour but rather depends on the relation, or fitness, of it to the situation. The behaviour of an Eskimo shaman, although psychotic by Western standards, is judged to be normal by his group because it occurs in a socially defined situation and is understandable in terms of the cultural beliefs. On the other hand the behaviour of a madman (*nuthkavihak*) occurs out of social context and is not comprehended by the group (Murphy, 1976). Devereux (1963) and Edgerton (1969) discuss the social criteria and the methods of diagnosis of mental illness in Western and non-Western societies. In an example from East Africa, Edgerton describes the subtle negotiations going on between the patient and his associates before the diagnosis is determined. In Western society, according to Balint (1957), a psychiatric diagnosis is also implicitly negotiated between the psychiatrist and his patient.

Once the behaviour of an individual, on account of its incomprehensibility, is defined as insane, an attempt is made to make sense of it and make it more predictable. A social stereotype of madness is attached to the behaviour in question. The person diagnosed as insane is cast by his social group into the role of the madman, conceived in terms of this stereotype. The stereotypes differ somewhat from culture to culture and from one period of history to another.

Scheff (1966) and Nunnally (1961) have investigated the American stereotype of madness as it is reflected in popular beliefs and mass media. A madman is believed to look different, has glassy eyes, his mouth is widely ajar, and he mumbles incoherent phrases or laughs uncontrollably. Goffman (1961) believes that culturally derived and socially ingrained stereotypes may influence the symptomatology of mental illness. According to him the moral career of a mental patient, by which he means the patient's mental hospital experiences, involving degradation and stigmatization rituals, affect his fate more than illness itself. Hollingshead and Redlich (1958) have found that in the American population the social class membership is associated with different conceptions of mental illness. While patients from higher socioeconomic strata perceive their disorders in terms of emotional and interpersonal problems, patients belonging to the lower classes tend to perceive their symptoms in terms of somatic conditions. The stereotypes of madness exist also in non-Western societies. The Bering Sea Eskimos describe somebody suffering from *nuthkavihak* (insanity) "as talking to oneself, screaming at someone, believing that a child or husband was murdered by witchcraft, and believing oneself to be an animal..." (Murphy, 1976). In some preliterate societies there are culture-bound psychiatric syndromes such as *latah,* found in Southeast Asia, *imu,* found among the Ainu of the Hokkaido island in Japan, *saka,* found in Kenya, and *pibloktoq,* found among Eskimos. These culture-bound syndromes suggest that the existing stereotypes of madness can shape the behaviour of mentally ill subjects. Devereux (1963) after surveying the field of comparative psychiatry has concluded that mental patients conform to cultural expectations of how symptoms should appear. To put it differently, being mentally ill involves playing a social role. In explicating the meaning of psychiatric diagnosis, Sarbin (1969) goes even further than Goffman and Devereux. He believes that mental illness does not exist and the term is used as a metaphor to describe undesirable behaviour. Undoubtedly, the claims of Goffman, Devereux, and Sarbin are exaggerated; however, attempts to make sense out of strange behaviour and experience apply not only to the patient's associates but also in some cases to the patient himself.

The Epidemiology of Mental Illness

There are two schools of thought on the subject of sociocultural causes of mental illness. One maintains that causes of mental illness are biological and social factors influence only the form that illness takes in a given culture. The other school attributes causation solely to the operation of social factors. The proponents of sociocultural models of mental illness belong to the second school of thought. They focus on social determinants, although making allowance for some biological predispositions. The issues drawn between the two schools can be resolved by finding the definitive answers to two questions. The first asks whether the prevalence and incidence of mental illness are the same all over the world. The second asks whether the clinical psychiatric syndromes or diseases are cross-culturally the same. An affirmative answer to these two questions would give support to the views of the biological school of thought. A negative answer would support a sociocultural explanation. However, even if there were differences in mental illness morbidity and in the frequency of various psychiatric syndromes in different societies, this would not preclude the possibility of a biological causation. These societies may represent *Mendelian populations* with differing gene pools and with varying frequencies of pathogenic genes (Murray & Hirsh, 1969). Also, the physical and biological factors in their geographical environments may produce different morbidity rates. For instance, vast areas of West Africa are afflicted by endemic trypanosomiasis, which causes "sleeping sickness" (Tooth, 1950). The clinical picture associated with this illness is very often similar to that of schizophrenia. Tropical malaria can produce acute psychotic episodes. Mental abnormalities may be associated with nutritional deficiencies such as pellagra and kwashiorkor disease.

Epidemiological studies of mental illness are fraught with serious methodological difficulties. The number of patients hospitalized for mental illness or treated as outpatients varies enormously from one society to another and depends on the presence of facilities and community tolerance of mental illness. Even in America, various subcultures differ a great deal. Eaton and Weil (1955) have found that Hutterites, who have a prevalence rate of psychosis similar to that of the general population, seek psychiatric help less often because they are more tolerant of the mentally ill than other groups. The only meaningful epidemiological studies are those that use systematic random sampling of the general population, such as the Stirling County Study (Leighton, 1959) and the Midtown Manhattan Study (Srole, Langner, Michael, Opler, & Rennie, 1962). Even then, however, the results depend on the criteria of mental abnormality. The Stirling County rates are significantly lower (57%) than those of the Midtown Study (81%). This discrepancy may be real. However, it is also possible that rural Nova Scotia is to a lesser degree a psychological society than Manhattan (Gross, 1978). The inhabitants of

Manhattan tend to define their difficulties in psychological terms to a greater extent than do the citizens of small towns in Nova Scotia. That the reported rates may change during relatively short time intervals is suggested by the follow-up of the Midtown Manhattan study, which has found lower rates of mental disorders than in the original study (Srole & Fischer, 1980). A recent review of epidemiological estimates of the rate of mental illness in the United States concludes that the prevalence rate is between 15 percent and 25 percent (Dohrenwend, Dohrenwend, Gould, Link, Neugebauer, & Wunsch-Hitzig, 1980).

It is impossible to review here the enormous literature on the epidemiology of mental illness (Plog & Edgerton, 1969). Rates of mental illness have been compared in populations differing in geographical locations, culture, ethnicity, and religion. Immigrants have been compared with native born, upper socioeconomic classes with lower, and urban with rural populations. The effect of social mobility on the rates of mental illness has been investigated, but the results are far from being clear, as studies often contradict one another. The reported differences often disappear when the data are adjusted for age and socioeconomic status. However, there seems to be a connection between the rate of mental illness and poverty. A low socioeconomic status tends to be conducive to mental illness (Hollingshead & Redlich, 1958; Srole et al., 1962). Srole mentions three factors related to impaired mental health in Manhattan: (1) the poverty complex, (2) role-discontinuity, and (3) the stigmatization-rejection mechanism. Brenner (1973) found that poverty produces social stress, which contributes to causation of psychotic breakdown. Kohn (1969) maintains that low social class membership and resulting poverty produce an orientation of fatalism, helplessness, distrust, and fearfulness. This leads to family disorganization and to a vulnerability to mental illness.

The best controlled cross-cultural studies were those by Leighton (1969). He found that the Yoruba of West Africa were familiar with most of the syndromes known to Western psychiatry with the exception of depression, phobia, and the obsessive-compulsive symptoms. For the urban Yorubas, Leighton found that the rate of mental illness was the same as for the Stirling county population; however, for the rural Yorubas it was lower. It seems that mental illness occurs in all societies, although sometimes at different rates. The early theories that associated mental illness with civilization and with social complexity have been by and large abandoned (Plog & Edgerton, 1969).

The question remains whether the Western nosological categories such as schizophrenia, manic-depressive psychosis, and neurosis are applicable to mental patients from other cultures. An early study attempting to answer this question was carried out by Emil Kraepelin. He noticed that in Java melancholia and mania were rare and patients suffering from melancholia did not express any guilt feelings. Alcoholic psychosis was absent. On the other hand, Kraepelin found *dementia praecox* in all non-European societies he visited. Since then, anthropologists and transcultural psychiatrists have been divided on the question of whether mental diseases are cross-culturally identical with only their overt forms modified or whether each culture produces indigenous clinical syndromes. To put it differently, the issue is whether the approach to transcultural psychiatry should be *etic* or *emic*. On the whole, psychiatrists have tended to favour the *etic* and anthropologists the *emic* orientation. They also differ in their stress on the importance of biological as opposed to social causation. Anthropologist Marvin Opler (Plog & Edgerton, 1969) states, "Those who claim schizophrenias (of modern type) are biogenetic in origin and therefore distributed randomly in population are simply ignorant of the anthropological data. Variations in the form and epidemiology of mental illnesses occur transculturally."

Leighton (1969), who is a psychiatrist, was struck by the similarity between the symptom patterns in the Yoruba and in the Stirling county in Nova Scotia, which made it possible to compare their incidence rates. However, there is no doubt that there is marked variation in the symptom patterns and in their social settings in different cultures. A common type of psychosis in West Africa is an acute, delirious confusional state of brief duration, brought about by a psychic trauma (Jilek & Jilek-Aall, 1970). Psychiatrists do not agree on whether to classify this confusional state as an acute schizophrenic episode or as a hysterical psychosis. Carothers (1953) and Tooth (1950) have found a low incidence of depression among the African natives. In Western culture depression is usually associated with guilt feelings, self-deprecation, and suicidal ideas. These features are absent in Far Eastern and African countries where depression is characterized by somatic symptoms such as fatigue and insomnia (Angst, 1973). The guilt feelings and self-deprecation may be a product of the Judeo-Christian tradition and, therefore, constitutes a cultural overlay on the somatic manifestations of depression. The differences in the symptomatology of mental illness are not limited to cultures that are as distant from one another as is the Western from the Oriental or the Western from the African. Various ethnic groups, within Western societies, differ in their symptom patterns. Thus, Opler and Singer (1956) in a well controlled study showed that, in New York City, Irish and Italian paranoid schizophrenics display different symptoms. While the Irish tend to be withdrawn and quiet, their Italian counterparts are noisy and aggressive. It seems that in the Irish a schizophrenic pathology affects mainly fantasy life while in the Italians it affects motility (see also Opler, 1956).

The most striking manifestation of cultural specificity are the so-called culture-bound reactive syndromes (Yap, 1974; Kiev, 1972). They have culturally specific form and context. Several of them have been described. They usually occur in primitive, isolated societies. Some examples will now be given. *Latah,* which occurs in Southeast Asia, is characterized by suggestibility, echolalia, echopraxia, echomimia, altered consciousness, depression, anxiety, and disorganization. A similar condition is known as *imu* among the Ainu of the Hokkaido Island of Japan and as *arctic hysteria* in Eastern Siberia. It is believed by the natives to be caused by a sudden fright or surprise. *Pibloktoq,* occurring among the Eskimos, is characterized by depression, brooding, screaming, crying, wild running, and occasionally by suicidal or homicidal behaviour (Kiev, 1972). Kiev regards it as a dissociative state. *Utox,* occurring among the Formosan aborigines, is a state of a hallucinatory clouding of consciousness precipitated, according to the natives, by an encounter with an evil spirit. *Susto,* or *espanto,* common to Latin America, is an acute anxiety state believed to be caused by sudden fright, bad air, witchcraft, or evil eye. All of which, according to the members of the culture, produces a soul loss. Somewhat similar conditions occur among African tribes and is known as *malignant anxiety.*

To this category of fright reactions belong *thanatomania,* a progressive psychophysiological disorganization with an expectation of an impending death, and also *voodoo death*. *Koro*, also called *suk yeong*, occurring in South China and Southeast Asia, is an episodic depersonalization state characterized by an acute anxiety and panic. The victim experiences a fear that his penis is about to shrink and be drawn into the abdomen. This is believed by the members of the culture to be caused by sexual excesses (Yap, 1974). *Amok*, occurring among Malayans, is a rage reaction leading to unprovoked murderous attacks made at random. *Windigo* was a psychotic reaction that occurred in the past among the Ojibwa Indians and other Algonquin speaking tribes such as the bush Crees who inhabit the northern forests of Canada. It was characterized by the delusion of possession by the cannibalistic evil spirit *windigo* and by acts of cannibalism. In several cultures, acute psychotic reactions occur that are characterized by beliefs of being possessed by evil spirits or deity and that are similar to the demonic possession psychosis common in Europe in the Middle Ages. For example, the acute spirit possession psychosis occurring in Haiti and known as *boufee delirante aigue* is characterized by confusion, excitation, and visual and auditory hallucinations. Linton (1956) distinguishes the nonpsychotic possession by spirits found in the context of religious rituals from the psychotic ones occurring outside the appropriate social situation with shared meaning. *Iich aa*, or moth craziness, is a violent psychotic episode characterized by disorganized behaviour occurring among the Navaho Indians. It is regarded by the members of the Navaho tribe as a punishment for brother-sister incest. These examples of culture-bound syndromes will suffice. Some of them, such as *latah*, are reactions to nonspecific stress situations or shocks. Others, such as moth craziness in the Navaho, thanatomania, and voodoo death are believed to be punishments for breaking taboos or brought about by a curse. They are also believed to result from witchcraft and sorcery.

Are culture-bound syndromes universal psychiatric diseases cast in a cultural mold, or are they the product of specific social and psychological processes existing in particular cultures? Proponents of the theory of biological causation of mental illness subscribe to the first alternative. Those who believe in social and cultural determinism opt for the second alternative. P. M. Yap (1974) has offered a model for transcultural psychiatry that attempts to reconcile the two points of view. Yap rejects the dualistic position that separates a biologically determined human organism from a culturally and socially determined human mind. Instead, he proposes a hierarchy of different levels of integration. It is a model similar to that of Henry Ey (1969) discussed in the previous chapter. The lower levels of integration of the organismic events and functions are within the framework of physiology and biology. The higher levels are within the sociocultural framework. These levels interpenetrate, although at times one is more important than the other. Together they constitute an open system of reciprocal causality and feedback.

In the structure of a mental illness, the biological and sociocultural factors inseparably interpenetrate with one another. Yap, although basically biopsychologically oriented, rejects the conventional disease or faulty-machine model. Instead, he opts for the Hippocratic-Galenian model of *dyscrasia*, which was described in a previous chapter as a constitutional model. The state of *dyscrasia* is a state of imbalance brought about by internal or external factors, both physical and sociocultural. Sometimes the former are more important, at other times the latter. It produces certain basic biopsychological reactions such as fear, rage, withdrawal, or a dissociative state. It also may lead to a regression, dedifferentiation, disintegration, and reorganization of behaviour. So every *dyscrasia* has both the passive dissolution and the active coping aspects. The typical universal reactive syndromes such as schizophrenia, depression, or neurosis are biopsychological reactions to *dyscrasias*. They are moulded by cultural factors present in more advanced societies belonging to the same broad cultural sphere. On the other hand, the atypical culture-bound syndromes, such as *latah, utox, piboloktoq,* or *windigo* psychosis, are encountered in isolated primitive cultures, far removed from the industrial, urbanized, rational societies of today. The biopsychological reactions to *dyscrasias* are shaped by the systems of exotic beliefs occurring in these cultures. Yap (1974) divides all the atypical culture-bound syndromes into three groups. There are those related to the biopsychological reaction of fear, an example being *latah*, those such as *amok*, which are related to rage, and those, such as possession psychoses, which are dissociative reactions.

The Intraindividual versus Interactionist Nexus of Causation

Before the different sociocultural models of mental illness are presented a few words need to be said about the way sociocultural causes are conceptualized in contrast to the biological and psychological ones. While in the medical and psychological models of mental illness the nexus of causation is placed inside the patient, in the sociocultural models it is placed in the interactions of the patient with other people or with the society at large. When considering mental illness, social scientists do not think in terms of individual pathology but in terms of a breakdown of social systems, which may be the society at large or a smaller unit such as family.

The sociocultural models of mental illness may be divided into two classes: the macrosocial and the microsocial. The first is concerned with large social units such as tribes, nations, cultures, and cities. The second deals with smaller units such as families, work groups, friendship cliques, and therapy groups. Cooley (1929) has called the large social units secondary groups and the small ones primary or face-to-face groups. In the primary groups the members are intimately acquainted with one another. These groups are based on close interpersonal relationships and interactions. In the secondary groups the social participation is through sharing common institutions, values, norms, and common ideology. Relationships are highly formalized and impersonal. As with any theoretical formulation the division to a great extent is artificial. The society at large exerts its influence on man, in great measure, through the primary groups. A child is socialized and acquires the cultural values in its family. Also, at the adult level social control is exercised, to a large extent, by approval or disapproval of one's behaviour by intimates. However, the division does serve a useful analytical purpose and allows one to focus on distinct aspects of social structures and processes.

THE MACROSOCIAL MODELS OF MENTAL ILLNESS

This category includes sociological theories of mental illness that take the society at large, the secondary group, as their frame of reference. Culturally determined social values, norms, and social structure of statuses and roles serve as the explanatory concepts. The macrosocial models can be further subdivided into the structural-functionalist (synchronic) and the conflict (diachronic) model.

The Structural-Functionalist (Synchronic) Model

The structural-functionalist theory of society is represented in sociology by Durkheim (1933), Parsons and Shils (1951), and Merton (1968), to mention the most prominent names. In anthropology it is represented by the so-called Functionalist school of B. Malinowski (1960) and of A. R. Radcliffe-Brown (1952). While there are important differences between the various structural-functionalist thinkers, there are also important similarities. Society is regarded literally or metaphorically as an organism similar to a biological organism. It is a whole composed of mutually related parts whose function is to preserve the integrity of the system and to maintain its boundary. An optimal functioning system depends on the coordination and harmony among its parts or, in the societal context, on consensus and conformity. It is identified with a state of equilibrium or homeostasis. The focus therefore is on the social statics, to use Spencerian terms, rather than on the dynamics. To borrow the distinction made by linguists and, in anthropology, by Levi-Strauss (1963), the stress is on the synchronic, timeless social order rather than on the diachronic process of change. This statement requires some qualifications. Even in a static social system certain processes recur in time, but the social structure does not change. Also, all the structural-functionalists recognize the reality of social change but regard it in terms of orderly growth and differentiation, similar to that occurring in biological organisms (Parsons, 1971). However, they have focused on social status quo rather than on social change. Of course, no society is perfectly static, devoid of conflict and changeless. Some primitive, isolated homogeneous societies approach this ideal, although not to the degree supposed by the nineteenth century sociologists. The changing pluralistic, heterogenous American society with various interest groups opposing one another is very far from it.

The structural-functionalist theory has been formulated most systematically by Talcott Parsons (1951). According to him, social structure is composed of a system of statuses. Each status has a social role associated with it. The incumbents of the statuses enter the roles, which they play vis-à-vis the others playing reciprocal roles. The roles have expectancies associated with them that determine the behaviour of the actors. This arrangement allows the incumbents to fulfill the obligations and enjoy the rights of their statuses. The roles are institutionalized and regulated by the social norms and values that have been internalized during the incumbent's socialization processes. The behaviour associated with playing the roles is highly predictable and enshrined in stable social institutions. The smooth functioning of a social system depends on (a) a proper interarticulation of the reciprocal social roles that complement one another, (b) the absence of confusion or ambiguity about the roles, (c) an internalization of cultural norms and values, and (d) a congruity of the value system. An internalization of role expectancies, of social norms and values, into the personality produces the necessary motivation to participate in a social system and act in accordance with its requirements.

Culture provides a pattern of symbols with shared meanings that allows the participants to communicate. It facilitates meshing in and coordination of the roles. On the subjective level, it provides a system of congruent beliefs and ultimate values, giving a meaning to life and affording a cosmic orientation. In a well-integrated sociocultural system, man lives in a predictable world, sharing meanings, beliefs, attitudes, sentiments, and values with the members of his group. His choices are determined by the cultural values. His behaviour is regulated by the social norms that have become his second nature and are not questioned by him. The system shapes the behaviour of the individual through the process of socialization in childhood and the mechanisms of social control throughout his life. Powerful social forces operate to ensure conformity and consensus, resulting in a state of equilibrium, harmony, and stability. Since the structural-functionalist model of society postulates the existence of a system of feedbacks and regulatory mechanisms, it can be fitted in the conceptual framework of general systems theory. Such a conceptual framework could be more formal and rigorous than the earlier versions of the model. Some recent developments in this direction are summarized by Buckley (1967).

The Social Disorganization-Anomie Model of Mental Illness

When applying the biological organism metaphor to a social system, the structural-functionalists sometimes use the term social pathology to describe deviations from its optimal functioning (Brown, 1946; Lemert, 1951). This line of thinking has led to speculations about the relationship between social pathology and individual psychopathology in the form of social deviance and mental illness. Since in a biological organism a mild degree of infection or stress is beneficial because it mobilizes the forces of resistance, it has been thought that a certain degree of deviance has been considered socially useful. Thus, Durkheim (1958) has argued that a moderate rate of crime serves a useful social purpose because it mobilizes collective sentiments, strengthens social control mechanisms, and enhances social solidarity. Similar speculations have been offered with regard to mental illness. Yap (1974) has suggested that some mental disorders may serve a socially useful purpose by serving as a warning that breaking certain taboos causes madness. Foucault (1965), in his speculations on madness and civilization, has implied that madness may play a culturally useful role of defining the range and limits of rationality.

While the structural-functionalist school of thought considers a moderate rate of social deviance to be compatible with and even beneficial to the proper functioning of a social system, it regards an excess to be harmful. Such an excess upsets the equilibrium and causes disorganization and dysfunction of the social system. The latter is threatened with disintegration and annihilation. Social disorganization and malfunctioning in turn cause individual maladjustment, personal disorganization, and psychopathology, which are only symptoms of social pathology. Consequently, social disorganization has been linked by some with increased rates of mental illness and is considered as one of its causes. A state of social disequilibrium subjects individual members of a society to strain, which causes an increase in the rates of deviance and mental illness. The factors that may produce such disequilibrium are rapid social change, rapid upward and downward social mobility, migration, cultural lag, cultural disorientation, cultural conflict, and role and value conflicts. A rapid social change is usually caused by a technological revolution, where a gap is created between the economic infrastructure and ideological superstructure, a condition known as cultural lag. It results in dislocations within social system and in status alterations. In a situation of cultural conflict two cultures, usually one advanced and dominant and the other primitive or in a minority position, come into contact. As a result the primitive or minority culture disintegrates. A member of a minority group who has lost his old culture but has not yet acquired the new one may be described as a marginal man, confused as to his identity (Stonequist, 1937). In this situation, the socialization of children goes astray. The values and norms fail to be internalized, and if they are, they are often in conflict because of the incongruous models presented to the child. There is confusion about role expectancies, which interferes with the proper role playing and synchronization. The conflict of values and ideology produces a cultural disorientation. Life loses meaning and purpose. People live for today without any roots in the past or orientation towards the future. They suffer from personal disorganization and a lack of integration into the society. This condition has been associated with senseless crime, juvenile delinquency, alcoholism, drug addiction, suicide, and mental illness.

So far, conditions have been described in which social disorganization is caused by some external factors extrinsic to the culture. There are also factors intrinsic to cultures that cause strain and social disequilibrium. They are described as cultural discontinuities (Benedict, 1938). To this category belong abrupt changes in the attitudes of the socialization agents, unresolved role and value conflicts that are built into the cultural matrix, and cultural means-ends discrepancies. Every culture involves some role and value conflicts. However, cultures differ in the way and the extent to which these conflicts are resolved. In some cultures, incongruities are controlled by situational compartmentalization. In others, role and value conflicts are internalized to produce strains in the social fabric. This situation may lead to deviance and personal psychopathology in individuals who have been thoroughly socialized and who are well integrated into the social structure. Originally the term social disorganization was applied to social disintegration caused by external factors, extrinsic to the culture. When factors were intrinsic, built into social structure and culture, the terms anomie or normlessness were preferred. However, in recent years the two terms have been used interchangeably and the concept of anomie has acquired a broader denotation to make it synonymous with social disorganization (De Grazia, 1948; Dunham, 1964). From the point of view of the structural-functional model of mental illness, social disintegration and anomie can be combined into one concept describing the processes involved in causation or precipitation of mental illness. The concepts of social disorganization and anomie have different historical roots. The first was developed by the Chicago School of Sociology in America during the twenties and thirties of this century and the second by Durkheim in France at the turn of the century.

The social disorganization theory of mental illness has its origin in the pioneering work on urban ecology of R. E. Park and E. W. Burgess (1925). These authors found that Chicago and other large American cities could be divided into three concentric zones: the central business district, the residential suburbs, and the transition zone between the two. The business district was the place of work where few people lived. The single family dwelling suburbs were inhabited by a stable population with family ties and roots in the community. The transition zone was a district of rooming houses, ethnic ghettos, houses of ill repute, and skid row. It was inhabited by unattached transients who were single and often foreign born members of ethnic minorities. This zone was found to have higher crime and suicide rates than the single family dwelling areas (Shaw & McKay, 1931; Cavan, 1928). Faris and Dunham (1939) investigated the epidemiology of mental illness in relation to these city areas. They found that the rate of mental illness was higher in the transition zone than in the areas of single family dwellings. When the rates were calculated for different diagnostic categories, it was found that the city center and the transition zone rates for schizophrenia, general paresis, alcoholism, and drug addiction were higher than those for residential areas. The same trend, although to a lesser extent, was shown for the rates of senile and arteriosclerotic dementias. Manic-depressive psychosis was an exception. There was no relation between its rate and the city zones. Similar findings were reported for other big cities. Hare (1956) found a high rate of schizophrenia in single-person households in Bristol, Great Britain. In a more recent study of Detroit, Dunham (1965) has essentially confirmed his original findings.

In the original Chicago study, Faris and Dunham (1939) stressed the link between schizophrenia and social isolation. The unattached inhabitants of the transition zone formed few lasting social relations. Consequently, they did not have the social reference framework for their private view of the world. The social feedback, which shaped their thinking, and conduct norm pattern was deficient. This lack of social control mechanisms led to seclusiveness, bizarre ideation, and grossly disorganized behaviour.

The social disorganization theory was deficient in scientific rigor. Moreover, it was influenced by certain biases and prejudices. These were the xenophobia rampant in the United States at that time, a tacit assumption of the superiority of the middle-class values, and a preference of the rural life-style to the urban. It was an expression of nostalgia for the simple life of small towns and farms in the preindustrial America (Plog & Edgerton, 1969).

The concept of anomie, or normlessness, was developed by Emile Durkheim (1933, 1951). It has firmer theoretical foundations and a greater objectivity than its American equivalent. Anomie conceptualizes disorganization phenomena as disturbances of social structure. In his book, *Suicide*, Durkheim (1951) has suggested that man's relation to society can be represented by two independent bipolar dimensions. The first, egoism-altruism axis, indicates the degree to which the individual is autonomous from or is integrated into society. The second, anomie-fatalism axis, describes the degree to which society exercises control over him. At the anomie pole the social controls or constraints are absent; at the fatalism pole they are excessive. The two axes describe four types of suicide: the altruistic, egoistic, anomic, and fatalistic. Anomic suicide is caused by an absence of norms regulating behaviour and usually results from dislocation of social and economic conditions. The individual loses the measure of what is proper or improper for his social status. He becomes motivated by excessive greed and ambition, which are never satisfied. The resulting frustration may lead to suicide. Egoistic suicide is caused by a loss of identification with society leading to a loss of meaning and purpose of life. Altruistic suicide results from a commitment to uphold social values or a code of ethics. It is exemplified by the highly ritualistic Japanese *hara-kiri*. The fatalistic suicide is a suicide of a slave, of a concentration camp prisoner, or of a person dying from cancer. Such individuals find themselves in a hopeless situation with no way out. Both the anomic and egoistic suicides are signs of disintegration of social fabric.

Durkheim has found some support for his speculations in higher rate of suicide in Protestant than in Catholic countries and in the relation of suicide rate to economic cycles. A more recent study by Naroll (1969) of fifty-eight preliterate societies showed that suicide rate is a good indicator of social pathology caused by rupture of social ties.

The concept of anomie has been introduced to American sociology by Robert Merton (1968). Merton distinguishes the cultural goals for which people are encouraged to strive from the institutionalized, legitimate means by which these goals are to be attained. Societies differ in the extent to which they focus on the goals or on the means. The American society stresses and clearly defines the goal of economic success but is less explicit about the means to achieve it. The imbalance between the two lends to social strain and anomie. Merton lists five types of individual adaptation to social strain, depending on the acceptance or rejection of the social goals and of the institutionalized means of their procurement. In conformity the individual accepts both the goals and the means. In innovation he accepts the goals but rejects the institutionalized means and substitutes his own, often criminal means. Ritualism is characterized by a preoccupation with institutionalized means at the expense of the goals. This adaptation characterizes the bureaucratic virtuoso and also the obsessional-compulsive personality. In retreatism both the goals and the means are rejected. This is the adaptation of vagabonds, drug addicts, chronic alcoholics, and in its extreme form, schizophrenics. The final adaptation is rebellion in which both new cultural goals and new means of their attainment are adopted. This is the adaptation of radicals, revolutionaries, or members of a counterculture.

Talcott Parsons (1951) has developed further the concept of anomie in relation to social deviance. He distinguishes six types of individual responses to social structure stresses. They can be viewed as pairs of poles of three orthogonal axes: conformity versus alienation, passive orientation versus active orientation, and orientation to social objects versus orientation to normative patterns. Various permutations of motivational responses along these three axes define different types of social deviance. According to Parsons, schizophrenia is the extreme of the deviance characterized by alienation, passivity, and withdrawal from social objects.

It has to be emphasized that anomie describes a disordered state of a social structure and not a state of an individual person. An individual participating in such a structure reflects subjectively the state of anomie. This reflection of anomie by an individual has been called "anomia" by Srole (1956), who has developed a personality scale to measure it. According to Meier and Bell (1959) the anomia scale measures despair, hopelessness, and discouragement, all of which indicate poor mental health. The concept of anomia is very close to that of alienation. However they have to be distinguished because they differ in their theoretical context and connotations, although descriptively they are very similar (Nettler, 1957; Seeman, 1959). The concept of anomie influenced the theoretical orientation of many epidemiological studies. Examples are the Midtown Study (Srole, Langner, Michael, Opler, & Rennie, 1962) and the Stirling County Study (Leighton, 1959). Leighton used the term social disintegration; however, he regarded it as synonymous with anomie.

Social stratification is another area that has been subjected to epidemiological studies. Frumkin (1955) found that persons engaged in low status occupations are more prone to mental illness than persons in higher status occupations. Powell (1958) made similar observations with regard to suicide. The most important study of social class and mental illness was conducted by Hollingshead and Redlich (1958) in New Haven, Connecticut. These authors found that social classes differed in the prevalence of mental illness. The overall prevalence of mental illness was higher in the lower than the upper social classes and was particularly high in the lowest (Class 5, as measured by Hollingshead's Index of Social Position). The prevalence of psychoneurosis was somewhat higher in the upper classes (Class 1 and 2). The opposite was true with respect to psychosis. Its rate was much higher in the lower classes (particularly Class 5). The incidence and prevalence rates of schizophrenia, organic psychosis, senile psychosis, and alcoholism are all higher in the lower (particularly Class 5) than the upper classes. The relation is somewhat weaker for affective psychosis. The further finding concerned the type of treatment received by patients belonging to different social classes. While the upper-class patients were treated by psychotherapy, the lower-class patients were treated by physical methods. The patients belonging to higher classes tended to define their difficulties in psychological terms in contrast to lower-class patients who defined them in terms of physical illness and demanded physical remedies. The relatives of the higher-class patients accepted mental illness, although they experienced shame and guilt. The relatives of the lower-class patients rejected the mentally sick, distrusted psychiatry, and displayed feelings of fear, anger, and resentment toward them.

Myers and Roberts (1959), as part of the New Haven study, investigated the psychodynamics of patients belonging to different social classes and also the effect of social mobility on the incidence of mental illness. They found that patients from the lower classes had a weaker ego and poorer control of impulses than those from the higher classes. They were more passive in their attempts to master external reality. Their social inhibitions were internalized to a lesser extent, and they tended to act out, while the upper-class patients tended to act in. The authors found that social upward mobility, particularly when not very successful—the strainer syndrome—led to psychological maladjustment. This last finding has a bearing on the anomie theory of mental illness. A subject who is straining to attain a higher social status but has insufficient means at his disposal becomes maladjusted and may react by developing a mental illness. This would be a case of means-ends imbalance and fits Merton's paradigm of anomie. In an open society, where vertical mobility is assumed to be high, members of the lower classes when they find it difficult to attain culturally desirable goals blame themselves for failure and are expected to have a higher incidence of mental illness.

Murphy (1969) has pointed to some methodological difficulties in studies attempting to find the relation between mental illness and social class. According to him, there is not one system of stratification in America but several, allowing an individual to use more than one frame of reference in defining his social status. Further, there is an important question whether in America social classes are discontinuous entities or whether there is one continuum of social statuses. If the latter is the case, there is no class consciousness. The cultural goals are the same for all the occupiers of the social status continuum. Since no class barriers are perceived, achieving a high status depends on one's effort and perseverance. If one fails, it is his own fault and he should blame only himself. This condition produces an anomie strain and increases the risk of mental illness in persons who occupy low social positions.

The anomie theory of mental illness is fraught with serious difficulties. First it deals with populations rather than with individuals. The association between high rates of mental illness and social structures does not explain why a particular individual becomes ill. Second, if mental illness is a form of social deviance, the theory of anomie does not explain why certain individuals become drug addicts, others hoboes, and still others schizophrenics. There must be some personality determinants responsible for the choice of deviance. Finally, most studies have established only an association between mental illness and particular social structures. They have not established causal relations. Alternative explanations to those offered by the anomie theorists have been suggested. Thus, the drift hypothesis has been offered as an explanation for the high rates of schizophrenia in the transition zone of the city and in the low social classes. According to the drift hypotheses, constitutionally handicapped, incompetent individuals who are incipient schizophrenics tend to drift to low cost housing and low status jobs (Myerson, 1941). If this hypothesis is true, we are dealing with social selection and, essentially, biological causation. Another theory is that of visibility of symptoms and tolerance of mental illness by the community (Buck, Wanklin, & Hobbs, 1955). According to this hypothesis the differences in the rates of schizophrenia may be due to a greater tolerance of its symptoms by some communities than others. It may also be that middle-class families tend to shield their sick relatives, while unattached patients draw the attention of strangers to themselves. The third hypothesis that has been offered (Gerard & Houston, 1953; Hare, 1956) is the opposite of the previous one. It states that schizophrenics or incipient schizophrenics seek anonymity because they find interpersonal relations trying. So as to secure social isolation, they migrate to big cities and live in rooming houses, where they are left to their own devices. More recent studies (Vaughn & Leff, 1976) indicate that social isolation and anonymity sought by incipient schizophrenics may be a defence mechanism preventing an overt psychotic breakdown. It shields them from interpersonal contacts and intense emotional relationships and the emotional expressiveness characterizing the milieu of their families. Again, the last two theories suggest the presence of social selection rather than of social causation. Dunham (1964) has proposed a social selection theory of schizophrenia. He believes that some individuals are by genetic constitution and personal experiences predisposed to develop schizophrenia. When the social structures they occupy tilt towards a state of disequilibrium, some of these potential schizophrenics are selected to play the schizophrenic roles. Consequently, a state of anomie does not cause schizophrenia but only selects predisposed individuals for schizophrenic roles.

To conclude our discussion of the macrosocial structural-functionalist model of mental illness, certain of its general features and assumptions will be mentioned. This model assumes that society is a system that strives to maintain a state of equilibrium. This presupposes an integration of parts and their subordination to the whole. The stress is on the statics of equilibrium rather than the dynamics of change. In terms of systems theory, the model has the features of a closed system with an emphasis on negative feedbacks. In societal terms, it implies the ideal of an unchanging, traditionalist society with an emphasis on consensus and conformity. The key concept is that of anomie or social disorganization described as social pathology. The latter is reflected in individual pathology, maladjustment, and deviant behaviour. Mental illness is regarded as a form of social deviance. A continuity is presupposed between a severe mental illness such as schizophrenia and such manifestations of social maladjustment as family breakdown, alcoholism, drug abuse, sexual promiscuity, illegitimate childbirth, juvenile delinquency, and crime. The model is therefore a continuity model in which psychosis merges into psychoneurosis and the latter into the manifestations of mild maladjustment. Moreover, these conditions merge with other forms of social deviance and are not essentially different from them. Causes and precipitating factors of mental illness are considered to lie in a malfunctioning of society. They arise from faulty socialization processes in childhood or from a warped social structure under strain. As far as therapy is concerned, the stress is on prevention rather than on cure. Mental illness could be prevented and perhaps also cured by amelioration of social conditions by piecemeal social engineering. No revolutionary, sweeping changes of the system are envisaged. Instead, social amelioration and prevention of mental illness are brought about within the existing system by propping it up. The system is taken for granted, and an endeavour is made to render it again functional and working. Mental health is synonymous with conformity and internalization of the existing social values and role expectancies.

The recent development of community psychiatry may serve as an illustration of the preventive and therapeutic measures inspired by this model of mental illness. Gerald Caplan, in an influential book *Principles of Preventive Psychiatry* (1964), points out that the important function of the community psychiatrist is to give advice to legislators regarding legislation that could affect mental health and to participate in the planning and administration of the governmental agencies dealing with mental illness. In short, he is perceived as a social engineer working to improve community mental health.

The Conflict (Diachronic) Model

The social conflict tradition in sociological theory is most conspicuously represented by Karl Marx (1946, 1963), Georg Simmel (1955), and more recently, Ralf Dahrendorf (1959) and Lewis Coser (1956). All these authors, although differing in many important respects, stress social processes and change rather than the static social order. They attach a great importance to conflicts among groups and between man and society. Conflict is regarded as a creative force working for change and shaping the destiny of man and his society. To use an analogy from linguistics, this model is *diachronic* since it emphasizes change over time rather than an equilibrium and a status quo. In terms of systems theory, society may be described as an open system, with many positive as well as negative feedbacks. Such a system is unstable and prone to change. Certain types of conflict and deviance are valued positively for initiating social change, while consensus and conformity are viewed as manifestations of stagnation leading to deadening sterility.

With regard to models of mental illness, the most important tradition stems from the early writings of Marx. In contrast to his later works in which he dealt mainly with economics and philosophy of history, in his early writings young Marx addressed humanistic problems, in particular to the problem of alienation (Kaufmann, 1970). He took the concept of alienation from Hegel and offered an interpretation within the context of his contemporaneous capitalist society. Marx was concerned with the plight of the industrial workers labouring in factories. In contrast to the artisans of Medieval society, these workers were alienated both from the product of their labour and from one another.

The concept of alienation is discussed in philosophical, theological, psychiatric, and sociological literature (Schacht, 1970). Three core meanings of alienation may be discerned: the alienation from nature, the alienation from society, and the alienation from self. The last two are particularly important in the present context. In sociological literature they cover such phenomena as subjective feelings of loneliness, lack of solidarity with others, meaninglessness of one's work, and powerlessness about controlling one's destiny and influencing the course of political events. Erich Fromm and Karen Horney use the concept of self-alienation in the clinical context to explain a stunted personality growth and the causation of psychoneurosis.

While anomie is the key concept for the explanation of mental illness and social deviance in the structural-functionalist framework, alienation is the key explanatory concept in the context of the conflict diachronic theories. While anomie refers to the state of a society, alienation refers always to the state of an individual. Although anomie constitutes a condition of the social system, it is reflected in subjective experiences characterized by a feeling that the world and oneself in it are adrift with no stable moorings and rules. Many authors have commented (Nettler, 1957; Seeman, 1959) on the similarity of the experiences associated with the states of anomie and of alienation. Both are described as feelings of meaninglessness, purposelessness, powerlessness, normlessness, loneliness, and estrangement from the cultural values. However, in spite of the superficial similarity the connotations and the theoretical contexts of the two concepts are quite different. Alienation implies a feeling of dissatisfaction with the existing social order and a desire to change it by revolutionary or evolutionary means. Individual dissatisfaction can be potentially channelled into a social movement aimed at social change.

In an important paper, *The dehumanization of anomie and alienation: A problem in the ideology of sociology*, John Horton (1964) points to different historical and ideological roots of the two concepts. The concept of anomie originated with Durkheim and that of alienation with Marx. These concepts stem from radically different ideologies with "different directives for action, they describe essentially the same behaviour and discontents, but from polar opposite perspectives, which look for different causes and call for different remedies" (Horton, 1964). While anomie is concerned with adequacy of social control, alienation is concerned with its legitimacy. It is concerned with the power structure of the society and the legitimacy of it. Durkheim and Marx had radically different conceptions of the relation of man to society. Durkheim had a transcendental conception of society, as something that is imposed on man to which he passively submits, accepting of its moral constraints. In contrast, Marx had an immanent conception of the relationship between man and the society. According to this view, society is an extension of man; it is his creation. Man actively creates society and in turn is moulded by it. The process is dialectic, in which both human nature is changing, attaining new values, and new social forms are created. Far from being a passive product of society, man is the creator of it. Society is an expression of the humanity of man and is eventually to become the embodiment of humanistic values. The dialectic relationship between self and society, the creative nature of man, and the importance of humanistic values have not been emphasized by all brands of Marxism.* These aspects, which are important for mental health, have been emphasized by the Frankfurt school of social philosophy as represented by the writings of Habermas (1971), Marcuse (1964), and Fromm.

The underlying assumption of the concept of anomie is a mechanistic model of man (Harre & Secord, 1972): man as a passive object buffeted by external forces, malleable, and cast in the mould of his culture, who becomes disoriented without social controls. In

---

*The orthodox version of Marxism stresses to a much greater extent the economic and the social class determinism of human behaviour. Also, according to the orthodox view, social change is determined to a greater extent by the laws of history than by individual choices.

contrast, the assumption underlying the concept of alienation is an anthropomorphic model of man (Harre & Secord, 1972), man as an active agent self-determining his behaviour in a dialectic spiral of interaction with the society. Further, the concept of anomie implies an acceptance of cultural relativism. Different sets of cultural values, as long as they are functionally consistent, can produce a stable social system. Its destabilization produces a state of anomie. On the other hand, the concept of alienation implies that man is free from alienation only in a society that embodies the humanistic values and humanistic ethics. Therefore, the state of genuine mental health is tantamount to the realization of humanistic values immanent in every human personality. Only societies embracing such values are healthy and are conducive to human growth and creativity. Anomie is a value-free concept, while the concept of alienation implies the acceptance of the humanistic values and ethics.

The Alienation Model of Mental Illness

The model of mental disease based on the concept of a sick society and the alienation of man has been developed by Erich Fromm (1941, 1955, 1961). In his discussion, Fromm goes beyond purely sociological and psychological considerations and enters the realm of philosophy. He is concerned with the human predicament of being endowed with consciousness and rationality, which alienates man from nature. Man tries either to enslave nature or to become disengaged from it. A new unity with nature can be achieved through productive work, creativity, and actualization of man's potential. However, the desire to be reunited with nature may misfire and lead to attempts to become submerged in the environment and regress to a prehuman existence. Within the social context this leads to a desire to merge with society, compulsive conformity, and self-alienation. Only a society that allows man to realize fully his creative human potential brings about a genuine reconciliation of man with nature. Fromm (1955) discusses such a society in his book *The Sane Society* and contrasts it with the present American capitalist society, which he considers to be sick. He asks whether a whole society can be sick and whether people who conform to such a society, although considered normal by their peers, are not also sick. He answers these questions in the following way (1955):

To speak of a whole society as lacking in mental health implies controversial assumption contrary to the position of *sociological relativism* held by most social scientists today. They postulate that each society is normal inasmuch as it functions, and the pathology can be defined only in terms of the individual's lack of adjustment to the ways of life in his society.

To speak of "sane society" implies a premise different from sociological relativism. It makes sense only if we assume that there can be a society which is *not* sane, and this assumption, in turn, implies that there are universal criteria for mental health which are valid for the human race as such, and according to which the state of health of each society can be judged. This position of *normative humanism* is based on a few fundamental premises.

Furthermore he states:

The approach of *normative humanism* is based on the assumption that as in any other problem, there are right and wrong, satisfactory and unsatisfactory solutions to the problem of human existence. Mental health is achieved if man develops into full maturity according to the characteristics and laws of human nature. Mental illness consists in the failure of such a development. From this premise the criterion of mental health is not one of individual adjustment to a given social order, but a universal one, valid for all men, of giving a satisfactory answer to the problem of human existence.

To attain maturity, man has to satisfactorily solve certain conflicts and satisfy certain needs. Fromm believes that the modern capitalist society does not satisfy the human needs for relatedness, love, creativity, rootedness, identity, and a frame of orientation. Therefore, it is a sick society in which men are exploited, have to perform monotonous, meaningless tasks, and are manipulated by mass media. The stress on competition, on marketing, and on contractual relationships leads to the dehumanization of man and to his self-alienation. The self-alienated man is a compulsive conformist, whose aim in life is to keep up with the Joneses. His personality growth is stunted. He fails to attain freedom, spontaneity, and genuine self-expression.

The social structure and the ideology of a capitalist society are associated with certain typical personality orientations. In the marketing orientation, man tries to sell himself in the market. To do that he has to be attuned to the demands of buyers and to please them. He has no inner standards but rather is guided by those of the marketplace. He is, to use David Riesman's term, an other-directed man (Riesman, Glazer, & Denney, 1950). The receptive orientation is that of consumerism, an unsatiated desire for material goods and for conspicuous consumption. This attitude fostered by the capitalist society stunts personal growth and limits freedom, spontaneity, and creativity. It produces a socially patterned personality defect, normative for the whole society. The majority of people handicapped by this defect are on the surface quite well-adjusted and are free from manifest neurotic and psychotic symptoms. However, their life lacks in meaning; they are not capable of genuine love, and their creativity is stunted. Some of them fail in their attempts to conform and succeed. They may develop an overt psychoneurosis. This type of neurosis has no potential for personality growth, productive orientation, and social change. However, a few may develop an existential type of psychoneurosis, which has a potential for positive personality development and for enhancement of mental health. These people become vaguely aware of the meaninglessness and purposelessness of their lives and of the lack of satisfaction of their human needs. In the attempt to regain self-autonomy, they become alienated from their society. Although from the point of view of the sick society, these individuals are maladjusted, by the standards of normative humanism they are mentally healthier than the conforming majority. They question the values of their society and may set up the nucleus of a social movement, bringing about a change. This creative deviance eventuates in genuine self-expression, originality, and a freedom from the shackles of conformity. However, sometimes alienation from the society becomes extreme and leads to schizophrenic withdrawal into a private, autistic world.

According to Fromm, the sane society, a society where man is not alienated but free to develop his human potential, is the one embodying the principles of humanistic commuterian socialism. Fromm rejects state socialism, as represented in Soviet Russia and China. In these systems, the capitalist employers are replaced by the state bureaucrats, and the state of alienation of the working masses continues. The commuterian society will stress the dignity and equality of man. It will encourage a participation of workers in decision-making processes. Creative aspects of work will be emphasized, and the productive orientation will replace the marketing and receptive ones.

In his theory of the insane and sane society, Fromm offers a sociological model of mental illness. The important feature of this model is the notion that adjustment and conformity to the demands of a sick society are manifestations of mental ill-health, while deviance and psychoneurosis may be manifestations of superior mental health. Mental illness is an expression of the state of alienation of man. Since the relation between the self and the society varies continually between the extreme of complete self-alienation and merging with the society and that of complete alienation from society, Fromm's theory is a continuity model of mental illness, with normality located somewhere near the middle between the two extremes of alienation.

The Labelling Model of Mental Illness

The labelling model of mental illness is an extension of the labelling model of social deviance. This model has both macrosocial and microsocial aspects. At the microlevel, its framework is provided by the theory of symbolic interactionism (Cooley, 1929; Mead, 1972; Blumer, 1969) and at the macrolevel by the conflict theory of society. Those authors who study social processes, by which the individuals labelled accept deviant roles, are operating mainly within the interactionist framework. Those who are dealing with the political implications of labelling operate mainly within the conflict theory framework.

The labelling model of social deviance is primarily applied to criminal behaviour. According to this model criminality is not intrinsic to the act itself but rather arises from the societal reaction to it — its social definition. Moreover, there is a subtle transference from the definition of acts as being criminal to the definition of individuals who commit them as criminals (Tannenbaum, 1938). In the process the labelled criminal or other social deviant becomes identified with the role into which the society casts him. Edwin Lemert (1951, 1964) postulated the existence of primary and secondary deviance. Many people occasionally break laws and violate norms due to momentary situational factors, but they do not perceive themselves as criminals. This is described by Lemert as primary deviance. If a violation of law leads to a criminal charge and has the consequence of branding the perpetrator as a criminal, a deviant, it may cause a rapid change in his self-image and his social status identification. The social stigmatization and the associated rejection by the conforming majority results in secondary deviance. The deviant role becomes dominant and the individual starts to perceive himself as occupying permanently that social role. He becomes committed to the new role and the new style of life, thereby becoming a member of a deviant subculture. His norms cease to be the norms of the conforming majority but become those of that subculture. Howard Becker (1963) talks about deviant careers—the sequence of events leading to a commitment to a deviant style of life. Each episode of stigmatization leads to a stronger identification with the deviant role. There is a discontinuity between primary and the secondary deviance. At a certain point in the transition process a break occurs, the individual's self-perception becomes restructured, and his perception of the deviant role becomes the most salient. Becker asks who set the rules that are broken by the deviant. His answer is that the rules are set by those wielding political and economic power over the poor and disadvantaged. Thus, labelling is an expression of a social conflict that pits the dominant, conforming group against deviant subcultures.

Thomas Scheff (1966, 1967, 1975) has extended the theory of labelling to mental illness. His particular interest is in the social processes by which a person is defined as a schizophrenic. In his *Being Mentally Ill*, Scheff (1966) offers a social system model of schizophrenia to complement the medical and psychological approaches without denying the validity of the latter two. From the social system point of view, psychotic behaviour involves a violation of social norms, which leads to negative social sanctions, as does any other case of deviance. His theory has two basic components: that of social role and that of societal reaction.

Mental illness, particularly in the chronic stage, involves playing a social role imposed on the individual by the societal reaction. This condition leads to repeated hospitalization and chronicity. The patient follows the slippery path of a deviant career. The theory does not apply to the initial stage but to the stage in which the patient has been stigmatized, labelled a schizophrenic, and segregated from the rest of the community. To put it differently, it applies to the stage of secondary deviance. Every type of deviance, such as crime, heresy, and sexual perversion, involves breaking social rules or norms. Some rules are clearly defined and even enshrined in law; others are part of a code of ethics or etiquette. All these rules are clearly defined, and a person who breaks them is labelled a criminal, a pervert, a sinner, or an ill-mannered person. There are, however, certain rules of behaviour and social interaction that are implicitly accepted by everybody, they go without saying, whose violation is unthinkable by the members of a society. A person who follows these rules is considered to behave sensibly and intelligibly. He can be understood and one can empathize with him. Thus, there are certain linguistic rules that make our speech coherent and intelligible to the members of our linguistic community and, hence, make communication possible. Similarly, there are implicit rules of social interaction described by Scheff as the residual rules and the act of breaking them is referred to as residual deviance. When confronted with criminal behaviour or moral depravity, we may condemn them and feel indignant. However, we feel that we can understand the motives behind the behaviour and its purpose. Confronted with residual rule-breaking we find it bizarre and we feel puzzled and flabbergasted. We cannot understand it. We feel that the assumptions of our consensual social world are undermined. The reaction to residual deviance, which people find threatening to their notion of rationality, reality, and predictability of the world, is to deny it or to categorize it by putting a culturally derived label on it.

Various labels are used in different cultures to categorize a motley of residual rule breaking. Residual deviance may be labelled as witchcraft, black magic, or spirit possession. In the Western culture it is labelled as mental illness or schizophrenia. Most instances of residual rule-breaking are ignored or explained away as a momentary aberration, joking, or personal eccentricity. Residual deviance may be due to a variety of causes such as fatigue, intoxication, some temporary indisposition, emotional stress, and acts of innovation or defiance. It is usually an evanescent condition of a short duration, without a tendency to become crystallized into a permanent behaviour pattern. Only a minority of cases of residual deviance are labelled as mental illness. Whether a residual rule-breaker is labelled as insane or schizophrenic depends on the visibility of his acts and on the severity of the social reaction. The latter, in turn, depends on the social status of the rule-breaker. If he is a person of a low social status, poor, or a member of a minority group, he is more likely to be labelled as insane than a high status person. The norm-bearers of the society, those who set the rules and are agents of social control, are members of the power elite. They are more likely to label as insane somebody far away on the social distance scale than somebody close by. In the latter case they use the mechanism of denial. Other factors are the tolerance level of the community for deviance and the availability of other labels such as, for instance, that of a religious mystic or a member of a counterculture.

Presumably, once an individual is labelled mentally sick, he is cast into a social role, which he is enjoined to play by the persons with whom he interacts. The role is that of a stereotyped madman or a schizophrenic. A mentally sick person becomes identified with his role. It determines his self-concept. His behaviour becomes crystallized and stabilized, and he enters the phase of the secondary deviance. He is rewarded for playing the role of a madman and punished for an attempt to abandon it. Goffman (1961) refers to this sequence of events as the moral career of mental patients. Michael Balint (1957) has postulated a similar role-shaping in neurotic and even organic patients by a doctor who has preconceived ideas about the symptoms of various diseases. In the early stages of therapy there is a process of bargaining between the doctor and the patient. By exercising his apostolic function the doctor by subtle means suggests what he expects the patient's symptoms to be. In most of the cases, the patient accepts the suggestion and starts playing the expected role. Similarly, in mental hospitals the psychiatric aides shape the behaviour of patients so that it conforms to the image of a chronic schizophrenia.

The stereotype of madman, which defines the role of the mental patient, is deeply ingrained in our culture. Its imagery is embedded in the common language, constantly reinforced by the mass media, and internalized by every child in the process of socialization. Consequently, a person so labelled has no difficulty in entering into the role of a schizophrenic. The process of becoming mad consists of a series of interactions. Society reacts to a residual deviance, which produces the label. The labelled person reacts to being labelled leading to further societal reaction, and so on. While the primary deviance phase is continuous with normality, the secondary one is discontinuous. In the eyes of the society, which does the labelling, the mentally sick belong to a qualitatively different category from normals.

The presentation of the labelling theory by Scheff (1966) emphasizes interaction processes rather than that of social conflict. This early version could fit well the structuralist-functionalist schema, with labelling representing a social control mechanism to maintain the stability of the society. In subsequent writings on the subject, Scheff (1975) has quite explicitly adopted the neo-Marxist version of the conflict model of society. In his paper entitled *Labelling Theory as Ideology and as Science,* Scheff (1975) states that labelling individuals as schizophrenics by psychiatrists and other medical doctors constitutes an affirmation of the ideology of the American capitalist society. The doctors are not making value-free judgements regarding objectively existing phenomena but rather are passing moral judgements on the behaviour of human beings. In doing so, they are upholding the values and the world view of the society to which they belong. They are social agents who endeavour to maintain the status quo. Referring to psychiatric symptoms, Scheff states, "Far from being culture-free such 'symptoms' are themselves offences against implicit understandings of particular culture" (1975). Following Mannheim (1936), Scheff believes that every culture or historical epoch has its ideology, an intense and unconscious commitment to a particular view of reality and to the status quo. This ideology is upheld by the ruling classes, the conforming majority, and social enforcement agents. It is threatened by psychiatric symptoms.

In his paper *On Reason and Society: Some Political Implications of Psychiatric Thought,* Scheff (1975) discusses the threat of residual deviance to the moral order of the society. An important dimension of the social view of reality is that of rationality-irrationality. In the tradition of the Western societies, this dimension is conceived of as sanity-insanity. According to Scheff, each culture and each historical epoch have different notions of what is rational and what is irrational. For instance, in the contemporary Western society an outgoing, extraverted, aggressive attitude is regarded as rational and mentally healthy. Introversion and exploration of the inner space is regarded as irrational and morbid. This can be illustrated by the social approval of such dangerous and costly achievements as climbing Mount Everest but the strong disapproval of experimentation with psychedelic drugs and the quest for mystical experiences.* Some tradi-

---

*This example is provided by the present author and not by Scheff.

tional Eastern societies had the opposite view of rationality and irrationality. Since it cannot be rationally explained, residual deviance is particularly threatening. It calls into question the basic assumptions of the culture about social and physical reality. By labelling a case of residual deviance as schizophrenia, the psychiatrist acts as a social agent upholding the current conception of rationality held by a particular society. He plays a political role by upholding the world view of his society and forestalling social change. Therefore, the concept of mental illness and mental health are not value-free. They do not refer to physical facts, but they imply "value choices about what kind of men we *should* be and what kind of values we *should* encourage in our society" (Scheff, 1975). When the psychiatrist describes a schizophrenic as withdrawn and showing thought disorders, hallucinations, and delusions, he passes a negative value judgement on a certain type of behaviour. He reaffirms social disapproval of passivity, inward-dwelling, and indulgence in private fantasy. The psychiatrist, therefore, functions as an accomplice in maintaining the current moral status quo.

In another paper entitled *Labelling Emotion and Individual Change*, Scheff (1975) takes a utopian perspective and discusses the possible amelioration of the present status quo. The present capitalist society places value on hierarchy, order, obedience, and repression of spontaneous emotions. It tends to alienate a man from other men, to categorize and pigeonhole him. The interpersonal relationships characteristic of capitalist society may be described, following Martin Buber (1958), as "I-It" and not as "I-Thou" relations. A society that could be characterized by "I-Thou" relationships would value equality, spontaneity, freedom, reverence for life, camaraderie, and play.

The relationship between schizophrenia and social stratification, as exemplified by the findings of Hollingshead and Redlich (1958), could be reinterpreted within the framework of the conflict theory of society. These authors have found that the incidence of schizophrenia is more common in the lowest social class than in the other classes. Also, patients in the lower social classes are committed more often to mental hospitals and treated by ECT and drugs than patients in the higher classes, who are treated privately by psychotherapy. The reported higher incidence of schizophrenia in the lower than in the higher classes may be a reflection not of a true difference in the rate of incidence but of a greater tendency to label members of the former classes as schizophrenics. The psychiatrist who does the labelling is a member of the upper middle class who perceives a greater social distance between himself and members of the lower classes than between himself and those of his own class. The same symptoms that are regarded as evidence of schizophrenia in a labourer may be viewed by him as an expression of personal eccentricity in a banker or of immaturity in a debutante. Linsky (1970) and Rushing (1971) have found that when the incidence rates of schizophrenia in the lower and upper classes are equated, the lower classes show a much higher rate of involuntary admissions. This finding indicates that the labelling and the degrading commitment procedure is more frequent in the lower than in the upper classes. Labelling of mental illness is therefore a function of the society's power structure. The powerful label the weak as mental patients.

When the structural-functionalist model of mental illness is compared with the conflict model, certain important differences are observed. While the former stresses the stable, unchanging aspect of society, the latter emphasizes social change and dynamics. Consequently, from the structural-functionalist standpoint mental illness and other types of deviance are seen as disturbances of social equilibrium. In the framework of the conflict model, these phenomena are thought to be manifestations of social change and may have positive as well as negative aspects. While the structural-functionalist model purports to be value-free, the conflict model is openly ideologically committed. It unashamedly espouses certain ethical values and advocates their implementation by social change. It rejects the position that mental illness is a value-free, purely scientific concept. The proponents of the conflict model argue that the structural-functionalist point of view is not really value-free. Hidden behind the facade of the supposedly value-free concepts such as anomie and social disintegration is the desire to maintain the status quo of the present society (Friedricks, 1970; Horton, 1964). Far from being ideologically neutral, the structural-functionalist theorists espouse the conservative ideology and the middle-class values of American society.

In the conceptual framework of conflict theory, mental illness is regarded as a product of alienation or of labelling, which occurs in a particular type of society: one torn by conflict, class struggle, and dissent. Therefore, it can be prevented and even cured only by a radical social change. A new, radically different social order will bring about a disappearance of alienation and abolish class struggle. Conditions will be created that allow everyone to self-actualize and attain mental health. In contrast to the structural-functionalist model, which envisages the prevention of mental illness by piecemeal social amelioration within the existing system, the conflict model implies that mental illness can be prevented by a revolutionary change creating a new social system. This change will be implemented by an ideological movement rather than by a pragmatic application of social science engineering.

THE MICROSOCIAL MODELS OF MENTAL ILLNESS

Theoretical Framework

The frame of reference for microsocial models of mental illness are small, face-to-face, primary groups. They may be natural groups such as families or artificial ones such as therapy groups. It is not easy to draw a distinction between micro- and macrosocial phenomena. An individual is embedded in a network of social relations, some of them are intimate face-to-face, others more impersonal occurring in institutionalized settings that are part of the fabric of the whole society. There is a continuum, with small groups such as families and friendship cliques at one end and large social groups such as nations at the other. In between there are groups of intermediate size such as hospitals, schools, villages, and neighbourhoods. Nevertheless, the distinction between the macro and micro points of view is useful because they focus on different aspects of social phenomena.

The microsocial model was influenced by four important theoretical formulations: the sociological theory of symbolic interactionism, the small group dynamics theory of Kurt Lewin, systems theory, and psychoanalytical theory of group psychology.

Symbolic Interactionism

The theory of interactionism, which deals with the problem of the relation of self and mind to society, is of a great importance for the analysis of microsocial phenomena. It considers self to be a product of interpersonal relations within a face-to-face primary group. The latter constitutes, as it were, the looking glass for the developing self (Cooley, 1929). According to Mead (1972) symbolic behaviour is a product of interpersonal interactions. The communicative interactions create shared meanings and reciprocal perspectives in the actors, each of whom takes the other's role and monitors his own role playing through the eyes of the other. The reciprocal relations become incorporated into the self and make speech and behaviour follow mutually shared social rules, appropriate to the situation. The metaphor used by Mead is that of a team playing a game, where the acts of the players have to be mutually congruent, reciprocal, and synchronized. The self-concept is derived from the perception of oneself by the others and from their attitudes. The introjected relations with individual others in the process of development coalesce into that of the generalized other representing the society at large. The self develops within the context of a dialectical relationship between "I" and "me," where the latter is a reflection of the self in the social mirror. This aspect of the symbolic interactionism was developed further by Herbert Blumer (1969) of the Chicago School. Human interaction, according to Blumer, is a creative and indetermined process. The development of self-identity is an ongoing process that cannot be reduced to the totality of the roles into which man is cast by the society.

In contrast, the interactionism of the Iowa school of Manford Kuhn (1964) tends to reduce the self-identity, the "core self," to the totality of the roles one is playing. The individual's behaviour is determined by the expectations associated with the role he is playing. As a result the reciprocal roles are meshed in, interarticulated, and coordinated, making for smooth interactions both at the symbolic and behavioural levels.

The developmental processes postulated by interactionist theory may go astray, leading to a confusion between the role played by the self and the role taken by the self. Faulty role taking may lead to a deficient self-monitoring. It results in impaired role playing and absence of reciprocity with other actors, which may be labelled by the group as strange, alien, or insane. In this framework schizophrenia has been attributed to a breakdown of communication due to faulty role taking and role playing that was caused by defective socialization (Cameron, 1950; Cameron & Magret, 1951). The schizophrenic patient's idiosyncratic thinking is dominated by private fantasy, which creates a paranoid pseudocommunity. As a result, self-perception is at variance with that of the group. This leads to a mistaken self-identity. The reciprocal perspectives of the self and of the imaginary other, the role one is taking and the role one is playing, are often confused, leading to such strange phenomena as hallucinations, delusions, and schizophrenic phenomena of passivity (feelings of thought control by an external agent, feelings that one's thoughts belong to someone else). A distortion in the perception of others that was attributed to defective role-taking has been reported in schizophrenic patients by Diamond (1958) and Milgram (1961). Gough (1948) has proposed a role-taking theory of psychopathy. He maintains that a psychopath cannot take the perspective of another person, cannot perceive himself as an object, and therefore cannot empathize with others.

The group dynamics theory of Kurt Lewin

The theory of group dynamics, proposed by Kurt Lewin and his students (Lewin, 1948; Hare, 1962), arose within social psychology. In the action research, carried out during World War II, these workers attempted to discover underlying dynamic processes responsible for group behaviour. They discovered that in order to obtain a change in the behaviour of its members the whole group had to be influenced. To put it differently, the group determines the behaviour of its members and not the other way around. A group constitutes a gestalt, being more than the sum of its parts. It is controlled by certain dynamic processes that are irreducible to the individual behaviour of its members. Such properties as its cohesiveness, group atmosphere, the degree of equilibrium, and the leadership style characterize the whole group. A group remains in a state of quasistationary equilibrium due to a balance of opposing forces. To change the equilibrium certain forces have to be increased or others reduced. Lewin's work on group dynamics led directly to the development of T-group (training group) techniques. His concepts have been subsequently applied to group therapy.

Systems theory

Lewin's group dynamics may be regarded as a precursor of general systems theory, which came to dominate more recently the area of small group and family research. The latter theory is concerned with the properties of self-regulating systems and was originally developed in the context of biology. According to von Bertalanffy (1966, 1968), the originator of the theory, every organism constitutes a system characterized by a dynamic, hierarchical ordering of parts and processes that interact reciprocally. A system is organized with parts so related to one another that a change in one part produces changes in the other parts of the system. Systems may be divided into closed and open. A closed system does not interact with the external milieu. It tends to attain a state of an irreversible equilibrium. The run-down universe presupposed by the second law of thermodynamics is an example of a closed system. Living organisms are open systems. They utilize external energy and information to maintain a highly improbable state of complexity and organization, a condition of negative entropy. An organism utilizes numerous homeostatic mechanisms to maintain its equilibrium and autonomy. It is separated from the external environment by a semipermeable boundary that controls the input of matter, energy, and information from the environment. A system may be subdivided into relatively autonomous subsystems forming an interdependent hierarchical organization, regulated by feedback mechanisms. An organism is capable not only of maintaining a steady state but also of growth and differentiation, or morphogenesis. It is flexible and may adjust to markedly changed environmental conditions by resetting its homeostatic mechanisms to different levels and reorganizing itself. While negative feedback mechanisms are responsible for maintaining a steady state, homeostasis, or morphostasis, positive feedbacks produce growth and change, or morphogenesis. These two feedback mechanisms, one maintaining the status quo and the other producing growth, change, and innovation, are important for both biological and social systems (Maruyama, 1963).

Although all living systems are basically open, some, depending on preponderance of positive over negative feedbacks, are more open than others. Also, within a living organism, such as human, some subsystems are more open and others more closed. The subsystems regulating purely vegetative functions, such as those maintaining the pH level (acidity) in the blood, are relatively closed. On the other hand, the subsystems responsible for processing external information, learning and symbolic behaviour, which are associated with cerebral functions, are relatively open. Thus, there is a continuum of systems stretching from relatively closed to relatively open. No biological or social system may be entirely closed or entirely open.

General systems theory has been adopted by sociology and, in particular, by the small group theory. Buckley (1967) characterizes a social system as complex and adaptive. While mechanical and biological systems are concerned primarily with the transmission of energy from one component to another, social systems depend on the transmission of information, communication, and symbolic behaviour. Consequently, social systems tend to approach the open end of the system continuum and are relatively unstable. From the point of view of the general systems theory there is a hierarchy of systems, starting at the lowest level with complex protein and DNA molecules, proceeding to cells, continuing through organ systems to the whole human organism. The latter is a part of a social system, such as a family, which in its turn is embedded in a larger social network—the society at large. The systems point of view avoids attributing concreteness and ultimate reality to any of the levels of system hierarchy. The basic principles of systems theory remain the same at all the various levels. However, the systems tend to become more open, more concerned with an exchange of information and symbolic processes, as one ascends the hierarchy from a bodily cell to a social group. The systems approach focuses on the relationships and transactions between parts rather than on the parts themselves. It also is concerned with the general principles underlying these relationships. Cybernetics and the Theory of Information have attempted to develop mathematical formalisms to describe precisely these principles.

The psychoanalytic theory of group psychology

The psychoanalytical contributions to group psychology include the Interpersonal psychiatry of Harry Stack Sullivan and the Object

Relation theory developed in Great Britain by Melanie Klein (1948) and W. R. D. Fairbairn (1954).

Freud, in *Group Psychology and the Analysis of the Ego* (1955a), outlined the psychoanalytical theory of group processes and their relation to the self. However, the individual patient always remained the focus of his theorizing and the target of psychotherapy. Melanie Klein (1948) has developed a theory of the early infant-mother relationship. In the first months of life the infant is not capable of integrating various experiences of the mother and to perceive the mother as a whole object. Instead, the infant perceives only part-objects such as her breast or her face. Moreover, since some of these experiences are associated with pleasure and others with frustration and pain the perceived part-objects are split into the good and bad. The boundary between the self and the external world is poorly defined, leading to the attribution of inner experiences to the external objects and the characteristics of the latter to oneself. There takes place a constant introjection and projection of bad and good part-objects. Klein describes this stage of development as the paranoid schizoid position. During the next developmental stage, the depressive position, the good part-objects are integrated into a whole object representing the mother. However, the integration is incomplete and there are strong ambivalent feelings attached to the introjected object. In later life, the early introjected objects, with the associated feelings and conflicts, become part of the inner world of fantasy. They serve as the models for future interpersonal relations. The bad objects are projected in fantasy on partners in adult relationships with, for example, spouses or children. As a result these relations become warped (Bowlby, 1969; Skynner, 1976). In the same vein, Harry Stack Sullivan (1953) formulated a psychodynamic theory of mother-infant interactions determining future dyadic relationships and having bearing on the etiology of juvenile schizophrenia.

The theory proposed by Fairbairn (1954) presents a more radical departure from the orthodox psychoanalysis. Fairbairn rejects the Freudian and Kleinian assumption that gratification of instinctual bodily needs is the most basic motive of life in human beings. To him the most basic motive is need for satisfactory relationship with other people, or as he calls it, object relationship. According to Barnard and Corrales (1979), the Fairbairnian formulation provides a bridge between intrapsychic dynamics and the interpersonal relations and transactions observed at the level of social systems such as a family or a small group. Fairbairn believes that satisfactory interactions with the significant others constitute the basic need of the human nature. Such interactions give rise to a mixture of satisfying and frustrating experiences. They lead to an introjection of bad and good objects, associated with ambivalent feelings of love and hate. The internal objects become part of the personality structure. Not only the objects but also the relations between the self and the significant others are internalized. The representation of the significant others and their relations to self is split not only to good and bad objects. In addition, each bad object is split further into a libidinal component representing unsatisfied emotional longing for the object and an antilibidinal component representing the hateful and destructive aspects of the relationship. The introjection of objects and their ambivalent relationships into the self leads to internal conflicts between various parts of the ego. These objects and conflicts are later externalized and tested in real situations. They are projected on current interpersonal relations causing these relations to be warped. However, if the current relationships are emotionally satisfying, the distorted images may be corrected, the real persons recognized for what they are, and a basic sense of trust in self and others developed. Many family therapists who use the psychodynamic approach have been influenced by the theories of Fairbairn, Melanie Klein, and Harry Stack Sullivan.

While macrosocial models of mental illness are important from the theoretical and ideological points of view, the microsocial models have practical applications in group psychotherapy. The basic assumption underlying the microsocial models of mental illness can be expressed by a quotation from the book *Family Therapy* by Maurizio Andolfi (1979). After discussing the traditional psychiatric approaches that isolate the sick organism from its context of significant relations (Andolfi, 1979) he states:

> In alternative approach, the individual is observed in an interactional context (family, school, neighbourhood, clan, etc.) in which his "different" behaviour has a specific meaning. Investigation begins by analyzing the relationships existing *here* and *now* between the individual and his interactional system. ...When we consider the family as an interactional system, we see it as something greater than the sum of individual behaviours, and it articulates them in a functional whole.

This statement applies not only to families but also to artificial groups, formed for the purpose of therapy. The emphases of different microsocial models vary. Some stress individual personality psychodynamics in the context of the family or the group, some the group as an emergent entity, and others the interactional processes occurring within the family or group. However, all these models place the locus of the illness not inside an individual but rather in the group as a whole or in its faulty interactions. In family therapy, the patient is the whole family and not the individual who presents symptoms.

The microsocial models can be divided into those related to artificial groups and natural groups. To the first category belong therapy groups and therapeutic communities, to the second nuclear and extended families, friendship cliques, and neighbourhood networks.

Microsocial Models of Mental Illness Related to Artificial Groups

Artificial groups such as those set up for therapeutic purposes are relatively free from institutionally prescribed norms and roles. Norms, roles, and values emerge as a result of group processes. Group psychotherapy and public relations training have a long history going back to the moral treatment of the insane and to social work groups such as one conducted by Jane Addams in the nineteenth century. This history is presented by Shaffer and Galinsky (1974).

Since the second world war, the popularity of group psychotherapy has increased tremendously and the field has burgeoned into a multitude of schools. This development may be attributed to several factors, such as wartime experience with the treatment of psychiatric casualties, a shortage of qualified psychiatrists, and last but not least, the positive value attached in America to the experience of togetherness. New helping professions such as clinical psychologists and social workers were ready to fill the new niche.

In their book, *Models of Group Therapy and Sensitivity Training*, John Shaffer and David Galinsky (1974) have provided a useful review of the area. They divide the whole field into group therapy and human relations, or sensitivity training. Group therapy is concerned with treatment of psychiatric patients, while human relation training deals with growth and development of healthy personalities. Since, with a few exceptions, group therapy methods are also concerned with growth and development of the personalities of the patients rather than a removal of their symptoms and solving specific problems, the division is artificial. Group therapy tries not only to cure diseases but also to improve the positive mental health of its participants. Shaffer and Galinsky further subdivide group therapy into the following seven categories: (1) social work, (2) psychoanalytic therapy, (3) group-dynamic, (4) existential-experiential, (5) psychodrama, (6) gestalt therapy workshops, and (7) behaviour therapy in groups. To these seven categories may be added another one: the transactional analysis developed by Eric Berne (1961), conducted in small groups.

Shaffer and Galinsky (1974) divide the human relations training methods into the following categories: (1) the Tavistock approach to groups, (2) T-groups, (3) the encounter groups, and (4) the theme-centered interaction method. The present concern is with group therapy and its relation to models of mental illness. Only the essential features of various methods will be summarized.

Social work groups

The social work group is concerned with solving social problems, such as deviance, unemployment, and housing, through the use of small group processes. It aims at the adjustment of clients to society, to the best satisfaction of the needs of both sides. This approach combines the group-dynamic conceptualizations such as interactions and group self-regulating processes with the didactic features of behaviour therapy. The group situation is structured, and the goals are clearly defined. The social work group techniques, as applied to psychiatric patients, are almost identical to those of the theme-centred interactional methods used with normals.

Psychoanalytical therapy groups

Psychoanalytical group therapy was originally concerned with psychodynamics of the individual members of the group and their mutual transferences. The horizontal or sibling dimension of transference on group members was stressed in contrast to the vertical or child-parent dimension that is important in the individual psychotherapy dyad (Foulkes, 1965). Since the patient's psychopathology originated in the matrix of family relations, it is believed to be best treated in the social network of a small group. The model of mental illness presupposed by psychoanalytic (psychodynamic) group therapy is basically the same as that based on a single patient. The unconscious motivation and ego defences in the group context are stressed. Importance is attached to the past history of childhood experiences that determine the present symptoms of individual patients and the disturbance of their interpersonal relations. The method of Whitaker and Lieberman (1965) combined the Freudian psychoanalysis with the Lewinian group dynamics.

Group-dynamic approach

Group dynamic therapy focuses on group processes as determinants of individual behaviour. A group attempts to solve the problems and conflicts that produce tension and upset its equilibrium. It establishes its own unique culture, unique values, norms, and role definitions. The deviant behaviour of its members is controlled by other members who become the norm bearers. The members are committed to the group's values and become strongly identified with each other. When a conflict is solved, tension abates and the group equilibrium is restored at a new level, eventuating in its growth. The group dynamic therapy assumes that human beings are members of small groups whose mental health depends on adequate group functioning. A group's malfunctioning, as exemplified by a lack of cohesion, disequilibrium, and dissension, leads to mental illness. These theoretical assumptions stem from the conceptual framework established by Kurt Lewin in his work on group dynamics. Apart from regarding the group as an entity that makes decisions and exerts pressures, this framework has postulated the importance of certain group values. A well functioning or healthy group is believed to be guided by the values of democracy and egalitarianism, while authoritarianism and anarchy cause group and individual sickness. Lewin's framework may be reinterpreted in terms of the systems theory. The latter regards a small group as a network of interpersonal relations and describes its control mechanisms as negative and positive feedbacks. Depending on which feedbacks predominate, a group may be relatively closed, conservative and stable, or open, unstable and changing. The health of the group and its members depends on the proper balance between the mechanisms maintaining stability and those leading to change. The model of mental illness envisaged by this approach focuses entirely on microsocial group processes to the exclusion of the individual.

Existential-experiential groups

The existential-experiential and the encounter group therapies have their roots in the philosophy of existentialism and in humanistic psychology. They focus on the subjective experiences of the group members. The intersubjectivity, the "I-Thou" (Buber, 1958) aspect of human relations, is emphasized. These topics will be discussed in detail in the next chapter. At present, it suffices to say that the existential-experiential method focuses on the immediate experience of the here and now and rejects intellectualization and preoccupation with past history. It denies that current experience and behaviour is determined by past events. The autonomous individual is free to make choices and self-actualize. Group phenomena creatively emerge from human interactions. Therefore, very little structure is imposed on the group. The aim of therapy is the growth and development of the total personality rather than the cure of symptoms. The interaction between the individual and the group leads to the growth of his personality and to evolution of the group to higher levels of functioning. Through interactions of the group members, a sense of a shared world (*Mitwelt*) is created that gives a new meaning to life. The feelings of alienation and loneliness are overcome, false social masks are discarded, and an encounter of authentic selves takes place. The encounter group technique is used in nonclinical settings. It is concerned with existential problems of the individual and his alienation from the dehumanized modern industrial society. Its purpose is to put an alienated individual into contact with himself, his emotional and bodily experiences, and other people. The social roles and labels such as psychiatrist, mental patient, disease, and normality are abandoned. The individual is made aware of the nature of his sensations and bodily feelings in order to break through his character armour (Reich, 1949) and enhance his human potential (Schutz, 1971). In this approach mental illness is equated with alienation, loneliness, and inauthenticity, while mental health is equated with authentic interpersonal relations and creative spontaneity.

The psychodrama technique of Jacob Moreno

The psychodrama technique of Jacob Moreno (1953) bears a great similarity to the existential-experiential group. Moreno, at a young age, developed an abiding interest in drama and believed that it could be utilized for therapeutic purposes. Aristotle, before him, believed that theatre spectators benefitted from watching the performance of a tragedy. They had their souls cleansed of pent-up emotions by the process of catharsis. Moreno maintained that acting out or playing a role is even more beneficial than watching somebody else performing it. Moreover, a minimum of constraint by a script enhances spontaneity and creativity of play acting—Moreno even opened a Theatre of Spontaneity in Vienna in 1921. In psychodrama, he has emphasized action, empathic identification, and catharsis. The stress is on the here and now of immediate experience while enacting a role rather than on the there and then recapitulation of past experiences. During a psychodrama session, a protagonist-patient is enacting spontaneously a role, supported by other players, called auxiliary egos, who empathize and interact with him. There is no constraint on the script and a complete openness about the outcome of the enacted story, which the actors create as they go along.

Gestalt therapy

Gestalt therapy, developed by Perls (1969), was discussed in the previous chapter. This mode of therapy is usually conducted in groups. The participants, in turn, occupy the center of the stage—the chair. They are very often asked to enact particular parts of their personalities or even parts of their bodies. The emphasis is on the moment-to-moment flow of awareness, the immediate experience of the here and now. Intellectualizing and delving into the past is discouraged.

Behaviour therapy in groups

Behaviour therapy, originally developed with individual patients, in recent years has been also applied in group settings. A shortage of trained behaviour therapists undoubtedly contributed to this new development. Three types of behaviour therapy groups are used: systematic desensitization, behavioural practice, and specific behaviour control therapy groups (Shaffer & Galinsky, 1974). Classical and operant techniques are combined with didactic instructions by the group leader who fills the role of expert and teacher. The focus is on the overt behaviour and specificity of behavioural control. The treatment goals are clearly stated and the treatment plan prepared, followed by an objective evaluation of the results. The techniques are concerned with the removal of specific symptoms rather than with curing disease or with personality growth and development. However, more recently the application of group atmosphere as a supportive and reinforcing agent has been stressed by various authors. The members of the group support and reinforce one another in their effort to change the behaviour inside and outside the group situation. This recent development may be viewed as an application to group behaviour therapy of the exchange theory (Homans, 1950; Turner, 1978). In behavioural practice groups, the emphasis is on role-playing and practising of new interpersonal skills, such as assertiveness. In that respect this technique is similar to psychodrama. However, while psychodrama stresses spontaneity and creativity, in behaviour practice groups the setting is rigidly structured and roles are specifically prescribed and articulated. The script is predetermined by the group leader. The implied model of mental illness is behaviouristic, as was discussed in the previous chapter. However, the group approach attaches a great importance to social reinforcement.

The transactional psychotherapy of Eric Berne

This is a proper place to describe briefly the transactional analysis psychotherapy of Eric Berne (1961), which was not included in the Shaffer and Galinsky review. The theory proposed by this author consists of two closely related parts. The first is a theory of personality structure, a variant of Freudian ego psychology. In his discussion of this topic, Berne refers very often to P. Federn (1952), an early ego psychologist. He calls mental structure, roughly corresponding to the Freudian id, the archeopsyche, the one to the ego neopsyche, and the one to the superego the exteropsyche. In contrast to the Freudian formulation, he regards the three parts of psyche as approaching the status of autonomous personalities. Each of them in turn may monopolize the field of consciousness, producing different ego states. The ego state dominated by the neopsyche is called the Adult, the one by the archeopsyche the Child, and the one by the exteropsyche the Parent. Phenomenologically different qualities of awareness characterize the three ego states. They are separated from one another by boundaries, but they can interpenetrate. According to Berne, in normals and neurotics the real self resides in the Adult, while in psychotics it is located in the Child. In neurotics the boundary between the Adult and the Child is poorly defined, and they tend to interpenetrate each other. Psychic life is a continuum with the ego states following one another. Normally, experiences are integrated with the help of dreams into the mainstream of mental development. However, traumatic experiences warp the smooth evolution of psyche producing dissociations or interpenetrations between certain ego states. Interpenetrations between the Parent and the Adult and the Child and the Adult may cause hallucinations and delusions.

The second part of Berne's theory addresses the problems of social psychiatry and the interpersonal transactions occurring in small groups, which serve as a vehicle of psychotherapy. Berne assumes that people have a strong need for patterned social interactions. These patterns are provided by social customs and rituals, which are called by him pastimes. However, some patterns are idiosyncratic and are called games. An individual playing a game programs his interactions in such a way as to draw other persons to be his partners. In his interpersonal relations, such an individual repeats the same game as a defence against intimacy and authenticity. Games, or ulterior transactions, are aimed at manipulating other people. In psychotherapeutic groups, transactions occur between members who may be experiencing different ego states. In such settings, the purpose of the analysis of transactions and games is to help the members of the group attain insight into their warped interpersonal relations. The individual psychodynamics, as reflected in the interpersonal transactions, are revealed. At the same time the importance of true self and the authentic intimacy, characterizing the "I-Thou" relations, is emphasized. The transactional analysis combines the features of the psychoanalytic and existential-experiential group psychotherapies. Therefore, it implies the model of mental illness that is a combination of the psychoanalytical and of the existential.

In their review of the subject, Shaffer and Galinsky (1974) single out the following dimensions along which group therapy methods can be compared: (1) the focus on the group versus the focus on the individual, (2) treatment of the symptoms, or disease, versus personality growth goals, (3) gratification of needs versus frustration of needs, and (4) a highly structured format versus a relatively unstructured one. To these four points, a fifth may be added: (5) a stress on the here and now present situation versus a stress on the there and then past history.

Therapeutic Community

In the discussion of microsocial models it is necessary to mention also some larger groups, such as the therapeutic community developed by Maxwell Jones (1953). The therapeutic community is a hospital community. It is larger than a therapy group but is still characterized by face-to-face group properties. The purpose of it is to replace the highly structured and hierarchical organization of the traditional hospital, where the patient and the various professional roles are rigidly defined (Stanton & Schwartz, 1954). Goffman (1961) has coined the name of "total institution" to describe the typical highly stratified and regimented mental hospital. A therapeutic community is egalitarian and democratic. There is no clear division between the roles of the staff and of the patients. The values and norms are not imposed from the outside but rather emerge as a result of group processes, providing a therapeutic milieu for the patients. In contrast, the traditional mental hospital is considered to be antitherapeutic.

Microsocial Models of Mental Illness Related to Natural Groups

By far the most important in this category are the models related to family therapy. In the past thirty years this therapeutic procedure has become very prominent. It has spawned an immense literature and has produced a great number of different schools. A detailed review of the topic is beyond the scope of this book. Sociologists, anthropologists, social and developmental psychologists, psychiatrists, clinical psychologists, social workers, linguists, and communication engineers have all made contributions to the field of family studies.

In contrast to the traditional medical model, family therapists locate the pathology not in an individual patient who may present the symptoms but in the whole family. In their theorizing, these workers stress interactions and communications processes within the whole family system, instead of linear causality. The family is both a cultural institution and a group of interacting unique personalities. As an institution it occupies a peculiarly crucial and central position. It is a social and cultural microcosm facing inwardly towards the individual and outwardly towards society. The family plays an important role in providing the individual with his earliest social experiences and in instilling in him the mores and values of his culture. It turns a biological organism into a person who is a member of a society by providing him with a self-identity within a matrix of interpersonal relations. Finally, it schools the child in the symbolic processes of thought, language, and communication. In addition, the family provides for satisfaction of biological needs, such as sexuality between the parents, and the needs for security and belongingness in all family members.

The differentiation of self depends on the internalization of social roles played by the family members. According to Parsons and Bales (1955), in the nuclear family of procreation the father, or the male, plays an adaptive-instrumental role and the mother, or the female, an integrative-expressive role. The generality of this statement is disputed by Elizabeth Bott (1957), who in her study in England has found a variety of conjugal roles, and by Jule Henry (1951), who argues that every family creates its own role definitions. Parsons and Bales (1955) view personality development and socialization as a process of a progressive differentiation brought about by internalization of the reciprocal role interactions of the family system. These formulations influenced many early workers in the field of family therapy. While anthropologists and sociologists are preoccupied mainly with the family as a cultural institution in the context of the general cultural pattern and social structure, the interest of social psychologists and psychiatrists lies in the family as a unity of interacting personalities (Burgess, 1926). In the context of mental health, the first approach addresses such problems as, for example, the effect of cultural value conflict on socialization processes. The second approach is concerned with family interpersonal dynamics and interactions involved in pathological and therapeutic processes. While the family as a social institution is of interest to the macrosocial approach to mental illness, the family as a uniquely interacting social group is the focus of the microsocial approach.

The Structure and Dynamics in Normal and Abnormal Families

The family as a social system is a structure maintained by dynamic forces that perform certain functions. Hess and Handel (1959) postulate four basic problems with which every family is confronted: (1) a proper balance between separateness (autonomy) of the family members and their connectedness (integration) as a family unit, (2) a satisfactory congruence of the family image or theme formed in the minds of its members, (3) the establishment of boundaries of the family world of experience (physical and social reality), and (4) satisfactory solution of such biosocial problems as sexuality, status, power, and generation boundary. Using the idiom of general system theory, Barnard and Corrales (1979) pointed out that a normally functioning or healthy family maintains a proper balance between stability and change. It maintains the self-identity and autonomy of its members combined with a sense of family solidarity. The latter is particularly important in the relationship between husband and wife. Within a normal family, person-to-person communications are clear, honest, direct, and unambiguous, and the generational boundaries (parental and child roles) are clearly defined. The characteristic of healthy families that is stressed by all family theorists is the individuality or separateness of family members in the context of their relatedness.

In recent years, the field of family study has come to be dominated by systems theory stressing the processes of interaction and communication. The concepts of boundary, positive and negative feedbacks, subsystems, and input and output have become paramount. Also, different types of normal families have been discerned, each having its own solution to optimal functioning. Thus, what is normal for one type of family may be abnormal for another. A theory of the processes occurring inside the family proposed by David Kantor and William Lehr (1975) illustrates the systems approach. According to them there are three basic subsystems in the family system: the family unit subsystem, the interpersonal subsystem, and the personal subsystem. They interact with each other as well as with the external world. The recurrent purposive patterns of interactions, which are meaningful to the participants, constitute family strategies concerned with attaining certain goals or targets. These targets are affect, power, and meaning. Families differ in the structural arrangement of their interactional process, particular strategies used to attain goals, and the optimal states aimed at. According to Kantor and Lehr there are three basic family types differing in the homeostasis models associated with them. The first is the closed type, the second open, and the third random. These terms are relative since a completely closed, open, or random family system could not function. The purpose of the closed family system is to maintain stability of family interactional processes. The open family system aims at adaptation of the needs of both the individuals and the family. The purpose of the random family system is free exploration. The ideals of the closed family are to be stable, to have clearly defined boundaries and a hierarchical power structure, and to maintain a permanent identity. Those of the open family system are the democratic exercise of power, decisions based on consensus, adaptive identity, rationality, tolerance, and authenticity. Finally, unlimited individual freedom, the *laissez faire* attitude, creativity, ambiguity, diversity, and originality are the ideals of the random family. There is a similarity between these three family system types and the social climates of groups subjected to the three different kinds of leadership, autocratic, democratic, and *laissez faire*, described by Lippitt and White (1943), who were students of Kurt Lewin.

Families as social systems are based on the reciprocal interactions of roles. In formulating a theory of the interactive processes, it is important to designate the elementary unit of interaction. The early theorists based their models on the dyadic interaction units. As the conceptual models of family grew in complexity, the triadic interaction, or the triangle, became the basic unit. A triad consists usually of two parents and a child who is used as scapegoat by the former. Fogarty (1972) defines a triangle as "a closed system with sum of the distance between the three members remaining fixed." Other triangles also may be formed, and the whole family may be described in terms of overlapping triadic interactions (Bowen, 1966). Kantor and

Lehr (1975) describe their basic unit as a four-player system consisting of mover, follower, opposer, and bystander roles. The mover initiates a certain strategy, the follower follows him, the opposer counteracts the strategy move, and the bystander watches from the sidelines.

In the sociological and psychiatric literature on the family, two basic dimensions of its functioning have often been described: adaptability and cohesion. Adaptability has already been mentioned in connection with the closed and open family systems. In a closed system, negative regulatory feedbacks predominate. They maintain a state of homeostasis or morphostasis. As a result, a closed family is stable, maintains the status quo, and tends to be rigid. It functions well when the changes of milieu are relatively limited so that the homeostatic mechanisms of the system can cope with them and maintain the status quo. However, more extreme changes put too much strain on these mechanisms and the system breaks down. It has a low adaptability. On the other hand, in an open system there is a preponderance of positive feedbacks that potentiates any slight deviation from the status quo and causes a change in the system. The latter is characterized by morphogenesis rather than morphostasis (Speer, 1970). An open family is more flexible, more adaptable, and even shows spontaneous growth. When the circumstances are markedly changed, such a family adapts better than a closed one. The closed and open are not discrete categories but two extreme poles of the adaptability continuum. If the terminology of Kantor and Lehr (1975) is used, the extreme ends of the continuum are respectively the closed and random (super-open) categories, with the open in the middle. Wertheim (1975) proposed a similar continuum with closed, partly open, and open categories. The dimension of adaptability of normal families was found to be important in time of crisis, transition, and social change (Hill, 1949; Rappaport, 1962). However, while adaptability is functionally beneficial, its excess leads to a lack of stability. In the context of family therapy the general consensus is that optimally functioning families lie in the middle range of the adaptability continuum, showing proper balance between flexibility and stability, or between the morphogenic and morphostatic processes (Wertheim, 1975). A family that is too unstable will develop centrifugal forces leading to its disintegration. On the other hand, a family that lacks in flexibility and is excessively rigid finds adjustment to society difficult and tends to stultify the personality development of its members.

The other dimension is that of cohesion, or the connectedness-separateness continuum, already mentioned in connection with the discussion of Hess and Handel's (1959) theory. This dimension has been of a great interest to family therapists, particularly those working with families of schizophrenic patients. It is related to the self-autonomy problem of a unique individual, who yet maintains a satisfactory relationship, bonding, to other family members. To quote Olson, Sprenkle, and Russell (1979), "the definition of family cohesion used in this model has two components; the emotional bonding members have with one another and the degree of individual autonomy a person experiences in the family system." As has already been mentioned, the problem of cohesion has preoccupied many family therapists, and a few examples follow.

Wynne and his collaborators (Wynne, Ryckoff, Day, & Hirsch, 1958), in their theory of pseudomutuality in families of schizophrenic patients, have suggested that in the reciprocal role playing by the members of these families no room is left for a mutual recognition of unique individuality and the development of self-identity. As a result, family roles become stereotyped, lacking in innovation and diversification. The family is separated from the external social world by a rubber fence. Since a diversification of role playing and role taking is necessary for the development of an autonomous self and for an acquisition of social skills, a child who comes from such an excessively cohesive family remains permanently bonded to the family roles and cannot function on his own in the outside society. Later Wynne introduced the concept of pseudohostility to describe families at the opposite end of the cohesion continuum (Barnard & Corrales, 1979). In such families, the lack of meaningful relationships, which is disguised by interminable, pointless bickering, precludes the normal development of self. Boszormenyi-Nagy (1967) believes that the self is an integral part of an interpersonal relationship in which the self actively defines itself and is passively defined by the other. George Herbert Mead (1972) talks in this connection about role taking and role playing. Since at the extremes of pseudomutuality and pseudohostility meaningful interpersonal relationships are lacking, the growth of self is stunted. According to Wynne and Singer (1963ab) both extremes are related to schizophrenia and cause thought abnormalities through disordered family transactions. These authors distinguish between amorphous and fragmented types of schizophrenic thought disorders related to different types of family interactions, presumably at the opposite ends of the cohesion continuum.

The idea of the separateness-connectedness dimension has been further elaborated by other family therapists, Murray Bowen, Helen Stierlin, and David Reiss, who have continued the research at the NIMH started by Wynne. Bowen (1966) has described extremely high family cohesion as undifferentiated family ego mass, or emotional fusion, and extremely low cohesion as emotional divorce. In a high cohesion state, the self of an individual has not differentiated from and remains fused with those of the other family members. The fusion is not only with the egos of the parents and the siblings but also with those of the grandparents—the process called by him transgenerational influence. In emotional divorce, the other end of the cohesion continuum, there is an emotional distance between parents and the parents and children, leading to family conflicts. Salvadore Minuchin (1974) views the family as the "matrix of identity" from which the self is derived, following continuous interactions between the individual and other family members. Minuchin conceives family as a system differentiated into various subsystems: individual members and their coalitions. The subsystems are divided from one another by boundaries. The latter may vary from being excessively rigid to being diffuse. A family characterized by rigid boundaries is described as disengaged and that with diffuse boundaries as enmeshed. Families in the middle range are described as having clear boundaries. Enmeshment implies belongingness, conformity, and connectedness. Conversely, disengagement refers to a state of impermeable boundaries, rendering communication and interaction between the subsystems difficult. The enmeshed state is synonymous with high family cohesion and the disengaged state with low cohesion. They occupy the two extreme ends of the continuum. The condition of clear boundaries, the middle range of the continuum, is conducive to the optimal functioning of the family and its members, which is characterized by their self-autonomy and meaningful communication. Similar dimensions of family integration and family adaptability were proposed by Angell (1936) in his study of the effect of economic depression on family life.

Using the two basic dimensions, adaptability and cohesion, Olson, Sprenkle, and Russell (1979) have constructed a circumplex model of family systems. The circumplex model was first described by Guttman (1954). It defines a space by orthogonal dimensions that can be subdivided into discrete areas. In the present case two dimensions were used to define a circular plane. The adaptability dimension was divided from low to high into four areas: rigid, structured, flexible, and chaotic. Similarly, the cohesion dimension was divided into disengaged, separated, connected, and enmeshed. Thus, the two dimensions produce 4×4 matrix with the resulting sixteen cells. Each cell describes a family type on two characteristics: adaptability and cohesion. The model is illustrated by Figure 5, reproduced with permission from the paper of Olson, Sprenkle, and Russell (1979). The middle area, the flexibly separated, the structurally separated, the flexibly connected, and the structurally connected types, represent well functioning families. The four types, either high or low on both adaptability and cohesion, represent malfunctioning families. The remaining eight types are less frequent. The authors use their model for family diagnosis and treatment planning. Thus they avoid such diagnostic categories as schizophrenia, psychopathy, or depression, which are borrowed from conventional psychiatry for the diagnosis of individual patients. They also have developed an assessment tool, the Family Adaptability and Cohesion Evaluation Scales (FACES), as a diagnostic aid.

Our discussion until now has treated the family system from the cross-sectional point of view. Presently, a few remarks will be made in regard to its longitudinal development. This distinction is analogous to the one between the synchronic and diachronic aspects of the macrosocial processes. However, the time scale is different. The microsocial time scale is concerned with changes occurring during the life span of the family. In contrast, the macrosocial scale compares changes in family development patterns from one historical epoch to another, over much longer periods of time. The contributions of Reuben Hill (1949, 1971), a distinguished sociologist, have provided a theoretical framework for the longitudinal studies of families.

The family is a system that undergoes constant development. The influences shaping this development come from inside and outside

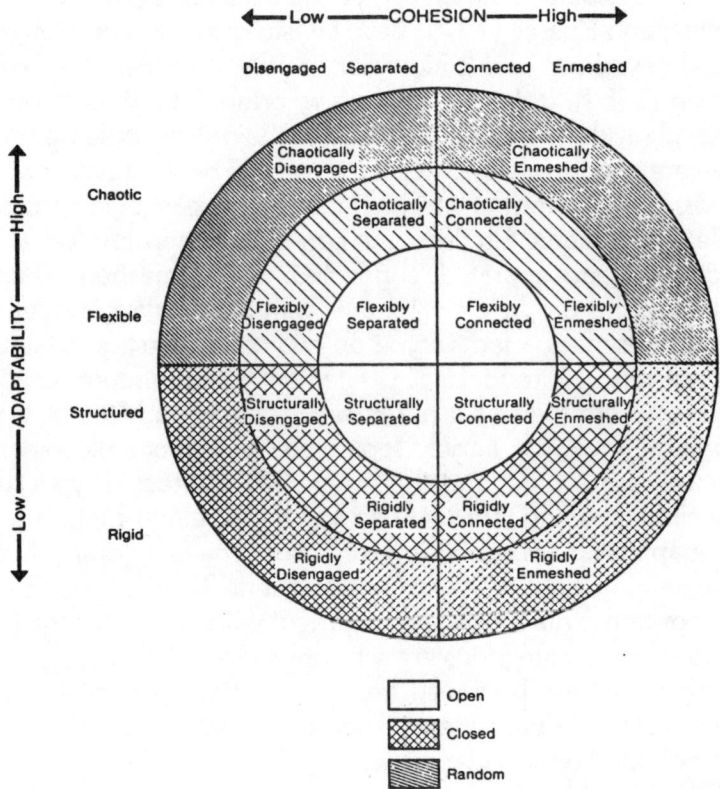

Figure 5. Sixteen possible types of marital and family systems derived from the circumplex model. By permission of Family Process, Inc., modified from Olson, Sprenkle, & Russell, 1979, p. 17.

the family. The most important factors are the biological life cycles of family members: the birth and maturation of children and the aging and death of parents. These factors produce certain discontinuities in family development. Consequently, the family life cycle can be divided into stages with associated periods of transition. These transitional phases subject the family system to stresses and strains, occasionally resulting in family and individual pathology. During these phases, the family system undergoes restructuring with a concomitant redefinition of the role relationships. The morphogenic processes take the upper hand over the morphostatic ones. The family is confronted with new developmental tasks with which it has to cope. A failure to make a successful transition leads to family disintegration and psychiatric symptoms in its members. Eventually, a new equilibrium is reached accompanied by a dominance of morphostasis.

In addition to these natural biological cycles, there are other more idiosyncratic and accidental factors influencing the development of families. The spouses bring into their marital relationship certain emotional attitudes from their families of origin, leading to unconscious processes of transference and projection of the old bonds on the new ones. However, each family constitutes a unique behavioural pattern emerging from the intimate relationship of its members. The accidental factors such as the death of a member, chronic illness, or divorce demand a drastic reorganization of role definitions and relationships with a resulting stress put on the family system. External factors such as economic depression, bankruptcy, unemployment, and war may disrupt normal family development and call for drastic readjustments.

Family Therapy With Schizophrenic Patients

Family therapy originated within the context of Freudian theory. The early pioneers in the field, such as Nathan Ackerman (1958), were psychoanalysts. They abandoned the practice of individual therapy and, instead, started treating whole family units. This innovation was prompted by the belief that individual psychodynamics are reflected in the dynamics of interpersonal relations in the family. The analysis of transference and countertransference processes between the patient and the therapist were extended to those of the members of the whole family. In Great Britain, early psychodynamic family therapists were influenced by the object-relation theory of Melanie Klein and Ronald Fairbairn (Skynner, 1976).

In the fifties, a great interest developed in the family relationships of schizophrenic patients as a possible etiological factor in this disease. The early formulations were in terms of one-way causality. The cause of schizophrenia was believed to lie with certain personality characteristics of the patient's mother. A cold, affectionless, domineering, and overcontrolling mother was said to be schizophrenogenic. She was the dominant partner in marriage. Her attitude towards the children was ambivalent. Under the surface of overprotectiveness there was hostility (Sanua, 1961; Farina, 1960). A variant of this approach was the scapegoat theory, which located the cause of mental illness of a child in both parents (Vogel & Bell, 1960). The parents solved their interpersonal difficulties and ambivalent feelings by selecting one child as a scapegoat and casting it into the role of a mental case.* The choice was determined by accidental characteristics of the child, which had an unconscious significance to the parents. It was a version of labelling theory in the family context. The one-way causality theories, apart from the tendency to oversimplify the issues, tended to put the blame on a parent or both parents for the child's mental illness. Consequently, the process of family therapy based on such theories was bound to produce feelings of guilt in one or both parents. In the course of time the concept of one-way causality has been replaced by that of interaction.

An early research with families of young schizophrenics was conducted by three groups of researchers: the Yale group led by Theodor Lidz, the Palo Alto group led by Gregory Bateson, and the NIMH group at Bethesda led by Lyman Wynne (Mishler & Waxler, 1965). Wynne's work has been discussed in the previous section in connection with the cohesion dimension of families. Lidz, Fleck, and Corelison (1965) investigated the families of fifty young schizophrenics who developed psychosis in their teens. These were well-to-do, middle-class families, characterized by interpersonal conflict or precarious adjustment. The conceptual framework for the study was provided by the theory of Parsons and Bales of family socialization and interaction (Parsons & Bales, 1955). According to this theory the internalized family system shapes the child's personality. A malfunctioning system, when internalized, produces role identifications and expectations that make the individual incapable of becoming a functional member of his society. Lidz focuses in particular on sex roles. The future social and marital adjustment depends on the proper identification with the parent of the same sex who serves as the role model. The abnormal role interactions occurring in the

---

*Andolfi (1979) divides the methods used by families to deal with a scapegoat into judicial, protective, and madness contexts. In the judicial context, the scapegoat is morally blamed. His behaviour is considered reprehensible. In the protective context, he tends to be overprotected and smothered with kindness. Finally, in the context of madness, the undesirable behaviour of the scapegoat is attributed to mental illness.

families of schizophrenic patients lead to intrafamilial communications that distort the symbolizations of reality in these patients. Thus, the intrafamilial environment of youthful schizophrenic patients transmits irrationality and instills in them thought patterns that are at variance with those of society (Lidz, Cornelison, Carlson, & Fleck, 1958).

Lidz et al. (1965) distinguish two types of families associated with schizophrenic offspring: the skew and the schism. The skewed family pattern is characterized by a passive, weak father and a domineering, seductive, and possessive mother. This pattern is associated with schizophrenia in male children, while schizophrenia in females is typically associated with schismatic families. The latter families are characterized by an aloof, devalued mother and a grandiose, narcissistic father. The schizophrenic families have a poorly defined intergenerational boundary. In schismatic families, daughters form very strong sexual attachment to their fathers that they find difficult to resolve. In skewed families, a boy forms not only a strong Oedipal tie with the mother but also tends to identify with her and, hence, becomes confused about his sex role. In this type of family the mother often displays paranoid beliefs and abnormal thought processes that she imposes on the whole family. While the skewed family maintains a precarious balance, the schismatic family is torn by more or less open conflict. In the latter type of family, one parent co-opts children into a coalition against the other parent, with the children being used as pawns in family squabbles. The theory of Lidz and his co-workers was a mixture of the psychodynamic and the social role structure theory, and it anticipated the more recent interactionist theories. Waring and Ricks (1965) distinguish three types of families that produce future schizophrenics. The first is the emotional divorce family characterized by distrust and hostility between the parents. The second, symbolic union type, is characterized by a domineering and a passive-submissive parent. In the third, family sacrifice type, there is open rejection of the child. The symptoms and severity of the subsequent illness depended on the type of the family.

A great deal of research concerned with families of schizophrenics has focused on communication processes (Jacob, 1975; Raush, Greif, & Nugent, 1979). Many studies have found that these families engage in verbal communication that is out of focus, inconsistent, and confusing. It lacks in clarity and accuracy and, therefore, is inadequate for conveying valid and explicit information. The verbal utterances of the schizophrenics' family members have been described as vague and ambiguous. Their exchanges are characterized by incomplete sentences, simultaneous speaking, interruptions, and inappropriate pauses. Normal communication processes possess enough redundancy to insure a smooth flow of information, and mutual understanding. In contrast, in families of schizophrenic children the redundancy tends to blur the conveyed meanings and to create misunderstandings. There is an imbalance between the symmetrical, stressing equality, and the complementary, stressing difference, in communication exchanges. The first, when used inappropriately, rejects the other person, the second invalidates his messages.

In the communication research of families with schizophrenic members, a lot of attention has been paid to metacommunication processes utilizing multiple channels. These channels can convey contradictory messages. The resulting disjunctive information may disqualify the communicator, cast doubt on his trustworthiness, and disconfirm the reality of the messages. It also may create discrepancies in punctuation (sequencing) of communicational exchanges. However, the most important application of the metacommunication concept is the double bind theory.

Gregory Bateson, an anthropologist and the leader of the Palo Alto group, focused on the communication processes occurring in the families of schizophrenic patients. He established a multidisciplinary group to investigate the problem. Don Jackson, Jay Haley, John Weakland, Paul Watzlawick, and more recently Virginia Satir have been the most important contributors to this project. The Palo Alto group has formulated the double bind theory of schizophrenia (Bateson, Jackson, Haley, & Weakland, 1956; Bateson, 1959). The basic assumption of this theory is the existence of different levels of communication. They may be described as the level of communications and that of metacommunications or of communications about communications. Bateson took the idea of different levels of communications from Bertrand Russell's theory of logical types (Whitehead & Russell, 1910). According to this theory there is a discontinuity between a class and its members because they belong to different logical types. A class cannot be a member of itself nor can a member be identified with the class. Bateson believes that the multilevelness of communication processes has a wider application than to formal logic and mathematics. Some of the examples are humor, metaphor, and play. All these activities have double meaning. The first meaning is literal, the second metaphorical, conveyed by the social and linguistic context. A normal adult has no difficulty in separating these two different levels of meaning. In a proverb the literal meaning level is distinguished from the metaphorical. In human beings direct communication occurs always on the verbal and the nonverbal levels (Reusch & Bateson, 1968). The first is linear and digital (denotative meaning), the second contextual and analogic (connotative meaning). The signals used in nonverbal communication are the tone of voice, facial expressions, posture, and gestures. They are usually an expression of unconscious affective attitudes rather than of conscious communicative intents. Nevertheless, they are purposeful and unconsciously intended to convey messages about interpersonal relations. The verbal and nonverbal messages may be congruent or they may contradict one another. Frigid politeness is an example of such contradiction. Usually the incongruity of the messages at the two levels is understood and reacted to appropriately. One of the important characteristics of schizophrenic thinking is their inability to differentiate between the levels of abstraction, as for instance between the literal and the metaphorical meanings of proverbs.

The double bind refers to a particular social learning context in which a child is subjected to contradictory messages, one on the verbal and the other on the nonverbal level. These messages convey contradictory injunctions, sanctioned by punishment or withdrawal of affection. Moreover, the child is forbidden to withdraw from the situation. In other words, the child is caught between the devil and the deep blue sea. It is a you are damned if you do and damned if you don't situation. In the early version of the theory, the rejecting mother was the villain and the child was the victim. Torn by ambivalent feelings towards her child, the mother covered up nonverbal expressions of hostility by verbal messages of love and affection. The child caught in a double bind did not learn to discriminate between the levels of communication, as he was also forbidden to comment on the contradictory nature of messages (Bateson, 1959). In a family characterized by double bind communication patterns, the child does not learn communicative skills. Later on, as an adult, such an individual is unable to engage in a successful social intercourse. He is confused about the levels of abstraction, treating literal statements as metaphorical and vice versa. Also, he tends to send contradictory messages through different channels of communication and to create double bind situations himself. Unable to communicate, he withdraws from social intercourse into a world of fantasy and is diagnosed as schizophrenic. According to Bateson et al. (1956), "The psychosis seems, in part, a way of dealing with double bind situations to overcome their inhibiting and controlling effect." Subsequently the idea of villain mother and of linear causality was abandoned in favour of a conception of the family as an interacting system.

Jay Haley (1963), who has reformulated the double bind theory, described the whole family as a communication network. In schizophrenic families there is a confusion about the metacommunicative rules. Nobody takes responsibility for these rules, as there is no clearly defined power structure. Recently Haley (1979) has tended to play down the double bind idea and to focus on family power structure. He believes that family pathology may be due to a hierarchical confusion. Bateson, Jackson, and Haley have emphasized the homeostasis of the family system, maintained by intercommunication processes (Jackson, 1957). These processes include, in addition to verbal and nonverbal messages, psychiatric symptoms conveying information about interpersonal relations. The mental sickness of one of the family members may be necessary for maintenance of the family equilibrium. Any attempt at change is resisted by the family system. A cure of the symptoms in one of the family members may be followed by the appearance of symptoms in others. While in earlier papers the emphasis was on homeostatic mechanisms, recently emphasis has shifted to processes that bring about family change (Haley, 1976; Watzlawick, Weakland, & Fish, 1974).

Somewhat similar to the double bind theory of schizophrenia is the interactional theory of depression proposed by Coyne (1976). This theory is not limited to the interactions and communications processes within families but applies to all small group interpersonal transactions. According to Coyne, depression is triggered by a disruption of the depressed individual's social field by a crisis situation. This disruption threatens the individual's identity and invalidates his experience. In his communications with significant others, the depressed subject conveys his feelings of despair, hopelessness, and helplessness. He demands from the others a reassurance of his worth and validity as a person. Since the others find the demanding behaviour of the depressed subject irritating and annoying, their messages to him often have a double meaning. On the one hand they convey reassurance and sympathy, but on the other also irritation and rejection. This type of communication process tends to aggravate and perpetuate the depressive state, which in turn increases rejection by the others. Depression is thus seen to be a result of distorted interpersonal communications and faulty interactions.

The Tavistock group in Great Britain, led by R. D. Laing, has pursued a similar enquiry to that of the Wynne and the Bateson groups (Laing, 1965a, 1965b, 1969, 1972; Laing & Esterson, 1970; Cooper, 1971). These workers have investigated young schizophrenic patients in the context of their families. They have focused on the development of self and the communication processes. However, their frame of reference has been different from that of the American researchers. Laing and his co-workers have approached the problems of self and of interpersonal relationships from the existential-phenomenological point of view, or from the subjective perspective of the patients. Since this group tends to reject the framework of objective science, the contributions of these authors will be discussed in greater detail in the next chapter, together with other philosophical and literary approaches. Only some features of Laing's theory pertinent to the sociological point of view will be briefly mentioned here. Similarly to Wynne's position, Laing (1965b) believes that a schizophrenic patient is lacking in self-autonomy as a separate being. This condition produces an existential fear of annihilation by being engulfed by the other, by being imploded by the external world, and by being rendered lifeless by petrification. Since relating to others requires a secure sense of self-identity, the patients tend to withdraw into a world of fantasy. A split develops between the real inner self and a false self that enters in a robot-like fashion into relations with others. The false self automatically complies with the expectations of other members of the family. It may be described as a mask of conventionality that the individual is presenting to the external world. His relations with others lack authenticity and fail to validate his reality as a person. The deficient reality of self leads to a flight into fantasy. It produces feelings of disembodiment and depersonalization. An acute psychotic attack is an attempt by the inner self to regain the sense of reality, to overcome the split from the false self, and to reach out to the external world. It is an attempt at self-integration, a recovery of one's sense of unity. "Indeed, what is called psychosis is sometimes simply the sudden removal of the veil of the false self, which had been serving to maintain an outer behavioural normality that may, long ago, have failed to be any reflection of the state of affairs in the secret self" (Laing, 1965b). According to Laing, if one knows the family context, one perceives the seemingly senseless behaviour of a schizophrenic patient as sensible and rational.

Influenced by Jean Paul Sartre's social philosophy of the *Critique of the Dialectical Reason,* Laing and his co-workers put the blame for the plight of the youthful schizophrenia patient squarely on the shoulders of his family members (Laing, 1965a, 1967, 1969; Laing & Esterson, 1970; Cooper, 1971). The latter are responsible for mystification of the information conveyed to the patient about the family and the world. They attribute to him the characteristics and roles that are useful to themselves as family members but not to the patient. They also invalidate the meaning of his acts and seduce him to accept a false self-identity (Laing, 1965a). By creating a pattern of interpersonal relations and networks of communications that invalidate the patient as an autonomous person, the family members, in collusion with the psychiatrist, cast him into the role of a schizophrenic. This is the conspiratorial (Siegler & Osmond, 1974) view of schizophrenia that blames family members, psychiatrists, mental health professionals, and society as a whole for driving the patient into insanity. This view is also shared by Thomas Szasz (1971). The patient is mystified further by certain family traditions and myths that have been handed down by the previous generations. These ideas are internalized by the patient in the form of patterns of interactions—"a matrix for dramas, patterns of space-time sequences to be enacted" (Laing, 1972). The internalized imaginary family is projected to the real family, leading to a distorted perception of reality. David Cooper (1971) goes further than Laing in criticizing the role of family. He believes that the family in a capitalist society prevents the actualization of self-identity and one's unique creative potential, and therefore it should be abolished.

There is a similarity between Wynne's pseudomutuality and Laing's false self concepts, as well as between Bateson's double bind and Laing's mystification ideas. However, Laing's frame of reference is the subjective experience of the patient rather than that of the group processes. He doubts the reality of collectivity or of social systems (Laing & Esterson, 1970; Siegler, Osmond, & Mann, 1971).

The Contemporary Schools of Family Therapy

In the past twenty years the field of family therapy has enormously expanded. The numbers of schools and techniques have multiplied. The focus of interest has shifted from the families of juvenile schizophrenics to a variety of other disorders, from marital difficulties to psychosomatic conditions. New techniques have been introduced such as family social network therapy (Speck & Attneave, 1973), multiple family therapy (Laqueur, 1972), and the method of cotherapy, using two or more therapists (Satir, 1967). In general, larger numbers of family members have been included, a development called by Jackson and Satir (1973) horizontal expansion. In a review entitled *Dimensions of Family Therapy,* Madaness and Haley (1977) have offered a classification of the schools of family therapy based on seven dimensions differentiating them. The discussion presented here follows closely the review by these authors. Madaness and Haley distinguish the following dimensions: (1) past versus present, (2) interpretation versus action, (3) growth versus presenting problem, (4) method versus specific plan for each problem, (5) unit of one, two, or three people, (6) equality versus hierarchy, and (7) analogical versus digital.

In the past versus present dimension, the distinction is made between the schools of family therapy that stress individual and group history and those that focus on the ongoing present processes. The interpretation versus action dimension differentiates between those schools that believe that an interpretation of past and present events will bring about a cure and those that believe that actual experiences and behaviour in the present are necessary to achieve this end. Schools of family therapy differ in whether they try to promote growth and development of the family group and of the personalities of its members or to restrict themselves to specific problems. Some schools are method oriented and use the same method irrespective of the problem. Others are problem oriented and choose different methods depending on the problems. The schools of family therapy that originated in individual therapy, for instance, the psychodynamic school, focus on individual patients, the feelings of the family members about each other, and each one's awareness of how he treats the others. On the other hand, the schools that stress interactive processes consider dyads, triads, or even larger groups to be the basic units. The equality versus hierarchy dimension distinguishes between those schools that disregard the role and power structures of the family and those that emphasize these structures. The former put stress on equality and democracy among the family members, while the latter try to reinforce the existing family hierarchy. The analogical versus digital dimension differentiates the schools that stress the contextual field and connotative aspect of family behaviour from those that conceive of the latter in terms of discrete bits or concrete events.

Using these seven dimensions, Madaness and Haley (1977) classify the various schools of family therapy as follows:

A. Schools of family therapy that originated from individual therapy
  (1) Psychodynamic therapy
  (2) The experiential school
  (3) The behavioural school
B. Schools of family therapy based on the conception of family as an interacting system.
  (1) Extended family systems
  (2) Communication networks
    (a) Communication: structural
    (b) Communication: strategic therapy

Table I, taken from the article of Madaness and Haley (1977), summarizes the differences between various schools of family therapy. For further details, the reader is referred to the above article. Some family therapists do not fit exactly this schema. Their methods combine the features of more than one school. A case in point is the

Table I
Comparison of Different Approaches to Family Therapy According to Various Dimensions

Dimensions	Schools				Communication	
	Psychodynamic	Experiential	Extended Family	Behavioral	Structural	Strategic
Past	X					
Unit 1 person	X	X		X		
Interpret (past)	X				X	
Interpret (present)	X		X			
Method	X	X	X			
Growth	X	X	X		X	
Analogical	X	X	X		X	X
Present		X		X	X	X
New Experience		X		X	X	X
Directives			X	X	X	X
Plan for therapy				X	X	X
Unit 2 people			X		X	X
Unit 3 people			X		X	X
Hierarchy			X		X	X
Presenting problem				X		X
Digital				X		X

From C. Madaness and J. Haley, Dimensions of family therapy, *Journal of Nervous and Mental Diseases*, 165:92, © 1977 The Williams & Wilkins Co., Baltimore.

technique of Virginia Satir (1967), which combines the communication and the experiential approaches.

Earlier, in the section dealing with group therapy, a distinction was made among four contemporary models of mental illness: the psychodynamic (psychoanalytical), the group dynamic, the existential-experiential, and the one based on behaviour therapy. It also was stated that the group dynamic model was originally based on notions stemming from Kurt Lewin's field theory and that these were later superseded by ones stemming from systems theory. The models of mental illness presupposed by various techniques of group therapy were discussed in some detail. All these models are continuity models. We may ask what additional light can be thrown on the subject from the discussion concerned with various approaches to family therapy. That family therapists subscribe to the continuity model of mental illness can be illustrated by a quotation from Olson, Sprenkle, and Russell (1979) after presenting their circumplex family model based on the cohesion and adaptability dimensions: "In defining these four extreme types (on the two dimensions), we believe that these behaviours are continuous with functional behaviour but represent an exaggerated version of it. Even the pioneer family therapists were impressed with the fact that 'normal' families displayed some of the same behaviour, albeit limited, as the clinical families they were describing as dysfunctional."

In the Madaness and Haley classification of family therapy schools, the first three categories (the psychodynamic, the experiential, and the behavioural) are almost identical with similar categories discussed in connection with group therapy. They presuppose basically the same three models of mental illness as the corresponding categories of group therapy. The basic features of these models have already been discussed. Since they derive from individual therapy methods, they focus on individual patients in the context of groups. These groups may be newly formed and unrelated to wider social networks, as in the case of group therapy, or they may have a long preexisting history and be embedded in a broader social nexus, as is the case with family therapy.

The remaining three schools of family therapy (the extended family system, the communication-structural, the communication-strategic) and their associated models of mental illness may be placed on a continuum of commitment to the systems theory point of view. All these schools view the family as a system. However, while the extended family systems school focuses on the formation of self in the context of role playing, the communication schools view the family as a cybernetic network that processes information (Keeney, 1979).

In the extended family systems school, the therapy task is to promote the differentiation of the autonomous self from the undifferentiated ego mass embedded in a tangle of the present and past family relationships (Bowen, 1966). The latter are conceived of as a hierarchical network of obligations, a system of rights and duties that have to be kept in balance. An upset of this balance offends the sense of fairness and justice. Some of these obligation-networks extend horizontally to the members of the present generation (horizontal bookkeeping). Others extend to past generations, the ghosts of which may be haunting the living descendants for failing to perform such obligations as mourning rituals (Paul, 1967; Whitaker, 1970). They constitute transgenerational processes (generational bookkeeping). The situation is similar to one described by anthropologists in primitive societies, where social relations are based on kinship systems (Levi-Strauss, 1969). The model of mental illness proposed by the extended family systems school, while differing from the medical model, is concerned with individual actors occupying statuses and playing roles within the family social system. Since it stresses the family role structure, hierarchy, and the intergenerational boundaries, it can be best discussed within the framework of the traditional sociological theories of role playing and symbolic interaction. Mental illness is believed to be associated with too tight or too loose family role interarticulations. In the first case, an autonomous self is not developed because the individual cannot dissociate himself from the social roles into which he has been cast by the family system. In the second, the socialization of the individual is impaired because he has not learned to interact and to communicate with the others. The locus of illness is placed in the self, although the latter has developed and exists only in the context of social interactions.

The communicational-structural school of family therapy maintains that the exchange of messages by family members defines their relationships and stabilizes the family system. The communication network, which is governed by implicit rules, is determined by the family structure and hierarchy. In their absence, the channels of communications are poorly defined causing a confusion of messages. The resulting chaotic communications produce an enmeshed, disorganized family. In a disengaged family, its subsystems do not intercommunicate (Minuchin, Montalvo, & Guerney, 1967).

While the structural variant of the communication school focuses on the communicators and on their channels of communication, the "strategic therapy" approach focuses on repeated, patterned sequences of messages, out of which the family structures are crystallized. The first is concerned with relatively static aspects of communication, the second with the flow of information and the reciprocal, simultaneous interactions (Haley, 1971, 1976, 1963; Montalvo, 1973; Watzlawick, Weakland, & Fish, 1974; Zuk, 1971).

The communication schools of therapy, in particular the strategic variety, presuppose a model of mental illness that makes a clear break not only with the medical and the traditional psychological models but also with the traditional epistemology, associated with the scientific outlook in Western culture. The proponents of the communication approach take a completely different point of view from the traditional one, when discussing a patient, his symptoms, his diagnosis, the family group, and the role of the therapist. They view the whole process of therapy in a completely different light. The inspiration and leadership for these new metatheoretical developments have come from Gregory Bateson, who combines an originality of thought with a cross-cultural perspective. As an anthropologist studying foreign cultures he has used the method of participant observation, which involved being drawn into the orbit of the culture by actively interacting with the people. In this process, both the observer and the culture are affected. Bateson (1958) believes that observation of a culture proceeds on three interweaving levels of degree of abstraction: the concrete ethnographic data, a picture or a schema representing one aspect of the culture, and the processes of thinking involved in information extraction. The third level of abstraction is concerned with epistemological and metaphysical assumptions underlying observation processes. Keeney (1979), following Wilden and Wilson (1976) distinguish two kinds of epistemology. The first is the traditional linear epistemology, exemplified by the medical model and psychiatric diagnosis. It is reductionistic, selective, atomistic, anticontextual, and follows analytical logic. This epistemology conceives of the world digitally in terms of discrete, isolated objects. It tends to reify the ongoing processes, thereby committing what Whitehead (1953) called "the fallacy of misplaced concreteness" (Keeney, 1979), and has a monadic view of man (Watzlawick, Beavin, & Jackson, 1967). The second epistemology has been called by Keeney (1979) and by Wilden and Wilson (1976) ecosystemic epistemology. It emphasizes interrelations, complexity, ecology, and whole interacting systems. The conceptual frameworks associated with it are that of cybernetics, ecology, systems theory, and analogical thinking. While in the paradigm of linear epistemology the observer actively selects certain information according to a preconceived scheme, in the paradigm of ecosystemic epistemology the observer passively immerses himself in the observed, becoming, as it were, part of it. He absorbs all the incoming information without any attempt to select and order it. The first paradigm is that of traditional Western science, the second is more consistent with Chinese Taoistic philosophy (Bateson, 1972). It is nonpurposive being-cognition—of being what is known (Maslow, 1966). In this paradigm the dichotomy between the observer and the observed, between man and society, and between the inside and the outside disappears. Man and society or family groups are open-linked systems in constant interaction (Wynne, 1967).

Keeney (1979) has offered a paradigm for the diagnosis and conceptualization of mental illness based on ecosystemic epistemology, cybernetics, ecology, and systems theory. While the traditional psychiatric diagnosis has been based on attaching a label to an individual to describe certain pathological symptoms, the ecosystemic diagnosis considers symptoms inextricably a part of relationship systems such that the site and nature of symptom manifestation may shift (Keeney, 1979). A change in one part of the system results in change in other parts. So the diagnosis and the model of mental illness associated with it are not concerned with individuals as receptors of lineal causal effects who become the sites of pathology. Instead, they are concerned with the circuitry of information flow in its total complexity and ramifications. Symptoms are viewed as messages used by the system to maintain a state of equilibrium. They are attributed to the total system and not to individuals, and their cure requires a change in the equilibrium of the whole system. A symptom is "an indicator or sign for the ecology of relationships" (Keeney, 1979). The therapist can diagnose a system only by interacting with it and becoming a part of it. He becomes part of an ecosystem (Bateson, 1974; Keeney, 1979). Minuchin (1974) calls this process interactional diagnosis. However, the fact that the therapist, or diagnostician, is not a monad but rather part of a preexisting system of social interactions adds further complexity. The process of diagnosis may be viewed as an interaction of two self-referential systems. It may be described as an interference of two interactional patterns, similar to that of an interference of two ripple patterns on the surface of the pond, or to a moire pattern in textile fabric. It is a hybrid of the two relational fields and comes under the heading of the cybernetics of the second order—the cybernetics of observing systems (Howe & von Foerster, 1975). Keeney concludes (1979), "This hybrid relationship network constitutes relationship system in diagnosis." In this kind of diagnosis no blame is put on any particular person and no cause is singled out to explain mental illness. An explanation that posits an agent or a cause is replaced by one based on the totality of simultaneous, reciprocal interactions.

To recapitulate, in addition to the anomie and alienation models of mental illness, distinguished in the context of macrosocial phenomena, the microsocial perspective is associated with the following additional models: the group version of the psychodynamic model, the experiential-existential, the behaviouristic, the group dynamic or social system, and the communication models. The last two are closely related to one another and deal with somewhat different aspects of the same social phenomena. The communication model is the most revolutionary and departs radically from the traditional paradigm of science. There is a similarity between the macrosocial anomie and the microsocial group dynamic (social system) models. Both attribute mental illness to a deficiency of role interactions within either macro or micro social systems. There is also a similarity between the macrosocial alienation and the microsocial experiential-existential models, particularly if the historicity aspect of the former is disregarded. Both attribute mental illness to subjectively felt meaninglessness of relations between the self and others.

In contrast to the macrosocial models that envisage only a prevention of mental illness through more or less sweeping social changes and reforms, the microsocial models offer concrete methods of group and family therapy. The latter models are more useful than the former, from the point of view of individual patients with concrete problems and from the point of view of the practitioners who treat them.

Chapter 6

PHILOSOPHICAL-MORAL MODELS

INTRODUCTION

The previous chapters presented models of mental illness that were based on the biological, behavioural, and social sciences. Although in the past two centuries the scientific outlook has had a great appeal, its application to the human mind and society has encountered widespread criticism. The critics often have argued that the legal and political system of our society is based on the assumption of individual freedom, moral responsibility, and mutual obligations of its citizens. They have argued further that subjective meanings and value judgements are the essential features of human conscious experience. Therefore, besides the natural order, which is the domain of science, there is also the moral order. Science, which stresses objectivity, predictability, and control of events, is not applicable to the moral order. The critics of scientism reject the deterministic metaphysics, the preoccupation with the general in contrast to the unique, and the reductionism of the scientific outlook. They stress that in addition to the animal aspect of human nature there is also a spiritual one that manifests in free moral choices and artistic creativity. This point of view is shared by both theists and humanists, irrespective of their differences with regard to the ultimate meaning of human existence. According to many of them, human experience and behaviour and, consequently, the social order should be approached by way of the humanities and moral philosophy rather than by way of natural sciences. Since the problems of mental patients are often moral, alternative models of mental illness have been proposed to those based on sciences.

The models of mental illness to be discussed in this chapter come from different philosophical traditions. They do not conform to one conceptual pattern and do not constitute one particular theory. They have in common an attitude towards the mental patient and his problems. This attitude is characterized by the implicit or explicit belief that mental illness is *not* a disease but that it involves problems of living encountered by morally free and responsible individuals. Therefore, the psychiatric symptoms are manifestations of real, moral, and philosophical problems, and they are not caused by a disease. Psychotherapy is then *not* merely a matter of treating a psychotic or a neurotic patient by a doctor, but it is a personal encounter between two unique human beings. The patient is not a passive object, manipulated by the psychiatrist but rather an active, free agent making decisions regarding his fate. Further, these models are characterized by a rejection of positivistic philosophy and of scientism. They are antireductionist and refuse to reduce human behaviour to animal drives, conditioning, or to the social roles played by man. Instead, they stress the individuality, uniqueness, and freedom of each person. Thus, there is a denial of both biological and social determinism.

HERMENEUTIC–LINGUISTIC MODELS

Hermeneutics and the *Verstehen* (Understanding) Method

The problem of methodology of humanities and social sciences, the so-called "methods controversy" (*Methodenstreit*), became the focus of academic debates in Germany in the latter part of the nineteenth century. While the method of natural sciences (*Naturwissenschaften*) was based on observation, induction, and experimentation aimed at establishing general laws, there was no similar method applicable to humanities (*Geisteswissenschaften*). It was proposed that hermeneutics should become such a method. The word derived from the Greek *hermeneutikos*, which means explaining or clarifying (Bauman, 1978). Originally, hermeneutics was a method connected with biblical scholarship and the interpretation of ancient texts. Its purpose was to derive the meaning of ambiguous words or sentences from their context and in the process clarify the latter. This procedure was called the "hermeneutic circle." During the Romantic period, the hermeneutic method was extended to literary and art criticisms. Its aim was to discover the personal message that a poet or an artist tried to convey. Friedrich Schleiermacher and Wilhelm Dilthey (1961), two important nineteenth century philosophers, established hermeneutics as the general method of the humanities. They described the method of understanding (*Das Verstehen*), which was applicable to the studies of history, culture, art, and literature. In its earlier version, understanding meant identifying empathically with another person, reliving the other's mental experiences, and seeing the world through the eyes of the other. The later version equated understanding with grasping the cultural context and meaning of particular historical events or documents.

Two neo-Kantian philosophers, Wilhelm Windelband (1901) and Heinrich Rickert (1962), denied that humanities and natural sciences are two different realms of discourse, using two different methods. Instead they suggested that, depending on the purpose, two methods, the idiographic and the nomothetic, could be used both in the humanities and in the natural sciences. The first method was synthetic and was concerned with understanding (*Verstehen*) unique individual subjects and events in their unique contexts. The second method was analytical. It was concerned with classes of subjects or events, and with their explanation (*Erklärung*) in terms of generally valid scientific laws. It tended to analyze observed phenomena into elementary, basic units and variables for the purpose of generalizations.

The relevance of the idiographic and nomothetic methods to psychology and social sciences was widely discussed in the context of the method controversy. Max Weber, a German sociologist-philosopher, proposed two kinds of sociology, one the *Verstehen*, the other objective sociology, and these would complement one another (Weber, 1949). He also divided the method of understanding into direct understanding and explanatory understanding. The first was an everyday, commonsense, intuitive understanding of behaviour and utterances of other people. The second went beyond the immediately given understanding to uncover the motives of behaviour by grasping the meaningful connections between past and present episodes. While the first was concerned with the "what" of behaviour, the second was concerned with the "why" of it. Explanations that used the category of ideal types lay somewhere between the *Verstehen* and the objective sociology. The ideal types constructed by the researcher helped him classify the observed phenomena. The methodology of hermeneutic understanding and the application of the ideal types played an important role in German psychology and psychiatry. For instance, Eduard Spranger claimed that psychology belonged to humanities rather than to natural sciences. In his important work on types of men, he used the *Verstehen* and ideal types methodology (Spranger, 1928).

Another thinker important for the humanistic tradition was Karl Jaspers (1883-1969). In his *General Psychopathology* (1963), he offered the method of descriptive phenomenology, which reconstructed another person's momentary state of consciousness. Jaspers also offered the *Verstehen* method of establishing meaningful connections between present and past events in the biography of a person. The notion of ideal types is evident in the typology of physique and character offered by Ernst Kretschmer (1925). Pure pyknics and asthenics with their typical personalities were never encountered in real life. People only approached these ideal types to a greater or lesser extent. Particularly in the description of characters Kretschmer relied on empathy and the *Verstehen* method.

The Verstehen *Model of Mental Illness, Summary*

Jaspers (1963) devotes a large section of his book *General Psychopathology* to the psychology of meaningful connections. The latter is one of the three approaches to psychopathology described by him. The other two are the descriptive phenomenology of the patient's conscious experiences and the objective description of his behaviour according to the principle of nomothetic science.

The psychology of meaningful connections is based on the *Verstehen* method. It attempts to understand the development of a unique personality. It also tries to understand the unique motives, purposes, and the character structure of the individual. The *Verstehen* psychology takes its inspiration from the works of such great authors as Shakespeare, Goethe, Dostoyevsky, and Balzac, masters of understanding and portrayal of human characters. Jaspers thus developed, alongside the other models, the *Verstehen* model of mental illness. This model uses literary intuition for understanding the personality of a patient on the basis of his unique biography. The psychiatrist empathizes with the patient in a way a reader empathizes with the hero of a novel. The discerned themes in the history of the patient are based on an intuitive grasping of the meaningful connections, rather than on application of scientific laws. The model is par excellence an idiographic one, dealing with patients as unique individuals rather than as members of classes. The model can be further described as continuous, since the patient is understood in the same way as is a normal person.

Philosophy of Language and Symbolic Forms — Approaches to Mental Illness Through Language

An area of great interest to humanistic scholars and philosophers is the field of symbolic behaviour and symbolic products. This extremely difficult and complex subject has been investigated by linguists, logicians, philosophers, and literary critics. Logicians have developed a formal theory of signs and symbols known as "semiotics" (Morris, 1946). The latter is concerned with the denotation (extension) and with the sense (intention) of symbols. Meaning is explained in terms of reference and of implications rather than in terms of causality. The search for meaning in such symbolic products as natural language and myth is the task of the broad domain of hermeneutics. In Germany, there has been a long tradition of linguistic philosophy and the philosophy of other symbolic forms. Wilhelm Von Humboldt described the inner form of language, which was responsible for a deep-rooted, subjective view of the world, a spiritual attitude, controlling the formation of concepts (Isham, 1967). Friedrich Schelling conceived of art and mythology as systems of symbols with their own a priori categories. These ideas had a great influence on the later philosophical theories of Ernst Cassirer.

Ernst Cassirer (1874-1945) was a German neo-Kantian philosopher. He succeeded in extending the Kantian critique to broader areas of human experience than those of the Kantian pure and practical reason. He also regarded categories that crystallized experience as being specific to the mode of symbolic representation and as nonstatic but continually undergoing development (Cassirer, 1957). According to him symbolic representation is an essential function of human consciousness. Man lives in a symbolic world or, rather, in several symbolic worlds. There are three symbolic systems, representing three types of reality and three corresponding modes of symbolic function. The first is the expressive function, which represents the primitive world of myth and magic. The second mode is the intuitive function, which represents the world of ordinary language discourse and of common sense. The third mode is the conceptual function, which constitutes the world of science. Thus, the humanities, sciences, and common sense use different symbolic forms, different thought processes, and different criteria of truth. The methods of enquiry used by the human and natural sciences are therefore different.

Hermeneutic-Linguistic (Symbolic) Approach to Mental Illness

Cassirer's philosophy has had a great influence in English-speaking countries. It was popularized by Suzanne Langer in her book *Philosophy in a New Key* (1948). The philosophy of symbolic forms also influenced some psychiatrists and neurologists. One example is the neurologist Kurt Goldstein (1939, 1948). He was influenced by the neo-Kantian philosophy of Cassirer, by phenomenology, as well as by holistic gestalt psychology. In his studies of brain damaged patients, aphasias, and schizophrenics, Goldstein came to the conclusion that the basic disorder underlying various abnormalities of speech and behaviour in these patients is a disorder of symbolic functions.

The philosophy of symbolic forms also influenced the work of M. Edelson (1971), who has reformulated Freudian psychoanalytical theory in terms of symbolic implications rather than as causal explanation. He has replaced the concept of cathexis (energy) by that of intentionality (meaning). Thus, the withdrawal of cathexis would mean the absence of intentionality, meaning, or significance (Wilden, 1968). According to Edelson psychoanalysis belongs to the humanities rather than to the natural sciences. Consequently, it should be approached by way of hermeneutics rather than by way of the natural science method. The new action language, proposed by R. Schafer (1976), for psychoanalysis redefines it in a similar way. In terms of action language the individual, who is a free agent, initiates purposeful actions for reasons related to the meanings of situations. The relationships between meanings and actions are implicative rather than causal.

The hermeneutic reinterpretation of Freudian theory by Paul Ricoeur. In his *Freud and Philosophy* (1970), Paul Ricoeur used the hermeneutic method to interpret Freud's texts and arrived at a conclusion similar to Edelson and Schafer regarding the nature of the psychoanalytical discipline. Ricoeur defines symbol as a sign (signifier) that possesses more than one meaning—usually two meanings. Symbols are equivocal and have double meaning. Usually one meaning is obvious, and the other is hidden and has to be deciphered. The task of hermeneutics is an interpretation of the hidden meaning. The method used by Ricoeur is described as hermeneutic phenomenology (Ihde, 1971) in contrast to structural phenomenology. While the latter lay bare the essential structures of experience, the former focuses its attention on the problematics of language. The interpretation of the full meaning of symbols and of cultural myths by hermeneutics reveals the foundation and roots of language. Ricoeur's hermeneutic method may be characterized as dialectical. Contrary approaches, such as the subjective experience and the objective scientific description, that oppose one another result in a synthesis. Symbols have two opposing purposes: that of revelation and that of dissimilation of meaning. Accordingly, hermeneutics has also two contrasting purposes: one is the restoration of meaning and the other is demystification, or the exposition of false meaning. The latter purpose motivates the philosophies of Karl Marx, Friedrich Nietzsche, and Sigmund Freud. Marx and Engels (1947) exposed false consciousness engendered by idealistic philosophy. Nietzsche (1966) uncovered selfish and base motives underlying our system of morals. Freud showed that our conscious motives and meanings are only a facade covering the unconscious ones. On the other hand hermeneutics when applied to biblical texts has the purpose of restoring meaning so the divine message (kerygma) might be revealed.

Another dialectic relation is the one between the archeology of subject, a concern of the Freudian theory, and the teleology of consciousness, as presented by Hegel in his *The Phenomenology of Mind* (1949). Freud's archeology of subject goes outside the phenomenological *Cogito*, given in immediate conscious experience, to the unconscious and forgotten roots of meanings and motives. It reconstitutes the individual's past history, so as to make his experience and behaviour understandable. The present apparent meaning is interpreted in the light of past meanings and is demystified by the revelation of the concealed real meaning buried in the deep strata of the past experience. While the Freudian archeology of the subject is concerned with the hermeneutics of demystification, the Hegelian teleology of consciousness is concerned with the hermeneutics of restoration and revelation. According to Hegel (1949), in the dialectical spiral of collective mind development, contradictory phases are reconciled by their synthesis, which gradually reveals their true meaning in the light of the purpose (*telos*) of the development. There is similarity between the existential project and the Hegelian *telos*, both reveal meaning by pointing to the future. The Freudian and the Hegelian points of view complement one another, and each is implied by the other.

Ricoeur denies that psychological phenomena can be explained in terms of energetics as products of conflicting forces. Their explanation is in terms of the exegesis of their hidden meaning carried out by hermeneutics. According to Ricoeur, psychoanalysis, in contrast to experimental psychology, is not an empirical, natural science dealing with the facts of behaviour but rather a humanistic discipline based on the method of hermeneutics. Therefore, it should not be judged by the canons of natural sciences. To quote Ricoeur, "No, psychoanalysis is not a science of observation; it is an interpretation, more comparable to history than to psychology" (1970). Psychoanalysis, according to him, is the "semantics of desire." Desires are represented by ambiguous symbols with double or multiple reference. For him the unconscious is the interface between the biological and symbolic processes. Based on this prelinguistic substratum, there rises a hierarchy of symbols that increase in their creativity. The lowest level of sedimented symbolism is constituted by stereotyped and fragmented remains of symbols. It is the level of dream symbolism, of legends, fairy tales, and neurotic symptoms. This is the language of the unconscious, which is outside the sphere of pure consciousness, as studied by the Husserlian phenomenology. At a higher level are symbolic processes on which the linguistic and social structures are based. They are the clockwork of the society. Finally, at the highest level come the prospective symbols, which use the second level symbols to create new meanings. They are oriented towards the future and are the domain of the teleological hermeneutics of restoration (revelation). Man, thus, is characterized by a polarity. The lower pole is constituted by his biological aspect and the higher pole by the *telos* of his consciousness, his *mythopoetic* aspect as the creator of new meanings.

Phenomenology and psychoanalysis complement one another. They both aim at making the subject a free agent aware of his intentionalities. A neurotic subject is alienated from the true meaning of the desires emanating from the id. He is also alienated from the moral code of the superego. These alien influences constrain his freedom. Psychoanalysis is conceived of as a discourse aiming at the hermeneutic clarification of symbolic products of the language of the unconscious. By this clarification the sphere of ego intentionalities is extended. "Where id was, there shall ego be" states Freud (1964).

Ricoeur has incorporated the biological notions of psychoanalysis into the concept of man conceived of as a product and a creator of symbolic forms. Moreover, he has brought about, by his dialectic method, a rapprochement between psychoanalysis and phenomenology. He has moved the psychoanalytical theory from the field of natural-biological sciences to that of humanities. It should be noted that Carl Gustav Jung, in his analytical psychology, was also concerned with symbolic functions and implicitly used the hermeneutic method.

Structural-Linguistic Approach to Mental Illness

The structural-linguistic reinterpretation of Freudian theory by Jacques Lacan. Jacques Lacan has interpreted psychoanalysis in terms of structural linguistics. The early work of Lacan (1966, 1968) was influenced by the phenomenology of Hegel and of Merleau-Ponty and by the Sartrean version of existentialism. However, later in life he abandoned phenomenology for structuralism. Influenced by the linguist Ferdinand de Saussure (1966), Lacan applied a structural linguistic model to psychoanalysis, which he reinterpreted in terms of linguistic discourse between the conscious and the unconscious (Lacan, 1968; Wilden, 1968).

To understand Lacan's position it is necessary to make a few remarks about the structuralist movement. French structuralism emerged as a reaction against both phenomenology and existentialism.

It was inaugurated by the structuralist anthropology of Claude Levi-Strauss (1963, 1969) and the sociology of Marcel Mauss (1954). It was adumbrated by structural linguistics, as exemplified by the work of de Saussure (1966) and of the Prague school. Two members of that school, N. S. Trubetzkoy and R. Jakobson, made an outstanding contribution to phonology by describing the structure of rules that underlie the differentiation of phonemes (Lacan, 1968). The structuralists believe that behind the appearance of things, the phenomena, there is an underlying, hidden, invariant structure. The latter is a system of relationships that can be expressed by a set of logical or mathematical rules. This system presents a symbolic order in which the meaning and the function of each element depends on the totality of elements and on their relationships. The symbolic order underlying social phenomena can be partitioned into several subsystems representing certain aspects of social and physical reality such as language, kinship (e.g., marriage rules), economic relationships, religion, art, and science.

The subjectivism of phenomenology and existentialism is rejected. The point of gravity is shifted from the individual to the society. The human mind reflects the social, cultural, and linguistic orders, which in their turn may be expressions of innate mental structures or potentialities. The unconscious, the reality of which was denied by the phenomenologists and existentialists, plays an important role in structuralist philosophy (Mauriello, 1975). It is a depository of structure, the system of rules regulating language, cognition, and social relationships. Since the unconscious, in contrast to the preconscious, contains the rules common to the whole society and not the individual memories, it is collective. As far as the individual is concerned, it represents the "other," the society. Human, social, and linguistic behaviour occur in the course of time, and form the diachronic aspect of social reality. In contrast, the symbolic structure of behavioural rules, which is timeless, constitutes its synchronic aspect. According to Levi-Strauss (1969) the rule forbidding incest and the rule regulating the exchange of women in marriage are the basic rules of the social order. Lacan calls the rule forbidding incest The-Name-of-the-Father law. He relates it to the Oedipus complex and to the mythical symbolic father of *Totem and Taboo* (Freud, (1953b). In primitive societies, which change slowly, the collective unconscious is expressed in the form of myths. The latter play an important role in shamanistic practices. The shaman relies on the collective myths in bringing about a cure in the way the psychoanalyst relies on private dreams. Consequently, myths can be described as collective dreams and individual dreams as private myths.

There is an intimate relationship between the structure of culture and that of language. Lacan is particularly concerned with the linguistic structure and its bearing on psychodynamic processes. He follows the linguistic theory of de Saussure. The latter distinguished two aspects of linguistic phenomena that he called language (*la langue*) and speech (*la parole*). The first is concerned with the synchronic rules of grammar and syntax, the second with the diachronic flow of speech, implementing the synchronic rules. According to de Saussure a linguistic sign has two aspects: the signifier (S) and the signified (s). Their relationship is usually denoted by the algorithm S/s. However, both de Saussure and Lacan deny that there is any one to one correspondence between a single signifier and a single signified. Rather, there is polyvalency with one signifier relating to many signified and one signified to many signifiers. To put it differently, the totality of signifiers refers to the totality of signifieds, and the meaning of a signifier is determined by other signifiers as well as by the signifieds. This is de Saussure's diacritical theory of meaning. The relationship between the signifier and the signified is quite arbitrary and depends on the structure patterns of the signifiers and the signifieds. An absence as well as a presence of a desired object may be indicated by this arrangement. According to Lacan, the unconscious, which is a collective unconscious, is the locus of deep language structure. It is equated with the system of signifieds giving meaning to the conscious signifiers and through them imposing an order on the domain of the Real. The domains of the Symbolic, the Imaginary, and the Real, according to Lacan, coexist and intersect in the subject. The Real is synonymous with what is real for the subject. The Imaginary constructs the ideal self, the alter ego, which becomes the Other. This image of the ideal self originates in childhood during the hypothetical stage of the mirror (*le stade du miroir*). The child at this stage when confronted with his reflection in a mirror has conceptual difficulties in reconciling the sameness and the otherness of the reflection in relation to the self. The ideal self becomes an aspect of the Other represented by the unconscious. The Symbolic, which constitutes the primary order, represents deep, unconscious structures and gives a meaning to the other two domains.

The Freudian ego defences are reinterpreted by Lacan in linguistic terms as symbol dynamisms. The Freudian mechanism of displacement is explained in terms of the speech figure of metonymy. In the metonymic structure, the missing signifier is replaced by signifiers that constitute its context. It is a displacement from one signifier to others in terms of the context of the message rather than in terms of the code. A desire is displaced diachronically from one signifier to other signifiers.

The Freudian mechanism of substitution and symptom formation is conceived in terms of the metaphoric figure of speech. One signifier is substituted by another on the basis of an unconscious code, which translates one signifier into another. Moreover, there is a return of the repressed and "the passage of the signifier into the signified" (Lacan, 1968), which distorts the signification of the message. The substituted signifier and the signified exist synchronically with the substituting signifier. A hysterical symptom may be regarded as a metaphor expressing a repressed thought. According to Freud (1957b) the mechanism of disavowal of reality rather than repression is the defence mechanism used in psychosis. Lacan equates the disavowal of reality with a rejection of the Name-of-the-Father law and, consequently, a rejection of the symbolic system. There is a dissociation of the signifier from the signified system. As a result, in severe psychosis all communication ceases, but speech does not. There is a coalescence between consciousness and the unconscious. The psychotic knows that he wants to murder his father and sleep with his mother, and he controls his desires by a disavowal and splitting of the ego. Since a psychotic cannot communicate, reality loses its significance and becomes meaningless.

Lacan presents a structural linguistic model of mental illness. Similarly to von Humboldt and to Levi-Strauss, he equates being human with the possession of language. Therefore, he tends to play down the biological aspect of man. The unconscious is identified with the deep-structure of language rather than with biological instincts and drives. Intentionality and reference replace causality.

This theme is developed further by Alphonse de Waelhens (1978), whose main interest is philosophical anthropology. Combining the psychoanalytical, linguistic, and existentialist approaches, de Waelhens proposes a theory of the unconscious and offers a model of schizophrenia and of paranoia. He stresses the primacy of language in the constitution of self-identity, in the experience of reality, and in the structuring of the unconscious. The discourse with the other in which meanings are elucidated, instead of the Cartesian cogito, is the ultimate touchstone of the experience of reality. This discourse has two strands of meanings. One strand is that of manifest meanings concerned with rational conscious thought. The other strand is concerned with latent, unconscious meanings and constitutes the existential framework of the rational conscious thought. As a result, there is an ambiguity of the meaning characterizing all the thoughts and utterances of the subject. The purpose of psychoanalysis is the elucidation of the latent meaning of the discourse.

The schizophrenic has never attained Lacan's stage of the mirror and has never established himself vis-à-vis the other. He has never separated himself as an autonomous being from the mother and has never reached the stage of the Oedipus complex. Therefore, he has never submitted himself to The-Name-of-the-Father law. As a result, the schizophrenic has not entered the linguistic symbolic order and is not capable of conducting a meaningful discourse with the other. His language is a pseudolanguage in which the signifiers are confused with the signified. Words are treated as concrete things. There is no distancing from and no transcending the immediate meaning of the situation, and there is no reaching for further meanings. As a result, a subjectivity open to the world is never established.

The schizophrenic is characterized by (a) a fragmented body-image, (b) a lack of accession to the symbolic order, (c) a profound disturbance of the Oedipal triangle, (d) a confusion of sexual roles and bisexuality, and (e) a tendency to confuse birth and death.

In paranoia, the stage of the mirror has been attained and there is only a confusion of sexual roles. However, the capability for fully meaningful discourse is absent, as the intersubjective validation of truth is replaced by an apodictic conviction about the truth of one's beliefs.

The reformulation of the Freudian theory by Ricoeur and Lacan in terms of philosophy of language and symbolic processes rejected

Freud's reductionistic, biological theory of human mind and presented it as a humanistic discipline.

Neither Ricoeur nor Lacan offers an explicit model of mental illness. However, on the basis of their reinterpretation of Freudian theory, it can be inferred that they consider mental illness to be a disorder of language and symbolic processes. Thought is seen as an autonomous system that is to a great extent independent of the biological substratum. Mental illness could be explained as a process of semantic distortions, misapplications of symbolic reference, and misuses of linguistic rules. Since these disorders may vary in degree, the linguistic model is a continuous one. Alfred Korzybski's (1941) application of semantics to the problem of mental health may be regarded as an early example of this model. De Waelhens, who offers a definite model of mental illness, combines the existentialist approach with the linguistic one. His model is a discontinuous one. According to him madness is a different mode of being-in-the-world from that of a normal person. It is an existence in a different order of reality.

PHENOMENOLOGICAL-EXISTENTIALIST MODELS

Phenomenology and Existentialism

Phenomenology, particularly Edmund Husserl's philosophical phenomenology, should not be identified with existentialism—the intents and purposes of the two philosophies are different (Spiegelberg, 1960). While in Germany there has been a tension and an antagonism between the Husserlian phenomenologists and the existentialists, in France, phenomenology and existentialism have been closely associated with one another. The tension between phenomenology and existentialism is largely due to the fact that while the Husserlian phenomenology has had a rationalistic appeal existentialism has appealed to the irrational voluntarism in men.

Both phenomenology and existentialism stem from the tradition of German transcendental idealism. Two problems posed by Immanuel Kant, the problem of the limitation of human pure reason and, therefore, of human knowledge (Kant, 1966b), and the problem of an apparent contradiction between the freedom of will of the *noumenal* (metaphysical) self and the causal determinacy of the phenomenal self (Kant, 1959) have given impetus to many attempts at their solution.

Phenomenology and existentialism, following the tradition of German transcendental idealism, are based on the Leibnitzian model of human mind, in contrast to empiricism and to experimental psychology, which are founded on the Lockean model (Allport, 1955; May, Angel, & Ellenberger, 1958). According to the Leibnitzian view, human mind is an active agent initiating cognitive and conative acts, by which it moulds and creates reality. The mental act is of basic importance for both phenomenology and existentialism. To make a gross generalization, phenomenology has been mainly concerned with the first problem of Kant and has tried to lay a foundation of human knowledge that is absolutely certain. It has concerned itself with epistemology. Existentialism, on the other hand, has applied itself to Kant's second problem, namely how to reconcile freedom of choice and moral responsibility with the causal determinism of the experienced world. To put it differently, existentialism has applied itself to the problem of the ultimate meaning of human life; it has been concerned with the questions of ontology—the meaning and nature of being—and of ethics—the moral predicament of man.

The Rise of Phenomenology

We may ask, "What does the concept of phenomenology mean?" There is more than one meaning of the term. The first meaning of phenomenology is an approach to science that stresses a pure observation and description without any preconceived ideas or attempts at causal and theoretical explanations. Any preconceived conceptual categorization is eschewed. The observer registers naturally-occurring types and groupings of phenomena.

The second meaning of phenomenology refers to a description of consciousness, of conscious states in all their richness and fullness, without a reduction to some presupposed basic elements such as sensations. Examples of this type of phenomenology are William James's stream of consciousness (James, 1950) and the stream of consciousness literature as exemplified by James Joyce's *Ulysses*. However, in a more technical sense, the description of states of consciousness of self or another person is based on a standardized technique. The examination of one's own consciousness uses the method of inner perception, which is not to be confused with introspection (Spiegelberg, 1960).

The third meaning of the concept of phenomenology refers to Husserl's phenomenological philosophy. Edmund Husserl (1859-1938)(1962) was an influential German philosopher who developed a school of phenomenological philosophy and started the so-called phenomenological movement. Husserl was a student of Franz Brentano, an Austrian philosopher who also taught philosophy to the young Sigmund Freud. Brentano (1874) proposed the theory of Act Psychology, which maintained that the proper subjects of psychology are mental acts or intentionalities. By these acts the individual relates himself meaningfully to the contents of his conscious experience. The intentionalities have become the subject of the Husserlian phenomenology (Husserl, 1962). They constitute the structure of the pure consciousness studied by his phenomenological method. By mental acts (intentionalities) relations of reference are established between the subject and the object. Consequently, consciousness is not a container filled with sensations and ideas from which the homunculus-ego infers the existence of the external world of objects (resembling a radar operator inferring the presence of planes and ships from the blips on a radar screen). Rather, consciousness is open to the world of real objects. It is to be found in the relations themselves of the subject to the objects. Consciousness is a dynamic activity (acts) rather than stuff (substance); it is doing rather than being.

Husserl has made a clean break with the Cartesian metaphysics of body-mind relationship, according to which the body, *res extensa*, the machine, and the mind, *res cogitans*, the ghost, were two entirely different substances. He has also abandoned the Cartesian epistemology, which leads inevitably to the position of Solipsism of or Humean scepticism. The phenomenologists' call of *Zur Sache* to the matter at hand was to put an end to metaphysical conundrums of unsolvable riddles. After all, the ultimate reality is the concrete experience. Husserl was mainly concerned with the problems of epistemology—the ultimate foundation of knowledge. His phenomenological method included the transcendental-phenomenological reduction, or *Epoche*. This involved suspending or bracketing judgement as to the physical or mental nature of objects and intuiting their meaning by phenomenological reflection (Spiegelberg, 1960). It was a suspension of the natural, commonsense, everyday attitude towards the external world and an assumption of a reflective attitude. In this way the factualness of objects is transcended and the source of their meaning in pure consciousness is revealed.

In the early phase, Husserl spoke of only descriptive phenomenology, using the method of transcendental-phenomenological reduction to grasp the meaning of concrete objects and situations. Later on, he went further and developed a second phenomenological method of eidetic reduction aimed at grasping the general essences of things and ideas, the so-called *Wesensschau* as a version of Platonic ideas. Husserl thought that this method would lead to an absolute, noncontingent knowledge. Many phenomenologists did not follow him in his quest for *Wesensschau* but stuck to the descriptive phenomenology of concrete intentionalities (Spiegelberg, 1960). This is true of the phenomenological method of Eugene Minkowski, Kurt Schneider, Erwin Straus, Jan Van der Berg, and Maurice Merleau-Ponty (Spiegelberg, 1972). These phenomenologists have been concerned not only with the problem of knowledge but also with the application of phenomenological method to the experiences of concrete individuals in their concrete worlds, to their feelings, perceptions, bodies, movements, and to their acts. There have been many phenomenological philosophers (Spiegelberg, 1960). Only a few, who are important for the concerns of the present chapter, will be discussed.

Merleau-Ponty (1962, 1963) made an exhaustive phenomenological analysis of perception and of the structure of human behaviour, taking as his point of departure the concrete-man-in-the-concrete-world. One can only separate man from his world by secondarily abstracting one from the other. For Merleau-Ponty, to-be-in-the-world is to perceive the world. Meaning emerges from the perception of the world. He believes that man seeks meaning because he is condemned to meaning. The perceived world is the real world, an inexhaustible source of meaning. The perceived world is both the physical and social and, therefore, intersubjective. In contrast to Husserl, Merleau-Ponty believes that phenomenology should be concerned not with pure consciousness but with the world of concrete life and social human existence. His phenomenology of the full bodied man-in-the-concrete world is important for the understanding of schizophrenic patients. The structure of behaviour embodies inseparably both consciousness and objectively observed movements. They are welded together in one gestalt. Merleau-Ponty's phenomenology is concerned not only with knowledge and meaning but also with the existence of the individual. Accordingly, this type of phenomenology has been of a much greater importance for psychiatry and psychology than the transcendental phenomenology of Husserl.

Two other phenomenological philosophers have to be mentioned. The first was Max Scheler (1874-1928)—a very influential German social philosopher of the first quarter of the twentieth century. Scheler (1954) was concerned with the problems of sympathy, ethics, and the hierarchy of values, conceived to exist objectively. In his philosophical work he used the phenomenological-hermeneutic method described by Ricoeur. Scheler's main contribution was in the field of phenomenology of emotions, both normal and abnormal. He even published an essay on pension (compensation) neurosis (Spiegelberg, 1972). His theories were important for the understanding of human personality, interpersonal relations, and psychotherapeutic processes. They influenced such phenomenological psychiatrists as Kurt Schneider, H. C. Rümke, Paul Schilder, and V. E. von Gebsattel. The second phenomenological philosopher, more recent, was Alfred Schuetz (1932), a phenomenologically-oriented social philosopher. He was particularly interested in the phenomenological analysis of intersubjectivity, which was the main focus of his philosophy. He was concerned with the phenomenology of the social world (Spiegelberg, 1960), and he made some important contributions to the structural analysis of this world.

The Impact of Phenomenology on Psychiatry

Philosophical phenomenology has had a great impact on psychiatry and psychology in Europe. However, these enterprises should not be confused as their purposes are different. While Husserl's transcendental phenomenology of pure consciousness is concerned with the ultimate foundations of human knowledge, phenomenological psychology and psychiatry are concerned with concrete subjective experiences of people. Psychiatrists use the phenomenological framework to describe and make sense of the subjective experiences of their patients. Blondel (1914), on the basis of his investigation of mental patients, came to the conclusion that these patients live in their subjective worlds that normal people cannot understand or enter. The phenomenological psychiatrists try to reconstruct the subjective worlds of their patients. Ellenberger distinguishes three main methods used by phenomenologically oriented psychiatrists: (1) the descriptive phenomenology, (2) the genetic-structural method, and (3) the categorical analysis (May, Angel, & Ellenberger, 1958).

The descriptive phenomenology of Karl Jaspers

The descriptive phenomenology was introduced by Karl Jaspers (1963, 1968), a member of the Heidelberg school, who considered it an important part of the psychiatric examination. In this method the psychiatrist attempts by empathy to reconstruct the contents of the patient's consciousness. The method is concerned with the momentary state of the patient's consciousness, the specious present. It grasps the contents of the other's consciousness by static understanding, which has to be distinguished from the genetic understanding of the meaningful connections used by the traditional *Verstehen* (understanding) method. The latter aims at an intuitive understanding of a particular person's behaviour in terms of its motives and purposes, and it covers a longer time span. The method of descriptive phenomenology involves an extraction of the common features from the flux of constantly changing contents of experience, which would make generalizations possible (Jaspers, 1968). Its purpose is to reveal the range of variation of the normal and abnormal contents and forms of consciousness, discover their distinguishing features, and classify them (Jaspers, 1968). Some of the abnormal forms of consciousness are continuous with the normal forms, some are discontinuous. The phenomenon of pseudohallucination serves Jaspers (1968) as an illustration. This phenomenon, described in the nineteenth century by the Russian psychiatrist Kandinsky (Jaspers, 1963, 1968), was found to be puzzling because it could not be classified either as a percept or as an image. The phenomenological method has established that pseudohallucination is like imagery because it occurs in the private space and has the character of an image. However, it is also like a percept because it is clearly cut and complete in detail, is stable, and cannot be voluntarily controlled.

The descriptive phenomenological approach has been widely used in Europe. Willy Mayer-Gross (1914) offered a phenomenological description of abnormal feelings of happiness. In a later study, Mayer-Gross (1924) provided a description of subjective experiences in mental confusion and dreamy states. Jakob Wyrsch (1937) described the inner states of acute and chronic schizophrenics. Kurt Schneider (1920), who was influenced by the philosophical anthropology of Max Scheler, studied the phenomenology of depression. In describing human personality, Scheler distinguished four levels: the sensuous, the vital, the psychic, and the spiritual. Kurt Schneider described two kinds of depression: endogenous and reactive. In the first, the emotional disturbance was at the vital level of the personality, in the second at the psychic level. In a subsequent publication, Kurt Schneider (1921) discussed the phenomenology of love and sympathy. He examined the disturbances of these sentiments by using the conceptual framework of Scheler's theory of emotions. He described four disturbances: (1) weakening of love and sympathy, (2) estrangement (*Entfremdung*) of feelings, (3) failure to experience feelings for others because of an immersion in one's own feelings, and (4) intensification of feelings for others based on the intensity of one's own feelings. In the estrangement of feelings there was a loss of their genuineness and authenticity. This was related to the syndrome of depersonalization, described by Schneider as due to a loss of authenticity of self. Feelings appeared only as contents of consciousness without being assimilated into the ego.

Emotions and feelings were also studied by the Dutch psychiatrist H. C. Rümke (1924), who published a monograph on the phenomenology of feelings of happiness. He analyzed happiness as a state of consciousness and described the subjective ways in which it was experienced. He distinguished the autochthonous feelings of happiness from the responsive ones and from the ones due to intoxication. Two other Dutch phenomenologists should be briefly mentioned: the psychiatrist J. H. Van den Berg (1955), who has studied the phenomenology of patient-doctor relationship, and the biologist F. J. J. Buytendijk (1952, 1962, 1968), who has written on the phenomenology of encounter, pain, and the psychology of women.

The genetic-structural and categorical phenomenology

In contradistinction to the strictly descriptive phenomenology, the genetic-structural and the categorical varieties seek the underlying structure and the categories of experience, which would explain its general character and its total gestalt (pattern).

Eugene Minkowski (1953, 1970) has studied the phenomenology of time and space experience in psychiatric patients. He was influenced by Henri Bergson's (1960) theory of time, particularly by the latter's concept of flowing time (*durée reelle*). In his book, *Lived Time,* Minkowski (1970) has distinguished the subjectively experienced lived time from the objective, abstract time of physics and astronomy. The lived time is characterized by a subjective feeling of flow, of duration, and of becoming. The flow of lived time is characterized by subjectively felt speed, by a feeling of relatedness to the past, and by an openness to the future. The latter is anticipated, lived, and planned for. In depression, lived time moves very slowly or is even at a standstill. The access to the future is blocked; it does not exist, and there may be a return into the past. In mania, on the other hand, lived time is speeded up. The experiences of certain schizophrenics and mystics are characterized by timelessness, or by being outside time. Some schizophrenics also experience a feeling of disconnection between the past, the present, and the future and an absence of synchrony with objective social time causing a loss of contact with the external world. Minkowski was also concerned with the phenomenology of space. The lived space, in contradistinction to the physical space, is characterized by an orientation in relation to the self and by subjectively felt vastness or constriction. It could be clear space, with open horizons and a possibility of movement from one point to another. On the other hand, dark space is characterized by obscurity, a lack of horizon, impenetrability, and inaccessibility. It is associated with the subjective world of persecutory delusions inhabited by paranoid schizophrenics. There is also luminous space, characteristic of mystical and ecstatic experiences.

Lived time and space together constitute the underlying structure of experience and determine its meaning. According to Minkowski, depression is characterized by a slowing of lived time and a blocking of future. In schizophrenia, the experience of space dominates that of time and is characterized by morbid geometrism (Minkowski, 1953). In addition to the categories of time and space, other categories of experience, such as causality and materiality, have been studied by phenomenologists (May, Angel, & Ellenberger, 1958). The experienced events may be perceived as determined by the subject or by external agents. They may be perceived as due to chance or to the intentions of some conscious beings. In depression, events appear to be determined by the past history; in mania, they appear to be due to chance. Paranoics tend to perceive all happenings as due to evil human intentions. The materiality (substance) of the world is absent in the derealization syndrome. Some patients may perceive all things as if they were made of stone or metal, as hard or soft, as fluid or viscous, and so on.

Erwin Straus (1966) has described the forms of spatiality and the phenomenology of lived movements. The main concern of his phenomenology (Straus, 1963) is the meaningful world of sensory experience in all its full richness. In the world of immediate sensory experience, events are meaningfully connected and lead from one to another. The individual through his sensory experience is directly related to and communicates with the outside world—the Allon. Psychopathology, according to Straus, is to be conceived of in terms of I-World (I-Allon) relations. This relation has been severed in depersonalization. In schizophrenic auditory hallucinations, voices have become autonomous and are dissociated from the speakers. They have ceased to be the voices of real persons.

The study of the phenomenology of obsessional compulsive states by Victor von Gebsattel (1954) provides another example of the genetic-structural analysis. Von Gebsattel has analyzed the world as experienced by the compulsive neurotic. The disturbing aspect of the world (the disturbing symptom) is its character of ugliness, dirtiness, and repulsiveness, which the patient finds disgusting. Everything in the compulsive neurotic's world has the physiognomy of rot, decomposition, and decay. This is a counter-world of decay and destruction, the world of anti-eidos. The patient is fighting against that world, which is, however, in the final analysis of his own making because of a failure on his part to realize himself (May, Angel, & Ellenberger, 1958).

The study of depersonalization by J. E. Meyer (1957) may serve as a final example. Meyer has discussed depersonalization from the phenomenological-existential point of view. He has stressed the fact that depersonalization and derealization phenomena are manifestations of the ego-outer world relations. He believes that obsessional-compulsive neurosis and depersonalization are two opposite poles of the same type of disturbance, which can be described as being either too close to or too far away from the external world. The obsessional-compulsive neurotic is completely controlled by the external world. He comes into a close contact with the world and cannot detach himself from it. The external world is too real for him. In contradistinction, the depersonalized patient has lost contact with the world. There is an unbridgeable gap between him and the external world.

The phenomenological model of mental illness, summary

This model stresses the subjective world experienced consciously by the patient. It is concerned with description and understanding rather than with the causal explanation. It is not concerned with the historical origin of symptoms or their development. Even genetic-structural phenomenological analysis is not concerned with the genesis of the phenomena but with their underlying structure and the physiognomic features of the experience. In contrast to the psychodynamic model, which posits the unconscious with its dynamic forces, the phenomenological model limits itself only to the consciousness of the patient. It tries to understand his experience in terms of the phenomenological features and in terms of the appearance of his subjectively perceived world. The phenomenological model, in contradistinction to the psychodynamic one, does not concern itself with motivation. Since mental patients dwell in subjective worlds, which are qualitatively different from one another and from the world of normal persons, the phenomenological model may be described as a discontinuity model. Because it is a noncausal, the phenomenological model is only concerned with the understanding of patients as unique human beings and is not concerned with their treatment. Therefore, the phenomenological model is compatible with and may complement both the medical and the psychodynamic models. It reveals a new dimension of the patient and may help to arrive at the diagnosis, in addition to providing an understanding of him as a unique human being. In contrast to some other philosophical-moral models, this model is not antiscientific; it supplements rather than supplants the scientific approach. The phenomenological description of the perceptual world of the patient may be supplemented by an experimental investigation of his perceptual processes (Ittelson & Kutash, 1961; Weckowicz, 1972).

The Rise of Existentialism

Existentialism is a philosophy of the predicament of man or, to put it differently, a philosophy that examines the question, "What does it mean to be man?" While Husserl was mainly concerned with epistemology, existentialists are concerned with ontology—the meaning and the nature of being. Modern existentialists have adopted Husserl's phenomenological method of the analysis of pure consciousness and have applied it to the analysis of being. Heidegger's version of the phenomenological method—hermeneutic phenomenology—not only deals with here and now consciousness but also examines the totality of man's life. It stresses the historicity of man, the existential time from birth to death (Heidegger, 1927).

Existential themes have tended to occupy philosophers since time immemorial. This preoccupation becomes more intense whenever there is a cultural crisis, when the old values are questioned, when the existing social order is disintegrating, and when the hitherto prevailing *Weltanschauung* is no longer meaningful nor valid. At such times, questions are asked about the meaning of human life and death and the meaning of individual existence.

Existential themes can be discerned in the writings of St. Augustine (1961), in the poetry of Omar Khayyam (Weckowicz, 1981), and in the writings of Pascal (1967). In the nineteenth century, Søren Kierkegaard and Friedrich Nietzsche turned to existentialist themes as a form of protest against such dehumanizing philosophies as positivism and rationalism. These two philosophies came into prominence against the background of social disintegration and psychological alienation brought about in the wake of the Industrial Revolution. Their teachings tended to disregard the meaning of unique individual existence and to lose the individual, as it were, in the objective world of things or in philosophical abstractions. Both Kierkegaard and Nietzsche strongly protested against this devaluation of the importance of the individual.

Søren Kierkegaard (1813-1855) (1941) passionately attacked rationalism and objectivity both in philosophy and theology. He insisted on subjective or personal meaning of truth and saw man condemned to loneliness, guilt, "sick unto death," and fear and trembling because he was irrevocably confronted with making choices for good or evil. He stressed the necessity of commitment to a particular faith and a way of life.

Another precursor of existentialism, Friedrich Nietzsche (1844-1900) (1966), rejected value systems based on the natural order and reason. He sought to elucidate the irrational, unconscious sources of man's drive to power and greatness, as well as of madness and of self-destruction. Nietzsche also stressed the importance for the individual to become his real self. Thus, Nietzsche may be regarded as a precursor of both existentialism and psychoanalysis.

The rise of existentialism in Europe in the twentieth century is associated with the social upheaval of the two world wars, crumbling social and political orders, the threat of a nuclear holocaust, the rise of mass society, and the alienation of man both from his culture and from himself (Schacht, 1970). There is more than one variety of existentialism. The existential themes were taken up by Karl Jaspers (1955), who rediscovered Kierkegaard and developed the method of elucidation of existence based on the Kierkegaardian leap of faith. Another important philosopher, Martin Buber (1958), was concerned with both theology and philosophy. He developed a theory of the relationship between subjects. According to him there were two types of relationship: I-it and I-Thou. The I-it relationship is impersonal, manipulative, and devoid of a reciprocity. The I-Thou relationship is intersubjective. It is an encounter of two conscious beings, of two personalities, who are aware of the reciprocity of their mutual experience. The I-Thou relationship is genuine and engages the total personality, while the I-it relationship is not genuine and is maintained with only a part of the person. The I-Thou relationship may characterize the relation between man and God, particularly during a mystical experience. The interpersonal relations between people may be of the I-Thou or the I-it character. In the latter case, the other person is treated as an object to be manipulated and used for one's own ends. The encounter, which is the backbone of the existential psychotherapy, is based on Buber's notion of the I-Thou relationship. For example, Sidney Jourard (1964) has developed the self-disclosure therapy system based on this notion.

Both Jaspers and Buber developed their versions of existentialist philosophy independently from Heidegger. However, the mainstream of twentieth century existentialism originated in, or at least was considerably influenced by, the systematic philosophy of Martin Heidegger. The latter examined existentialist themes in the light of his method of hermeneutic phenomenology. In his most important book, *Sein und Zeit* (*Being and Time*), Heidegger (1927) is concerned with ontology—the problem of *being* in general. Human beings are special kinds of beings. They are beings who are conscious of their own being. He has asked the question, "What is the predicament of human beings who are conscious of their being?" The predicament is their finitude and temporality. Thrown into the world without the ability to exercise any choice in the matter, they are faced with the absolute certainty of their death, total dissolution, and nothingness. Heidegger calls the being conscious of its own being, which is always being-in-the-world, *Dasein*, literally translated as "There is." The *Dasein* is embedded in the network of meaningful involvements with his world. It seeks self-understanding, searching for the meaning of its existence and of the world it encounters. The *Dasein* orients itself in time, relating to the past, while at the same time projecting itself towards the future. The method of intuitively grasping by understanding the meaning of *Dasein* in relation to the general problems of being is called *Daseinsanalytik*. It is an ontological analysis of *Dasein* or *Existenze*, not to be confused with Binswanger's *Daseinsanalyse*, which is an attempt to establish a philosophical anthropology. Each *Dasein* is characterized by an individuality, *Jemeinigkeit*, but his world is also *Mitwelt*; he shares his world with the others with whom he communicates. The *Dasein* is confronted by the facticity of his world, which to some extent limits his freedom, but he also has the possibility of making free choices and of facing his existence and his death. The most important choice is that of an authentic life as against an inauthentic life. The *Dasein* shows concern (*Sorge*) about his destiny; at the same time, he tends to escape into the facticity of the world, to be occupied by social conventions and trivia (*Das man*). He tries to escape from anxiety (*Angst*), which is not a fear of any particular object or situation but rather the fear of nothingness, the consequence of the temporality of human existence. However, death gives meaning to the human life and the human life gives meaning to death. The authentic existence has to face squarely this predicament. You have, after all, to live your own life and to die your own death, as was so poignantly portrayed by Leo Tolstoy in *The Death of Ivan Ilyich* (1960).

The French philosopher Jean-Paul Sartre, during his existentialist period, had a great influence not only on the French existentialist movement but also on the general intellectual climate of Europe. He and the existentialist-phenomenologist Merleau-Ponty (1962, 1963) have made a lasting impact on both psychology and psychiatry. Sartre's existentialism, as presented in his book *Being and Nothingness* (1956) as well as several of his plays, short stories, and essays, is perhaps the most radical version of existential philosophy. It stresses subjectivity of experience and the absurdity of the human predicament. Consciousness, the *pour soi*, is nothingness (nonbeing). In contrast to inanimate objects, the *en soi*, it can only attain being by relating to other objects. Sartre's most famous pronouncement is that "existence precedes essence." The meaning of this statement is that consciousness—*pour soi*—creates its own nature out of nothingness. By free acts and free choices, man constantly transcends himself. To put it still differently, he is what he does, hence his aspiration to godliness. Many Christian existentialists, for instance, Paul Tillich (1952, 1962) and Gabriel Marcel (1965), have rejected this position and assumed the presence of a polarity between essence and existence. According to Sartre, *pour soi* or human consciousness, in contrast to causally determined objects, *en soi*, is free and projects itself into the future by anticipating events. Since freedom of action and choice has its roots in nothingness, it produces anguish or existential anxiety, which tends to be suppressed by bad faith, an approximate equivalent of Heidegger's inauthentic existence. The predicament of man is that he has to make free choices and to establish his human dignity in a Godless, absurd world, devoid of any purpose or grand design.

Sartre has developed a method for understanding concrete human beings and their psychological experiences. This method is called by him "phenomenological existential analysis," and it is modelled on Freudian analysis. However, there are important differences; he rejects the notion of unconsciousness and substitutes for it the prereflective consciousness. He also rejects the division of the psyche into id, ego, and super-ego, while regarding psyche as a total gestalt. His most famous existential analyses are those of Jean Genet, a thief who was also a literary figure (Sartre, 1952), that of P. Ch. Baudelaire, and more recently that of Gustave Flaubert.

In later years Sartre dissociated himself from existentialism and came closer to the position of humanistic Marxism, based on the writings of the young Marx. He criticized his own earlier assertions, expressed during his existentialist period, about the absolute moral autonomy and the freedom of the individual. Both the moral autonomy and freedom are restricted by the fact that the individual lives in an exploitive society full of violence. The individualistic moral theory was replaced by a dialectical sociology that attempted to reconcile Marxism with existentialism (Sartre, 1960). The existentialist phenomenology of Merleau-Ponty was already briefly described in the discussion of phenomenology.

The Impact of Existentialism on Psychiatry

Continental psychiatry has been greatly influenced by existentialist philosophy. In France, Angelo Hesnard (1957), Daniel Lagache (1956), Antoin Vergote (1958), and the early Lacan were influenced by Sartre and Merleau-Ponty. By rejecting Freudian metapsychology and by replacing the concept of transference with that of existential encounter, they produced a phenomenological-existentialist reinterpretation of Freudian psychoanalysis. Heidegger's formulations made a great impact on a group of Swiss psychiatrists, Ludwig Binswanger (Needleman, 1963), Medard Boss (1963), and Roland Kuhn (1963), as well as on a group of young German psychiatrists, Heinz Hafner, Karl Peter Kisker, and Hubert Tellenbach (Spiegelberg, 1972). This latter group, under the leadership of Walter von Bayer, has formed the new Heidelberg School of Psychiatry. While the older Heidelberg school, following the lead of Karl Jaspers, limited itself to phenomenology, the new school has an existentialist orientation. The three Swiss psychiatrists mentioned earlier have been trained in Freudian psychoanalysis and have been practising it as a method of psychotherapy. They added *Daseinsanalyse* as an anthropological framework to help them to understand their patients better. A new dimension was added, making for a fuller and richer picture of man. While biological and psychodynamic factors accounted for some aspects of the life history of the patient, the *Daseinsanalyse* accounted for other aspects. Thus, an attempt was made to create a phenomenological anthropology: a framework within which human beings could be fully understood. It was an example of philosophical anthropology applied to the problem of mental illness. Such an anthropology offers a philosophical interpretation for the discoveries of science concerning the nature of man and of the human condition. It studies both man as a creature of the natural order and man as the creator of cultural values, transcending his biological nature. Philosophical anthropology has developed in Germany and has synthesized the contributions of Dilthey's *Lebensphilosophie*, phenomenology, existentialism, as well as those of Marx, Nietzsche, and Freud. Max Scheler and Helmuth Plessner were important philosophical anthropologists. Viktor von Gebsattel (1954) laid the foundations of philosophical anthropology as applied to medicine. He has adopted the general conceptual framework of Heidegger's *Sein und Zeit*. Von Gebsattel regarded neurosis as a disturbance, a blocking, of becoming. However, the most important contributions of philosophical anthropology to the problem of mental illness were made by Binswanger.

Phenomenological anthropology of Ludwig Binswanger

Binswanger was one of Freud's early Swiss followers, and, despite his subsequent involvement with the phenomenological and existential movements, he and Freud remained on friendly terms (Binswanger, 1957a). The main feature of Binswanger's phenomenological anthropology is the concept of *Daseinsanalyse* (Binswanger, 1942). In this concept, the stress is put not on being as such but on concrete being-in-the-world, on the concrete individual-in-his-world. Thus, Binswanger's concerns are *ontic* rather than ontological, with concrete individuals rather than with general categories of being. The accent of *Daseinsanalyse* is on the existentialist *Mitwelt*—the relatedness to other human beings—rather than on the *Umwelt* and the *Eigenwelt*. In existentialist terminology the *Umwelt* is the world of man as a biological organism without self-awareness, the *Mitwelt* is the world of social relationships and encounters with others, and the *Eigenwelt* is the world of self-reflection and self-identity, the world in which man transcends his biological and social determinants.* Heidegger's concept of concern is developed by Binswanger into that of love. Love has spiritual connotations and transcends Freud's biological libido. It is an encounter between two unique individuals, a unique I–Thou relationship, a We-ness. Love, in its spirituality, transcends man's temporality. An example of the *Daseinsanalyse* of a schizophrenic patient is provided by the case histories of Ilse and Ellen West (May, Angel, & Ellenberger, 1958; Binswanger, 1957b). Schizophrenic *Dasein* is characterized by the breaking apart of the consistency of natural experience, splitting of experience into rigid alternatives, different experiential worlds, and the attempt to cover up the attrition caused by these tensions. For example, the patient Ellen West alternates between the airy world of fantasy, the earthy world of practical affairs, and the subterranean world of desires. These worlds are characterized by different spatiality, temporality, and motility. The air world is a world of flying, of freedom, of irresponsibility, of winged wishes, of highest ideals, and of ethereal dreams. It is oriented towards an inauthentic future. The subterranean world has a sepulchral quality. It is a world of crawling, constrained and bound by an inauthentic past. It is a world of pressing down of burdening encumbering desires. The earthy world of striding and practical pursuits is characterized by a disintegrating temporality (falling apart). Each world has its characteristic spatialization, lighting and colouring, and material consistency. It represents a particular contextual totality. The world of a manical patient is characterized by lightness, softness, brightness, colourfulness, and luminosity (Binswanger, 1960). The unfolding *Dasein* of a particular person represents a unique structure of meanings. It cannot be reduced to general psychological mechanisms as in the case of psychoanalysis. The meaning of events in the course of history of the individual and

---

*As a gross oversimplification, one could state that phenomenological psychiatry is mainly concerned with the *Umwelt*, existential psychiatry with the *Mitwelt*, and existential philosophy with the *Eigenwelt*.

the meanings of his acts are quite unique. They have to be interpreted from the point of view of his *Dasein*.

One important innovation of *Daseinsanalyse* is the claim that the schizophrenic's experiences can be intuitively understood in the same way as those of a psychoneurotic. The contrary claim of Karl Jaspers (1963) that schizophrenic mental processes are incomprehensible is rejected.

Since the death of Binswanger, the most important representative of the *Daseinsanalyse* school is Medard Boss, who calls his method the phenomenological *Daseinsanalytik,* thus indicating a closer adherence to Heidegger's ontology. Boss (1963) is also a psychoanalyst, as was Binswanger, and regards his phenomenological *Daseinsanalytik* as a frame of understanding rather than as a psychotherapeutic method. He is interested in the relation between psychoanalysis and *Daseinsanalysis*. For Boss, psychoanalysis is concerned with man as a creation of nature (*homo naturae*). The Heideggerian nonnaturalistic conception of man corrects the limited psychoanalytical approach and reveals man as a manifestation of being in the ontological sense. Thus, *Daseinsanalytik* discloses the philosophical meaning of man's existence. The function of psychotherapy is liberation of the patient's phenomenal experience both in the waking state and in dreams. Experience provides its own meaning. It is taken on its face value and is not interpreted. Patients do not have feelings of guilt, which are a manifestation of an illness, or of unconscious complexes. They *are* guilty of forfeiting their potentialities and of not realizing their being. They *are* also guilty because they are alienated from nature as a whole (separation guilt). Perhaps Boss's most important contribution is his phenomenological analysis of dreams. He rejects both the Freudian and the Jungian theories of dreams. For him, dreams are not a symbolic expression of unconscious complexes, conflicts, or archetypes. They are the expressions of *Dasein* and have to be taken as phenomena in their own right, similar to those occurring in waking life.

Another important follower of Binswanger is Roland Kuhn (1954) who has given a phenomenological interpretation of the Rorschach test. According to him, some Rorschach inkblot responses, such as masks, are a manifestation of the anonymous mode of *Mitwelt*. This mode is characteristic of men living in anonymous collectivities.

Logotherapy of Viktor Frankl

So far we have discussed existential psychiatrists who have used the Heideggerian philosophical system as the framework for their theories of mental illness and psychotherapy. However, several psychiatrists and psychotherapists in their orientation follow existential philosophy without committing themselves to the Heideggerian system and terminology. One of these is Victor Frankl (1963, 1968, 1973), who developed his method of existential analysis of *ontoanalysis* together with his method of *logotherapy,* independently of the *Daseinsanalytik* of Heidegger and of the *Daseinsanalyse* of Binswanger. Frankl was originally a follower of Alfred Adler, but he became dissatisfied with the latter's exclusive emphasis on biological and social motivations. He believes that in every man and in every psychoneurosis there is, in addition to the biological, psychological, and sociological dimensions, also a spiritual one. Every man has the will to meaning and wants to find meaning in his life, in his death, and even in his suffering. Men can give meaning to their lives by realizing certain existential eternal values: creative, experiential, and attitudinal values. The first are concerned with artistic and scientific achievements, the second with the experience of goodness, truth, and beauty, and third with giving meaning to one's suffering and death. A confrontation with death, with nonbeing, produces an increased vitality and immediacy of existence. It enhances the consciousness of oneself, of one's world, and of others around him. In the routine of suburban life, this feeling of vitality and immediacy of existence, as well as the consciousness of oneself, tends to be reduced, is vapid, humdrum, unreal, and submerged in conformity. A proper attitude towards one's death and one's suffering gives meaning to one's life and realizes attitudinal value. The confrontation with death and suffering and with the human nature at its rawest during his death camp experiences led Frankl to adopt the philosophy of existentialism (Frankl, 1963). He is an existentialist philosopher who not only has preached his philosophy from an armchair but also, like Socrates, has lived it. His experiences in the concentration camp produced his passionate commitment to the existentialist *Weltanschauung.* The latter stresses freedom of will, will to meaning, and reverence for human life. For Frankl, every human existence has its significance and dignity, and every neurosis and psychosis has a spiritual dimension. In his psychiatric credo he states, "An incurable psychotic may lose his usefulness but yet retain the dignity of a human being" (1963).

Frankl distinguishes two types of psychoneurosis. The first is due to a conflict of biological drives and should be treated by psychoanalysis or by Adlerian psychotherapy. The second is a product of moral conflict and arises as a result of spiritual problems. One such problem is the existential frustration, which results from meaninglessness, and may manifest itself as a psychoneurosis. Frankl calls this a *noögenic* neurosis. It is an existential neurosis suffered by people who find their lives devoid of meaning. The meaninglessness of such barren lives produces existential anxiety, resulting in neurotic symptoms. Sometimes *noögenic* neurosis assumes the proportions of a collective affliction, distorting the lives of whole groups of people. Such a collective neurosis is characterized by a planless and fatalistic attitude towards life, by collective thinking, by fanaticism, and by submergence in a collectivity. It robs man of his freedom, his responsibility, and his spirituality. Logotherapy is the treatment for *noögenic* neurosis.

Frankl perceives the doctor's role as one not only of treating the body but also as that of ministering to the spiritual needs of the soul of the patient. Thus, the doctor reverts to the role of a medicine man in primitive society, where medical practice and priesthood were not separated. *Noögenic* neurosis is not a manifestation of psychopathology but rather a resultant of the human condition. Anxiety and guilt accompanying it are not imaginary symptoms of an illness but valid experiences, expressing spiritual realities. To quote Frankl (1973), "We would certainly not be entitled to brand something as 'true' because it was 'healthy,' or, vice versa, something as 'false' because it was 'sick.'" His method of logotherapy deals with existential frustration and with the ultimate meaning of life and death. It stresses the freedom of the individual and the responsibility for his life. Its aim is to lead the patient from the state of a "patiens" to that of an "agens." Schizophrenia, according to Frankl (1973), is a manifestation of an extreme passivity in which an active subject becomes a passive object. However, even in the most deteriorated schizophrenic there is an intact spiritual core and therefore hope for recovery. Frankl passionately takes a stand against reductionistic and deterministic theories of human behaviour and of mental illness. These theories degrade and dehumanize man. To quote him again, "I am absolutely convinced that the gas chambers of Auschwitz, Tremblinka, and Maidanek were ultimately prepared, not in some Ministry or other in Berlin, but rather at the desks and in the lecture halls of nihilistic scientists and philosophers" (1973).

The existential analysis of R. D. Laing

Existentially oriented psychiatry has been practised in England by a group of psychiatrists at the Tavistock Clinic in London. Under the leadership of R. D. Laing, D. G. Cooper, and A. Esterson, Sartre's and Merleau-Ponty's phenomenological-existential analysis and Martin Buber's and Alfred Schuetz's analysis of intersubjectivity has been used with schizophrenic patients and applied to their interpersonal relationships. In the *Divided Self,* Laing (1965b) presents the existential model of schizophrenia based on Sartrean phenomenological-existential analysis of the subjective experiences in schizophrenic patients. He tries to understand the lives of his patients in terms of their unique being-in-the-world. He also focuses on the family interpersonal relationships and patterns of communication (Sedgwick, 1971).

Laing's model of schizophrenia based on family communication networks was discussed in the previous chapter. However, even when focusing on family patterns of intercommunication, Laing never abandoned the individual patient's subjective experience perspective as his frame of reference. Following Lionel Trilling (1955), Laing contrasts the basic existential position of ontological security with one of ontological insecurity. Franz Kafka's heroes, as for instance Gregor Samsa in *The Metamorphosis* (Kafka, 1972) who is turned into a beetle, are characterized by an ontological insecurity. They have difficulty in maintaining their self-identity and are lacking in the feeling of reality and of continuity in time. As a result, they are continuously threatened by annihilation and nonbeing. According to Laing, schizophrenic patients and schizoid individuals are, similarly to Kafka's heroes, characterized by this ontological insecurity. They feel more unreal than real and more dead than alive (Laing, 1965b). Their identity, autonomy, and sense of temporal continuity are always in question. They also may feel partially divorced from their bodies or disembodied. These individuals are obsessed with a fear of annihilation, and they desperately contrive to preserve their existence by various defensive strategies. Since they lack personal autonomy, relating to other people is associated with a fear of being engulfed by others and of losing their identity. Their defence against engulfment is isolation and a withdrawal into a world of autistic fantasy. However, the autistic fantasy is destructive, it produces an existential void, a feeling of emptiness and nothingness. This feeling is associated with a fear of implosion of the external world into the subject, bringing about his instantaneous annihilation. The external world is seen as a malign persecutor. Under the withering gaze of the persecutor, the ontologically insecure individual may shrivel and become petrified and depersonalized. He becomes an object, an *en soi*, in the regard of the other, and he loses autonomy and spontaneity and is turned into a lifeless automaton. Sometimes the individual plays possum, pretending to be dead, or turns himself into a stone in order to stay alive. In Tillich's words he avoids his "non-being by avoiding being" (1952). Laing's (1965b) patient, Julie, a chronic schizophrenic, illustrates many of these points. She is a ghost in the weed garden, inhabiting a desolate, arid landscape scorched by the rays of a black sun, in the glare of which she has shrivelled and withered to nothingness. The black sun is the gaze of the persecuting external world, which is also her mother. She is a ghost, a phantom, empty, and devoid of life. And, yet, deep down there is "something of great worth deeply lost or buried inside her, as yet undiscovered by herself or by anyone" (Laing, 1965b).

An ontologically insecure person is disturbed not only in his relation to the others and the external world but also in his relation to himself. The unity of mind and body, stressed by Merleau-Ponty (1962), that characterizes the ontologically secure individual is absent in the ontologically insecure one. There develops a split between mind and body. The ontologically insecure individual becomes disembodied and exists as an incorporeal self. His body becomes foreign to him, a part of the external world. "The body is felt more as one object among other objects in the world than as a core of the individual's own being" (Laing, 1965b). One consequence of the body-mind dissociation is a division of the self. The disembodied self becomes the inner, real self, while the false self remains attached to the body. The objective or public existence of the individual, playing social roles, becomes the expression of the false self. The activity of the individual becomes automatic, devoid of spontaneity, and automatically follows social expectations. It compulsively complies to the will of others. The perceptions of the false self are unreal and its action futile, devoid of meaning. The inner self lives in the world of autistic fantasy, cherishing the lofty private ideals of honesty, freedom, omnipotence, and creativity, however without realizing them in action. A similar interpretation of schizophrenia within the framework of John Dewey's theory of action was offered by Ernest Becker (1964).

In hysteria there is also a split between the inner and the false self. A hysteric dissociates himself from much of what he does; he evades responsibility and is guilty of bad faith in the sense used by Sartre (1956). However, the hysteric manipulates his false self as a vehicle for the gratification and fulfilment of the inner self. This does not occur in schizophrenia in which the false self is controlled by the external world, while the inner self deprived of gratification lives in the world of autistic fantasy. In a schizoid individual, the false self-system maintains for a period of time a mask of sanity and social conformity. A frankly psychotic breakdown is associated with a sudden removal of the veil of the false self and a revelation of the real life-world, the being-in-the-world, of the individual. According to Laing, an understanding of the existential predicament of schizophrenic patients is important for their psychotherapy.

The existentialist model of mental illness, summary

There are several similarities between the phenomenological and existentialist models. Both models reject the split of man into mind and body, which has been inherited from Cartesian dualism. Both models stress subjectivity and the meaning of experience. However, there are important differences. While the phenomenological model can be regarded as being related to scientific psychiatry, the existentialist model is concerned with a different dimension, a different aspect of reality from that which is the concern of science. Phenomenology, particularly descriptive phenomenology, carefully describes and classifies mental phenomena that can be investigated scientifically. It may be regarded as a preliminary step to undertaking a scientific analysis of normal and abnormal phenomena. The existentialist approach on the other hand is either antagonistic (e.g., Kierkegaard, 1941) or indifferent to the scientific approach. Existentialism deals with a different dimension of the human condition from that with which science is concerned. It is not concerned with a description and explanation but rather with an active living through.

The existentialist model deals with the spiritual dimension of the patient, his living values, his projects, and the ultimate meaning of his life. It is concerned with the unique existence of the patient from his birth to his death. The model stresses an honesty in the doctor-patient relationship and a respect for a unique being-in-the-world and way of life. It opposes any interference or control of the other's style of life. Instead, it envisions an authentic encounter between two unique individuals who are equal. According to Rollo May (May et al., 1958) there cannot be any special school of existential psychotherapy. Existentialism is an attitude; it is an approach to fellow human beings. The existentialist model is concerned with philosophical presuppositions and basic orientations rather than specific techniques. It implies a humanistic attitude that is a corrective to soulless professionalism, an attitude with which specific psychotherapies are carried out. However, while the existentialist attitude is compatible with insight elucidating psychotherapies, like psychoanalysis (both Binswanger and Boss have used it), it is not compatible with behaviour modification techniques in which the client is manipulated as an object. On the other hand, some European psychiatrists find the existentialist approach compatible with the use of psychotropic drugs. Roland Kuhn, for instance, introduced the antidepressant drug Tofranil® (Spiegelberg, 1972). Some types of psychotherapy are more compatible with the existentialist attitude than others. Van Kaam (1962) believes that the Rogers's client-centred therapy is most compatible of all psychotherapies with the existentialist attitude and orientation.

Each existence is unique with its own historical time and future. It inhabits its own peculiar world or several worlds in turn. Therefore, the existential model of mental illness is a discontinuous one. Each patient is a unique being-in-the-world.

HUMANISTIC MODELS

Humanism

The label humanistic is applied to so many different systems of ideas that apart from pointing to man as the measure of all things it denotes very little else. Obviously, Protagoras the sophist, Socrates, Thomas Hobbes, John Locke, Jean-Jacques Rousseau, Immanuel Kant, Jeremy Bentham, John Stuart Mill, the young Karl Marx, John Dewey, the existentialists, and the American humanistic, Third Force psychologists, to mention only a few, all have been concerned with man, regarding him as the measure of all things. However, the conceptions of man held by these different humanistic thinkers have often differed a great deal.

Historically, humanism denotes a philosophical and literary movement associated with the Renaissance period of the fifteenth and the sixteenth centuries, which originated in Italy. It was characterized by a revival of interest in classical Greek and Roman culture and literature. By the beginning of the nineteenth century the concept of humanism had ceased to be predominantly associated with classical scholarship and the Italian Renaissance. By and large, there are two humanistic traditions, the rationalist and the romantic. The first has its roots in the philosophy of the Enlightenment, in rationalism, and in the scientific revolution of the seventeenth century. It has given impetus to social reforms and is characterized by a faith in progress and the goodness of man. This tradition inspired the English Utilitarians and was responsible for the social reforms brought about in the wake of the American and French revolutions. This brand of humanism is optimistic. It believes that through social reforms and scientific progress man will become liberated from hunger, poverty, sickness, ignorance, and superstition. Man will become the master of the world and the master of himself. He may even replace God of traditional religion as the pinnacle of being. The code of ethics based on the commandments of God will be replaced by humanistic ethics based on the essential nature of man. Autonomous morality will replace heteronomous morality. This type of humanism seeks the liberation of man through progress and struggle against the orthodoxy of the established religion. Its three main pillars are rationalism, empiricism, and scientific method. Alfred Adler, Erich Fromm, and even B. F. Skinner can be mentioned as examples of the humanistic psychologists in this tradition.

The other humanistic tradition is rooted in the romantic cult of the unique individual and his inwardness. It stresses the importance of feelings and of spiritual, intuitive, mystical, and esthetic experiences. It is based on the philosophy of irrationalism and voluntarism. It also stresses the autonomy of the individual, his self-actualization, his artistic creativity, and his absolute freedom. This tradition perceives man as pitted against society, which is intent on crushing him and turning him into a mindless robot. The romantic humanists have tended to glorify an encounter between unique individuals, the unique relationships of romantic love and of intimate friendship between two individuals or those characteristic of small groups. They have tended to distrust secondary social groups and social institutions. The encounter groups are a present-day manifestation of this tendency. The romantic humanistic tradition is basically antiscientific. With some qualifications, it may be said that existentialism belongs to this second humanistic tradition.

The American Movement of Humanistic Psychology

This section is concerned with the group of American psychologists known under the general name of Humanistic Psychologists or as the Third Force. The group includes such people as Gordon Allport, Carl Rogers, Abraham Maslow, Charlotte Bühler, Rollo May, James Bugental, B. M. Moustakas, Sidney Jourard, and Erich Fromm. On the European continent it is represented by Casimir Dabrowski (1964) and by Roberto Assagioli (1971), the creator of the psychosynthesis method of psychotherapy. Carl Gustav Jung and Otto Rank, although usually classified as representatives of the psychodynamic school, may be regarded as precursors of the humanistic approach.

General Characteristics of Humanistic Psychology

The humanistic psychologists have formulated their theories of personality and their approaches to psychotherapy independently of the European phenomenological and existentialist traditions but have subsequently converged, to a greater or a lesser extent, towards existential psychology and psychiatry. Although there are important differences between the theories of this group of psychologists, their theories also share important similarities. All of them are holistic-organismic and stress the integration of the whole person. Thus, they are against the Cartesian dualism, the Freudian division of man into the ego, id, and super-ego, or the behaviouristic focus on the elementary, atomistic units such as reflexes and habits. All humanistic psychologists emphasize the self as the integrative and the control center of the personality. Further, all humanistic psychologists postulate a continuous personality growth and self-actualization. This latter concept was introduced by Kurt Goldstein (1939) as the basic drive of a healthy organism and was adopted under the names of self-actualization, self-realization, or individuation by all humanistically oriented psychologists.

There is a similarity to the Aristotelian notion of *entelechy,* or potency, and also to the notion of essence by which the goals of personality growth and thus the state of mental health are defined. Self-actualization, or personality growth, is the most important notion of this school of psychology. It can be interpreted in three ways. The first interpretation is the Aristotelian one wherein human beings are endowed at birth with an *entelechy,* or potency, to develop the essence of humanness (the perfect man). Development towards this goal is teleologically determined—the essence is already present, potentially, in the *entelechy* and it precedes, or determines, existence. Individual differences are accidental and are played down. The second interpretation stresses individual differences in the developmental or genetic endowment potentials. If optimal environmental conditions are provided, individuals will divergently develop their unique characteristics. Essence still precedes existence, but it is no longer the common human essence but a unique, individual essence. Finally, the third approach maintains that the individual is not determined by an *entelechy* but that he transcends himself by his creative acts. To put it differently, the individual creates himself. Existence precedes essence. Existentialism, at least the Sartrean version, espouses the third approach to self-actualization.

It is not always clear where the American humanistic psychologists stand on this issue. A quotation from Maslow, the leading theoretician of the group, will illustrate this point. In a little book entitled *Towards a Psychology of Being,* Maslow (1962) devotes a chapter to "What psychology can learn from existentialists." After indicating that the American humanistic psychologists have been independently developing the same ideas as the European existentialists, he expresses scepticism about terms like essence, existence, and ontology used by existential philosophers and considers only the concept of personality identity as useful, because it "can be worked with empirically" (Maslow, 1962). As far as the interpretation of the process of self-actualization is concerned, he (1962) states:

> The Europeans are stressing the self-making of the self, in a way that the Americans don't. Both the Freudians and the *self-actualization and growth theorists* in this country talk more about discovering the self (as if it were there waiting to be found) and of *uncovering* therapy (shovel away the top layers and you'll see what has been always lying there, hidden). To say, however, that the self is a project and is *altogether* created by the continual choices of the person himself is an *extreme* overstatement in view of what we know, e.g., the constitutional and genetic determinants of personality. This clash of opinion is a problem that can be settled experimentally (italics added).

Further, in connection with the time dimension and the orientation towards future in existential philosophy, Maslow (1962) states:

> I think it fair to say that no theory of psychology will ever be complete which does not centrally incorporate the concept that man has his future within him, dynamically *active at this present moment.* In this sense the future can be treated as *a-historical in Kurt Lewin sense* (italics added).

It seems that the goals, situated in the future, are conceptualized as the Aristotelian potencies or *entelechies* determining the growth of the organism in a certain direction, thus implying that the essence precedes existence. Allport (1955), in his book *Becoming,* also devoted a few pages to the problem of personal freedom and implied that although personal freedom is experienced subjectively, nevertheless, from the objective point of view, when all the factors are known, the behaviour is predictable and therefore determined.

According to Maslow self-actualized people are mature. They are characterized by a clear perception of reality, openness to experience, personality integration, spontaneity, and expressiveness. Further, they display self-acceptance, autonomy, uniqueness, and the acceptance of others. The self-actualized people are creative, original, have a democratic character structure, and are problem centered. They have the capacity to give and to receive love. Finally, they are characterized by self-transcendence and a high frequency of peak experiences. Maslow has compiled the above list of character traits and values from his observation of mature, superior persons who, he believes, have achieved self-actualization. During peak experiences, which have a profound mystical quality, the state of self-actualization becomes enhanced. The self-actualizing people enjoy superior mental health, have high moral standards, and come close to being perfect specimens of human species. Maslow, of course, does not minimize the importance of the unique characteristics and idiosyncrasies of each individual personality, but he focuses on general properties of humanness. The latter is the essence of man, which Maslow defines as "fulfilling the concept of 'human being' " (1962). A person is born with the potential to attain full humanness, in the same way as an acorn has the potential of becoming an oak tree.

There is a similarity between Maslow's views and those of Aristotle, particularly as expressed in the latter's *Nicomachean Ethics*. According to Aristotle the end, or purpose, of each object is to be itself. The purpose of each man is to actualize himself to be himself, to achieve the state of *eudaimonia*, or self-fulfillment. This state is synonymous with attaining goodness and happiness. Both Aristotle and Maslow believe in naturalistic ethics: the values are inherent in the nature of man, to be discovered and realized by him. However, there is an important difference. Aristotle had a static conception of human nature. He identified the fulfillment of man with the fulfillment of his function, conceived to be his social role. His fulfillment depended on how effectively he performed it. Therefore, the fulfillment of a free man was different from that of a slave. For Maslow self-fulfillment, or self-actualization, means attaining certain personality and cognitive characteristics that are independent of one's social role and culture. There is another difference between Aristotle and Maslow. For Aristotle, the self-actualization of man meant the realization of his intellectual potential, of his reason. In contrast, Maslow's concept of self-actualization comprises the realization of both the intellectual and the emotional potentials. For Maslow, emotions and feelings are of equal importance to the intellect.

However, it seems that Maslow comes close to the Aristotelian interpretation of self-actualization when he describes the characteristics of the self-actualizing man as the ideal, final goal of personality development and of mental health. On the other hand, Rogers and Allport stress individuality, uniqueness, and the divergence of human developments, thus coming close to our second interpretation of self-actualization. In addition, Maslow associates striving with deficiency needs and self-actualization and mental health with the final state of being. In contrast, Allport and Rogers identify the process of becoming and of constant growth of personality with mental health. Maslow appears to subscribe to the Aristotelian notion of the final state, the natural equilibrium, as the ideal goal of development and to the notion of the Paramenidean unchanging ultimate reality. Allport and Rogers, on the other hand, seem to view man and the world in terms of the Heraclitean notion of constant change and flux.

Another feature that characterizes humanistic psychology is antireductionism. Both behaviourism and the Freudian theory attempt to reduce human behaviour to a few simple, elementary, biological processes such as physiological drives, animal instincts, and conditioned reflexes. Similarly, some social scientists reduce the unique individual to the social roles he is playing. The behaviourists explain complex human behaviour, such as religious or esthetic experiences, ideological commitments, and artistic creativity, as products of a few physiological drives (hunger, thirst, pain avoidance, and sex) and by simple Pavlovian and operant conditioning. The psychoanalysts explain the higher reaches of human behaviour as a manifestation of oral, anal, or urethral libidinal impulses and as a manifestation of psychosexual fixations during the first four years of life. Both behaviourism and Freudian psychoanalysis use the homeostatic model as an explanation of human and animal motivation. According to this model, a physiological need produces a drive that the organism tries to reduce by performing the appropriate act. As soon as the drive is reduced, a state of equilibrium is achieved and the organism becomes quiescent. In general, the behaviourists reduce the human to the animal behaviours, using the white rat or the pigeon in the Skinner box as a model. The anthropormorphism of the nineteenth century animal psychologists has been replaced by the zoomorphism of the twentieth century behaviourists. Moreover, the behaviourists do not make allowance for species differences. According to them, the same laws of behaviour apply to the goldfish, to the white rat, and to man. They do not take into consideration the possibility that, apart from the level of intelligence, there may be some behaviour characteristics that are peculiar to man, as there are some peculiar to the cat or white rat.

Humanistic psychologists object to reductionism; they explain such complex behaviour as artistic creativity or religious experience on its own level. This explanation may be based on new principles and new laws and may require the development of new research methods. Moreover, it may be pointed out that the behaviourists and the Freudians have laboured under wrong assumptions regarding biological organisms. Experimental studies have shown that homeostasis does not explain animal behaviour. Animals find sensory deprivation and monotony stressful. They actively seek novel stimulation and information input even when their organic needs are satisfied. Animals exercise their functions and master skills without any extrinsic reinforcements. The homeostatic model is based on the mistaken notion of the organism as a closed instead of an open system (von Bertalanffy, 1968).

The humanistic psychologists subscribe to a concept of man that is different from that of the behaviourists and the orthodox psychoanalysts. Allport (1955) distinguishes two traditional views on the nature of man. The first one is the Lockean. This view assumes that the human mind is a *tabula rasa* on which the impressions coming from the physical and social milieu are imprinted. Man is regarded as basically passive and only reacting to external forces. He is molded by the external environment to which he becomes adapted by social learning. This view stresses the average man and adjustment and tends to regard behaviour as being determined by past conditioning and learning.

Allport calls the second view of human nature Leibnitzian. According to this view, man is an active agent, initiating actions. He is not merely a passive object reacting to environmental forces but is the source of purposive acts that actualize his potential. Consequently, man's behaviour is not mainly determined by his past learning but also by goals and purposes that lie in the future. Thus, human behaviour is self-determined rather than externally determined. This distinction between the Lockean and the Leibnitzian idea of man is almost identical to that made by Harré and Secord (1972) between a mechanistic and an anthropomorphic model of man. The humanistic psychologists accept the Leibnitzian view of man, while the behaviourists subscribe to the Lockean one. The Freudian position lies somewhere in the middle.

Two other diametrically opposing views of man are those of Thomas Hobbes and Jean-Jacques Rousseau. The Hobbesian view is that natural man is intrinsically bad, animal-like, and that he becomes civilized and humanized by society. Accordingly, the society is the source of higher levels of human behaviour and the source of values and morals. In contrast, Rousseau, and before him John Locke, regarded natural man as intrinsically good, although corrupted by civilization. According to the Hobbesian view there is a split, a discontinuity, between the natural order and the moral order. The roots of the former originate in the physical world, while the roots of the latter lie in the society. Rousseau, however, envisages a continuity between the natural and the moral orders. The latter emerges from the former. Therefore moral values can be discovered in the natural order. Humanistic psychologists have tended to adopt Rousseau's view of man, while the Freudians and the behaviourists adhere to the Hobbesian one. They maintain that the animal side of man is basically evil and has to be suppressed by society. Accordingly, only a civilized man, a member of a society, is capable of moral and esthetic feelings, of altruism, and of religious experiences. Humanistic psychologists, on the other hand, believe that the potentialities for these capacities exist in man as a biological organism waiting to be actualized. They can probably only be fully actualized by a superior man who enjoys perfect mental health, is creative, and who epitomizes the design for a good life. Such a life realizes moral and esthetic values, which are the beacons guiding the personality towards its full actualization. Moral and esthetic values, which are at the bottom identical with one another, exist objectively in the natural order to be discovered empirically. Thus, some humanistic psychologists subscribe quite explicitly to ethical naturalism. Together with the ancient Stoics, they claim to be able to discover what ought to be in what is. Consequently, they reject ethical subjectivism and cultural relativism. Further, they believe that positive mental health is identical with superior morality and the implementation of ethical and esthetic values. One could ask, How are values to be discovered and how may the criteria of positive mental health be established? The answer of the humanistic psychologists to this question is clearly spelled out by Maslow (1962): it can be found by observing superior, self-actualizing people. Full self-actualization is an ideal approached only by few. It cannot be defined by averaging human characteristics and by using the average man as the norm. Other humanistic psychologists, such as Carl Rogers (1961), discover the criteria for mental health and valuation in the unfolding growth of an individual personality in the course of psychotherapy.

The problem of the role of values in psychotherapy is discussed by Charlotte Bühler (1962). In contrast to Heinz Hartmann (1960), who believes that the psychotherapist is a technologist and as such is neutral as far as the patient's values are concerned, Charlotte Bühler believes that the psychotherapist has to help the patient to attain the proper value orientation. According to her view, many cases of psychoneurosis are due to a commitment by the patient to a wrong value system or to a value conflict. A psychotherapist cannot be value-neutral, because every system of psychotherapy implies a set of values. For instance, Philip Rieff (1959) has suggested that the Freudian system advocates a certain set of moral values that are embodied by the mature, genital character. Charlotte Bühler believes that a psychologically healthy individual establishes a clear hierarchy of values. Healthy development is associated with the realization of values intrinsic to the personality, the values of maturity, self-fulfillment, and values stressing meaningfulness of life. On the other hand, a neurotic development is guided by values extrinsic to the personality, by a quest for success, and by the achievement of social status. Similar views are held by Maslow and Allport. According to the former, psychotherapy is a search for inner, intrinsic values. It is a search for self-identity, the true self. Similarly to Socrates, Maslow believes that unexamined life is not worth living. Self-knowledge leads to enlightenment and makes it possible to distinguish the right conduct from the wrong. Self-knowledge, therefore, produces a knowledge of virtue, which is self-rewarding. Allport believes that psychoneurosis may be due to stunted personality growth and to valuelessness, a lack of purpose in life. On the other hand, positive mental health is associated with self-determined, oriented becoming. It is based on free choices and a consistent value system.

The relationship between morality and psychotherapy has been critically discussed from the point of view of analytical philosophy by Joseph Margolis (1966). He does not share the view of some humanistic psychologists that moral values can be discovered by empirical enquiry, and he accuses them of the naturalistic fallacy. Moreover, while there are some value judgements, Margolis calls them findings, such as the state of physical health, which are relatively objective; they do not apply to the characteristics of a self-actualizing personality. The latter belong to the category of appreciative judgements, such as those of works of art that express personal preferences. According to Margolis, positing the ideally self-actualized man as the criterion of perfect mental health represents a quest for human essence. The attribution of essence can be made to an object that, like a knife, performs a definite function. Such an attribution does not apply to man. Man has no essence.

Historically, the theory of morals and ethics may be seen in terms of two traditions. Some moral philosophers, such as Aristotle and the English Utilitarians, have based morality on human happiness, well-being, and on the concept of good. These are the *eudaimonistic* ethical systems. Others, such as Kant, have regarded morality as being founded on duty, justice, and the concept of right. The ethical system advocated by Humanistic psychologists and implied in their concept of positive mental health is *eudaimonistic*. It represents morality based on the quest for happiness and good. The problem of human happiness is an important point of disagreement between the humanistic psychologists and the existentialists. There is a kind of pollyannaish optimism about the goodness of human nature and of the world in the writings of the American humanistic psychologists that is not shared by the existentialists.

The emphasis on happiness and well-being may be illustrated by Maslow's theory of motivation. Maslow (1954) has proposed a theory of motivation based on the hierarchy of needs. The lower needs are deficiency needs. They continue to be aroused so long as they are not satisfied, after which they become quiescent. The lowest in the hierarchy are physiological deficiency needs such as those for food, water, sleep, or sex. Higher in the hierarchy come psychological deficiency needs such as the ones for safety and security; still higher come the needs for love, belongingness, esteem by others, and self-esteem. At the top of the need hierarchy are growth needs such as those for knowledge and creativity. The highest is the need for self-actualization. According to Maslow the deficiency needs have to be satisfied before the individual can begin self-actualization. This is contrary to the beliefs of existentialists such as Frankl (1968). The latter found his personal meaning of life while he was in a state of extreme physical deprivation in a concentration camp. The same applies to an artist who creates great works of art while starving in a garret (Maddi, 1968). This point has also been stressed by Casimir Dabrowski (1964) in his theory of positive disintegration. Dabrowski maintains that higher and new personal values are created through suffering and a disintegration of the previous personality adjustment at a lower level. This idea is in agreement with the general ethos of existentialism.

It is believed by the humanistic psychologists that by investigating man and society scientifically, it will be possible to discover humanistic ethics based on nature and therefore the essence of man. Further, it is believed that when the society is based on humanistic ethics, the millenium will arrive. This theme is particularly prominent in the writings of Erich Fromm (1965). The existentialists do not share this optimistic faith in Utopia. Humanistic psychologists often identify the quest for happiness with positive mental health. Existentialism, on the other hand, is not a philosophy of happiness—it is a philosophy of courage and emphasizes human dignity as its key value, and as such, although not based on the Kantian categorical imperative, it comes closer to espousing a morality of duty rather than that of happiness.

The humanistic psychologists have distinctive views on science and on scientific methodology. In contrast to the existentialists and to more romantically oriented humanists, they do not reject science. They only maintain that the behaviourists have adopted a wrong paradigm of science that is based on classical, Newtonian physics. This classical paradigm as well as the doctrine of logical positivism associated with it have recently been questioned by contemporary philosophers of science (Feyerabend, 1970; Kuhn, 1962; Polanyi, 1958). Abraham Maslow (1966), who offers a clearly articulated description of a model for humanistic science, may serve as the spokesman for the whole group: "I believe mechanistic science (which in psychology takes the form of behaviourism) to be not incorrect but rather too narrow and limited to serve as a *general* or comprehensive philosophy" (1966). These views are shared by Floyd Matson (1964), who considers the model of physical science when applied to human beings as dehumanizing and mechanistic. Maslow (1966) suggests that the orthodox science of human behaviour is preoccupied with its negative aspects such as mental illness, subnormality, and crime. It disregards the higher forms and positive aspects of human behaviour such as artistic creativity, mystical experiences, and altruism. The preoccupation of psychology and of sociology with the inferior, the pathological, and the troublesome has also been pointed out by Pitrim Sorokin (1950, 1956).

Furthermore, behaviouristic psychology is mainly concerned with the average man, disregarding superior and outstanding people, and thus is oblivious to the higher reaches of human nature. This psychology considers only objective behaviour as amenable to scientific investigation, and ignores subjective experiences. It uses nomothetic rather than idiographic methods. In contrast, the humanistic science of psychology studies complex and superior manifestations of human behaviour; it studies the outstanding and gifted people, who display creativity and superior mental health. It focuses on subjective, conscious experiences and on human uniqueness. Self-knowledge and the immediate inner experiences are considered important and serve as guides to self-actualization, to mental health, and to moral behaviour. Therefore, humanistic psychology tends to use, in personality research, the idiographic rather than nomothetic method. It studies the whole man rather than fragments of behaviour. Humanistic psychology is interested in the present state, the subject's goals and orientation towards the future, rather than in causal explanations and past determinants of behaviour. Furthermore, the humanistic researcher does not manipulate his subjects by conducting experiments. He takes the passive attitude of a naturalistic observer, being receptive to emerging truth rather than imposing his theories on observations. This method is called by Maslow Taoistic science.* Above all, the humanistic researcher is problem rather than methods oriented.

Contributions of Individual Humanistic Psychologists

The space available does not permit presenting in detail the views of all humanistic psychologists. Only a few of the most important points are singled out for discussion.

Carl Gustav Jung and Otto Rank, originally followers of Freud, may be considered important European precursors of the contemporary American Third Force humanistic psychology. Although they sought to explain human behaviour by psychodynamic forces originating in the unconscious, they made a clear breakaway from Freudian reductionism. These authors stressed in their writings personality growth, self-actualization, and the spirituality of man.

According to Jung (1953) the goal of personality growth was self-individuation and self-realization. It aimed at the differentiation of underdeveloped personality functions and their integration into the self. Jung's explanations were teleological, stressing purpose and orientation towards the future. He emphasized the spiritual needs of man. Psychoneurosis according to Jung was due to a thwarted personality development and a failure of self-realization. It caused suffering, but it could also have a positive effect, because the regression occurring in it was associated with a mobilization of creative unconscious forces.

Otto Rank (1932, 1950, 1964), who was influenced by the philosophies of Arthur Schopenhauer and Friedrich Nietzsche, stressed in his writings irrationalism and voluntarism as the key concepts to the understanding of human nature. He also stressed the freedom of

---

*There is a similarity between Maslow's Taoistic approach to science and that of Francis Bacon (1965). In *The New Organon*, the latter advocates laying to rest the idols of the Tribe, the Den, the Marketplace, and the Theatre, and observing the external world with an open mind without any preconceptions. As a result of this procedure, the regularities in the observed facts would be inducted, and truth would be revealed to a passive mind. This approach to science is vigorously opposed by Karl Popper (1965), who believes that truth has to be actively extracted by making conjectures and attempting to refute them.

will and the self-determination of the ego. Rank replaced the concept of Freudian super-ego by that of self-ideal, which was not, however, an internalized parental figure. He believed that it embodied the intrinsic values created by the self instead of the extrinsic parental ones. He also emphasized individuality, uniqueness, and creative self-actualization as the goals of personality development. He saw man as being torn by conflicts: will versus impulse, individuality versus conformity, spirituality versus biological instincts, and the most important, the fear of life versus fear of death. Consequently, there was a conflict between the desire to procreate biologically and the desire to assert man's spirituality by attaining cultural immortality as a hero or an artist. The normal, average man was a conformist. He did not assert his individuality and did not self-actualize. He played safe by conforming to collective norms. The hero asserted his individuality by creating new ethical values and the artist by creating new esthetic ones. The neurotic was a failed hero or a failed artist (*artiste manqué*). He detached himself from the collectivity in an attempt to become an autonomous individual. However, his fear of life prevented him from achieving full self-actualization. He was alienated from the society, disoriented, and overcome by existential guilt because he did not realize his potential. His level of development was higher than that of the normal, conforming man but lower than that of the artist or the hero.

The contemporary Third Force humanistic psychologists can be divided into those who emphasize becoming, the process of personality growth, and those who stress being, the final state of self-actualization and the goal of personality growth.* In addition, the first group emphasizes the individuality and the uniqueness of each person, while the second focuses on the general characteristics of self-actualizing people who enjoy a superior mental health. Thus, according to the first group, individual developments diverge, while according to the second they converge towards a common goal. These emphases are, of course, only relative, as both groups admit the existence of general and well as of unique personality traits. The

---

*The first group of humanistic psychologists embrace the Heraclitean concept of man, man as a flux of becoming. The second subscribe to the Aristotelian-Parmenidean concept of man as tending towards the final, immobile state of being.

views of Gordon Allport and of Carl Rogers exemplify those of the first group, while the already discussed views of Abraham Maslow those of the second.

Gordon Allport (1937, 1955) has opposed the reductionistic trends of behaviourism and of psychoanalysis. He has developed a theory of functional autonomy of motives and of personality traits. Although motives can originate from primitive biological drives, they become entirely changed during their development. Allport is interested in the spirituality and in the religious experiences of men. He believes that psychology should be concerned with humanistic problems and focused on the individual person. Consequently, its method should be idiographic rather than nomothetic. Allport (1955) sees the human personality as a process of becoming without a final goal. An arrest of this process leads to stagnation and psychological ill health. During this continuous personality growth an individual is developing an autonomous schema of values to guide him. Consequently, clinical psychology cannot be value-free. He points out that the moral treatment of the insane, introduced by Philippe Pinel, gave better results than the treatment based on scientific psychology.

Carl Rogers (1959, 1961, 1965; Van Belle, 1980) is perhaps the most important American humanistic psychologist, who has profoundly influenced psychotherapy and clinical psychology. In his earlier period, Rogers (1965, 1959) was concerned with personality structure and the concept of self. He believed that psychoneurosis was caused by a perceived discrepancy between the ideal self and the actual self. The ideal self was often founded on extrinsic standards alien to the person and originating with others. The conflict between the extrinsic and intrinsic valuations led to a stunted personality growth and regression to more primitive levels of development. The nondirective client-centred therapist had to accept the client totally as a unique person and to give him unconditional positive regard. In such a permissive, accepting climate the awareness of actual self expanded and was followed by the natural personality growth towards the goal of self-actualization. The psychotherapist did not impose his standards and interpretations on the client but rather let his natural development unfold. Rogers believed that each client was unique and that applying diagnostic labels was meaningless and even harmful.

More recently, Rogers (1961) has abandoned his previous interest in personality structure and has come to view man as continuous actualization process that strives to enhance itself. It is an ongoing, unending Heraclitean flux, ever thrusting forward towards more mature, complex forms of development. Under the influence of Eugene Gendlin (1962), Rogers has come close to the European existentialist point of view. He focuses now on the actual act of experiencing, rather than on its contents, and on the interpersonal encounter. Following the tradition of Wesleyan Evangelical brand of American Protestantism (Hudson, 1961), Rogers puts the individual above the society and stresses the freedom of man. He may be classified, according to our scheme, as a romantic humanist. However, he believes that there is a communality underlying all unique individual values making possible the existence of a social order. In recent years, Rogers has focused on the role of the existential encounter in psychotherapy.

The theory of encounter has been further elaborated by Sidney Jourard (1964) as the psychotherapy of self-disclosure. Jourard believes that open communication without dissemblance is essential for personality growth and self-actualization. In a genuine existential encounter based on I-Thou instead of I-It relationship (Buber, 1958), the mask of deception is dropped and the authentic self, which was hiding previously behind a social role, is revealed both to the subject and his partner. This process leads to personal growth, spontaneity, and self-actualization, associated with a superior mental and physical health.

The Humanistic Model of Mental Illness, Summary

The humanistic model of mental illness is similar to the existentialist one. From the practical point of view there is little difference. Both models envisage the same kind of psychotherapy—the existential encounter. Van Kaam (1962) regards the Rogersian client-centred therapy as being of an existential type. The basic attitudes towards the client are the same, although there may be some differences in the metaphysical assumptions regarding human nature. Moreover, in recent years there has been a significant convergence of the views of the American humanistic psychologists with those of the European existentialists. The points made in the previous discussion of existential psychotherapy apply, therefore, in the present context.

The humanistic psychologists envisage a continuity model of mental illness. According to them psychoneurosis is caused by a failure of personal growth. They have been strong advocates of the positive mental health concept. Actually, they appear to be more interested in mental health than in mental illness. Mental health is not identified with the idea of an average, reasonably well-adjusted, man. It is an ideal state that only a few superior individuals approach. The envisaged continuum stretches from the ideal of perfect mental health at the positive end to severe mental illness at the negative end. The ideal of perfect mental health coincides with the state of full self-actualization, which is also only an ideal approached by few. Theoretically, the standards provided by ideal mental health might be valid for the whole human species (*Homo sapiens*), for members of a culture or a historical epoch, and finally for each unique individual. Humanistic psychologists are unanimous in rejecting cultural relativism, and they regard the criteria of positive mental health to be transcultural. They are less clear about the other two options. Maslow appears to believe that the characteristics of the fully self-actualized man and therefore the standards of positive mental health are valid for the whole human species. Rank and Rogers seem to favour the other option. They appear to believe that each unique individual provides his own idiosyncratic ideal standard for self-actualization and positive mental health. The continuum, which stretches from maximally positive to maximally negative mental health, presents a spectrum of varying conditions. Self-actualizing persons occupy the positive end of the continuum. The relatively well-adjusted, noncreative conformists, who constitute the bulk of the population, occupy the middle range. The overt psychoneurotics can be placed closer towards the negative end, and the severely sick psychotics are at the negative end of the continuum.

There are some similarities between the theories of the humanistic psychologists and those of the psychoanalysts, in particular of the ego psychology variety. The humanistic psychologists place the self at the core of conscious experience. Organismic experiences, which are outside of the self, are disowned and repressed. The purpose of psychotherapy is to expand the self so that it will encompass the totality of organismic experiences. Thus, there is a similarity between the non-self's organismic experiences and the Freudian unconscious. However, there is one important difference. Humanistic psychologists regard the non-self's organismic experiences as beneficial, a source of creativity and humanity. The influences that turn an animal into the human do not come from the external social world. They come from the inside, from the core of the personality. The orthodox Freudians, in contrast, regard the unconscious as the source of evil and of antisocial impulses that have to be kept in check by the society. The external social forces mould a biological organism into a human being.

In contrast to the existentialists, who are neutral on the issue, the humanistic psychologists altogether reject the medical model. They find it dehumanizing and instead view mental illness as a moral problem of an individual who fails to become a complete person. This moral problem is a disease only if the latter term is used in a metaphorical sense.

Supersanity Models of Mental Illness

Supersanity models are offshoots of the humanistic model of mental illness. Their proponents identify themselves with the humanistic movement. Their views on the nature of man are essentially the same as those of humanistic psychologists. They emphasize personality growth and self-actualization. However, they regard mental illness, or some of its types, as a positive development beneficial to the subject. According to this model some types of mental illness are manifestations of a personality development towards higher emotional and spiritual levels of functioning. The sequel is a state of enlightenment, a better insight, a better integration, and a revelation of the true self.

Several authors have mentioned that in some cases regression to more primitive stages of personality development, occurring in mental illness, could have a beneficial effect on personality growth and on creativity. Kris (1952) described regression in the service of the ego. Wild (1965) referred to the same phenomenon as an adaptive regression. Rank (1932) regarded the neurotic as a failed artist (*artiste manqué*), who was at a higher level of personal development than a normal conformist. Jung (1953) stated that psychoneurosis and even schizophrenia could in some cases have a beneficial effect, because it would lead to the mobilization of unconscious forces, followed by an integration of the personality on a broader basis. Erich Lindmann (1960), in his theory of psychological crisis caused by a loss of significant interpersonal relations, made allowance for the possibility of subsequent personality reintegration at a higher level. Anton Boisen (1936), on the basis of his own brief psychotic experience and of his work as a hospital chaplain, came to the conclusion that psychosis represented a character crisis. As a result of this crisis an individual may either regress in the direction of deterioration or may progress toward character reorganization on an ethically and socially higher level. French and Kasanin (1941) presented the hypothesis that schizophrenic episodes may be transitions from inferior to superior levels of adjustment. Perry (1962) has stressed the self reconstitutive aspects of psychopathology. Two more recent theories of mental illness are firmly based on the supersanity model. The first one is the theory of positive disintegration developed by Casimir Dabrowski. The second one is the psychedelic model of schizophrenia proposed by R. D. Laing and his collaborators. While the positive disintegration model applies only to psychoneurosis, the psychedelic model is concerned with psychosis.

Dabrowski's positive disintegration model

Casimir Dabrowski (1902-1980) (1964, 1967, 1972), in several books and articles, presented a theory of positive disintegration of personality and of mental illness. Dabrowski is a personality growth theorist who believes that every human being has a propensity for personality development that aims at attaining higher levels of its integration and functioning. Dabrowski is a neo-Jacksonian (a follower of Hughlings Jackson, 1932). Like Jackson, he maintains that the nervous system contains a hierarchical organization of the levels of neural function integration. One of these is always actively dominant. Before the dominance shifts from lower to higher levels of integration, however, there must be a dissolution of the functions of the lower level and vice versa, from higher to lower levels. The higher levels of integration are associated with the complex psychological and symbolic functions that constitute human personality. Dabrowski uses the term personality only to describe the highest level of integration.

He defines it "as a self-aware, self-chosen, self-affirmed, and self-determined unity of essential psychic qualities, of fundamental individual and universal 'essences' " (Dabrowski, 1972). Only few people reach the stage of personality, attain the status of personhood, or become real persons. The term individuality is used by Dabrowski to describe those who have attained only lower levels of development. Personal growth occurs throughout life but proceeds at a different rate in different individuals. The rate depends on the constitutional and the social-environmental factors. However, a higher level of development is accompanied with the appearance of the third factor, which produces the self-determination of growth. At higher levels of development man becomes autonomous and relatively independent from his hereditary endowment and his social environment. He attains freedom, and his humanness is enhanced.

Dabrowski distinguishes the following levels of personality integration, from lower to higher: primary integration, unilevel disintegration, spontaneous multilevel disintegration, organized multilevel disintegration, and secondary integration. An individual at the level of primary integration is largely only a biological organism; his main motives are physiological needs. He tends to adjust passively to the environment. From the psychological point of view he may be described as a closed system. Such an individual is not capable of higher feelings and empathy with other people. The unilevel disintegration is characterized by recurrent conflicts among physiological, instinctive drives at the same level of psychological functioning. These conflicts result in ambivalencies and ambitendencies towards external objects. The individual has no control over his condition and no insight into it. The unilevel disintegration manifests in physiological disturbances and psychosomatic symptoms. The stage of spontaneous multilevel disintegration is characterized by the simultaneous existence of lower and higher levels of personality integration (multilevelness) and by a conflict between those levels. There are different sets of values associated with the two levels. The multilevelness is further characterized by a tension that is due to the directionality of development, from heteronomy to autonomy, and from the world of facts to the world of ideals. The individual's behaviour comes to be influenced to a greater degree by the inner psychic milieu than by the external factors. The individual experiences disquietude, astonishment, and dissatisfaction with himself, as well as the feelings of inferiority and of guilt. He is prone to self-reflection. At the stage of organized multilevel disintegration the growth of personality becomes self-controlled and shaped to measure up to the ideal standards posited by the individual. Such dynamism as subject-object in oneself and the third factor come to dominate psychic transformations. The conduct becomes self-determined and guided by the values and ideals intrinsic to the personality. There is growing preoccupation with spiritual, philosophical, and ethical concerns. The final stage of the secondary integration, or of the full self-actualization, remains for the great majority of people an unattainable ideal. Dabrowski postulates the existence of a natural and objective system of values that constitutes a hierarchy of higher and lower values. This system becomes evident to the individual during the unfolding of his personal growth.

The process of growing from lower to higher levels is painful and is associated with maladjustment, suffering, and unhappiness. It is commonly described as psychoneurosis. In his book, *Psychoneurosis is not an illness*, Dabrowski (1972) states:

> The majority of psychopathological conditions, such as nervousness, neuroses and psychoneuroses, are—from the standpoint of the theory of positive disintegration—behavioural patterns of inner, mental changes of a positive character.... By "positive" we imply here changes that lead from a lower to a higher (i.e., broader, more controlled and more conscious) level of mental functioning. The process of change may involve mental disharmony, loosening of functions or even mental disorder.

Thus, for Dabrowski psychoneurosis is a creative process, causing suffering, but also leading to higher levels of personal development. Moreover, it is conducive to literary, artistic, and philosophical creativity, as illustrated by such authors as Fyodor Dostoyevsky, Franz Kafka, and Marcel Proust, such painters as Vincent Van Gogh and Toulouse Lautrec, and such philosophers as René Descartes and Søren Kierkegaard. Certain types of psychoneuroses are associated with the lower levels of development, certain others with the higher ones. Organ neurosis (psychosomatic conditions) and hysteria are associated with the lower, while existential (noögenic) psychoneurosis is associated with the higher levels of disintegration. The level of primary integration is often associated with constitutional psychopathy, characterized by a superficial adjustment, but also by a stunted personality growth.

In addition to positive disintegration there exists also the negative disintegration. It consists of dissolution of higher psychological functions and a regression to a lower level of development. The causes of this condition are usually organic. Dabrowski considers schizophrenia, and generally psychosis, as a product of negative disintegration. However, there are a few benign cases of psychosis in which under certain fortunate environmental conditions, or in the presence of a well-developed inner psychic milieu, the regression is arrested and reversed. Personality growth is resumed and the outcome is positive, leading to a higher level of development than before the illness. According to Dabrowski, Clifford Beers (1948), the originator of the Mental Hygiene movement, was one of such cases.

The psychedelic model of schizophrenia

The term psychedelic was used by Siegler, Osmond, and Mann (1971) to describe R. D. Laing's theory of schizophrenia, which he views as a spiritual healing process. To appreciate it fully, Laing's theory must be examined within its historical and cultural context.

The rise of the counterculture (Roszak, 1969) of the sixties revived interest in mystical, transcendental, and occult experiences. It also has revived interest in esoteric, oriental religions and cults. Many authors (e.g., Ornstein, 1972) have pointed out that in addition to the ordinary mode of consciousness, concerned with practical matters and everyday reality, there is another mode of consciousness that occurs in mystical and transcendental experiences. These experiences take place outside of normal time and space and are characterized by the disappearance of boundaries separating individual objects and of the polarity between the subject and the object. The horizon of consciousness is expanded, phantasies become real, and the impossible becomes possible. There is a novel perception of the world and a deep insight into its nature. There is a feeling of enlightenment and a feeling that a transcendental truth has been revealed about the self and the universe. These states often have a deeply religious, *numinous* character—a feeling of being in touch with the absolute. Sometimes they are accompanied by schizophrenic-like experiences such as hallucinations, feelings of influence, and of telepathic communication. At the same time, many authors who have studied the schizophrenic experiences have suggested, that some of them are similar to the mystical. Jaspers (1963) describes experiences in schizophrenic patients that possess the character of transcendental states. Conrad (1958) has studied the *apophanous* experiences, occurring in early schizophrenia and bearing a striking similarity to those reported by mystics. The schizophrenic language, full of pseudometaphors and allegories, has been compared to the language of mystics and prophets.

In the past, mystical experiences were associated with various religious systems and cults in literate and preliterate cultures. They were achieved by the practice of meditation, of physical exercises, of asceticism, and by withdrawal from social contacts. In some cultures, such as those found in Central America, mystical experiences were induced by ingestion of hallucinogenic substances found in plants. All the great religions of the world have had mystical traditions. The Christian mysticism is exemplified by such mystics as St. John of the Cross and St. Theresa of Avila. However, the tradition of mysticism in the Oriental countries has been much stronger than in Europe. This tradition is represented by the Sufis and Dervishes in the Moslem world, by Yogis in India, and by Zen-Buddhists in Japan.

In the West, in the course of the past two or three hundred years the tradition of mysticism has been suppressed and has waned. Modern Western man has tended to turn away from inner experiences and has become preoccupied with the external world, regarded by him as the touchstone of reality. The social institutions that used to canalize mystical experiences have ceased to exist. As a result, Western man has lost a frame of reference and the skills necessary for handling these experiences when they occur spontaneously.

The studies of different cultures, both preliterate and literate, have indicated that mystical experiences may play an important role in solving the problems of the individuals and of the society. They may be used to heal spiritual and physical ills, as when the state of *satori*, or enlightenment, is attained through Yoga practices. Mystics who become prophets may perform an important social role by pointing out a new direction for cultural development and paving the way to important social reforms. Every culture develops its own mode of adjustment to the environment. It produces its own technology and its own way of thinking and categorizing reality. The members of a tribe tend to perceive the world selectively through the spectacles of culturally preconceived ideas. Often, a large part of reality is ignored, since it has no cultural relevance. Such behaviour on the part of the group is adaptive so long as the environmental and economic conditions to which an adjustment has been made do not change. However, a change in the objective conditions is not always immediately followed by new adaptation because of the presence of the cultural lag. In this case the old ways of perceiving and thinking and the old practices become maladaptive. The mystic who turns out to be a prophet is capable of shedding the cultural blinkers and perceiving reality in a novel way. He develops new ways of thinking and points to new direction for his people. This was the role played by the prophets of the Old Testament and by the great religious reformers. In the contemporary Western world, this phenomenon is exemplified, on a smaller scale, by avant-garde artistic movements, such as Impressionism at the end of the nineteenth century. The world is perceived and painted by the avant-garde artists in a novel way that violates the old ways of perceiving and the accepted canons of art. Since the capacity for mystical experience and a novel way of perceiving is biologically useful, the genes determining this capacity occur with a certain frequency in the gene pool of a given population, sufficient to assure that there are always a number of potential mystics available. To put it differently, the predisposition to mystical experiences may be genetically determined. In cultures in which there are institutions for socially valid channeling of mystical experiences, a potential mystic will come to occupy the role of a prophet, guru, or shaman. In a culture where such institutions do not exist he may become a schizophrenic. A schizophrenic, therefore, may be a failed mystic. To paraphrase Otto Rank, he may be a *mystique manqué*.

The counterculture in the sixties revived the interest in mysticism in the West. The hallucinogenic drugs such as mescaline, LSD, psilocybin, and hashish were used widely to induce mind-expanding, psychedelic experiences. These experiences, if the trip was good, were equated with mystical experiences. Earlier on, Osmond and Smithies (1952) pointed out the similarities that existed between the experiences induced by hallucinogenic drugs and those occurring in schizophrenia. This suggestion gave rise to speculations that schizophrenia was caused by a metabolic abnormality or variation that resulted in production of an endogenous bodily substance with hallucinogenic properties. Speculations of this nature gave further impetus to the notion that the schizophrenic may be a failed mystic, and resulted in the development of a "psychedelic" model of schizophrenia.

Gregory Bateson (1961), in a brief introduction to a nineteenth century autobiography of a schizophrenic patient, suggested that schizophrenia is a painful initiation rite, induced by the subject on himself. In the course of this initiation ceremony, the patient embarks upon a voyage of discovery to the nether regions of the mind and returns back to the normal world with new insights, denied to those who never made the voyage. The whole process involves the spiritual death of the subject followed by his rebirth. This theme was developed further by R. D. Laing (1967) and his collaborators. According to Laing (1967), "Madness need not be all breakdown. It may also be break-through. It is potentially liberation and renewal as well as enslavement and existential death." He believes that schizophrenia is "a natural way of healing our own appalling state of alienation called normality" (Laing, 1967), during which the light breaks "through the cracks in our all-too-closed mind" (Laing, 1967). The doors of perception (Huxley, 1954) are wide open. Laing postulates two kinds of experience: the *egoic* and the *ego-less*. The egoic experience is the normal experience, concerned with the external reality and occurring in the space and time shared with others. The ego-less experience is a transcendental or mystical experience occurring in inner space and time. It is described as a "voyage from the outer to the inner; from life to a kind of death; from going forward to a going back; from temporal movement to temporal standstill; from mundane time to 'aeonic' (eonian) time; from the ego to the self; from being outside (post-birth) back into the womb of all things (pre-birth)" (Laing, 1967). The voyage from the outer to the inner is ideally followed by a return to the normal, everyday world and an existential rebirth. However, because they lack skills to handle mystical experience, many people who embark on the voyage to the nether regions of the mind become wrecked and fail to return. They become disoriented, confuse the inner and outer reality, and remain entangled in the web of unconscious fantasies. As a result, for the rest of their lives they remain chronic schizophrenic patients in the back wards of mental hospitals. If the individual returns safely, he is integrated on a higher level of personality development and is psychologically and spiritually healthier than before he undertook the journey.

In his thinking Laing was clearly influenced by the ideas of Jung (1953). In the Jungian terms, the voyage from the outer to the inner meant a descent into the collective unconscious and a reintegration of the personality on a higher level with the help of archetypes. During his voyage to the dark, netherworld of the interior of mind, the individual needs a guide, a sensitive person, who preferably has before made the voyage himself. Thus, the schizophrenic patient needs a guru, a spiritual guide, to help him to avoid the perils of the spiritual voyage rather than a medical doctor to treat him. A critique of the psychedelic model can be found in the Siegler, Osmond, and Mann (1971) paper.

MORAL-LEGAL MODELS

The moral-legal models of mental illness are related to the humanistic models. However, they are not based on a growth or self-actualization theory of personality. Instead, they emphasize individual freedom, human rights, and moral responsibility. In contrast to the self-actualization models, the moral-legal models separate the moral order from the natural order and do not subscribe to a naturalistic theory of ethics. They are based on the morality of right and duty rather than on that of happiness, good, and *eudaimonia,* which constitute the moral foundations of the self-actualization humanistic school.

The moral-legal models regard the antisocial behaviour of mental patients as a breach of social or divine laws. Since these patients are free agents, responsible for their acts, they should suffer the legal consequences. At the same time, their legal rights should be protected, as are the rights of all other citizens. According to the proponents of the moral-legal model the label of mental illness on the one hand shields people from moral and legal responsibility, and on the other it interferes with their human, political, and spiritual rights. Justice, freedom, and responsibility are considered the most important values by the proponents of this school.

The Libertarian Model of Thomas Szasz

In several books and articles, Thomas S. Szasz (1961ab, 1963, 1965ab, 1970, 1971, 1976, 1977) has discussed the concept of mental illness, the ethics of psychiatric treatment, drug addiction, and suicide. He is concerned with the logic and semantics of the language of psychiatry and with the moral implications of psychiatric practices. His book, *The Myth of Mental Illness* (1961a), offers a critique of the concept of mental illness and a semantic analysis of the psychiatric language. He believes that the terms illness or disease are inappropriate as a denotation for a socially deviant behaviour. It amounts to a category mistake, which results from applying terms belonging to a different universe of discourse from the one that is appropriate to the matter at hand. Following Ryle (1949), Peters (1958), and other members of the English ordinary language school of philosophy, Szasz distinguishes two kinds of descriptions of human behaviour: the first is in terms of physical movements and the second in terms of intentional acts. The former uses the causal type of explanation, based on the laws of natural science. The latter explains behaviour in terms of intentionalities, meanings, purposes, and rules. The first assumes that behaviour is causally determined, the second that it is rule governed. Finally, the first operates in the framework of biology, physiology, anatomy, and biochemistry. The second operates in the framework of semiotics and the communication, game, and role playing theories. Although they have the same referent, these two descriptions are in terms of two different languages that are mutually intranslatable. The term illness or disease belongs to the language of biology, physiology, and biochemistry. Therefore, it should not be used in the framework of describing interpersonal communication and games or descriptions concerned with the ethical problems of living. To quote Szasz (1961a):

> It is customary to define psychiatry as a medical specialty concerned with the study, diagnosis, and treatment of mental illness. This is a worthless and misleading definition. Mental illness is a myth. Psychiatrists are not concerned with mental illnesses and their treatment. In actual practice they deal with personal, social, and ethical problems in living.

The use of the term illness is only valid in cases where there is a definite organic, pathological lesion or physiological abnormality in the brain or other bodily system that causes an impairment of psychological functioning. Since such lesions have not been found in functional psychoses and psychoneuroses, the use of the term illness is in these cases inappropriate. They should be described and explained in terms of normative disciplines, which Szasz calls the moral sciences. These include logic, ethics, game theory, semiotics, and structural linguistics—all concerned with sets of rules.

Following Wittgenstein (1953), Szasz conceptualizes interpersonal communication and behaviour in terms of language games. The latter can be divided into object language and several metalanguages dealing with progressively higher levels of abstraction. In addition to those there is a protolanguage characteristic of the early stages of human development. It is an iconic language, concerned only minimally with conveying information but mainly with expressing affect and influencing other people. Hysteric patients in their interactions with other people use the iconic body protolanguage to communicate a state of helplessness and to cry for help. They are misunderstood by their game partners who use a different language. A psychotherapist tries to understand the patient's iconic bodily language and the game he plays in social settings.

In subsequent books Szasz discusses mental illness and psychiatric treatment from broad ethical, social, legal, political, and historical perspectives. He believes that since the so-called psychiatric problems are concerned with the conduct of a free and responsible individual they belong to the moral order and cannot be separated from ethical issues. Szasz takes a Libertarian stand on these issues. He does not believe in a naturalistic ethics. "We ought to know, however, that there is no necessary connection between facts and values, between what is and what ought to be" (Szasz, 1977). Consequently, Szasz does not assume the existence of objective humanistic values. Instead, he believes in pluralism and diversity in society. For him the highest values are individual freedom, liberty, and dignity. These are more important to him than making people happy and relieving their suffering. The individual's rights come before those of the collective. In his thinking, then, Szasz follows the tradition of such social philosophers as John Locke, Thomas Jefferson,

John Stuart Mill, the Scottish moral philosophers, Richard von Mises, Karl Popper, and F. A. Hayek, who put the rights of the individual above those of the society. He contrasts this tradition with that of philosopher kings, utopian reformers, and social engineers, starting with Plato, continuing with the French Encyclopedists, Comte de Saint-Simon, August Comte, Karl Marx, and finishing with such contemporary authors as Harold D. Lasswell and B. F. Skinner. The latter tradition puts the rights of the society or the state above those of the individual. It tries to apply the method of natural sciences to moral problems. Saint-Simon suggested even that "the government of persons should be replaced by the administration of things" (Szasz, 1970). Szasz believes that our social-moral order is based on the concept of the free individual who is morally and legally responsible. Such an individual enjoys certain unalienable rights and enters freely contracted obligations. He is an autonomous person, whose behaviour is self-determined and who exercises a free will and makes free choices. The society is based on the rule of law that protects the individual rights. The conflicts among individuals and between the individual and the state are settled in law courts by the adversary process according to strictly observed procedures that safeguard individual rights. According to Libertarian ethics, the individual should be allowed a maximum amount of freedom, compatible with the freedom of other individuals (Mill, 1945). Therefore, no laws should exist on the books against victimless crimes. The citizens should exercise a complete freedom of access to narcotic drugs, should exercise freely their sexual preferences, and should have the right to end their lives, if they so choose. They should also be allowed to express bizarre beliefs and indulge in eccentric behaviour, as long as it does not constitute a danger to others. Any restriction of individual freedom has a dehumanizing effect. It turns a free man into a slave and even into an object.

Szasz (1963, 1965a) perceives institutionalized psychiatry as a menace to individual freedom. Individuals who express bizarre beliefs or display bizarre behaviour, deviating from the norm, are considered to be dangerous by the state to the prevailing ideology. Deviants are a modern version of medieval heretics and witches. The institutional psychiatrist, acting as an agent of the state and using his medical authority, labels a social deviant as mentally ill, classifies him under a certain clinical rubric, and incarcerates him in a mental hospital. Using the pretext of making a medical diagnosis, the psychiatrist denies to the psychiatric patient the due process of law, denies to him a fair trial, acts as the prosecutor, the judge, and the jury, and sentences him to an indeterminate term. Moreover, while inside the mental hospital, the patient does not have the same rights as a convict in prison. He ceases to be a person and becomes an object. He can be forced against his will to undergo different kinds of therapy, such as drugs, electroshock, or behaviour modification. Szasz sees the institutional psychiatrist as the modern version of the medieval inquisitor who sent heretics and witches to be burned at the stake. In the Middle Ages, the burning of witches was a part of the game played between the forces of good and of evil. Witches were sacrificed to maintain the stability of the social order. The commitment of a psychiatric patient to mental institutions may, nowadays, perform a similar function: the function of affirming the mental health ideology—the modern, scientific, version of theology. Szasz (1971) believes that since the maintenance of psychiatric institutions and the vitality of mental health ideology depends on a regular supply of mental patients the psychiatrists, at the present and in the past, have manufactured madness and have done so in the same way as the medieval witch-hunters manufactured witches.

Szasz, along with Scheff (1966), Laing (Laing & Esterson, 1970), and Cooper (1970) have implicitly proposed in their writings a conspiratorial model of mental illness (Siegler & Osmond, 1974). According to Szasz (1971) and Scheff (1966) the psychiatrist in collusion with the state labels certain social deviants as mental patients, deprives them of their freedom, and subjects them to the modern medical version of torture. In the Laing and Cooper version of the conspiratorial model, the collusion is between the members of the patient's family and the psychiatrist. All these authors voice very strong antipsychiatry sentiments. They believe that psychiatrists and psychiatric institutions are detrimental to the welfare of the patients and constitute a threat to human rights. They go further than anybody else in condemning the medical model, finding it not only irrelevant but also actively detrimental and evil.

Szasz is against state medicine and against state institutions employing psychiatrists as the agents of the state. According to him, the only acceptable role for the psychiatrist is that of an agent or an attorney for the patient. In this role the psychiatrist promotes the patient's interests in his interpersonal conflicts and the problems of living. The psychiatrist is under a contract with the patient to promote his interests and help him to untangle his problems of living. Szasz (1965b) proposes a new version of the ethics of psychoanalysis. He suggests that the psychiatrist should view the patient not as medically ill but as a fellow man morally striving to solve his personal problems. He should not try to suppress or control the patient's conduct but instead should create conditions that would allow the patient to be free and make responsible choices for his own benefit. The influence of the psychiatrist on the patient should not extend beyond the therapeutic situation, so as to not encroach on the latter's autonomy. The ethical value inherent in the psychoanalytical procedure should be cooperation among equals. The patient should be helped to learn new communicative techniques and play new games that are more adaptive than the old ones.

The Moral Transgression Model of Mental Illness of Hobart Mowrer

The moral transgression model, or sin model, of mental illness has been proposed by Hobart Mowrer (1961, 1962). The idea that mental illness could be caused by sin is not a new one. Early in the nineteenth century, August Heinroth, a member of the German Psychological (*Psychotiker*) school of psychiatry, equated mental illness with sin. He believed that both were caused by a loss of the freedom of will and by a fall from grace. Earlier theories attributing mental illness to possession by the devil or to witchcraft were of the same nature. Modern psychiatry, based on scientific medicine and scientific psychology, have explained mental illness in naturalistic, morally neutral terms. Mowrer strongly disagrees with this explanation. According to him, "personality disturbance can be adequately understood only in an interpersonal, social, moral matrix" (Mowrer, 1961), and further that " 'neurosis' is just a medical euphemism for a 'state of sin' and social alienation. . . . " (Mowrer, 1961). Neurosis is a moral problem caused by real, not imaginary, guilt feelings, resulting from a real moral transgression or sin.

Mowrer (1961) believes that scientific materialism and positivism, associated with the development of natural sciences in the nineteenth century, had disastrous consequences when applied to the problems of the human mind and of human society. Man has lost his soul, his spirituality, and he has been relieved of moral responsibility for his deeds. Under the influence of the Darwinian theory of evolution, the human mind has come to be regarded essentially as an organ of adaptation used by a biological organism in its struggle for survival. This view of the human mind influenced both the Freudian psychoanalysis and the American functionalist school of psychology, the forerunner of behaviourism. Consequently, man has been regarded as a biological organism to be studied by the natural sciences. Mowrer separates the natural order from the moral and believes that the human mind and human society belong to the latter. The moral order is based on a system of absolute values, on the freedom of will, on moral responsibility, and on the conception of man as a spiritual being. As such, he relates to God and to other human beings. In his psychological theory, Mowrer is concerned mainly with the horizontal relations to other humans rather than with the vertical relation to God. Hudson (1961) distinguished two Protestant traditions: the Puritan tradition, which emphasized the objectively revealed will of God and stressed submission to law and order, and the more liberal Wesleyan tradition, which stressed personal religious experience and individuality. Van Belle (1980) classifies Carl Rogers as belonging to the Wesleyan tradition. It seems that Mowrer belongs to the Puritan tradition, although he rejects its Calvinistic ingredients, in particular the doctrine of predestination and the doctrine of salvation by faith and by the grace of God. He believes that good works are an important ingredient of one's salvation.

Mowrer (1961), similarly to Emile Durkheim, relates the concept of God to human society. A man who is estranged from other human beings is also estranged from God. Mental illness is not a medical condition; it is a state of sin, of estrangement from other human beings, and of a fall from grace. In these views he follows Anton Boisen (1936), who regarded mental illness as a moral problem:

> ... the real evil in mental disorder is not to be found in conflict but in the sense of isolation or estrangement. It is the fear and guilt which result from

the presence in one's life of that which one is afraid to tell. For this reason I do not consider it necessary to lower the conscience threshold in order to get rid of the conflict. What is needed is forgiveness and restoration to the fellowship of that *social something which we call God* (italics added) (Boisen, 1936).

Mowrer (1961) chooses the Freudian psychoanalytical theory of psychoneurosis, based on a biological conception of man, as his prime target for attack. According to this theory, psychoneurosis is caused by a repression of those instinctual impulses emanating from the id by an excessively severe super-ego. Because of his strict upbringing, the individual is oversocialized. He is too inhibited to enjoy pleasures, and he has to punish himself constantly for no apparent reason. He suffers from imaginary guilt feelings and from destructive anxiety. The psychoanalytical treatment aims at relieving the patient from the burden of the oversevere super-ego and at releasing sexual and aggressive instinctual impulses. To put it briefly, according to Freud the psychoneurotic condition is due to a strong super-ego and to a weak id. The patient's torments and sufferings are due to too much inhibition. They are considered imaginary products of a diseased mind. A cure is brought about by an insight into the groundlessness of the feelings of depression and anxiety.

Mowrer disagrees with this position. He believes that, in addition to being ineffective, psychoanalysis may turn the analysand into an immoral psychopath and that it destroys the moral fabric of society. A psychoanalytical ideology permeates the whole of American society. The Freudian ethic (La Piere, 1959) affects the upbringing of children, the administration of justice, and even theological writings. Mowrer considers this influence to be detrimental to the moral fiber of society, resulting in overpermissiveness and in condoning sin. He questions the validity of the Freudian model of psychoneurosis. By way of refutation, he points out that some psychoanalysts who broke away from Freud, such as Wilhelm Stekel (1950), described a type of psychoneurosis that was produced by the pangs of conscience over real misdeeds. Mowrer believes that this is the state of affairs that occurs in every psychoneurosis and functional psychosis. According to him a person who becomes a mental patient has committed a misdeed or sin that caused harm to another person. As a result he is bothered by his conscience and feels guilty, contrite, and a need for making restitution. However, the future patient is dishonest with himself and with other people, and he suppresses the voice of conscience. Yet conscience is the voice of God, the root of man's spirituality, and it cannot be suppressed. It comes back to haunt the ill-doer in the way MacBeth was haunted by the spectre of the dagger. The suppressed guilty conscience manifests itself as depression, anxiety, and in other psychiatric symptoms. The patient is severely punished by his conscience; he experiences hell-on-this earth. His guilt and anxiety are constructive; they make him realize the enormity of his misdeed, and they focus his mind on the need for atonement, expiation, and restitution. To put it briefly again, in contrast to Freud, Mowrer believes that the psychoneurotic condition is due to a strong id and a weak or suppressed super-ego. However, Mowrer believes that conscience is more than the super-ego. It has a metaphysical significance, which has been characterized by various authors as immanent God in residence, inner light, guidance of the spirit, or omnipresence of Divine influence (Mowrer, 1961). Immanuel Kant calls it the categorical imperative. Mowrer (1961), following Van Dusen (1958), equates human conscience with the Holy Spirit. Through it man is enlightened; but also, if he has committed a sin, man, through it, is smitten by the wrath of God. Mental illness, therefore, is a moral problem concerned with the spiritual welfare of man and requires a pastoral guidance rather than medical treatment.

In the last chapter of his book, Mowrer (1961) offers a more detailed model of mental illness. According to Freud, the psychopath (sociopath) has an extremely weak super-ego, or conscience, the psychoneurotic has an extremely strong super-ego, while the normal occupies the intermediate position. Mowrer offers a different character typology. According to him the position of the neurotic falls between that of the psychopath, on the one hand and that of the normal person on the other. The latter has the strongest super-ego (conscience), followed by the psychoneurotic, who has a weak, repressed, super-ego. The super-ego of the psychopath is the weakest of the three. A depressed patient experiences his conscience, from which emanates guilt feelings, as located inside. In contrast, a paranoid or a schizophrenic projects his bad conscience outside and experiences it in the form of accusatory voices and tormenting influences. For this reason the prognosis in his case is worse than in that of a depressive.

The main criticism of Mowrer is directed against Freudian theory and the psychoanalytical practice. However, he also attacks biological psychiatry, which attempts to treat patients with electroconvulsive therapy and drugs and disregards the moral and spiritual aspects of mental illness. He disapproves of the Rogersian client-centred therapy, because of the nonjudgemental attitude towards the patient. He believes that a nonjudgemental attitude, conveyed by the unconditional regard for the patient, potentially condones immoral behaviour. It is the duty of the psychotherapist to take a stand on moral issues. According to Mowrer, psychotherapy or pastoral counselling should encourage the client to confess his sins and misdeeds not only to the counsellors but also to the significant others. Mowrer envisages public confession to a group of people, presumably of intimates, as the best psychotherapeutic technique. The confession should be followed by atonement for the misdeed, expiation of guilt, contrition, and most importantly by a restitution to the party that was wronged. As a result, redemption is achieved by the guilty individual, who attains, at the same time, a state of grace. Mowrer equates the latter with a state of mental health.

The Social Irresponsibility Model of Mental Illness of William Glasser

William Glasser (1960, 1975) has developed a new approach to the treatment of mental illness, which he calls Reality therapy. This therapy may be described as a form of moral education. The existence of mental illness, conceived as a medical condition, is denied. Instead, psychiatric patients are regarded as irresponsible individuals who deny social reality and who indulge in immoral behaviour. For Glasser psychiatric diagnoses are labels that should be " ... considered only as descriptions of irresponsibility, nothing more" (1975). He equates mental health with responsibility and mental illness with irresponsibility. Psychiatric patients, according to him, are not mentally ill but people who have run into social difficulties on account of their immoral behaviour.

Glasser postulates two basic human needs: the need for relatedness and the need for respect. These needs are not satisfied unless the person becomes emotionally involved with the significant others and unless he maintains satisfactory standards of behaviour. These are moral standards, since "all society is based on morality" (Glasser, 1975). An individual should not only be able to distinguish the morally right behaviour from the wrong but also to choose the right one. He should be a socially responsible person, so that his conduct would give him a feeling of self-worth and a feeling that he is worthwhile to others. Psychiatric patients refuse to face social reality, are irresponsible, do not choose the right behaviour, and fail to become emotionally involved with other people. The various psychiatric diagnostic categories, such as psychoneurosis, schizophrenia, or psychopathy, do not mean very much, because they describe different forms of basically the same irresponsibility and call for the same treatment. The implied model of mental illness is a continuity model, in which there is a gradation of irresponsibility from mild one, occurring in normal people, to severe one occurring in psychotic patients. Individuals described as mental patients have not been sufficiently socialized in consequence of a deficient emotional involvement early in life with the significant others. They have not learned how to satisfy their basic needs. However, Reality therapy is not concerned with the past and with the causes of irresponsible behaviour. It is concerned with the present problems of irresponsible behaviour and the choice between right and wrong. Psychotherapy cannot be value-neutral; it has to face the moral issues. The psychotherapist, like a good parent, has to instruct the patient in how to make correct choices. He must enforce a degree of firm discipline combined with an emotional acceptance of the patient. The psychotherapeutic contacts should have the character of relations between two real people and not one between transference figures. Reality therapy is not concerned with insights, with uncovering unconscious conflicts and motives, but rather is concerned with reeducation. It focuses on the moral quality of present behaviour and its social consequences. There is a danger that a focusing on the unconscious conflicts and motives could provide the patient with pleas and excuses for his immoral behaviour. Diagnosing irresponsible behaviour as sick does a disservice to both patient and society. The patient must learn to accept the idea that society is based on mutual obligations and ethical norms, not only at the verbal level but also at the level of actual conduct. Reality therapy involves a special kind of moral education with the psychotherapist playing the role of a teacher. In this respect it is not different from the activity of parents, teachers, clergymen, counselors, and others who try to raise children to be responsible citizens. Reality therapy is conducted mainly in groups of juvenile delinquents.

One can draw a similarity between the new approach to psychiatry, advocated by Glasser, and the moral treatment of the insane advocated by the early nineteenth century psychiatrists. The role of the psychotherapist as a teacher or an educator rather than that of a medical doctor has also been emphasized by E. Fuller Torrey (1974).

The Moral-Legal Model of Mental Illness, Summary

The moral-legal model is a continuity model, regarding mental illness as a form of transgression or social deviance. As such, mental illness is continuous with crime and generally with eccentric behaviour. It is initiated through free choice by an individual who is fully responsible, morally and legally, for his acts. The mental patient therefore has the same rights, duties, and responsibilities as any other normal citizen. Consequently, mental illness is equated with crime, sin, or eccentricity and should be treated accordingly. This model regards man as a citizen of a polity, which entails the possession by him of certain rights and the fulfillment of certain duties. For Szasz the envisaged utopian polity is libertarian, for Mowrer it is theocratic. Glasser accepts the existing society as the basis for moral order.

Chapter 7

EPILOGUE: WHITHER PSYCHIATRY, MONISM OR PLURALISM?

The preceding chapters described various models of mental illness. Seven major varieties of models have been described. Three are scientific: medical, psychological, and sociocultural. Four are philosophical-moral: hermeneutic-linguistic, phenomenological-existential, humanistic, and moral-legal. Most of these major varieties can be divided into more circumscribed models giving rise to a total number of fifteen. In turn, some of these may be further divided into submodels. Thus, there are three psychodynamic, three behaviouristic, two cognitive, two macro- and two microsocial, two linguistic-symbolic, two phenomenological, two humanistic, two hypersanity, and three moral-legal submodels. The detailed classification of the models of mental illness is presented in Table II.

This system of classification may appear to be cumbersome and too detailed. However, a complex system is necessary in order to describe the range of theories and the variety of concepts associated with the topic. For practical purposes the number of models could be reduced to reflect only the major differences of current opinion and practice on the North American continent. The resulting list would contain six perspectives, or models: the medical (both the disease and the constitutional), psychodynamic (primarily psychoanalytic), behaviouristic, macrosocial (social), microsocial (family and small group interactions), and humanistic. These six perspectives encompass the main theoretical orientations with regard to mental illness and the main types of therapy (Price, 1978). They also deal with the three main aspects of mental illness: subjective distress, social disability, and violation of social norms (Price & Lynn, 1981).

Siegler and Osmond (1974) in their book, which deals mainly with schizophrenia, proposed eight models: the medical, moral,

Table II
The Detailed Classification of Models

Main Groups	Major Varieties	Models	Submodels
Scientific	1. Medical	a. Disease b. Constitutional (dyscrasia)	
	2. Psychological	a. Psychodynamic	i. Intrapersonal developmental ii. Interpersonal developmental iii. Interpersonal situational
		b. Developmental	
		c. Behaviouristic	i. Pavlovian (classical conditioning) ii. S–R Hullian iii. Skinnerian operant conditioning
		d. Cognitive	i. Cognitive Structures ii. Inefficient behavioural strategy
	3. Socio-cultural	a. Macrosocial	i. Structural-Functionalist (synchronic) ii. Conflict (diachronic)
		b. Microsocial	i. Artificial groups ii. Natural groups (family)
Philosophical-Moral	1. Hermeneutic-Linguistic	a. Understanding (*Verstehen*)	
		b. Linguistic-Symbolic	i. Hermeneutic-linguistic ii. Structural-linguistic
	2. Phenomenological-Existential	a. Phenomenological	i. Descriptive ii. Structural-genetic
		b. Existential	
	3. Humanistic	a. Humanistic	i. Becoming ii. Being
		b. Hypersanity	i. Positive disintegration ii. Psychedelic
	4. Moral-Legal	Moral-Legal	i. Libertarian ii. Theocratic iii. Social reality

impaired, psychoanalytic, social, psychedelic, conspiratorial, and the family interactions. Their impaired model is similar to the constitutional model, which is discussed in this book. Their moral model is similar to the behaviouristic model. The present author feels that the term moral in this context is inappropriate, because it implies moral responsibility, guilt, and punishment rather than mechanical conditioning. It is preferable to distinguish the behaviouristic model based on the deterministic assumptions from the moral, which is based on the indeterministic assumptions and the acceptance of free will. Finally, Siegler and Osmond's conspiratorial model coincides with the labelling model of schizophrenia proposed by Thomas Scheff (1966, 1975). It also encompasses Thomas Szasz' (1961a, 1971) notion that mental illness is a myth, manufactured by psychiatrists.

COMPARISON OF THE MODELS

The models presented in this book vary in many respects, and it is important to establish the dimensions on which these models can be compared. All the models can be divided into two major groups: the scientific and the moral-philosophical. Radnitzky (1968) in his discussion of metascience has distinguished two schools of philosophy associated with different presuppositions regarding the nature of man and of human science. The first is that of logical empiricism and the second that of the hermeneutic-dialectical school of philosophy. By and large, the scientific models described in this book are representative of the first school, while the moral-philosophical ones belong to the second. This statement has to be qualified in the case of the sociocultural models. Some of these models, particularly the conflict-diachronic macrosocial model, come closer to representing the hermeneutic-dialectical rather than the logical-empiricist school of philosophy. These two schools are based on very different assumptions, so that it is difficult to compare the models of mental illness belonging to one school with those of the other. The models based on the logical-empiricist thinking are deterministic, so it makes sense in their case to talk about the causes, the etiology, of mental illness or about prognosis. The models stemming from the hermeneutic-dialectical tradition are associated with the view of man as a free agent, a subject actively shaping his own destiny, rather than an object buffeted by internal biological and external environmental forces. Since these two kinds of models view man from entirely different perspectives, they may be applied simultaneously without contradicting each other. For instance, the medical and psychodynamic models are concerned with causal explanation of mental illness, its prognosis, and its treatment, while the phenomenological-existential model is concerned with understanding the patient's experience as a unique human being. They may complement each other and are often applied by the European psychiatrists to the same patient. The difficulty arises when the "nothing but" attitude is taken and thinking proceeds in terms of exclusive polarities rather than of complementarities (Radnitzky, 1968).

The models stemming from the logical-empiricist thinking and those belonging to the hermeneutic-dialectical tradition may be meaningfully compared in regard to where they stand on the four outstanding philosophical issues arising from the discussions of mental health that were spelled out in the first chapter.

On the first, the mind-body issue, the logical-empiricist (scientific) models tend to take the materialistic position while the hermeneutic-dialectical (moral-philosophical) models tend to have an idealistic orientation. The first focus on the body and the second on the mind. Those belonging to the first category, which claim to be psychological, conceive of mind in mechanistic terms.

The view, inspired by Cartesian dualism, that the body is a complex machine, qualitatively different from the mind, has tended to encourage either *the* somatic or *the* psychological approach as the valid one to the exclusion of the other. It has led to the necessity of an either-or choice, forcing a split between the psychologically and somatically oriented schools of psychiatry. The contemporary conflict between biological psychiatry on the one hand and the psychodynamic and psychological approaches on the other illustrates the point. The rigid, almost irreversible separation of the two perspectives is perpetuated by the traditional Cartesian conceptualization of mind and body as two mutually incompatible categories. Only a rejection of the traditional metaphysical categories, deeply ingrained in Western thought, would do away with the body-mind or the psychological-somatic polarization. This would, in turn, undermine the institutionalized divisions between biological and social sciences and between medicine and psychology. It would also weaken the intellectual and professional commitment to the two alternative approaches. A rejection of such old metaphysical categories as substance, matter, mind, or causality, as advocated by some phenomenologists and existentialists, may be one approach towards this solution. Another approach is offered by the general systems theory, which disregards the concept of substance, either material or mental, and concentrates on the principles of organization. The latter vary in the level of complexity. There are however no gaps as those separating qualitatively different substances.

On the second issue, of determinism versus indeterminism, the dividing line is clearly drawn. The philosophical-moral models of mental illness take an indeterministic stand as far as human behaviour is concerned. They stress freedom of will, freedom of choice by the individual, and his moral responsibility. The scientific (logical-empiricist) models, on the other hand, assume that human behaviour is, to a greater or lesser extent, determined. The proponents of the latter approach attempt to make valid predictions regarding human behaviour and discover the laws governing it with a view to exercising control. This is the most important issue because it is associated with two diametrically opposing views of man. The attempt at a reconciliation of these views will be discussed below.

Closely related to the issue of determinism versus indeterminism is the third issue of a value-free versus morally judgemental theory of mental illness and of psychotherapy. This is part of a broader issue of value free social science. As a consequence of their stand on the previous issue, the proponents of philosophical-moral models take a morally judgemental position while the advocates of scientific models are inclined towards the value-free, nonjudgemental point of view.

With regard to the fourth issue of autonomy versus conformity, the philosophical-moral models stress individual autonomy while the scientific models stress social conformity as the index of mental health.

The next two sets of comparisons deal separately with the scientific and the philosophical-moral models. The relevant dimensions of comparison are different for the two groups.

The comparison of the scientific models

The common dimensions important for the comparison of scientific models are (1) the locus of causation (etiology), (2) the importance of diagnosis (classification), (3) the time and the character of the onset, (4) continuity, (5) the importance of theoretical constructs, (6) treatment, and (7) the concept of man implied by the model. Undoubtedly, the proposed list of dimensions is not exhaustive. There are alternatives that could be suggested. Thus, Siegler and Osmond (1974) in their comparison of models of madness use twelve dimensions, and Price (1978) uses six when comparing different perspectives on abnormal behaviour. However, the focus of these authors is somewhat different from the one in the present book, which is on the theoretical frames of reference and the concepts of man implied by the various models of mental illness. Table III presents the comparison of the scientific (medical, psychological, and sociocultural) models on the seven dimensions listed above.

The dimension of continuity requires some further comments. In this book the continuity-discontinuity theme has played the most prominent role in the discussion of the various models of mental illness and of illness in general. This dimension distinguishes the two historically most important models in medicine: the disease, a discontinuous model, and the constitutional, a continuous one. It also distinguishes two contrasting views of psychopathology. According to the continuity view psychopathological phenomena are extreme deviations of the normal, while the discontinuity view regards them as qualitatively different and as alien. Historically, the discontinuity position has been largely associated with the active and aggressive treatment of a passive patient. The continuity view, on the other hand, has tended to rely more on the natural recuperative powers of the organism to regain its equilibrium and on natural personality growth. The continuity hypothesis implies that there are no intrinsic, qualitative differences between mental illness and mental health. A cogent argument, of course, could be made that a large quantitative difference would produce a qualitative one, so the distinction could be artificial. However, the advocates of the discontinuity position assume that there are intrinsic qualitative differences between health and illness, irrespective of the severity of the latter.

Table III
COMPARISON OF SCIENTIFIC MODELS

Variety of Models	Models	Dimensions		
		Causation (etiology)	Diagnosis (Classification)	Onset
Medical	Disease	Somatic (localized or systemic); mental symptoms are epiphenomena	Stress on classification into nosological (disease) categories	A definite point of onset at any time in life; appears to be extrinsic to personality development
Medical	Constitutional (dyscrasia)	Somatic-organismic (The totality of biological make-up)	Diagnosis of somatotype and temperament	Inborn; intrinsic to personality development
Psychological	Psychodynamic	Unconscious psychological conflicts	Diagnosis of unique unconscious psychodynamic forces (idiographic)	Early childhood experience causing unconscious conflict
Psychological	Developmental (orthogenic)	Arrest of maturational process or regression to an earlier more primitive stage	Diagnosis of the level of orthogenic development	Development stops at a certain stage, or there is regression to an earlier, primitive, one
Psychological	Behavioristic	Conditioning; learning of faulty habits	Precise diagnosis of circumscribed faulty habits	At any time in life. Presently existing habits are important and not their history
Psychological	Cognitive	Distorted representation of the world and faulty behavior strategies	Diagnosis of the cognitive representation of the world	At any time in life, although more likely early in life
Socio-Cultural	Macro-social	Disintegration of social fabric or social conflict	Diagnosis of social structure in which individuals participate	At any time, but early socialization processes are important
Socio-Cultural	Micro-social	Faulty interpersonal relations and communications in small groups	Diagnosis of small group processes in which individuals participate	At any time, but early family relations are important

Table III
COMPARISON OF SCIENTIFIC MODELS (cont'd.)

Dimensions			
Continuity vs. Discontinuity	**Theoretical Constructs**	**Treatment**	**Concept of Man**
Discontinuity of mental disease and mental health	Disease *(morbus)*; disease process	Somatic: mainly drugs, but also ECT and psychosurgery	Man is a complex physio-chemical machine in which some components may become faulty
Continuity of mental health and illness; (although an arbitrary cut-off point may be established)	Body and temperament types or dimensions	Custodial and symptomatic	Man is a bio-psychological organism which functions as a whole
Continuity: mild emotional disturbances are continuous with neurosis and the latter with psychosis	Psychological apparatus and mechanisms: id, ego, super-ego, defence cathexis, etc.	Insight psychotherapy	Man is motivated by non-rational forces in conflict with one another and with social mores
Continuity of mental health and illness, although there may be discontinuity between the stages of development	Such orthogenic constructs as maturity, differentiation, integration, etc.	Remedial education	Man is a developing organism passing from a low primitive to a high complex level
Continuity of mental health and illness. There is no intrinsic difference between "right" and "wrong" habits	The model, particularly its Skinnerian version eschews theoretical constructs	Behavior therapy	Man is an assembly of reflexes and habits
Continuity of mental health and illness. Abnormal cognitive structures continuous with normal ones	Such constructs as belief, expectancy, congruity and cognitive structure	Rational psychotherapy	Man is a rational information processing system
Continuity of mental health and illness. Mental illness continuous with social deviance	Such constructs as social structure, role, institution, anomie and alienation	Social engineering	Man is a link in the social fabric and mirrors social relations, structures, values and institutions
Continuity of mental health and illness; abnormal small groups continuous with normal ones	Such constructs as roles, dyads, and channels of communication	Group psychotherapy	Man is a link in group dynamic processes such as family relationships

Another fact that confuses the continuity versus discontinuity issue is the possibility of imposing arbitrary cutoff points on continuous dimensions. Such cutoff points may be established to separate, for pragmatic reasons, the mentally ill from mentally healthy or the intellectually subnormal from normal. There is a general tendency of the human mind to break down natural continuities into discrete categories, or classes, for conceptual or pragmatic reasons. These extrinsic classes have to be distinguished from the naturally occurring discontinuities. The classical concept of disease that existed, for example, in eighteenth century nosologies assumed intrinsic discontinuities between different diseases and the state of health. The eighteenth century view of nosology, because of the ignorance regarding the pathological processes causing symptoms of mental diseases, has persisted in psychiatry much longer than in the other branches of medicine. One of its manifestations is the search for the essential features of schizophrenia. The tendency to separate the observed phenomena into discrete classes was characteristic of the early science, such as the Aristotelian physics. According to this view the properties of objects and events depended on their class membership. The new science of the seventeenth century, as exemplified by the Gallilean physics, replaced the concept of classes by that of continuous dimensions and variables. Medicine and psychology followed suit. In medicine, Claude Bernard (1961) substituted a set of parameters describing physiological mechanisms for discrete disease categories. A deviation beyond a certain value or values on these parameters produced pathology. Similarly, the psychology of discrete faculties and types was replaced by that of continuous dimensions and variables.

The models of mental illness also differ in the type and the extent of the theoretical constructs they use. Theoretical constructs are entities not directly observable. They are only inferred from observations and are used as explanatory tools. The psychodynamic model relies heavily on theoretical constructs, which form the structure of its metapsychology and provide an explanation of the observed events. On the other hand, the behaviouristic model, particularly in its Skinnerian version, eschews theoretical constructs altogether and is limited in scope to observable events and their correlations.

The scientific models, the characteristics of which were summarized in Table II, are explicitly or implicitly based on the logical-empiricist philosophical outlook. They stress objectivity, the consensual validation of knowledge claims, and the confirmation of predictions from theory by observations. The philosophic-moral models, which may be described after Radnitzky (1968) as hermeneutic-dialectical, rely to a great extent on subjective experiences and valuations. They also are less inclined to separate the observing subject from the object of observation. To these models we now turn.

The comparison of the philosophical-moral models

The dimensions of comparison for this group of models are less obvious than those for the previous one. They are concerned more with the nature of man revealed through mental illness than with the empirical features of the latter. The following six dimensions can be suggested: (1) continuity, (2) historicity, (3) attitude towards conventional science and medical psychiatry, (4) phenomenological description versus the assumption of deep structure, (5) objectivity of values (naturalistic versus social versus subjective), (6) counselling (treatment), and (7) the concept of man implied by the model.

The continuity dimension is concerned with the same problem as the one in the comparison of the scientific models. Historicity is concerned with the time dimension of each unique human existence as reflected by the different models of mental illness. It conceives of the client as anchored in his past and as reaching towards the future. The ahistorical view is concerned only with the present experiences of the subject.

The philosophical-moral models differ in their attitude towards conventional science and medical psychiatry. Some of them reject the scientific and medical models as being incompatible with the freedom and dignity of man. The proponents of these models redefine mental illness in their own exclusive terms, which replace those of the medico-scientific approach. An example of this attitude towards the medical and scientific models are the antipsychiatry sentiments voiced by Thomas Szasz and by R. D. Laing and his associates. By and large, the phenomenological and existential models are neutral on this issue. Their proponents believe that the phenomenological and existentialist approaches provide additional dimensions that offer a better understanding of the patients as unique human beings. Further, they believe that these additional dimensions can be accommodated with other dimensions, or points of view, such as the biological or the psychodynamic, and do not exclude the latter. Similarly, the humanistic model does not reject the scientific approach. However, it maintains that the conventional science, which has been developed in the context of the study of physical objects, is too narrow and is not applicable to the behaviour and experiences of human beings. In the context of psychology it should be replaced by a new humanistic science, better suited to deal with mental phenomena.

The dimension of phenomenological description versus the assumption of deep structure differentiates the models as to how much weight they attach to the immediate conscious experiences, as against the deep unconscious structure underlying these experiences. The phenomenological model with its preoccupation with the data of consciousness represents one end of this continuum. The linguistic model, particularly in its Lacanian, structuralist version, represents the other.

The philosophical-moral models differ as to the theory of value and the type of ethics they follow. The humanistic model subscribes to the objective, naturalistic theory of values and seeks their source in the developmental potential of man, viewed as a special biological organism— *homo sapiens*— unique in its characteristics. The existentialists take a subjectivist point of view and believe that man creates his values by his free choices. Finally, the proponents of the moral-legal model seek the source of values in a utopian society. According to Szasz this is a society based on the libertarian ethics. For Mowrer it is a theocratic society based on the divine law. However, Glasser, in contrast to the other two proponents of the model, seems to take the existing society as the basis for his notion of social reality and as the source of values.

In describing the therapeutic interventions, the term counselling instead of treatment is used. The term counselling implies an encounter between two individuals who interact and in the process of interaction influence one another. The term treatment implies an active manipulation of a passive patient, an object, by an expert, a doctor, or a scientist. This term better suits the type of therapy associated with the scientific models of mental illness, while the term counselling is more in keeping with the therapy advocated by the philosophical-moral models.

The concept of man implied by a particular model of mental illness deals with the philosophical-anthropological assumptions underlying it. Thus, according to some interpretations of the humanistic model, such as that proposed by Maslow, the human personality actualizes its potential. Accordingly, the human essence precedes existence. On the other hand, according to the existential model existence precedes essence. Therefore, man creates his own personality by his free choices. Another aspect of this dimension concerns the place of man in the order of things. According to the humanistic-secular point of view man represents the highest value and is the master of himself and of the world. The humanistic-theistic view places the highest value on God and expects man to obey the divine commandments and laws. The purpose of man is to glorify God rather than himself.

Some models stress individualism, others interpersonal relations, and still others membership in a community with the resulting duties, rights, and obligations. Table IV presents the comparison of philosophical-moral models on the seven dimensions, discussed in this section.

This concludes the section dealing with the comparisons of the models. The next section attempts to answer the question whether the various models of mental illness can be reconciled. A positive answer would make it possible to substitute a meaningful discourse in place of the babble of confused voices that characterizes, at the present, the debates about mental health.

TOWARDS A PERSPECTIVIST VIEW OF MENTAL ILLNESS

In the contemporary discussions of different theories and models of mental illness, usually one is singled out as the only true model. Other models are criticized as false, misleading, and resulting in harmful practices. Thus, Siegler and Osmond (1974), in their book *Models of Madness, Models of Medicine,* take up the cudgels in the defence of the medical model as the most appropriate for dealing with schizophrenia and other functional psychoses. They also advocate narrowing the field of psychotherapy to a purely medical variety,

Table IV
COMPARISON OF PHILOSOPHICAL - MORAL MODELS

Variety of Models	Models	Dimensions		
		Continuity	Historicity	Attitude Towards Science and Medicine
Hermeneutic-linguistic	Understanding (Das Verstehen)	Continuity of "normal" and "pathological" characters	Historical development of personality, its past and its future are important	*Das Verstehen* is an alternative method to the scientific one
Hermeneutic-linguistic	Linguistic-symbolic	Ambiguous on this issue. Symbolic forms in psychosis may be discontinuous with ones in the normal states	Two aspects: the synchronic which is ahistorical, and the diachronic which is historical	Ambiguous on this issue
Phenomenological-existential	Phenomenological	Discontinuity: each mental patient lives in a different *umwelt* from that of normal people	The model is ahistorical. It relies on the study of momentary states of consciousness	A parallel approach, but not contradictory to the scientific
Phenomenological-existential	Existential	Discontinuous: each *Dasein* is unique	The historicity of *Dasein* is important	A parallel approach, but not contradictory to the scientific
Humanistic variety	Humanistic	Stress on positive mental health. Superior mental health is continuous with normality and with mental illness.	Stress on natural development of personality and its self-actualization, rather than on historicity	Rejection of the conventional science, as inapplicable to man, and its replacement by the humanistic science
Humanistic variety	Supersanity (Psychedelic)	Mental illness is a stage of personality development leading to superior mental health	Stress on the natural development and social memories, rather than the unique historicity of the individual	Rejection of the conventional science, as inapplicable to man, and its replacement by the humanistic science
Moral-legal variety	Moral-legal	There is a continuity (identity) of "mental" illness" with crime and social deviance	Irrelevant	Rejection of scientific-medical explanation of normal and abnormal behavior

Table IV
COMPARISON OF PHILOSOPHICAL - MORAL MODELS (cont'd.)

Dimensions			
Phenomenological Description Vs. Assumption of Deep Structure	Objectivity Vs. Subjectivity of Values	Counselling	Concept of Man
Common sense understanding of motive and reasons behind the observed behavior	In most cases subjectivity of values	Common sense counselling	Each human character to be understood by literary intuition
Stress on the unconscious deep structure and hidden meaning	Ambiguous on this issue. However values may be construed as existing objectively in the deep structure	Modified psycho-analysis	Man is a reflection of the linguistic-symbolic system
Phenomenological description of consciousness	Phenomenological study of values is inclined towards the objectivity position	Irrelevant	The "man-in-the-world" experience is the basis for the understanding of man
Rejection of the unconscious, hermeneutic understanding of the structure of the *Dasein*	Subjective values created by each individual by his free choices	Existential encounter and logotherapy	Man is an unique *Dasein* embedded in his historicity and facticity oriented towards his death
The unconscious is the source of creativity, but there is no stress to the deep structure	Naturalistic, objective theory of values	Non-directive counselling or existential encounter	Man is equated with a developing and actualizing self
The unconscious, particularly the collective unconscious is a source of creativity	The positive-disintegration theory stresses to objectivity of values. The psychedelic theory is ambiguous on this issue.	A "guru" guides the subject through his psychedelic experiences	Man is equated with a developing and actualizing self
Rejection of the unconscious and of the deep structure	Values are embedded in the social-moral order	Moral re-education	Man is a person in the legal sense, a citizen of a polity

leaving other varieties to educators, clergymen, and gurus. By implication they reject the idea of positive mental health and equate normality with the absence of a disease. Thomas Szasz (1961a), on the other hand, rejects the medical model and replaces it by a moral model, based on the ethical theory and on language games. Similarly, E. Fuller Torrey (1974), in *The Death of Psychiatry*, rejects the medical model and advocates its replacement by the educational one. These three examples will suffice, as they are typical of the ongoing polemics. The arguments have a nothing-but character: for example, that schizophrenia is nothing but a disease caused by a crooked chemical molecule in the brain or schizophrenia is nothing but an accumulation of faulty habits. One point of view, or perspective, is adopted, the others are criticized and rejected. Radnitzky (1968) characterizes this approach to scientific theories as the polarity stage. If two theories appear to contradict one another, one is totalized to the exclusion of the other. According to Radnitzky this stage in the development of science is superseded by one of the complementarity, as illustrated by the Bohr's well-known complementarity thesis in physics. The two theories do not contradict but rather complement each other.

Before the themes of complementarity and perspectivism are further developed, it is necessary to consider the possibility of constructing a unitary supermodel of mental illness. Such a model would supersede the existing models; however, on its way it would be required to overcome many obstacles. It would have to deal with the traditional split between mind and body and also with the split between the natural sciences and *Geisteswissenschaften* (humanities and social sciences). The supermodel would have to reconcile the Lockean and the Leibnitzian views of man. Finally, the supermodel would have to breach the barriers between traditional disciplines and cope with the vested professional interests.

Reductionism

The reductionist approach was an early attempt to breach these barriers. It advocated that social and cultural phenomena were to be reduced to the psychological. The latter, in turn, were to be reduced to biological phenomena, and so on down to the phenomena described by the subatomic physics. In this way the humanities and social sciences were to be reduced to the natural sciences. A sophisticated version of reductionism was offered by logical positivists in the form of the principle of unity of science. Two members of this school, Rudolf Carnap, a physical scientist, and Otto Neurath, a social scientist, maintained that all scientific propositions whether pertaining to social, psychological, biological or physical sciences can be stated in a physicalistic language and, therefore, are about physical objects. According to the principle of unity of science, all empirical sciences are fundamentally one. The division into different disciplines is accidental and purely practical. The proponents of unity of science believed the same scientific method is applicable to physical, biological, psychological, and social sciences. According to Carnap (1959) psychology can be reduced to the description of physical behaviour without any loss of meaning. This assertion became the cornerstone of logical behaviourism.

If the unity of science principle were followed to its logical conclusion, the supermodel of mental illness could be constructed at the microlevel in terms of the molecular biochemistry and biophysics. It would probably be concerned with the neurosynaptic events and the synaptic receptors. The supermodel, therefore, would be a scientific-medical one. Alternatively, the reduction could stop at the macrolevel of overt behaviour, described in the physicalistic language, and result in a radically behaviouristic supermodel. However, the reductionistic strategy fails and has to be rejected because it can be shown that it is impossible to translate propositions belonging to a higher level theory into those of a lower level without a considerable loss of meaning. It is impossible logically to derive a higher order scientific laws from a lower order ones. Also a community of scientists, intercommunicating, interpreting research data, and clarifying their meaning, is a precondition of any science, including the natural. This condition implies the necessity of a hermeneutic discourse among the scientists.

General Systems Theory

General systems theory, which is explicitly antireductionist, has come to play an important role in the biological and social sciences. It has also influenced psychiatric thinking (Gray, Duhl, & Rizzo, 1969; von Bertalanffy, 1966, 1968). This theory has already been described in Chapter 5 in connection with the discussions of small group interactions. For further details the reader is referred to the reviews by von Bertalanffy (1968), by Weiss (1969, 1977), and by Miller (1978). General systems theory views the world as a hierarchy of systems differing in the complexity of organization. It attempts to reconcile the Newtonian mechanistic outlook with the organismic one. It also tries to find the common characteristics of and the differences between the servomechanical, the biological, and the sociocultural systems. The theory is concerned with the abstract, organizational principles describing the relations among the components of systems rather than with the components themselves. According to Gray and Rizzo (Gray, Duhl, & Rizzo, 1969) it is a logical-mathematical theory dealing with the problems of wholeness, dynamic interaction, and organization. It is also concerned with integration, differentiation, growth, and communication. One of its interests is in the apparent teleology of the behaviour of the systems, called the principle of equifinality. Cybernetics, computer science, the information and communication theories, system engineering, operations research, and the games and decision theories are specialized formal disciplines that come under the general umbrella of systems theory and deal with specific areas of its application.

Although systems vary in complexity, certain of their features are isomorphic. This allows one to derive general laws applicable to all systems. Systems are governed by interactions and feedbacks rather than by linear causality. This characteristic is responsible for their self-regulation, a relative autonomy of the systems from the environment, and the development in the direction of negative entropy.

As it was pointed out in Chapter 5, systems vary in the degree to which they are closed or open and in the degree to which they are concerned with the transformations of energy or with the information and communication processing. Ludwig von Bertalanffy (Gray, Duhl, & Rizzo, 1969) maintains that the system at the human level creates a symbolic universe of language, thought, and art that becomes an important part of man's environment. Jurgen Ruesch (Gray, Duhl, & Rizzo, 1969), for example, has applied the general systems theory to human communication. It can thus be seen that the systems theory principles are applicable from the level of the

DNA molecule to the level of complex social processes.

The features of general systems theory provide an integrative potential for unification of science (Boulding, 1956; von Bertalanffy in Gray, Duhl, & Rizzo, 1969). Its contribution to the goal of the unity of science is more promising than the previous reductionist attempts of the logical positivists. According to its proponents the theory could provide a general framework for various special disciplines such as biology, medicine, psychology, sociology, cultural anthropology, and linguistics. It would provide a common language for the specialists in these different disciplines and would facilitate their intercommunication. General systems theory would not supersede the special disciplines but rather would allow them to establish meaningful relationships. Von Bertalanffy (Gray, Duhl, & Rizzo, 1969) uses the term perspectivism to describe this approach to the integration of scientific knowledge. The theories and models proposed by different disciplines would not be replaced by a new supertheory or a supermodel but would become compatible with one another because of the general underlying principles. This notion of perspectivism differs somewhat from that of Price (1978). He believes that the prevalence of various perspectives in the field of mental health is due to the unsettled period of a scientific revolution (Kuhn, 1962) to be followed by a period of normal science. During the latter period one perspective will be selected as paradigmatic. In contrast, von Bertalanffy assumes that knowledge in general, and in particular knowledge about man, will always require several perspectives, and its acquisition cannot be reduced to one paradigm. Perspectivism has to be dissociated from a thoughtless eclecticism. Eclecticism implies casual borrowing of concepts and ideas from different theories and models to suit the occasion. The procedure is quite unsystematic. In the approach advocated by von Bertalanffy, the various levels of theorizing form an orderly hierarchy that prevents a random selection of concepts from different theories.

The perspectivism of the general systems theory has offered hope that different models of mental illness (the medical, the psychological, the sociocultural, and even the humanistic) could be reconciled and made mutually compatible. Following this line of thought, Grinker (1967) and his collaborators have attempted to develop a unified theory of human behaviour based on the systems approach to serve as a general scientific framework. Menninger's theory of vital balance (Menninger, 1963), dealing with the problems of mental health and illness, has also been influenced by the concepts of general systems theory. Arieti (1955; Gray, Duhl, & Rizzo, 1969), applying systems principles to an interpretation of schizophrenia, has suggested that in addition to causing a dedifferentiation of the personality structure the schizophrenic process has some features of an open system with a tendency to increase negative entropy. The delusions tend to proliferate, to ramify, and to become more complex and elaborated. As time goes on an increasingly wide range of experiences is drawn to and organized around the original delusional nucleus.

George Engel (1977, 1980) has developed a biopsychosocial model of illness and of the patient's care based on systems theory. It is applicable to both physical and mental illness. This model stresses holism and the hierarchy of systems from the cell to the society. It views man both as a biological organism and as a person interacting with other persons. The biopsychosocial model is destined, according to Engel, to replace the reductionist biomedical model, which is at the present the dominant model in medicine. Thus, it is destined to bridge the schism between natural science and humanism by creating a holistic framework of human science.

The psychobiological model of disregulation, proposed by G. E. Schwartz (1977) to explain psychosomatic disorders, provides another illustration of systems theory as applied to medicine. Schwartz has described a system of information inputs and feedbacks between the environment, the brain, and the bodily organs. In this system of interactions the brain is the main regulatory center controlling both the behaviour of the organism and the function of the bodily organs. Psychosomatic diseases, such as a peptic ulcer or hypertension, are caused by a disturbance of the regulatory processes of the information processing system.

A general systems theory framework is useful for the integration of various approaches to mental illness, but only up to a point. It is sometimes criticized as being so general and abstract as to be empty. There are also objections from the humanistic point of view. Jurgen Ruesch (Gray, Duhl, & Rizzo, 1969) has warned of the danger that a system-oriented world view will replace the person-oriented one, with man becoming an expendable unit of a system. Further, while the humanistic model of personality and mental illness can be accommodated to the systems point of view, the existentialist and phenomenological models are incompatible with it. Although the behaviour of some sophisticated systems may appear to be indetermined, systems theory implies a deterministic point of view (not a linear causality but the simultaneous interactions of multiple feedbacks). On the other hand, existentialism presupposes the indeterminism of human behaviour and a freedom of individuals to make choices. The systems concept postulates an objective hierarchy of values and therefore the naturalistic theory of ethics. The ethical norms are derived from systems principles and are set either by the system itself or by its supersystem (Miller in Gray, Duhl, & Rizzo, 1969). This naturalistic theory of values is shared by both systems theory and the humanistic model. In this respect the two theories are different from existentialism, which presupposes that values are created by free choices of the individual. Finally, systems theory is confronted with the problem of consciousness and of subjectivity. Some new developments in the theory and in the higher order cybernetics attempt to deal with these problems. In this context, Francisco Varela (1979) has discussed self-referential systems, which he believes have many characteristics of conscious experiences. However, not everybody finds his arguments convincing.

Perspectivism

There are some other theoretical orientations that lend themselves to a perspectivist view. Adrian Van Kaam, a Dutch existentialist psychologist who came to America and has had training in client-centred therapy, in his book entitled *Existential Foundations of Psychology* (1966) has presented a version of perspectivism. He takes an existentialist point of view that encompasses the totality of man-in-his-world. Within this general, encompassing view, there can be differentiated perspectives, broader or narrower, dealing with particular aspects of man—the biological, psychodynamic, societal, and so on. These perspectives abstract certain aspects of the concrete man. They are of limited scope and usefulness, but each serves a purpose. Single perspectives do not present the complete view of man and do not tell the whole truth about him. However, they complement one another without exhausting the totality of knowledge about him and the full meaning of his existence.

The final version of perspectivism to be discussed is that proposed by Apel (1967) and Radnitzky (1968). These authors are concerned with the relation of the natural sciences to the humanities and social sciences, or to be more technical, the relationship of the logical-empiricist and the hermeneutic-dialectic views of man. The first explains human behaviour in terms of causes, the second in terms of reasons, meanings, and free choices. This version of perspectivism does not focus on ontology such as that of the hierarchy of systems but rather on the epistemology of various approaches to knowledge. Jurgen Habermas (1972) has proposed a three-fold classification of various disciplines: the empirical-analytic, historical-hermeneutic, and empirical-critical. These three groups are associated with three distinct human interests and fields of activity. The empirical-analytical disciplines are associated with work and technology and with the mastery of the external world. They are embedded in the technological progress of humanity and are concerned with value-free natural facts. The historical-hermeneutic are associated with language communication, interpretation, semantics, and self- and other understanding. The empirical-critical group of disciplines is concerned with the steering and control of the self and with the self-emancipatory interests. By critical self-reflection and the critique of society man frees himself from irrational constraints. He reaches a state of higher enlightenment and rationality. The three groups of disciplines use different methods, have different criteria of validity, and the most important, serve different human interests. However, they complement one another to create the totality of knowledge. According to this schema, the biological sciences, as applied to the field of mental illness, belong to the group of empirical-analytical disciplines and fall under the umbrella of logical-empiricism. The *Verstehen* (understanding) model of mental illness, the existentialist approach, and some aspects of the psychoanalytical procedure belong to the historical-hermeneutic category. They are concerned with explication and clarification of private meanings conveyed by verbal and nonverbal communications of the client. The behavioral and social sciences and the models associated with them belong, or should belong, to the empirical-critical group, although they are very often treated as if they were members of the empirical-analytical category.

Most of psychoanalytical theory and method should be classified as empirical-critical.

Apel (1967) and Radnitzky (1968) have somewhat modified the schema proposed by Habermas and spelled out more clearly the notion of the complementarity between the naturalistic and the hermeneutic approaches. They distinguish only two groups of disciplines among those concerned with man: the naturalistic (logical-empiricist) and the hermeneutic-emancipatory (hermeneutic-dialectic). Psychoanalysis as a purely scientific discipline, to be distinguished from its clinical application, occupies the central position with regard to the understanding of man and of making him self-transparent and rational. It offers the key to his emancipation by revealing to him his unconscious motives and freeing him from their bondage. At the level of society the discipline of social critique plays a corresponding role. According to Apel (1967) psychoanalysis combined the hermeneutic dialogue between the analysand and the analyst with quasi-naturalistic phases. During the hermeneutic dialogue phase the analyst, using the *Verstehen* (understanding) method, tries to understand the reasons for the analysand's ideation and behaviour. He tries to discern the means utilized by the latter to achieve his ends and explicate the meaning of his ideas. The dialogue takes place on the level of common sense and of the ordinary language. When the hermeneutic dialogue arrives at a barrier that prevents further understanding of the analysand's behaviour and thinking a switch to the quasinaturalistic phase occurs. During that phase the analyst objectifies the analysand. He treats his utterances as symptoms caused by the unconscious forces and mechanisms. As soon as the analysand achieves an insight into his unconscious motives, starts treating them as the reasons for his behaviour, and controls them, the hermeneutic dialogue is resumed. In this way the analysand becomes emancipated from the irrational constraints on the freedom of his behaviour. A similar interpretation of psychoanalysis has been offered by De Waelhens (1961).

The example of psychoanalysis indicates the manner in which the naturalistic and the hermeneutic approaches can complement each other, similarly to the complementarity in the subatomic physics as enunciated by Bohr's principle. The complementarity view of different approaches has to be contrasted with the polarity view. In the latter case, one approach or theory is totalized to the exclusion of the others. According to Radnitzky (1968) in the development of science the complementarity view supersedes that of polarity. For the science of man the complementarity thesis offers a version of perspectivism in which the biological, psychological, social, and spiritual points of view complement one another in a coordinated fashion. There is a continuous interaction among the pursuits of knowledge, associated with different points of view, increasing the degree and the precision of their coordination. The recent developments in the areas of physiological psychology and brain research offer an example of a growing coordination between the somatic and the psychological approaches. In the context of the models of mental illness, the complementarity view, as proposed by Apel and Radnitzky, would place the psychodynamic model in the central position. This model would bridge the gap between the medical (biological) and the behaviouristic models on one hand and the *Verstehen*, the phenomenological, and the existentialist on the other. The first group is based on the logical-empiricist paradigm of science, the second on the hermeneutic. The dialectic of psychoanalysis reconciles and brings together the two approaches.

The answer to the question posed in the title of the present chapter—"Whither psychiatry, monism or pluralism?"—should be pluralism. Psychiatry, and generally the disciplines dealing with the problem of mental illness, should pursue pluralistic goals rather than strive to attain a monistic solution. However, the pluralistic goals should be coordinated in a meaningful scheme or *Weltanschauung* (world view). More than one *Weltanschauung* is possible. The frameworks for integrating models of mental illness discussed in the present chapter included general systems, the existentialist, and the one offered by the social critique school of philosophy of science. Other frameworks could possibly be adopted to serve as the philosophical-anthropological frameworks for coordinating various models of mental illness.

REFERENCES

Abramowitz, S. I. Locus of control and self-reported depression among college students. *Psychological Reports,* 1969, *25,* 149-150.

Abramson, L. Y., Seligman, M. E. P., & Teasdale, J. D. Learned helplessness in humans: Critique and reformulation. *Journal of Abnormal Psychology,* 1978, *87,* 49-74.

Ackerman, N. W. *The psychodynamics of family life.* New York: Basic Books, 1958.

Adler, A. *The practice and theory of individual psychology.* Paterson, N. J.: Littlefield & Adams, 1963.

Adler, A. *Problems of neurosis.* New York: Harper & Row, 1964.

Allport, G. W. *Personality: A psychological interpretation.* New York: Holt, 1937.

Allport, G. W. *Becoming, basic considerations for a psychology of personality.* New Haven: Yale University Press, 1955.

American Psychiatric Association, *Diagnostic and statistical manual of mental disorders (DSM 11, 1968; DSM 111, 1980).* Washington, D.C.: American Psychiatric Association, 1968, 1980.

Andolfi, M. *Family therapy: An interactional approach.* New York: Plenum Press, 1979.

Angell, R. *The family encounters the depression.* New York: Charles Scribner's Sons, 1936.

Angst, J. Masked depression viewed from the cross-cultural standpoint. In P. Kielholz (Ed.), *Masked depression.* Bern: Hans Huber, 1973.

Apel, K. O. *Analytic philosophy of language and the "Geisteswissenschaften", Foundations of Language, Supplement Series (Vol. 5).* Dordrecht: Reidel, 1967.

Arieti, S. *Interpretation of schizophrenia.* New York: Robert Brunner, 1955.

Arnkraut, A., Solomon, G. F., Allowsmith, M., & McLellan, B. Immunoglobulin and improvement in acute schizophrenia reaction. *Archives of General Psychiatry,* 1973, *28,* 673.

Arnold, M. *Emotion and personality.* New York: Columbia University Press, 1960.

Assagioli, R. *Psychosynthesis.* New York: The Viking Press, 1971.

Axelrod, J. Methylation reactions in the formation and metabolism of catecholamines and other biogenicamines. *Pharmacological Review,* 1966, *18,* 95-113.

Axelrod, J. Noradrenaline. *Science,* 1971, *173,* 598-606.

Ayllon, T. Intensive treatment of psychotic behaviour by stimulus satiation and food reinforcement. *Behaviour Research and Therapy,* 1963, *1,* 53-61.

Ayllon, T., & Azrin, N. *The token economy: A motivational system for therapy and*

rehabilitation. New York: Appleton-Century-Crofts, 1968.
Ayllon, T., & Michael, J. The psychiatric nurse as the behavior engineer. *Journal of Experimental Analysis of Behaviour*, 1959, *2*, 323-334.
Bacon, F. The New Organon. In S. Warhaft (Ed.), *Francis Bacon: A selection of his works*. Toronto: Macmillan, 1965.
Bain, J. A. *Thought control in everyday life*. New York: Funk & Wagnalls, 1928.
Baldwin, A. L. *Theories of child development*. New York: John Wiley, 1967.
Balint, M. *The doctor, his patient, and the illness*. New York: International Universities Press, 1957.
Bandura, A. *Principles of behavior modification*. New York: Holt, Reinhart, & Winston, 1969.
Bandura, A. *Social learning theory*. Englewood Cliffs, N.J.: Prentice-Hall, 1977. (a)
Bandura, A. Self-efficacy: Towards a unifying theory of behavior change. *Psychological Review*, 1977, *84*, 191-215. (b)
Bandura, A., & Walters, R. H. *Social learning and personality development*. New York: Holt, Rinehart, & Winston, 1963.
Bannister, D. *Perspectives in personal construct theory*. London: Academic Press, 1970.
Barachas, J., & Usdin, E. *Serotonin and behavior*. New York: Academic Press, 1973.
Barnard, C. P., & Corrales, R. G. *The theory and techniques of family therapy*. Springfield, Illinois: Charles C Thomas, 1979.
Baruk, H., Bidermann, M., & Albane, A. Tuberculose et démence précoce: Réactions allergiques et encéphalite toxique. *Paris Medical*, 1932, *2*, 166-172.
Bateson, G. *Naven* (2nd ed.). Stanford, California: Stanford University Press, 1958.
Bateson, G. Cultural problems posed by a study of schizophrenic process. In A. Auerback (Ed.), *Schizophrenia, an integrated approach*. New York: Ronald Press, 1959.
Bateson, G. (Ed.). *Percival's narrative: A patient's account of his psychosis 1830-1832*. Stanford, California: Stanford University Press, 1961.
Bateson, G. *Steps to an ecology of mind*. New York: Ballantine Books, 1972.
Bateson, G. Draft: Scattered thoughts for conference on "Broken Power." *Co-Evolution Quarterly*, 1974, *4*, 26-27.
Bateson, G., Jackson, D., Haley, J., & Weakland, J. Towards a theory of schizophrenia. *Behavioral Science*, 1956, *1*, 251-264.
Bauman, Z. *Hermeneutics and social science*. London: Hutchinson, 1978.
Beck, A. T. *Depression: Clinical, experimental and theoretical aspects*. New York: Hoeber, 1967.
Beck, A. T. Cognitive therapy: Nature and relation to behaviour therapy. *Behavior Therapy*, 1970, *1*, 184-200.
Beck, A. T. The development of depression: A cognitive model. In R. J. Friedman & M. M. Katz (Eds.), *The psychology of depression: Contemporary theory and research*. New York: Wiley & Sons, 1974.
Becker, E. *Revolution in psychiatry*. New York: The Free Press, 1964.

Becker, H. S. *Outsiders*. New York: The Free Press of Glencoe, 1963.
Becker, H. S., Geer, B., Hughes, E. C., & Strauss, A. L. *Boys in white: Student culture in medical school.* Chicago: Chicago University Press, 1961.
Beckett, G. S. I. Clinical aspects of schizophrenia: Pointers to a biochemical causation. In L. L. Iversen & S. P. Rose (Eds.), *Biochemistry of mental illness*. London: Biochemical Society, 1973.
Beers, C. W. *A mind that found itself: An autobiography.* New York: Doubleday, 1948.
Belle, Van, H. A. *Basic intent and therapeutic approach of Carl R. Rogers*. Toronto: Wedge Publishing Foundation, 1980.
Bem, D. J. Self-perception: An alternative interpretation of cognitive dissonance phenomena. *Psychological Review,* 1967, *2,* 411-420.
Benedict, R. Anthropology and the abnormal. *Journal of Genetic Psychology,* 1934, *10,* 59.
Benedict, R. Continuities and discontinuities in cultural conditioning. *Psychiatry,* 1938, *1,* 161-167.
Benedict, R. *Patterns of culture*. New York: Mentor Books, 1959.
Bergson, H. *Time and free will: An essay on the immediate data of consciousness.* (transl.) F. L. Pogson. New York: Harper & Row, 1960.
Bernard, C. *An introduction to the study of experimental medicine*. (transl.) H. C. Green, (introd.) L. J. Henderson. New York: Collier Books, 1961. (Original 1865).
Berne, E. *Transactional analysis in psychotherapy*. New York: Grove Press, Evergreen Books, 1961.
Bibring, E. The mechanism of depression. In P. Greenacre (Ed.), *Affective disorders*. New York: International University Press, 1953.
Binswanger, L. *Grundformen und Erkenntnis menschlichen Daseins*. Zurich: Niehaus, 1942.
Binswanger, L. *Sigmund Freud: Reminiscences of a friendship*. New York: Grune & Stratton, 1957. (a)
Binswanger, L. *Schizophrenie*. Pfullingen: Neske, 1957. (b)
Binswanger, L. *Melancholie und Manie*. Pfullingen: Neske, 1960.
Birnbaum, K. *Der Aufbau der Psychose: Grundzuge für psychiatrichen Strukturanalyze.* Berlin: J. Springer, 1923.
Blashfield, R. K., & Draguns, J. G. Evaluative criteria for psychiatric classification. *Journal of Abnormal Psychology,* 1976, *85,* 140-150.
Bleuler, E. P. *Dementia Praecox: A group of schizophrenias*. New York: International University Press, 1950. (Original, 1911)
Blondel, C. *La conscience morbide*. Paris: Alcan, 1914.
Blumer, H. *Symbolic interactionism: Perspective and method*. Englewood Cliffs, N.J.: Prentice-Hall, 1969.
Bockoven, J. S. *Moral treatment in American psychiatry*. New York: Springer Publishing, 1963.
Boisen, A. T. *The exploration of the inner world*. New York: Harper & Bros., 1936.

Boring, E. G. *A history of experimental psychology.* New York: Appleton-Century-Crofts, 1957.

Boss, M. *Psychoanalysis and daseinsanalysis.* (transl.) L. B. Lefabre. New York: Basic Books, 1963.

Boszormenyi-Nagy, I. Relational modes and meaning. In G. H. Zuk & I. Boszormenyi-Nagy (Eds.), *Family therapy and disturbed families*, Palo Alto, California: Science and Behavior Books, 1967.

Bott, E. *Family and social network.* London: Tavistock Publications, 1957.

Boulding, K. E. General systems theory—the skeleton of science. *General Systems: Yearbook of the Society for the Advancement of General Systems*, 1956, 1, 11-17.

Bourdillon, R. E., Clarke, C. A., Ridges, A. P., Sheppard, P. M., Harper, P., & Leslie, S. A. Pink spot in the urine of schizophrenics. *Nature*, 1965, 208, 453-455.

Bowen, M. The use of family theory in clinical practice. *Comprehensive Psychiatry*, 1966, 7, 345-374.

Bowlby, J. *Attachment and loss, Vol. 1 & Attachment, Vol. 2: Separation, anxiety and anger.* New York: Basic Books, 1969.

Braestrup, C., & Nielsen, M. Searching for endogenous benzodiazepine receptor ligands. *Trends in Pharmacological Sciences*, 1980, 1, 424-427.

Breger, L., & McGaugh, J. L. Critique and reformulation of "learning-theory" approach to psychotherapy and neurosis. *Psychological Bulletin*, 1965, 63, 338-358.

Brenner, M. H. *Mental illness and the economy.* Cambridge, Mass.: Harvard University Press, 1973.

Brentano, F. *Psychologie vom empirischen Standpunkt.* Leipzig: Dunkker & Humblot, 1874.

Breuer, J., & Freud, S. *Studies on hysteria* (1895) (transl.) J. Strachey. New York: Basic Books, 1957.

Brown, L. G. *Social pathology.* New York: Appleton, 1946.

Buber, M. *I and Thou.* New York: Scribner, 1958.

Buchwald, A., & Young, R. D. Some comments on the foundations of behavior therapy. In C. M. Franks (Ed.), *Behavior therapy: Appraisal and status.* New York: McGraw-Hill, 1969.

Buck, C., Wanklin, J. M., & Hobbs, G. E. Symptom analysis of rural-urban differences in first admission rates. *Journal of Nervous and Mental Diseases*, 1955, 122, 80-82.

Buckley, W. *Sociology and modern systems theory.* Englewood Cliffs, N.J.: Prentice-Hall, 1967.

Budzynski, T. H., & Stoyva, J. M. An instrument for producing deep muscle relaxation by means of analog information feedback. *Journal of Applied Behavior Analysis*, 1969, 2, 231-237.

Bühler, C. *Values in psychotherapy.* New York: The Free Press of Glencoe, 1962.

Bunney, B. S., & Aghajanian, G. K. Central dopaminergic neurons: A model for predicting the efficacy of putative antipsychotic drugs. In D. J. Ingle & M. H.

Shein (Eds.), *Model systems in biological psychiatry.* Cambridge, Mass.: MIT Press, 1975.
Bunney, W. E., Janowsky, D. S., Goodwin, F. K., Davis, J. M., Brodie, H. K. H., Murphy, D. L., & Chase, T. N. Effect of L-DOPA on depression. *Lancet,* 1969, *1,* 885-886.
Burgess, E. W. The family as a unit of interacting personalities. *Family,* 1926, *7,* 3-9.
Burgess, E. The modification of depressive behavior. In R. Rubin & C. Franks (Eds.), *Advances in behaviour therapy.* New York: Academic Press, 1968.
Buscaino, V. M. Production of hallucinations, catatonia and Parkinsonism by action of amines (indol). *Revista di Patologia Nervosa e Mentale,* 1929, *34,* 162-165.
Buytendijk, F. J. J. *Phenomenologie de la rencontre.* Paris: Desclee de Brouwer, 1952.
Buytendijk, F. J. J. *Pain.* (transl.) Eda O'Shiel. Chicago: University of Chicago Press, 1962.
Buytendijk, F. J. J. *Woman.* (transl.) D. J. Barret. Glen Rock, N.J.: Newman Press, 1968.
Cameron, N. Reasoning, regression and communication in schizophrenics. *Psychological Monographs,* No. 1, Vol. 50, 1938.
Cameron, N. Role concepts in behavior pathology. *American Journal of Sociology,* 1950, *44,* 464-467.
Cameron, N., & Margaret, A. *Behavior pathology.* Boston: Houghton-Mifflin, 1951.
Caplan, G. *Principles of preventive psychiatry.* New York: Basic Books, 1964.
Carnap, R. Psychology in physical language. (transl. G. Schick). In A. J. Ayer (Ed.), *Logical positivism.* Glencoe, Ill.: Glencoe Press, 1959.
Carnegie, D. *How to stop worrying and start living.* New York: Simon & Schuster, 1948.
Carothers, J. C. *The African mind in health and disease: A study in ethnopsychiatry.* Geneva: WHO Monograph Services, 1953.
Carson, N. A., Cusworth, D. C., Dent, C. E., Field, C. M. B., Neill, D. W., & Westall, R. G. Homocystinuria: A new inborn error of metabolism associated with mental deficiency. *Archives of Diseases in Childhood,* 1963, *38,* 425-436.
Cassirer, E. *Philosophy of symbolic forms (3 vols.).* (transl. R. Manheim). New Haven: Yale University Press, 1957.
Cautela, J. R. Treatment of compulsive behavior by covert sensitization. *Psychological Record,* 1966, *16,* 33-41.
Cautela, J. R. Covert reinforcement. *Behavior Therapy,* 1970, *1,* 33-50.
Cautela, J. R. Covert extinction. *Behavior Therapy,* 1971, *2,* 192-200.
Cavan, R. S. *Suicide.* Chicago: University of Chicago Press, 1928.
Chase, T. N., & Murphy, D. L. Serotonin and central nervous system function. *Annual Review of Pharmacology,* 1973, *13,* 181-197.
Chein, I. The image of man. *Journal of Social Issues,* 1962, *18,* 1-35.
Chomsky, N. *Syntactic structures.* The Hague: Mouton, 1957.
Chomsky, N. *Language and mind.* New York: Harcourt, Brace, & World, 1968.
Colby, K. M. *Energy and structure in psychoanalysis.* New York: Ronald Press, 1955.

Colby, K. M. *Paranoia: A computer simulation of paranoid processes.* London: Pergamon Press, 1975.
Conrad, K. *Die beginnende Schizophrenie. Versuch einer Gestaltanalyse des Wahns.* (Beginning of schizophrenia. An attempt at a *gestalt* analysis of delusions). Stuttgart: Thieme, 1958.
Cooley, C. H. *Social organization.* New York: Scribner, 1929.
Cooley, C. H. *Social process.* Carbondale: University of Illinois Press, 1966.
Coombs, C. M., Dawes, R. M., & Tversky, A. *Mathematical Psychology.* Englewood Cliffs, N.J.: Prentice-Hall, 1970.
Cooper, D. *Psychiatry and anti-psychiatry.* London: Paladin, 1970.
Cooper, D. *The death of the family.* New York: Vantage Books, 1971.
Cooper, J. E., Kendell, R. E., Gurland, B. J., Sharpe, L., Copeland, J. R. M., & Simon, R. J. *Psychiatric diagnosis in New York and London: A comparative study of mental hospital admissions* (Maudsley Monograph 20) London: Oxford University Press, 1972.
Cooper, J. R., Bloom, F. R., & Roth, R. H. *The biochemical basis of neuropharmacology* (3rd ed.). New York: University Press, 1978.
Coppen, A. Indolamines and affective disorders. *Journal of Psychiatric Research,* 1972, *9,* 163-171.
Cotton, H. A. The relation of chronic sepsis to the so-called functional disorders. *Journal of Mental Science,* 1923, *69,* 434-365.
Coser, L. *The function of social conflict.* London: Free Press of Glencoe, 1956.
Coué, E. *The practice of autosuggestion.* New York: Doubleday, 1922.
Coulter, J. *Approaches to insanity: A philosophical and sociological study.* New York: John Wiley, 1973.
Coyne, J. C. Toward an interactional description of depression. *Psychiatry,* 1976, *39,* 14-27.
Cumming, E., & Cumming, J. Affective symbolism, social norms and mental illness. *Psychiatry,* 1956, *19,* 77-85.
Dabrowski, K. *Positive disintegration.* Boston: Little, Brown, 1964.
Dabrowski, K. *Personality-shaping through positive disintegration.* Boston: Little, Brown, 1967.
Dabrowski, K. *Psychoneurosis is not an illness.* London: Gryf Publications, 1972.
Dahrendorf, R. *Class and class conflict in industrial society.* Stanford, California: Stanford University Press, 1959.
Davis, D. A. On being detectably sane in insane places: Base rate and psychodiangosis. *Journal of Abnormal Psychology,* 1976, *85,* 416-422.
Davis, K. Mental hygiene and class structure. *Psychiatry,* 1938, *1,* 55-56.
Davison, G. C., & Valius, S. Maintenance of self-attributed behavior change. *Journal of Personality and Social Psychology,* 1969, *11,* 25-33.
DeGrazia, S. *The political community: A study of anomie.* Chicago: The University of Chicago Press, 1948.
Deleon-Jones, F., Maas, J. W., Dekirmenjian, H., & Sanchez, J. Diagnostic subgroups of affective disorders and their urinary excretion of catecholamine

metabolites. *American Journal of Psychiatry,* 1975, *132,* 1141-1148.
Devereux, G. Primitive psychiatric diagnosis: A general theory of the diagnostic process. In I. Galdston (Ed.), *Man's image in medicine and anthropology.* New York: Universities Press, 1963.
Diamond, M. D. Role-taking ability and schizophrenia. *Journal of Clinical Psychology,* 1958, *14,* 321-324.
Dilthey, W. *The meaning of history.* (Ed.) H. G. Rickmann. London: Allen & Unwin, 1961.
Dimond, S., & Beaumont, J. G. (Eds.), *Hemisphere function in the human brain.* London: Paul Elek, 1974.
Dobzansky, T. *Mankind evolving.* New Haven: Yale University Press, 1962.
Dohrenwend, B. P., Dohrenwend, B. S., Gould, M. S., Link, B., Neugebauer, R., & Wunsch-Hitzig, R. *Mental illness in the United States, epidemiological estimates.* New York: Praeger, 1980.
Dollard, J., & Miller, N. E. *Personality and psychotherapy.* New York: McGraw-Hill, 1950.
Douglas, J. D., & Johnson, J. M. (Eds.), *Existential sociology.* New York: Cambridge University Press, 1977.
Draper, G., Dupertius, C. W., & Caughey, J. L. *Human constitution in clinical medicine.* New York: Paul Holber, 1944.
Dunham, W. H. Anomie and mental illness. In M. B. Clinard (Ed.), *Anomie and deviant behavior.* New York: The Free Press of Glencoe, 1964.
Dunham, H. W. *Community and schizophrenia: An epidemiological analysis.* Detroit: Wayne State University Press, 1965.
Dunlap, K. *Habits: Their making and unmaking.* New York: Liveright, 1932.
Durkheim, E. *The division of labor in society.* New York: Macmillan Co., 1933.
Durkheim, E. *Suicide.* New York: The Free Press of Glencoe, 1951.
Durkheim, E. *The rules of sociological method.* New York: The Free Press, 1958.
Durkheim, E. The dualism of human nature and its sociological conditions. In K. H. Wolff (Ed.), *Essays in sociology and philosophy.* New York: Harper Torchbooks, 1964.
Dusen, Van, H. P. *Spirit, son and father.* New York: C. Scribner's Sons, 1958.
Eaton, J. W., & Weil, R. C. *Culture and mental disorders: A comparative study of the Hutterites and other populations.* Glencoe, Ill.: The Free Press, 1955.
Edelson, M. *The idea of mental illness.* New Haven: Yale University Press, 1971.
Edgerton, R. B. On the recognition of mental illness. In S. C. Plog & R. B. Edgerton (Eds.), *Changing perspectives in mental illness.* New York: Holt, Rinehart, & Winston, 1969.
Elenmeyer-Kimling, L., & Paradowski, W. Selection and schizophrenia. *American Naturalist,* 1966, *100,* 651-665.
Ellenberger, H. F. *The discovery of the unconscious: The history and evolution of dynamic psychiatry.* New York: Basic Books, 1970.
Ellis, A. *The essence of rational psychotherapy: A comprehensive approach to treatment.* New York: Institute for Rational Living, 1970.

Ellis, A. *Humanistic psychotherapy: The rational-emotive approach.* New York: Julian Press, 1973.
Endicott, J., Spitzer, R. L., Fleiss, J. L., & Cohen, J. The global assessment scale. *Archives of General Psychiatry,* 1976, *33,* 766-771.
Engel, G. L. The need for a new medical model: A challenge for bio-medicine. *Science,* 1977, *196,* 129-136.
Engel, G. L. The clinical application of the biopsychosocial model. *The American Journal of Psychiatry,* 1980, *137,* 535-544.
Erikson, E. *Childhood and society.* New York: Norton & Company, 1963.
Everitt, B. *Cluster analysis.* London: Heinemann, 1974.
Ey, H. Outline of an organo-dynamic conception of the structure, nosography and pathogenesis of mental diseases. In E. Straus, M. Natanson, & H. Ey (Eds.), *Psychiatry and philosophy.* New York: Springer Verlag, 1969.
Eysenck, H. J. *The scientific study of personality.* London: Routledge & Kegan Paul, 1952. (a)
Eysenck, H. J. The effects of psychotherapy: An evaluation. *Journal of Consulting Psychology,* 1952, *16,* 319-324. (b)
Eysenck, H. J. Learning theory and behavior therapy. *Journal of Mental Science,* 1959, *105,* 61-75.
Eysenck, H. J. (Ed.). *Behavior therapy and the neuroses.* New York: Pergamon, 1960.
Eysenck, H. J. Classification and the problem of diagnosis. In H. J. Eysenck (Ed.), *Handbook of Abnormal Psychology.* New York: Basic Books, 1961.
Eysenck, H. J. Personality and drug effects. In H. J. Eysenck (Ed.), *Experiments with drugs.* New York: Macmillan, 1963.
Eysenck, H. J. *The biological basis of personality.* Springfield, Ill.: Charles C Thomas, 1967.
Fairbairn, W. R. D. *An object relation theory of personality.* New York: Basic Books, 1954.
Farina, A. Pattern of role dominance and conflict in parents of schizophrenic patients. *Journal of Abnormal and Social Psychology,* 1960, *61,* 31-38.
Faris, R. E. L., & Dunham, H. W. *Mental disorders in urban areas.* Chicago: University of Chicago Press, 1939.
Federn, P. *Ego psychology and the psychoses.* New York: Basic Books, 1952.
Feighner, J. P., Robins, E., Guze, S. B., Woodruff, R. A., Winokur, G., & Munoz, R. Diagnostic criteria for use in psychiatric research. *Archives of General Psychiatry,* 1972, *26,* 57-63.
Fenichel, O. *The psychoanalytical theory of neurosis.* New York: W. W. Norton, 1945.
Ferster, C. B., Nurnberger, J. I., & Levitt, E. B. The control of eating. *Journal of Mathetics,* 1962, *1,* 87-110.
Festinger, L. *A theory of cognitive dissonance.* Stanford: Stanford University Press, 1962.
Feyerabend, P. Consolations for the specialist. In Lakatos & A. Musgrave (Eds.),

Criticism and growth of knowledge. Cambridge: Cambridge University Press, 1970.

Fish, F. J. *Schizophrenia.* Bristol: John Wright, 1962.

Fleiss, J. L., & Zubin, J. On the method and theory of clustering. *Multivariate Behavioral Research,* 1969, *4,* 235-250.

Flor-Henry, P. Psychosis, neurosis and epilepsy: Developmental and gender-related effects and their aetiological contribution. *British Journal of Psychiatry,* 1974, *124,* 144-150.

Fodor, J. A., Bever, T. G., & Garrett, M. F. *The psychology of language.* New York: McGraw-Hill, 1974.

Fogarty, T. Family structure in terms of triangles. In J. Brandt & C. Moynihan (Eds.), *Systems therapy.* Washington, D.C.: Groome Child Guidance Center, 1972.

Foucault, M. *Madness and civilization.* (transl.) R. Howard. New York: Random House, 1965.

Foulkes, S. H. *Therapeutic group analysis.* New York: International University Press, 1965.

Frankl, V. E. *Man's search for meaning: An introduction to logotherapy.* New York: Washington Square Press, 1963.

Frankl, V. E. *Psychotherapy and existentialism, Selected papers on Logotherapy.* New York: Clarion Books, 1968.

Frankl, V. E. *The doctor and the soul.* Harmondsworth, England: Penguin Books, 1973.

Franks, C. M. Alcohol, alcoholism and conditioning: A review of the literature and some theoretical considerations. *Journal of Mental Science,* 1958, *104,* 14-33.

French, T., & Kasanin, J. Psychodynamic study of the recovery of two schizophrenic cases. *Psychoanalytic Quarterly,* 1941, *10,* 1-22.

Freud, Anna. *Normality and pathology in childhood.* New York: International University Press, 1965.

Freud, S. The interpretation of dreams (1900). In J. Strachey (Ed.), *The standard edition of the complete psychological works of Sigmund Freud.* Volume IV, V. London: The Hogarth Press, 1953. (a)

Freud, S. Totem and taboo (1913). In J. Strachey (Ed.), *The standard edition of the complete psychological works of Sigmund Freud.* Volume XIII. London: The Hogarth Press, 1953. (b)

Freud, S. Group psychology and the analysis of the ego (1921). In J. Strachey (Ed.), *The standard edition of the complete psychological works of Sigmund Freud.* Volume XVIII. London: The Hogarth Press, 1955. (a)

Freud, S. Beyond the pleasure principle (1920). In J. Strachey (Ed.), *The standard edition of the complete psychological works of Sigmund Freud.* Volume XVIII. London: The Hogarth Press, 1955. (b)

Freud, S. On narcissism: An introduction (1914). In J. Strachey (Ed.), *The standard edition of the complete psychological works of Sigmund Freud.* Volume XIV. London: The Hogarth Press, 1957. (a)

Freud, S. Repression (1915). In J. Strachey (Ed.), *The standard edition of the* complete psychological works of Sigmund Freud. Volume XIV. London: The Hogarth Press, 1957. (b)

Freud, S. Mourning and melancholia (1917). In J. Strachey (Ed.), *The standard edition of the complete psychological works of Sigmund Freud*. Volume XIV. London: The Hogarth Press, 1957. (c)

Freud, S. *The origins of psychoanalysis: Letters, drafts and notes to Wilhelm Fliess.* M. Bonaparte, E. Mosbacher, & J. Strachey (Eds.). Garden City, N.Y.: Doubleday, 1957. (d)

Freud, S. Psychopathology of everyday life (1901). In J. Strachey (Ed.), *The standard edition of the complete psychological works of Sigmund Freud.* Volume VI. London: The Hogarth Press, 1960.

Freud, S. The ego and the id (1923). In J. Strachey (Ed.), *The standard edition of the complete psychological works of Sigmund Freud*. Volume XIX. London: The Hogarth Press, 1961. (a)

Freud, S. Civilization and its discontents (1930). In J. Strachey (Ed.), *The standard edition of the complete psychological works of Sigmund Freud*. Volume XXI. London: The Hogarth Press, 1961. (b)

Freud, S. New introductory lectures on psycho-analysis (1933). In J. Strachey (Ed.), *The standard edition of the complete psychological works of Sigmund Freud.* Volume XXII. London: The Hogarth Press, 1964.

Freud, S. *A general introduction to psychoanalysis.* New York: Washington Square Press, 1967.

Friedhoff, A. J., & Hollister, L. E. Comparison of the metabolism of 3-4 dimethoxyphenylethylamine and mescaline in humans. *Biochemical Pharmacology,* 1966, *15,* 269-273.

Friedricks, R. W. *A sociology of sociology.* New York: Free Press, 1970.

Fromm, E. *Escape from freedom.* New York: Holt, Rinehart, & Winston, 1941.

Fromm, E. *The sane society.* New York: Holt, Rinehart and Winston, 1955.

Fromm, E. *Marx's concept of man.* New York: Frederick Ungar, 1961.

Frumkin, R. M. Occupation and major mental disorders. In A. Rose (Ed.), *Mental health and mental disorder: A sociological approach.* New York: Norton, 1955.

Garfinkel, H. *Studies in ethnomethodology.* Englewood Cliffs, N.J.: Prentice Hall, 1967.

Gaylin, W. *The meaning of despair.* New York: Science House, 1968.

Gebsattel, von, V. *Prologomena zu einer medizinischen Antropologie.* Berlin: Springer, 1954.

Gedo, J. E., & Goldberg, A. *Models of the mind: A psychoanalytic theory.* Chicago: University of Chicago Press, 1973.

Gendlin, E. T. *Experiencing and creation of meaning.* Glencoe, Ill.: Free Press, 1962.

Gerard, D. L., & Houston, L. G. Family setting and social ecology of schizophrenia. *Psychiatric Quarterly,* 1953, *27,* 90-101.

Gjessing, R. Disturbances of somatic functions in catatonia with a periodic course, and their compensation. *Journal of Mental Science,* 1938, *84,* 608-621.

Gill, M. M. Topography and systems in psychoanalytic theory. *Psychological Issues*, Vol. 3, No. 2, Monograph 10. New York: International University Press, 1963.

Glasser, W. *Mental health or mental illness?: Psychiatry for practical action*. New York: Harper & Row, 1960.

Glasser, W. *Reality therapy: A new approach to psychiatry*. New York: Harper & Row, 1975 (original, 1965)

Goffman, E. *Asylums*. Garden City, N.Y.: Doubleday, 1961.

Goldfried, M. R. Systematic desensitization as training in self-control. *Journal of Consulting and Clinical Psychology*, 1971, 37, 228-234.

Goldstein, K. *The organism*. New York: American Book Company, 1939.

Goldstein, K. *Language and language disturbances*. New York: Grune & Stratton, 1948.

Gottesman, I. I., & Shields, J. A polygenic theory of schizophrenia. *Proceedings of the National Academy of Sciences*, 1967, 58, 199-205.

Gough, H. G. A sociological theory of psychopathy. *American Journal of Sociology*, 1948, 53, 359-366.

Gray, W., Duhl, F. J., & Rizzo, N. D. (Eds.), *General systems theory and psychiatry*. Boston: Little, Brown, 1969.

Grinker, R. Sr. A dynamic story of a homoclite. In J. H. Messerman (Ed.), *Science and psychoanalysis*. New York: Grune & Stratton, 1963.

Grinker, R. Sr. (Ed.). *Towards a unified theory of human behavior*. (2nd ed.). New York: Basic Books, 1967.

Gross, M. L. *The psychological society*. New York: Random House, 1978.

Guthrie, E. R. *The psychology of learning* (revised). New York: Harper, 1952.

Guttman, L. A new approach to factor analysis: The radex. In P. F. Lazarsfeld (Ed.), *Mathematical thinking in the social sciences*. Glencoe, Ill: Free Press, 1954.

Habermas, J. *Towards rational society*. (transl.) J. J. Shapiro. London: Heinemann, 1971

Habermas, J. *Knowledge and human interests*. (transl.) J. J. Shapiro. London: Heinemann, 1972.

Haley, J. *Strategies of psychotherapy*. New York: Grune & Stratton, 1963.

Haley, J. (Ed.). *Advanced techniques of hypnosis and therapy: Selected papers of Milton H. Ericson*. New York: Grune & Stratton, 1971.

Haley, J. *Problem solving therapy*. San Francisco: Jossey Bass, 1976.

Haley, J. Ideas that handicap therapy with young people. *International Journal of Family Therapy*, 1979, 1, 29-45.

Halmos, P. *Towards a measure of man*. London: Routledge & Kegan Paul, 1957.

Hare, A. P. *Handbook of small group research*. New York: Free Press, 1962.

Hare, E. H. Mental illness and social condition in Bristol. *Journal of Mental Science*, 1956, 102, 349-351.

Harley-Mason, J., Laird, A., & Smythies, J. R. The metabolism of mescaline in the human. *Confinia Neurologica*, 1958, 10, 152-155.

Harré, R., & Secord, P. F. *The explanation of social behaviour*. Oxford: Blackwell, 1972.

Hartmann, H. *Ego psychology and the problem of adaptation.* New York: International University Press, 1958.
Hartmann, H. *Psychoanalysis and moral values.* New York: International University Press, 1960.
Heath, R. G. An antibrain globulin in schizophrenia. In H. W. Hemwich (Ed.), *Biochemistry: Schizophrenia and affective illnesses.* Baltimore: Williams & Wilkins, 1970.
Hebb, D. O. Drives and the C.N.S. *Psychological Review,* 1955, *62,* 243-254.
Hegel, G. W. F. *The phenomenology of mind.* (transl.) J. B. Baillie. New York: Humanities Press, 1949.
Heidegger, M. *Sein und Zeit.* Halle: Niemeyer, 1927.
Heider, F. *The psychology of interpersonal relations.* New York: Wiley, 1958.
Hempel, G. C. Problems of taxonomy. In J. Zubin (Ed.), *Field studies of mental disorders.* New York: Grune & Stratton, 1961.
Henry, J. Family structure and the transmission of neurotic behavior. *American Journal of Orthopsychiatry,* 1951, *21,* 800-818.
Hesnard, A. L. *Psychoanalyse du lien interhumane.* Paris: P.U.F., 1957.
Hess, R. D., & Handel, G. *Family worlds: A psychosocial approach to family life.* Chicago: University Press, 1959.
Hill, R. *Families under stress.* Westport, Conn.: Greenwood Press, 1949.
Hill, R. Modern systems theory and the family: A confrontation. *Social Science Information,* 1971, *10,* 7-26.
Hoffer, A., Osmond, H., & Smythies, J. Schizophrenia: A new approach. Part 2, Result of a year's research. *Journal of Mental Science,* 1954, *100,* 24-45.
Hollingshead, A. B., & Redlich, F. C. *Social class and mental illness: A community study.* New York: John Wiley, 1958.
Holmberg, A. R. *Nomads of the long bow.* Washington, D.C.: Smithsonian Institute, Institute of Social Anthropology No. 10, 1950.
Holroyd, K. A. Stress, coping and the treatment of stress related illnesses. In J. R. McNamara (Ed.), *Behavioral approaches in medicine: Application and analysis.* New York: Plenum, 1979.
Holzman, M. *The significance of the value systems of patient and therapist for the outcome of psychotherapy.* Unpublished doctoral dissertation. University of Washington, 1961.
Homans, G. C. *The human group.* New York: Harcourt, Brace, & Jovanovich, 1950.
Homans, G. C. *The nature of social science.* New York: Harcourt, Brace, & World, 1967.
Homme, L. E. Perspectives in psychology: XXIV. Control of coverants, the operants of the mind. *Psychological Record,* 1965, *15,* 501-511.
Horney, K. *Neurosis and human growth.* New York: W. W. Norton, 1950.
Hornykewicz, O. Neurohumoral interactions and basal ganglia function and dysfunction. In M. D. Yahr (Ed.), *Basal Ganglia.* New York: Raven Press, 1976.
Horton, J. The dehumanization of anomie and alienation: A problem in the

ideology of sociology. *British Journal of Sociology,* 1964, *15,* 283-300.
Hoult, T. F. The humanistic perspective. In S. G. McNall (Ed.), *Theoretical perspectives in sociology.* New York: St. Martin's Press, 1979.
How, R., & Foerster, H. Introductory comments to Francisco Varela's calculus for self-reference. *International Journal of General Systems,* 1975, *2,* 1-3.
Hudson, W. S. *American Protestantism.* Chicago: University of Chicago Press, 1961.
Hughes, J., Smith, T. W., Kosterlitz, H. W., Fothergill, L. A., Morgan, B. A., & Morris, H. R. Identification of two related pentapeptides from the brain with potent opiate agonist activity. *Nature,* 1975, *258,* 577-579.
Hull, C. L. *Principles of behavior.* New York: Appleton-Century-Crofts, 1943.
Hull, C. L. *A behavior system.* New Haven, Conn.: Yale University Press, 1952.
Hume, D. *A treatise of human nature.* (Ed.) L. A. Selby-Bigge. Oxford: Clarendon Press, 1896.
Husserl, E. *Ideas: General introduction to pure phenomenology.* New York: Collier, 1962.
Huxley, A. *The doors of perception, and heaven and hell.* New York: Harper & Row, 1954.
Ihde, D. *Hermeneutic phenomenology: The philosophy of Paul Ricoeur.* Evanston, Ill.: Northwestern University Press, 1971.
Isaacs, W., Thomas, J., & Goldiamond, I. Application of operant conditioning to reinstate verbal behavior in psychotics. *Journal of Speech and Hearing Disorders,* 1960, *25,* 8-12.
Isham, H. Wilhelm von Humboldt. In P. Edwards (Ed.), *The Encyclopedia of Philosophy.* New York: Macmillan, 1967.
Ittelson, W. H., & Kutash, S. B. *Perceptual changes in psychopathology.* New Brunswick, N.J.: Rutgers University Press, 1961.
Jacob, T. Family interaction in disturbed and normal families: A methodological and substantive review. *Psychological Bulletin,* 1975, *82,* 33-65.
Jacobson, E. *Progressive relaxation.* Chicago: University of Chicago Press, 1938.
Jacobson, Edith. Contribution to the metapsychology of cyclothymic depression. In P. Greenacre (Ed.), *Affective disorders.* New York: International University Press, 1953.
Jackson, D. D. The question of family homeostasis. Part 1. *Psychiatric Quarterly Supplement,* 1957, *31,* 79-90.
Jackson, D., & Satir, V. A review of psychiatric developments in family diagnosis and family therapy. In D. Jackson (Ed.), *Therapy, communication and change.* Palo Alto, Calif.: Science and Behavior Books, 1973.
Jackson, H. J. (1884). *Croonian Lectures.* Reprinted *Selected Writings.* London: Hodder & Stoughton, 1932.
Jahoda, M. *Current concepts of positive mental health.* New York: Basic Books, 1959.
James, W. *The principles of psychology* (Vol. 1). New York: Dover Publications, 1950 (1890).
Janet, P. *L'Automatism Psychologique (Psychological Automatism).* Paris: Alcan, 1889.

Jaspers, K. *Reason and existenz.* New York: The Noonday Press, 1955.
Jaspers, K. *General psychopathology.* (transl.) J. Hoening & M. W. Hamilton. Manchester: Manchester University Press, 1963.
Jaspers, K. The phenomenological approach in psychopathology. *British Journal of Psychiatry,* 1968, *114,* 1313-1323.
Jilek, W. G., & Jilek-Aall, L. Transient psychoses in Africans. *Psychiatric Clinics,* 1970, *3,* 337-367.
Jones, M. C. The elimination of children's fears. *Journal of Experimental Psychology,* 1924, *7,* 382-390.
Jones, M. *The therapeutic community.* New York: Basic Books, 1953.
Jourard, S. *The transparent self: Self-disclosure and well-being.* New York: Van Nostrand, 1964.
Jouvet, M. Biogenic amines and the state of sleep. *Science,* 1969, *163,* 32-41.
Jung, C. G. *Collected works.* (Eds.) V. Read, M. Fordham, and G. Adler. New York: Pantheon Books, 1953.
Kaam, van, A. Counselling from the viewpoint of existential psychology. *Harvard Educational Review,* 1962, *32,* 403-415.
Kaam, van, A. *Existential foundations of psychology.* Pittsburgh: Duquesne University Press, 1966.
Kafka, F. *The metamorphosis.* (transl.) S. Corngold. New York: Bantam Books, 1972.
Kallmann, F. J. The genetic theory of schizophrenia. *American Journal of Psychiatry,* 1946, *103,* 309-322.
Kallmann, F. J. *Heredity in health and mental disorders.* New York: Norton & Co., 1953.
Kanfer, F. H., & Phillips, J. S. A survey of current behavior therapies and a proposal for classification. In C. M. Franks (Ed.), *Behavior therapy: Apprisal and status.* New York: McGraw-Hill, 1969.
Kant, I. *Foundations of the metaphysics of morals.* New York: The Liberal Arts Press, 1959.
Kant, I. Versuch Uber Krankheiten Des Kopfes (1764). W. Weischedel B. I *Immanual Kant, Vorkritische Schriften bis 1768.* Darmstadt: Wissenschaftliche Buchgesellschaft, 1966. (a)
Kant. I. *Critique of pure reason.* New York: Anchor Books, 1966. (b)
Kantor, D., & Lehr, W. *Inside the family.* San Francisco: Jossey-Bass, 1975.
Kantor, R. E., Wallner, J. M., & Winder, C. L. Process and reactive schizophrenia. *Journal of Consulting Psychology,* 1953, *17,* 157-162.
Kaplan, A. *The conduct of inquiry: Methodology for behavioral science.* San Francisco: Chandler Publishing Company, 1964.
Kardiner, A., with collaboration of Linton, R., DuBois, C., & West, J. *The psychological frontiers of society.* New York: Columbia University Press, 1945.
Kaufmann, W. The inevitability of alienation: An introductory essay. In R. Schacht, *Alienation.* Garden City, N.Y.: Doubleday, 1970.

Kazdin, A. E. Covert modeling and the reduction of avoidance behavior. *Journal of Abnormal Psychology*, 1973, *81*, 87-95.

Keeney, B. F. Ecosystemic epistemology: An alternative paradigm for diagnosis. *Family Process*, 1979, *18*, 117-129.

Kelly, G. A. *The psychology of personal constructs*. New York: Norton, 1955.

Kelly, H. H. *Causal schemata and the attribution process*. Morristown, N.J.: General Learning Press, 1972.

Kendell, R. E. *The classification of depressive illness* (Institute of Psychiatry, Maudsley Monograph 18). Oxford: Oxford University Press, 1968.

Kendell, R. E. The classification of depressions: A review of contemporary confusion. *British Journal of Psychiatry*, 1976, *129*, 15-28.

Kessler, S. The etiological question in mental illness. *Science*, September, *26*, 1969, 1341-1342.

Kierkegaard, S. *Concluding unscientific postscript of the philosophical fragments*. Princeton, N.J.: Princeton University Press, 1941.

Kiev, A. *Transcultural psychiatry*. New York: The Free Press, 1972.

Kiloh, L. G., & Garside, R. F. The independence of neurotic depression and endogenous depression. *British Journal of Psychiatry*, 1963, *109*, 451-463.

Klein, M. *Contributions to psycho-analysis, 1921-1945*. London: Hogarth Press, 1948.

Klein, M. *The psycho-analysis of children*. London: Hogarth Press, 1949.

Kleinberg, O. *Social psychology*. New York: Holt, Rinehart, & Winston, 1954.

Kohn, M. L. *Class and conformity: A study in values*. Homewood, Ill.: Dorsey Press, 1969.

Kohut, H. *The analysis of the self*. Psychoanalytic study of the child. Monograph series. New York: International University Press, 1971.

Kora, T. Morita therapy. *International Journal of Psychiatry*, 1965, *1*, 611-645.

Korzybski, A. *Science and sanity*. Lancaster, Pennsylvania: The International Non-Aristotelian Library Publishing Company, 1941.

Kotarbinski, T. *Praxiology: An introduction to the science of efficient action*. (transl.) O Wojtasiewicz. Oxford: Pergamon, 1965.

Kraepelin, E. *Lectures on clinical psychiatry* (transl. and ed.) J. Johnstone. London: Bailliere & Cox, 1913.

Krasner, L. The therapist as a social reinforcement machine. In H. H. Strupp & M. Luborsky (Eds.), *Research in psychotherapy* (Vol. 2). Washington, D.C.: American Psychological Association, 1962.

Krasner, L. Behavior modification-values and training: The perspective of a psychologist. In C. M. Franks (Ed.), *Behaviour therapy: Appraisal and status*. New York: McGraw-Hill, 1969.

Kretschmer, E. *Physique and character*. (transl.) W. J. H. Sprott. New York: Harcourt Brace, 1925.

Kris, E. *Psychoanalytic exploration in art*. New York: International University Press, 1952.

Kubie, L. S. The fundamental nature of the distinction between normality and

neurosis. *Psychoanalytic Quarterly*, 1954, *23*, 182-185.
Kuhn, M. Major trends in symbolic interaction theory in the past twenty five years. *Sociological Quarterly*, 1964, *5*, 61-84.
Kuhn, R. *Die Maskendeutungen in Rorschachversuch*. Basel: Karger, 1954.
Kuhn, R. Daseinsanalyse und Psychiatrie. In H. B. Brühle (Ed.), *Psychiatrie der Gegenwert*. Berlin: Springer, 1963.
Kuhn, T. S. *The structure of scientific revolution*. Chicago: University of Chicago Press, 1962.
Lacan, J. *Ecrits*. Paris: Seuil, 1966.
Lacan, J. *The language of the self*. Baltimore: John Hopkins Press, 1968.
Lagache, D. Psychoanalyse et psychologie. *L'evolution psychiatrique*. 1956, *21*, 269-295.
Laing, R. D. Mystification, confusion and conflict. In I. Boszormenyi-Nagy & J. Framo (Eds.), *Intensive family therapy*. New York: Harper and Row, 1965. (a)
Laing, R. D. *The divided self*. New York: Penguin Books, 1965. (b)
Laing, R. D. *The politics of experience, and the bird of paradise*. Harmondsworth, England: Penguin Books, 1967.
Laing, R. D. *The self and others*. New York: Pantheon Books, 1969.
Laing, R. D. *The politics of family*. New York: Vintage Books, 1972.
Laing, R. D., & Esterson, A. *Sanity, madness and the family*. London: Tavistock Publications (2nd ed.), 1970.
Lakatos, I. Falsification and the methodology of scientific research programmes. In I. Lakatos & A. Musgrave (Eds.), *Criticism and the growth of knowledge*. Cambridge: Cambridge University Press, 1970.
Langer, S. *Philosophy in a new key*. New York: Penguin Books, 1948.
La Piere, R. *The Freudian ethic*. New York: Duell, Sloan, & Pearce, 1959.
Laplin, I. P., & Oxenkrug, G. F. Intensification of the central serotoninergic processes as a possible determinant of the thymoleptic effect, *Lancet*, 1969, *1*, 132-136.
Laqueur, H. P. Multiple family therapy. In A. Ferber, M. Mendelsohn, & A. Napier (Eds.), *The book of family therapy*. New York: Science House, 1972.
Ledwidge, B. Cognitive behavior modification: A step in the wrong direction? *Psychological Bulletin*, 1978, *85*, 353-375.
Lehmann, H. E. Classification of depressive states. *Canadian Psychiatric Association Journal*, 1977, *22*, 381-390
Leighton, A. *My name is legion*. New York: Basic Books, 1959.
Leighton, A. A comparative study of psychiatric disorder in Nigeria and rural North America. In S. C. Plog & R. B. Edgerton (Eds.), *Changing perspectives in mental illness*. New York: Holt, Rinehart, & Winston, 1969.
Lemert, E. L. *Social pathology*. New York: McGraw-Hill, 1951.
Lemert, E. L. *Human deviance, social problems and social control*. Englewood Cliffs, N.J.: Prentice-Hall, 1964.
Leonhard, K. *The classification of endogenous psychoses* (5th ed.). (Ed.) E. Robins, (transl.) R. Berman. New York: Irvington, 1979 (original, 1957).

Levi-Strauss, C. *Structural anthropology*. (transl.) C. Jacobson & B. G. Shoepf. New York: Basic Books, 1963.
Levi-Strauss, C. *The elementary structures of kinship*. (transl.) J. H. Bell, R. von Sturmer, R. Needham. Boston: Beacon Press, 1969 (Original 1949).
Lewin, K. *Resolving social conflicts*. New York: Harper, 1948.
Lewinsohn, P. M. A behavioral approach to depression. In R. J. Friedman & M. M. Katz (Eds.), *The psychology of depression: Contemporary theory and research*. Washington, D.C.: V. H. Winston, 1974.
Lewis, A. J. States of depression: Their clinical and etiological differentiation. *British Medical Journal*, 1938, *12*, 875–878.
Lewis, N. D. A. *Research in dementia praecox*. New York: National Committee for Mental Hygiene, 1936.
Lidz, T., Cornelison, A., Carlson, D. T., & Fleck, S. Intrafamilial environment of the schizophrenic patient: The transmission of irrationality. *Archives of Neurology and Psychiatry*, 1958, *79*, 305–316.
Lidz, T., Fleck, S., & Cornelison, A. R. *Schizophrenia and the family*. New York: International Universities Press, 1965.
Lindmann, E. Psycho-social factors as stressor agents. In J. M. Tanner (Ed.), *Stress and psychiatric disorders*. Oxford, England: Blackwell, 1960.
Linsky, A. F. Who shall be excluded: The influence of personal attributes in community reaction to mentally ill. *Social Psychiatry*, 1970, *5*, 166–171.
Linton, R. *The cultural background of personality*. New York: Appleton-Century-Crofts, 1945.
Linton, R. *Culture and mental disorders*. Springfield, Ill.: Thomas, 1956.
Lippit, R., & White, R. K. The "social climate" of children's groups. In R. G. Barker, J. S. Kounin, & H. F. Wright (Eds.), *Child behavior and development*. New York: McGraw-Hill, 1943.
Locke, E. A. Is "Behaviour Therapy" behavioristic? (An analysis of Wolpe's psychotherapeutic methods.). *Psychological Bulletin*, 1971, *76*, 318–327.
Lunberg, G. A. *Foundations of sociology*. New York: Macmillan, 1939.
Lundberg, G. A. *Can science save us?* New York: Longmans, Green, 1961.
Luria, A. *The role of speech in the regulation of normal and abnormal behavior*. New York: Liveright, 1961.
Maas, J. W., Fawcett, J. A., & Dekirmenjian, H. Catecholamine metabolism, depressive illness and drug response. *Archives of General Psychiatry*, 1972, *152*, 35–75.
MacIver, R. M. *Society*. New York: Farrar & Rinehart, 1937.
Madaness, C., & Haley, J. Dimensions of family therapy. *Journal of Nervous and Mental Diseases*, 1977, *165*, 88–98.
Maddi, S. R. *Personality theories: A comparative analysis*. Homewood, Ill.: Dorsey, 1968.
Mahoney, M. J. *Cognition and behavior modification*. Cambridge, Mass.: Ballinger, 1974.
Malinowski, B. *Sex and repression in savage society*. London: Routledge & Kegan Paul, 1953.

Malinowski, B. *A scientific theory of culture and other essays.* New York: University of North Carolina Press, 1960.
Mannheim, K. *Ideology and utopia.* London: Routledge & Kegan, 1936.
Marcel, G. *Being and having.* London: Collins, 1965.
Marcuse, H. *One-dimensional man.* Boston: Beacon Press, 1964.
Margolis, J. *Psychotherapy and morality.* New York: Random House, 1966.
Marie, A., & Toporkoff, N. Démence précoce et syphilis. *Archive International de Neurologie,* 1929, *1,* 163-178.
Maruyama, M. The second cybernetics: Deviation-amplifying, mutual causal processes. *American Scientist,* 1963, *51,* 164-179.
Marx, K. *Capital.* New York: Modern Library, 1946.
Marx, K. *Early writings.* (Ed. and transl.) T. E. Bottomore. New York: McGraw-Hill, 1963.
Marx, K., & Engels, F. *The German ideology.* (Ed.) R. Pascal. New York: International Publishers, 1947.
Maslow, A. *Motivation and personality.* New York: Harper, 1954.
Maslow, A. *Towards psychology of being.* New Jersey: Van Nostrand, 1962.
Maslow, A. *The psychology of science, A reconnaissance.* New York: Harper & Row, 1966.
Matson, F. W. *The broken image: Man, science and society.* New York: Brazilier, 1964.
Mauriello, V. Unmasking Lacan. Paper presented at the Second Annual National Scientific Meeting of the Canadian Psychoanalytic Society. Toronto, June 7, 1975.
Mauss, M. *The gift.* (Transl.) I. Curnison. Glencoe, Ill.: Free Press, 1954.
May, R., Angel, E., & Ellenberger, H. F. *Existence.* New York: Basic Books, 1958.
Mayer-Gross, W. A. Zur Phanomenologie abnormer Glucksgefühle. *Zeitschrift für Pathopsychologie,* 1914, *2,* 588-601.
Mayer-Gross, W. A. *Selbstschilderungen der Verwirrtheit: Die oneiroide Erlebnisform.* Berlin: Springer, 1924.
McGuire, W. J. A syllogistic analysis of cognitive relationships. In C. I. Hovland & M. J. Rosenberg (Ed.), *Attitude orientation and change.* New Haven: Yale University Press, 1960.
McIsaac, W. M. A biochemical concept of mental disease. *Postgraduate Medicine,* 1961, *20,* 111-118.
Mead, G. H. *Mind, self and society from the standpoint of social behaviorist.* Chicago: University of Chicago Press, 1972 (Original 1934).
Mechanic, D. Some factors in identifying and defining mental illness. *Mental Hygiene,* 1962, *46,* 66-74.
Mechanic, D. Response factors in illness: The study of illness behavior. *Social psychiatry,* 1966, *1,* 11-20.
Mednick, S. A. A learning theory approach to research in schizophrenia. *Psychological Bulletin,* 1958, *55,* 316-327.
Meehl, P. E. Schizotaxia, schizotypy, schizophrenia. *American Psychologist,* 1962, *17,* 827-838.

Meehl, P. E., & Rosen, A. Antecedent probability and the efficacy of psychometric signs, patterns, or cutting scores. *Psychological Bulletin*, 1955, *52*, 194-216.

Meichenbaum, D. *The nature and modification of impulsive children*. Paper presented to the Society for Research in Child Development, Minneapolis, 1971.

Meichenbaum, D. *Cognitive-behavior modification*. Morristown, N.J.: General Learning, 1974.

Meichenbaum, D., & Cameron, R. Stress innoculation: A skill training approach to anxiety management. Unpublished manuscript, University of Waterloo 1973 (a), quoted by M. J. Mahoney, *Cognition and behavior modification*. Cambridge, Massachusetts: Ballinger, 1974.

Meichenbaum, D., & Cameron, R. Training schizophrenics to talk to themselves: A means of developing attentional controls. *Behavior Therapy*, 1973, *4*, 515-534. (b)

Meier, D. L., & Bell, W. Anomia and differential access to the achievement of life goals. *American Sociological Review*, 1959, *24*, 189-208.

Melzack. R. *The puzzle of pain*. Harmondsworth, England: Penguin Publishing Co., 1973.

Mendels, J., & Cochrane, C. The nosology of depression: The endogenous-reactive concept. *American Journal of Psychiatry*, 1968, *129*, supplement 1-11.

Menninger, K. Influenza and schizophrenia: Analysis of post-influenzal dementia praecox as of 1918 and 5 years later. *American Journal of Psychiatry*, 1926, *5*, 469-524.

Menninger, K. *The vital balance*. New York: The Viking Press, 1963.

Merleau-Ponty, M. *Phenomenology of perception*. New York: Humanities Press, 1962.

Merleau-Ponty, M. *The structure of behavior*. Boston: Beacon Press, 1963.

Merton, R. K. *Social theory and social structure*. New York: Macmillan, 1968.

Merton, R. K., Reader, G. G., & Kendall, P. L. (Eds.), *The student-physician: Introductory studies in the sociology of medical education*. Cambridge: Harvard University Press, 1957.

Meyer, A. *Psychobiology: A science of man*. Springfield, Illinois: C. C. Thomas, 1957.

Meyer, J. E. Studien zür Depersonalization, II Depersonalization und Zwang als polare Störungen der Ich-Aussenwelt-Beziehung. *Psychiatrie und Neurologie*, 1957, *133*, 63-79.

Michaels, J. W., & Green, D. S. Behavioral sociology emergent forms and issues. In S. G. McNall (Ed.), *Theoretical perspectives in sociology*. New York: St. Martin's Press, 1979.

Milgram, N. A. Role-taking in female schizophrenic patients. *Journal of Clinical Psychology*, 1961, *17*, 409-411.

Mill, J. S. *On liberty*. London: Watts, 1945.

Miller, J. G. *Living systems*. New York: McGraw-Hill, 1978.

Miller, N. E. Liberalization of basic S-R concepts: extensions to conflict behaviour, motivation, and social learning. In S. Koch (Ed.), *Psychology: A*

study of a science. New York: McGraw-Hill (Vol. 2), 1959.
Miller, N. E. Learning of visceral and glandular responses. *Science*, 1969, *163*, 434-445.
Miller, W. R., & Seligman, M. E. P. Depression and learned helplessness in man. *Journal of Abnormal Psychology*, 1975, *84*, 228-238.
Minkowski, E. *La schizophrenie: Psychopathologie des schizoides et des schizophrenes.* (2nd ed.). Paris: Desclee de Brouwer, 1953.
Minkowski, E. *Lived time.* Evanston, Ill.: Northwestern University Press, 1970.
Minuchin, S. *Families and family therapy.* Cambridge: Harvard University Press, 1974.
Minuchin, S., Montalvo, B., & Guerney, B. *Families of the slums.* New York: Basic Books, 1967.
Mishler, E. G., & Waxler, N. E. Family interaction processes and schizophrenia: A review of current theories. *Merrill-Palmer Quarterly of Behavior and Development*, 1965, *11*, 269-315.
Montalvo, B. Aspects of live supervision. *Family Process*, 1973, *12*, 343-359.
Moreau de Tours, J. J. *Du haschisch et de l'aliénation mentale: Etudes psychologiques.* Paris: Fortin, Masson, 1845.
Morel, B. A. *Traite des maladies mentales.* Paris: Masson, 1860.
Moreno, J. L. *Who shall survive?* Beacon, N.Y.: Beacon House, 1953.
Morris, C. W. *Signs, language and behavior.* New York: Prentice-Hall, 1946.
Mowrer, O. H. *Learning theory and personality dynamics.* New York: Ronald Press, 1950.
Mowrer, O. H. *The crisis in psychiatry and religion.* Princeton, N.J.: Van Nostrand, 1961.
Mowrer, O. H. Guilt in social sciences. In H. Schoeck & J. W. Wiggins (Eds.), *Psychiatry and responsibility.* Princeton, N.J.: Van Nostrand, 1962.
Murphy, R. J. Stratification of mental illness issues and strategies of research. In S. C. Plog & R. B. Edgerton (Eds.), *Changing perspectives in mental illness.* New York: Holt, Rinehart, & Winston, 1969.
Murphy, J. M. Psychiatric labelling in cross-cultural perspective. *Science*, 1976, *191*, 1019-1028.
Murray, H. G., & Hirsch, J. Heredity, individual differences and psychopathology. In S. C. Plog & R. B. Edgerton (Eds.), *Changing perspectives in mental illness.* New York: Holt, Rinehart & Winston, 1969.
Myers, J. K., & Roberts, B. H. *Family and class dynamics in mental illness.* New York: John Wiley, 1959.
Myerson, A. Review of mental disorders in urban areas. *American Journal of Psychiatry*, 1941, *96*, 995-997.
Nagel, E. *The structure of science.* London: Routledge & Kegan Paul, 1961.
Naroll, R. Cultural determinants and the concept of the sick society. In S. C. Plog & R. B. Edgerton (Eds.), *Changing perspectives in mental illness.* New York: Holt, Rinehart & Winston, 1969.
Needleman, J. *Being-in-the-world.* New York: Basic Books, 1963.

Neisser, U. *Cognitive psychology.* New York: Appleton-Century-Crofts, 1967.
Nettler, G. A measure of alienation. *American Sociological Review,* 1957, *22,* 670-677.
Nietzsche, F. The geneology of morals. In W. Kaufmann (Ed.), *Basic writings of Nietzsche.* New York: Modern Library, 1966.
Nunnally, J. C. *Popular conceptions of mental health, their development and change.* New York: Holt, Rinehart, & Winston, 1961.
Offer, D., & Sabshin, M. *Normality.* New York: Basic Books, 1966.
Olds, J., & Milner, P. Positive reinforcement produced by electric stimulation of septal area and other regions of rat brain. *Journal of Comparative and Physiological Psychology,* 1954, *47,* 419-427.
Olson, D. H., Sprenkle, D. H., & Russell, C. S. Circumplex model of marital and family systems: 1. Cohesion and adaptability dimensions, family types, and clinical applications. *Family Process,* 1979, *18,* 3-28.
Olson, L., Nystrom, B., & Seiger, A. Monoamine fluorescent histo-chemistry of human postmortem brain. *Brain Research,* 1973, *63,* 231-247.
Opler, M. K. *Culture, psychiatry and human values.* Springfield, Ill.: Charles C Thomas, 1956.
Opler, M., & Singer, J. L. Contrasting patterns of fantasy and motility in Irish and Italian schizophrenics. *Journal of Abnormal and Social Psychology,* 1956, *53,* 42-47.
Ornstein, R. E. *The psychology of consciousness.* San Francisco: W. H. Freeman, 1972.
Osgood, C. E. *Method and theory in experimental psychology.* New York: Oxford University Press, 1953.
Osmond, H., & Smythies, J. Schizophrenia: A new approach. *Journal of Mental Science,* 1952, *98,* 309-315.
Park, R. E., & Burgess, E. W. *The city.* Chicago: University of Chicago Press, 1925.
Parsons, T. *The social system.* Glencoe, Ill.: Free Press, 1951.
Parsons, T. *Social theory and modern society.* New York: Free Press, 1967.
Parsons, T. *The system of modern societies.* Englewood Cliffs, N.J.: Prentice-Hall, 1971.
Parsons, T. Definition of health and illness in the light of American values and social structure. In E. G. Jaco (Ed.), *Patients, physicians and illness.* New York: Free Press, 1972.
Parsons, T., & Bales, R. *Family, socialization and interaction process.* Glencoe, Ill.: Free Press, 1955.
Parsons, T., & Shils, E. (Eds.), *Towards a general theory of action.* Cambridge, Mass.: Harvard University Press, 1951.
Pasamanick, B., Roberts, D. W., Lemkau, P. W., & Krueger, D. B. Survey of mental disease in urban population: Prevalence by race and income. In Reisman, F., Cohen, J., & Pearl, A. (Eds.), *Mental health of the poor.* New York: Free Press, 1964.
Pascal, B. *Pensées.* (transl.) H. F. Stewart. New York: Modern Library, 1967.

Paul, G. L., & Lentz, R. J. *Psychological treatment of chronic mental patients: Milieu vs. social learning programs.* Cambridge, Mass.: Harvard University Press, 1978.
Paul, N. The use of empathy in the resolution of grief. *Perspectives in biology and medicine,* 1967, *11,* 153-169.
Pavlov, I. P. *Conditioned reflexes and psychiatry.* New York: International Publishers, 1941.
Perls, F. G. *Gestalt therapy verbatim.* Lafayette, Calif.: Real People Press, 1969.
Perls, F., Hefferline, R. E., & Goodman, P. *Gestalt therapy: Excitement and growth of the human personality.* New York: Dell, 1951.
Perris, C. A study of bipolar (manic-depressive) and unipolar recurrent depressive psychoses. *Acta Psychiatrica Scandinavica,* 1966, *42,* Suppl. 194, 1-189.
Perry, J. R. Reconstitutive process in the psychopathology of the self. *Annals of the New York Academy of Science,* 1962, *96,* 853-876.
Perry, T. L., Hansen, S., & Macintyre, L. Failure to detect 3,4-dimethoxyphenylethylamine in the urine of schizophrenics. *Nature,* 1964, *202,* 519-520.
Peters, R. W. *The concept of motivation.* London: Routledge & Kegan Paul, 1958.
Phares, E. J. *Locus of control: A personality determinant of behavior.* Morristown, N.J.: General Learning Press, 1973.
Piaget, J. *The construction of reality in the child.* New York: Basic Books, 1954.
Piaget, J. *The moral judgement of the child.* New York: The Free Press, 1965.
Piaget, J. *Structuralism.* New York: Basic Books, 1971.
Pilowsky, I., Levine, S., & Bolton, D. M. The classification of depression by numerical taxonomy. *British Journal of Psychiatry,* 1969, *115,* 937-945.
Plog, S. C., & Edgerton, R. B. (Eds.), *Changing perspectives in mental illness.* New York: Holt, Rinehart & Winston, 1969.
Polanyi, M. *Personal knowledge.* Chicago: University of Chicago Press, 1958.
Pollin, W., Cardon, P. V. Jr., & Kety, S. S. Effects of aminoacid feedings in schizophrenic patients treated with iproniazid. *Science,* 1961, *133,* 104-105.
Pollitt, J. Depression and the functional shift. *Comprehensive Psychiatry,* 1960, *1,* 381-390.
Popper, K. R. *Conjectures and refutations: The growth of scientific knowledge.* New York: Basic Books, 1965.
Popper, K. *The open society and its enemies.* London: Kegan Paul, 1945.
Post, F. The management and nature of depressive illness in late life: A follow-through study. *British Journal of Psychiatry,* 1972, *121,* 393-404.
Powell, E. H. Occupation status and suicide. *American Sociological Review,* 1958, *23,* 131-139.
Praag, Van. H. M. Towards biochemical typology of depression. *Pharmakopsychiatrie, Neuro-Psychopharmakologie,* 1974, *7,* 281-292.
Praag, Van. H. M. Significance of biochemical parameters in the diagnosis, treatment and prevention of depressive disorder. *Biological Psychiatry,* 1977, *12,* 101-131.
Praag, Van, H. M., Flentge, F., Korf, J., Dols, L. C. W., & Schut, T. The influence of probencid on the metabolism of serotonin, dopamine and their

precursors in man. *Psychopharmacologia,* 1973, *33,* 141-151.
Premack, D. Toward empirical behavior laws. I: Positive reinforcement. *Psychological Review,* 1959, *66,* 219-233.
Price, R. H. *Abnormal behavior: Perspectives in conflict* (2nd ed.). New York: Holt, Rinehart, and Winston, 1978.
Price, R. H., & Lynn, S. J. *Abnormal psychology in the human context.* Homewood, Ill.: The Dorsey Press, 1981.
Prince, M. *The dissociation of a personality.* New York: Longmans, Green, & Co., 1906.
Psathas, G. (Ed.). *Phenomenological sociology: Issues and applications.* New York: Wiley-Interscience, 1973.
Quetelet, A. *A treatise on man and the development of his faculties.* Edinburgh: W. & H. Chambers, 1842. (*Sur l'homme et development de ses facultes où Essai de physique sociale.* 2 vol. Paris: Bachelier, 1835.)
Radcliffe-Brown, A. R. *Structure and function in primitive society.* Glencoe, Ill.: Free Press, 1952.
Radnitzky, G. *Contemporary schools of metascience (Vols. 1 & 2).* Goteborg: Akademiforlaget, 1968.
Rank, O. *Art and artist.* New York: Alfred Knopf, 1932.
Rank, O. *Will therapy, and truth and reality.* New York: Alfred Knopf, 1950.
Rank, O. *The myth of the birth of the hero, and other writings.* (Ed.) P. Freund. New York: Alfred Knopf, 1964.
Rapaport, D. The structure of psychoanalytical theory. *Psychological Issues,* Monograph 6, Vol. 2, No. 2. New York: International University Press, 1960.
Rapaport, D., & Gill, M. M. The points of view and assumptions of metapsychology. *International Journal of Psychoanalysis,* 1959, *40,* 153-162.
Rappaport, R. Normal crises, family structure, and mental health. *Family Process,* 1962, *2,* 68-79.
Raush, H. L., Greif, A. C., & Nugent, J. Communication in couples and families. In W. R. Burr, R. Hill, F. J. Nye, and I. L. Reiss (Eds.), *Contemporary theories about the family: Research based theories* (Vol. 1). New York: Free Press, 1979.
Reich, W. *Character analysis.* New York: Orgone Institute Press, 1949.
Reusch, J., & Bateson, G. *Communication: The social matrix of psychiatry.* New York: Norton, 1968.
Rickert, H. *Science and history.* (transl.) G. Reisman. Princeton: Van Nostrand, 1962.
Ricoeur, P. *Freud and philosophy: An essay on interpretation.* (transl.) D. Savage. New Haven: Yale University Press, 1970.
Rieff, P. *Freud: The mind of the moralist.* New York: Viking, 1959.
Riesman, D., Glazer, N., & Denney, R. *The lonely crowd.* New Haven: Yale University Press, 1950.
Rimm, D. C., & Masters, J. C. *Behavior therapy: Techniques and empirical findings* (2nd ed.). New York: Academic Press, 1979.
Rimon, R., & Halonen, P. Antibody levels to viruses in psychiatric illness. In E. S.

Gershon, R. H. Belmaker, S. S. Kety, and M. Rosenbaum (Eds.), *The impact of biology on modern psychiatry.* New York: Plenum Press, 1977.

Rogers, C. R. A theory of therapy, personality and interpersonal relations. In S. Koch (Ed.), *Psychology: A study of science.* New York: McGraw-Hill, 1959.

Rogers, C. R. *On becoming a person.* Boston: Houghton-Mifflin, 1961.

Rogers, C. R. A theory of therapy, personality and interpersonal relationships, as developed in the client-centred framework. In S. Koch (Ed.), *Psychology: A study of a science.* New York: Basic Books, 1963.

Rogers, C. R. *Client-centered therapy.* Boston: Houghton-Mifflin, 1965, (original 1951).

Roheim, G. *Psychoanalysis and anthropology: Culture, personality and the unconscious.* New York: International University Press, 1950.

Rosenhan, D. L. On being sane in insane places. *Science,* 1973, *179,* 250-258.

Rosenow, E. C. Specific types of alpha streptococci in the etiology and streptococcal thermal antibody in diagnosis and treatment of diverse diseases. *Journal of Nervous and Mental Diseases,* 1955, *122,* 238-247.

Rosenthal, D. Changes in some moral values following psychotherapy. *Journal of Consulting Psychology,* 1955, *19,* 431-436.

Rosenthal, D. *Genetic theory and abnormal behavior.* New York: McGraw-Hill, 1970.

Rosenthal, D. *Genetics of psychopathology.* New York: McGraw-Hill, 1971.

Rosenthal, D. *Evidence for a spectrum of schizophrenic disorders.* Presented at the Annual Meeting of the American Psychological Association. Montreal, Canada, August, 1973.

Roszak, T. *The making of counterculture: Reflections on the technocratic society and its youthful opposition.* City, N.H.: Doubleday, 1969.

Rotter, J. B. Generalized expectancies for internal versus external control of reinforcement. *Psychological Monographs,* 1966, *86:* Whole No. 609.

Rümke, H. C. *Zur Phänomenologie und Klinik des Glücksgefühls.* Berlin: Springer, 1924.

Rushing, W. A. Individual resources, societal reaction, and hospital commitment. *American Journal of Sociology,* 1971, *77,* 511-526.

Ryle, G. *The concept of mind.* Hammondworth: Penguin Books, 1949.

Ryle, J. A. The meaning of normal. *Lancet,* 1947, *1,* 4-5.

Saint Augustine. *The confessions of Saint Augustine.* (transl.) E. B. Pusey. New York: Collier Books, 1961.

Sanua, V. Socio-cultural factors in families of schizophrenics: A review of the literature. *Psychiatry,* 1961, *24,* 246-265.

Sarbin, T. S. The scientific status of the mental illness metaphor. In S. C. Plog & R. B. Edgerton (Eds.), *Changing perspectives in mental illness.* New York: Holt, Rinehart, & Winston, 1969.

Satir, V. *Conjoint family therapy.* Palo Alto, California: Science and Behaviour Books, 1967.

Sartre, J. P. *Saint Genet: Comedien et martyre.* Paris: Gallimard, 1952.

Sartre, J. P. *Being and nothingness*. New York: Philosophical Library, 1956.
Sartre, J. P. *Critique de la raison dialectique*. Paris: Gallimard, 1960.
Saussure, F. de. *Course in general linguistics*. (Eds.) C. Bally & A. Sechehaye. (transl.) W. Baskin. New York: McGraw-Hill, 1966.
Schacht, R. *Alienation*. New York: Doubleday, 1970.
Schachter, S., & Singer, J. E. Cognitive, social and physiological determinants of emotional state. *Psychological Review*, 1962, *69*, 379-399.
Schafer, R. *A new language for psychoanalysis*. New Haven: Yale University Press, 1976.
Shaffer, J. B., & Galinsky, M. D. *Models of group therapy and sensitivity training*. Englewood Cliffs, N.J.: Prentice-Hall, 1974.
Schank, R. C. *Conceptual information processing*. New York: American Elsevier Inc., 1975.
Scheff, T. J. *Being mentally ill: A sociological study*. Chicago: Aldine, 1966.
Scheff, T. J. *Mental illness and social process*. New York: Harper & Row, 1967.
Scheff, T. J. (Ed.). *Labeling madness*. Englewood Cliffs, N.J.: Prentice-Hall, 1975.
Scheler, M. *The nature of sympathy*. New Haven: Yale University Press, 1954.
Schildkraut, J. J. The catecholamine hypothesis of affective disorders: A review of supportive evidence. *American Journal of Psychiatry* 1965, *122*, 509-522.
Schneider, K. Die Schichtung des emotionalen Lebens und der Aufbau der Depressionzustände, *Zeitschrift für die gesamte Neurologie und Psychiatrie*, 1920, *59*, 281-286.
Schneider, K. Pathopsychologische Beiträge zur phenomenologischen Psychologie von Liebe und Mitfühlen, *Zeitschrift für der gesamte Neurologie und Psychiatrie*, 1921, *65*, 109-140.
Schneider, K. *Psychopathic personalities*. London: Cassel, 1958.
Schneider, K. *Clinical psychopathology*. New York: Grune & Stratton, 1959.
Schuetz, A. *Der sinnhafte Aufbau der sozialen Welt*. Vienna: Springer, 1932.
Schutz, W. C. *Here comes everybody*. New York: Harper and Row, 1971.
Schwartz, G. E. Psychosomatic disorders and biofeedback: A psychobiological model of disregulation. In J. D. Maser & M. E. P. Seligman (Eds.), *Psychopathology: Experimental models*. San Francisco: Freeman, 1977.
Sedgwick, P. R. D. Laing: Self, symptom and society. In R. Boyers (Ed.), *R. D. Laing & Anti-psychiatry*. New York: Harper & Row, 1971.
Seeman, M. On the meaning of alienation. *American Sociological Review*, 1959, *24*, 783-791.
Seligman, M. E. P. Depression and learned helplessness. In R. J. Friedman & M. M. Katz (Eds.), *The psychology of depression: Contemporary theory and research*. New York: Wiley & Sons, 1974.
Seligman, M. E. P. *Helplessness: On depression, development, and death*. San Francisco: Freeman, 1975.
Seligman, M. E. P., & Maier, S. F. Failure to escape traumatic shock. *Journal of Experimental Psychology*, 1967, *74*, 1-9.
Selye, H. *The stress of life*. New York: McGraw-Hill, 1956.

Selye, H. On the real benefit of eustress. *Psychology Today,* March, 1978, 60-63, 69-70.
Shaver, K. G. *An introduction to attribution processes.* Cambridge, Mass.: Winthrop, 1975.
Shaw, D. M. Mineral metabolism, mania and melancholia. *British Medical Journal,* 1966, ii, 262-267.
Shaw, C. W., & McKay, H. D. *Report on the causes of crime.* National Commission on Law Observance and Enforcement. Washington, D.C.: United States Government Printing Office, 1931.
Sheldon, W. H. *The varieties of human physique: An introduction to constitutional psychology.* London: Harper & Brothers, 1940.
Sheldon, W. H. *The varieties of temperament: A psychology of individual differences.* London: Harper, 1942.
Shoben, E. J. Psychotherapy as a problem in learning theory. *Psychological Bulletin,* 1949, *46,* 366-392.
Siegler, M., & Osmond, H. *Models of madness, models of medicine.* New York: Macmillan, 1974.
Siegler, M., Osmond, H., & Mann, H. Laing's models of madness. In R. Boyers (Ed.), *R. D. Laing and anti-psychiatry.* New York: Harper & Row, 1971.
Sigerist, H. *Man and medicine.* London: Allen & Unwin, 1932.
Simmel, G. *Conflict and the web of group affiliation.* Glencoe, Ill.: The Free Press, 1955.
Skinner, B. F. *Walden Two.* New York: Macmillan, 1948. (a)
Skinner, B. F. "Superstition" in the pigeon. *Journal of Experimental Psychology,* 1948, *38,* 168-172. (b)
Skinner, B. F. *Science and human behavior.* New York: Macmillan, 1953.
Skinner, B. F. What is psychotic behaviour? In F. Gildea (Ed.), *Theory and treatment of the psychoses.* Washington University Studies Committee on Publications, St. Louis, MO.: Washington University, 1956.
Skinner, B. F. *Beyond freedom and dignity.* New York: Alfred A. Knopf, 1971.
Skynner, A. C. R. *Systems of family and marital psychotherapy.* New York: Brunner/Mazel, 1976.
Sorokin, P. A. (Ed.). *Explorations in altruistic love and behavior.* Boston: Beacon Press, 1950.
Sorokin, P. *Fads, foibles in modern sociology and related sciences.* Chicago: Regnery, 1956.
Speck, R. V., & Attneave, C. *Family networks.* New York: Pantheon Books, 1973.
Speer, D. Family systems: Morphostasis and morphogenesis, or "Is Homeostasis enough?" *Family Process,* 1970, *9,* 259-278.
Spence, D. P. (Ed.). *Psychoanalysis and contemporary science: An annual of integrative and interdisciplinary studies* (Vol. 4), 1975. New York: International Universities Press, 1976.
Spence, K. W., & Taylor, J. A. The relation of conditioned response strength to

anxiety in normal, neurotic and psychotic subjects. *Journal of Experimental Psychology,* 1953, *45,* 265-272.

Spiegelberg, H. *The phenomenological movement—A historical introduction* (2 vols.). The Hague: Nijhoff, 1960.

Spiegelberg, H. *Phenomenology in psychology and psychiatry.* Evanston: Northwestern University Press, 1972.

Spitzer, R. S. On pseudoscience in science, logic in remission and psychiatric diagnosis: A critique of Rosenhans' "On being sane in insane places." *Journal of Abnormal Psychology,* 1975, *84,* 442-452.

Spitzer, R. L., & Endicott, J. Diagno: A computer program for psychiatric diagnosis utilizing the differential diagnosis procedure. *Archives of General Psychiatry,* 1968, *28,* 746-756.

Spivack, G., & Shure, M. B. *Social adjustment of young children: A cognitive approach to solving real-life problems.* San Francisco: Jossey-Bass, 1974.

Spranger, E. *Types of men.* (transl.) J. W. Pigors. Halle: Max Niemeyer Verlag, 1928.

Srole, L. Social integration and corollaries: An experimental study. *American Sociological Review,* 1956, *21,* 709-716.

Srole, L., & Fischer, A. K. The midtown Manhattan longitudinal study vs. "the mental paradise lost" doctrine. *Archives of General Psychiatry,* 1980, *37,* 209-221.

Srole, L., Langner, T. S., Michael, S. T., Opler, M. K., & Rennie, T. A. C. *Mental health in the metropolis: The midtown Manhattan study.* New York: McGraw-Hill, 1962.

Stampfl, T. C., & Levis, D. J. Essentials of implosive therapy: A learning theory-based psychodynamic behavioral therapy. *Journal of Abnormal Psychology,* 1967, *72,* 496-503.

Stanton, A. H., & Schwartz, M. S. *The mental hospital.* New York: Basic Books, 1954.

Stein, L. Psychopharmacological aspects of mental depression. *Canadian Psychiatric Association Journal,* 1966, *11* (special supplement), 14-49.

Stein, L., & Wise, C. D. Possible etiology: Progressive damage of the noradrenergic reward mechanism by endogenous 6-hydroxydopamine, *Science,* 1971, *171,* 1032.

Stekel, W. *Das liebe Ich: Grundris einer neuen Diatetik der Seele.* Berlin: Otto Stalle, 1927.

Stekel, W. *Technique of analytical psychotherapy.* New York: Liveright, 1950.

Stevenson, C. *Ethics and language.* New Haven: Yale University Press, 1944.

Stoll, W. A. Lysergsäure-diäthylamid, ein Phantastikum aus der Mutterkorngruppe, *Schweizer Archiv für Neurologie und Psychiatrie,* 1947, *60,* 279-323.

Stonequist, E. *The marginal man.* New York: Scribner & Sons, 1937.

Straus, E. *The primary world of senses: A vindication.* Glencoe, Ill.: Free Press, 1963.

Straus, E. *Phenomenological psychology: Selected papers.* (transl.) E. Eng. New York: Basic Books, 1966.

Suinn, R. M., & Richardson, F. Anxiety management training: A nonspecific behavior therapy program for anxiety control. *Behavior Therapy,* 1971, *2,* 498-510.

Sullivan, H. S. *Interpersonal theory of psychiatry.* New York: W. W. Norton, 1953.
Susser, M. *Causal thinking in the health sciences: Concepts and strategies in epidemiology.* New York: Oxford University Press, 1973.
Swanson, D. W., Bohnert, P. J., & Smith, J. A. *The paranoid.* Boston, Mass.: Little, Brown, 1970.
Swets, J. A., Tanner, W. P. Jr., & Birdsall, T. G. Decision processes in perception. *Psychological Review,* 1961, *68,* 301-390.
Szasz, T. S. *The myth of mental illness: Foundations of a theory of personal conduct.* New York: Harper & Row, 1961, (a)
Szasz, T. S. The uses of naming and the origin of the myth of mental illness. *American Psychologist,* 1961, *2,* 59-65. (b)
Szasz, T. S. *Law, liberty and psychiatry: An inquiry into the social uses of mental health practices.* New York: Macmillan, 1963.
Szasz, T. S. *Psychiatric justice.* New York: Macmillan, 1965. (a)
Szasz, T. S. *The ethics of psychoanalysis: The theory and method of autonomous psychotherapy.* New York: Basic Books, 1965. (b)
Szasz, T. S. *Ideology and insanity: Essays on the psychiatric dehumanization of man.* Garden City, N.Y.: Doubleday, Anchor Press, 1970.
Szasz, T. S. *The manufacture of madness, a comparative study of inquisition and the mental health movement.* New York: Delta Book, Dell Publishing, 1971.
Szasz, T. S. *Schizophrenia: The sacred symbol of psychiatry.* New York: Basic Books, 1976.
Szasz, T. S. *The theology of medicine.* Baton Rouge: Louisiana State University Press, 1977.
Tannenbaum, F. *Crime and the community.* New York: Columbia University Press, 1938.
Taylor, C. *The explanation of behaviour.* London: Routledge & Kegan Paul, 1964.
Taylor, C. *Action and purpose.* Englewood Cliffs, N.J.: Prentice Hall, 1966.
Thoresen, C. M., & Mahoney, M. J. *Behavioral self-control.* New York: Holt, Rinehart, & Winston, 1974.
Tienari, P. Schizophrenia in monozygotic male twins. In D. Rosenthal & S. S. Kety (Eds.), *The transmission of schizophrenia.* London: Pergamon Press, 1968.
Tillich, P. *The courage to be.* New Haven, Conn.: Yale University Press, 1952.
Tillich, P. Existentialism and psychotherapy. In H. M. Ruitenbeck (Ed.), *Psychoanalysis and existential philosophy.* New York: Dutton, 1962.
Tinbergen, N. *The study of instinct.* London: Oxford University Press, 1951.
Tolstoy, L. *The death of Ivan Ilyich and other stories.* New York: New American Library, 1960.
Tomkins, S. S. *Affect, imagery, consciousness* (Vol. 2). The negative affect. New York: Springer, 1963.
Tooth, G. *Studies in mental illness in the Gold Coast.* London: H. M. Stationery Office, 1950.
Torrey, E. F. *The death of psychiatry.* Radnor, PA: Chilton Book Co., 1974.

Torrey, E. F., & Peterson, M. R. Slow and latent viruses in schizophrenia. *Lancet,* 1973, *2,* 22-24.
Trilling, L. *The opposing self.* New York: Viking Press, 1955.
Turner, J. H. *The structure of sociological theory.* Homewood, Illinois: The Dorsey Press, 1978.
Ullmann, L. P. Behavior therapy as social movement. In C. M. Franks (Ed.), *Behavior therapy: Appraisal and status.* New York: McGraw-Hill, 1969.
Ullmann, L. P., & Krasner, L. What is behavior modification. In L. P. Ullmann and L. Krasner (Eds.), *Case studies in behavior modification.* New York: Holt, Rinehart & Winston, 1965.
Ullmann, L. P., & Krasner, L. *A psychological approach to abnormal behavior* (2nd ed.). Englewood Cliffs, N.J.: Prentice-Hall, 1975.
Vaihinger, H. *Philosophy of the as if* (Die Philosophie des als Ob.) Berlin: Reuther and Reichard, 1911.
Van den Berg, J. H. *A phenomenological approach to psychiatry.* Springfield, Ill.: Charles C Thomas, 1955.
Varela, F. *Principles of biological autonomy.* North Holland Series in General Systems Research, Vol. 2. Amsterdam, New York: Elsevier-North Holland, 1979.
Vaughn, C. E., & Leff, J. P. The influence of family and social factors on the course of psychiatric illness: A comparison of schizophrenic and depressive patients. *British Journal of Psychiatry,* 1976, *129,* 127-137.
Vergote, A. L'interet philosophique de la psychologie Freudienne. *Archives de Philosophie,* 1958, *21,* 26-59.
Vogel, E. F., & Bell, N. W. The emotionally disturbed child as the family scapegoat. In N. W. Bell and E. F. Vogel (Eds.), *A modern introduction to the family.* Glencoe, Ill.: Free Press, 1960.
von Bertalanffy, L. General system theory and psychiatry. In S. Arieti (Ed.), *American Handbook of Psychiatry* (Vol. 3). New York: Basic Books, 1966.
von Bertalanffy, L. *Robots, Men and Minds.* New York: George Braziller, 1967.
von Bertalanffy, L. *General system theory: Foundations, development, applications.* New York: Braziller, 1968.
von Wright, G. H. *The varieties of goodness.* London: Routledge & Kegan Paul, 1963.
Vygotsky, L. S. *Thought and language.* Cambridge: M.I.T. Press, 1962.
Waelhens, de, A. *Schizophrenia: A philosophical reflection on Lacan's structuralist interpretation.* (transl.) W. Ver Eecke. Pittsburgh: Duquesne University Press, 1978.
Waelhens, de, A. *La philosophie et les experiences naturelles.* The Hague: Martinus Nijhoff, 1961.
Waring, M., & Ricks, D. Family patterns of children who became adult schizophrenics. *Journal of Nervous and Mental Disease,* 1965, *140,* 351-364.
Watson, J. B. Psychology as the behaviorist views it. *Psychological Review,* 1913, *20,* 158-177.
Watson, J. B. *Behaviorism.* New York: Norton, 1930.
Watson, J. B., & Rayner, R. Conditioned emotional reactions. *Journal of Experimental Psychology,* 1920, *3,* 1-14.

Watzlawick, P., Beavin, J., & Jackson, D. *Pragmatics of human communication.* New York: Norton, 1967.

Watzlawick, P., Weakland, J., & Fish, R. *Change: Principles of problem formation and problem resolution.* New York: Norton, 1974.

Weber, M. *The theory of social and economic organization.* New York: Free Press, 1947.

Weber, M. *The methodology of social sciences.* (transl.) E. A. Shils & H. A. Finch. New York: The Free Press, 1949.

Weckowicz, T. E. Depersonalization-derealization syndrome and perception: A contribution of psychopathology to epistemology. In J. R. Royce & W. W. Rozeboom (Eds.), *Psychology of knowing.* New York: Gordon & Breach, 1972.

Weckowicz, T. E. The impact of phenomenological and existential philosophies on psychiatry and psychotherapy. In J. R. Royce & L. P. Mos (Eds.), *Humanistic psychology: Concepts and criticisms.* New York: Plenum Press, 1981.

Weckowicz, T. E., & Liebel-Weckowicz, H. Typologies of the theory of Behaviorism since Descartes. *Sudhoffs Archiv,* 1982, 66, 129-151.

Weiner, B. *Theories of motivation: From mechanism to cognition.* Chicago: Rand McNally, 1972.

Weiner, B., Freize, J., Kukla, A., Reed, L., Rest, S., & Rosenbaum, R. M. *Perceiving causes of success and failure.* Morristown, N.J.: General Learning Press, 1971.

Weiss, J. M., Glazer, H. I., & Pohorecky, L. A. Coping behavior and neurochemical changes: An alternative explanation for original "learned helplessness" experiments. In G. Serban & A. Kling (Eds.), *Relevance of the animal model to the human.* New York: Plenum Press, 1976.

Weiss, P. The living system: Determinism stratified. In A. Koestler & J. R. Smythies (Eds.), *Beyond reductionism.* New York: Macmillan, 1969.

Weiss, P. The system of nature and the nature of systems: Empirical holism and practical reductionism harmonized. In K. E. Schaefer, H. Hensel, & R. Brody (Eds.), *Toward a man-centred medical science.* Mt. Kisco, N.H.: Futura Publishing, 1977.

Werner, H. *Comparative psychology of mental development.* Chicago: Follet, 1948.

Werner, H. The concept of development from a comparative and organismic point of view. In D. Harris (Ed.), *The concept of development: An issue in the study of human behavior.* Minneapolis: University of Minnesota Press, 1957.

Wertheim, E. The science and typology of family systems. II. Further theoretical and practical considerations. *Family Process,* 1975, 14, 285-308.

Whitehead, A. *Science and the modern world.* New York: The Free Press, 1953.

Whitehead, A. N., & Russell, B. *Principia Mathematica.* Cambridge: Cambridge University Press, 1910.

Whitaker, C. The territory chart as a platform for family therapy. *Voices,* 1970, 2, 95-97.

Whitaker, D. S., & Lieberman, M. A. *Psychotherapy through the group process.* New York: Atherton Press, 1965.

Wild, C. Creativity and adaptive regression. *Journal of Personality and Social Psychology*, 1965, *2*, 121-169.
Wilden, A. Lacan and the discourse of the other. In J. Lacan, *The language of the self: The function of language in psychoanalysis*. (transl.) A. Wilden. Baltimore: John Hopkins University Press, 1968.
Wilden, A., & Wilson, T. The Double Bind: Logic, magic and economics. In C. Sluzki & D. Ransom (Eds.), *Double bind: The foundation of the communicational approach to the family*. New York: Grune & Stratton, 1976.
Williams, R. J. *Biochemical individuality*. New York: John Wiley, 1956.
Williams, R. J., & Siegel, F. L. Propetology, a new branch of medical science. *American Journal of Medicine*, 1961, *31*, 325-327.
Winch, P. *The idea of social science*. New York: Humanities Press, 1958.
Windelband, W. *History of philosophy* (transl.) J. H. Tufts. New York: Macmillan, 1901.
Winett, R. A. Attribution of attitude and behavior change and its relevance to behavior therapy. *Psychological Record*, 1970, *20*, 17-23.
Wing, J., & Nixon, J. Discriminating symptoms in schizophrenia. *Archives of General Psychiatry*, 1975, *32*, 853-859.
Wittgenstein, L. *Philosophical investigations*. Oxford: Blackwell, 1953.
Witz, J. P., Anavi, R., & Weisenbeck, H. A tissue-binding factor in the serum of schizophrenic patients. In E. S. Gershon, R. H. Belmaker, S. S. Kety, and M. Rosenbaum (Eds.), *The impact of biology on modern psychiatry*. New York: Plenum Press, 1977.
Wolf, H. G. *Stress and disease*. (Ed. and rev.) S. Wolf and H. Goodell. Springfield, Ill.: Charles C Thomas, 1968.
Wolpe, J. Experimental neuroses as learned behaviour. *British Journal of Psychology*, 1952, *43*, 243-268.
Wolpe, J. *Psychotherapy by reciprocal inhibition*. Stanford: Stanford University Press, 1958.
Wynne, L. Discussion. In D. Jackson (Ed.), The individual and larger contexts. *Family Process*, 1967, *6*, 139-154.
Wynne, L., Ryckoff, I., Day, J., & Hirsch, S. Pseudo-mutuality in the family relations of schizophrenics, *Psychiatry*, 1958, *21*, 205-220.
Wynne, L., & Singer, M. Thought disorder and the family relations of schizophrenics: I. A research strategy. *Archives of General Psychiatry*, 1963, *9*, 191-198. (a)
Wynne, L., & Singer, M. Thought disorders and family relations of schizophrenics: II. A classification of forms of thinking. *Archives of General Psychiatry*, 1963, *9*, 199-206. (b)
Wyrsch, J. *Ueber akute schizophrene Zustande, ihren psychopathologischen Aufbau und ihre praktische Bedeutung*. Basel: Karger, 1937.
Yap, P. M. *Comparative psychiatry: A theoretical framework*. Toronto: University of Toronto Press, 1974.
Yates, A. J. The application of learning theory to the treatment of tics. *Journal of Abnormal and Social Psychology*, 1958, *56*, 175-182.

Zborowski, M. Cultural components in response to pain. *Journal of Social Issues,* 1952, *8,* 16-30.

Zigler, E., & Philips, L. Psychiatric diagnosis and symptomotology. *Journal of Abnormal Psychology,* 1961, *63,* 69-75.

Zimmerman, D. H. Ethnomethodology. In S. G. McNall (Ed.), *Theoretical perspectives in sociology.* New York: St. Martin's Press, 1979.

Zubin, J. (Ed.). *Field studies in the mental disorders.* New York: Grune & Stratton, 1961.

Zubin, J., & Spring, B. Vulnerability: A new view of schizophrenia. *Journal of Abnormal Psychology,* 1977, *86,* 103-126.

Zuk, G. *Family therapy: A triadic-based approach.* New York: Behavioural Publications, 1971.

NAME INDEX

A

Abramowitz, S. I., 154, 343
Abramson, L. Y., 155, 156, 343
Ackerman, N. W., 229, 343
Addams, J., 213
Adler, A. 106, 115, 116, 118, 276, 283, 343
Aghajanian, G. K., 77, 346
Albane, A., 68, 344
Allowsmith, M., 69, 343
Allport, G. W., 35, 259, 283, 285, 287, 288, 290, 291, 296, 343
Anavie, R., 69, 373
Andolfi, M., 212, 230, 343
Angel, E., 259, 263, 266, 274, 360
Angell, R., 226, 343
Angst, J., 178, 343
Apel, K. O., 339, 340, 343
Arieti, S., 337, 343
Aristotle, 27, 34, 286, 291
Arnkraut, A., 69, 343
Arnold, M., 150, 152, 343
Assagioli, R., 283, 343
Attneave, C., 237, 368
Augustine, Saint, 92, 366
Axelrod, J., 70, 76, 343
Ayllon, R., 139, 140, 343, 344
Azrin, N., 139, 140, 343

B

Bacon, F., 294, 344
Bain, J. A., 147, 344
Baldwin, A. L., 126, 344
Bales, R., 221, 230, 363
Balint, M., 173, 202, 344
Balzac, H., 248
Bandura, A., 140, 154, 159, 160, 344

Bannister, D., 148, 344
Barachas, J., 70, 344
Barnard, C. P., 211, 222, 225, 344
Baruk, H., 68, 344
Bateson, G., 230, 232, 233, 234, 237, 242, 243, 306, 344, 365
Baudelaire, P. C., 272
Bauman, Z., 246, 344
Bayes, T., 42
Beaumont, J. G., 80, 349
Beavin, J., 242, 372
Beck, A. T., 137, 151, 152, 344
Becker, E., 5, 12, 200, 280, 344
Becker, H. S., 19, 345
Beckett, G. S. I., 77, 345
Beers, C. W., 303, 345
Bell, N. W., 230, 371
Bell, W., 189, 361
Bem, D. J., 154, 345
Benedict, R., 32, 169, 185, 345
Beneke, 83
Bentham, J., 135, 282
Bergson, H., 265, 345
Bernard, C., 37, 327, 345
Berne, E., 214, 218, 219, 345
Bernheim, H., 104
Bever, T. G., 145, 351
Bibring, E., 151, 345
Bidermann, M., 68, 344
Binswanger, L., 270, 272, 273, 274, 275, 345
Birdsall, T. G., 44, 370
Birnbaum, K., 60, 345
Blashfield, R. K., 64, 345
Bleuler, E. P., 59, 60, 61, 345
Blondel, C., 263, 345
Bloom, F. R., 74, 75, 348
Blumer, H., 199, 207, 345
Bockoven, J. S., 138, 345

Bohnert, P. J., 164, 370
Bohr, N., 333, 340
Boisen, A. T., 300, 313, 345
Bolton, D. M., 62, 364
Bonhoeffer, K., 52, 70
Boring, E., 86, 346
Boss, M., 272, 275, 346
Boszormenyi-Nagy, I., 225, 346
Bott, E., 221, 346
Boulding, K. E., 336, 346
Bourdillon, R. E., 76, 346
Bowen, M., 223, 226, 241, 346
Bowlby, J., 211, 346
Braestrup, C., 71, 346
Breger, L., 12, 346
Brenner, M. H., 176, 346
Brentano, F., 260, 346
Breuer, J., 7, 346
Brodie, H. K. H., 71, 347
Brown, L. G., 184, 346
Buber, M., 204, 216, 269, 270, 278, 297, 346
Buchwald, A., 132, 346
Buck, C., 191, 346
Buckley, W., 183, 210, 346
Budzynski, T. H., 140, 346
Bugental, J., 283
Bühler, C., 283, 290, 346
Bunney, B. S., 77, 346
Bunney, W. E., 71, 78, 347
Burgess, E., 153, 347
Burgess, E. W., 186, 347, 363
Buscaino, B. M., 68, 69, 347
Buytendijk, F. J. J., 264, 347

C

Cameron, N., 123, 208, 347
Cameron, R., 161, 361
Caplan, G., 193, 347
Cardon, P. V., Jr., 76, 364
Carlson, D. T., 231, 359
Carnap, R., 334, 347
Carnegie, D., 147, 347
Carothers, J. C., 177, 347
Carson, N. A., 76, 347
Cassirer, E., 164, 249, 250, 347
Caughey, J. L., 56, 349
Cautela, J. R., 139, 158, 347
Cavan, R. S., 186, 347

Cervantes, 83
Charcot, J. M., 104
Chase, T. N., 79, 71, 347
Chein, I., 135, 347
Chomsky, N., 101, 102, 145, 347
Clarke, C. A., 76, 346
Cochrane, C., 62, 361
Cohen, J., 38, 350
Colby, K. M., 162, 163, 164, 347, 348
Comte, A., 167, 310
Conrad, K., 304, 348
Cooley, C. H., 118, 181, 199, 207, 348
Coombs, C. M., 44, 45, 348
Cooper, D., 235, 236, 278, 311, 348
Cooper, J. E., 39, 348
Cooper, J. R., 74, 75, 348
Copeland, J. R. M., 39, 348
Coppen, A., 78, 348
Cornelison, A., 230, 231, 359
Corrales, R. G., 211, 222, 225, 344
Coser, L., 193, 348
Cotton, H. A., 68, 348
Coué, E., 147, 348
Coulter, J., 172, 348
Coyne, J. C., 234, 348
Cumming, E., 172, 348
Cumming, J., 172, 348
Cusworth, D. C., 76, 347

D

Dabrowski, K., 283, 292, 300, 301, 302, 303, 348
Dahrendorf, R., 193, 348
Davis, D. A., 42, 43, 348
Davis, J. M., 71, 347
Davis, K., 133, 348
Davison, G. C., 154, 348
Dawes, R. M., 44, 45, 348
Day, J., 225, 373
De Giovani, 83
DeGrazia, S., 186, 348
Dekirmenjian, H., 63, 73, 348, 359
Deleon-Jones, F., 73, 348
Denney, R., 197, 365
Dent, C. E., 76, 347
Descartes, R., 92, 101, 302
Devereux, G., 173, 174, 349
de Waelhens, A., 256, 258, 340, 371

Dewey, J., 282
Diamond, M. D., 208, 349
Dilthey, W., 247, 273, 349
Dimond, S., 80, 349
Dobzansky, T., 24, 349
Dohrenwend, B. P., 38, 176, 349
Dohrenwend, B. S., 38, 176, 349
Dollard, J., 34, 128, 130, 161, 349
Dols, L. C. W., 79, 364
Dostoyevsky, F., 248, 302
Douglas, J. D., 166, 349
Draguns, J. G., 64, 345
Draper, G., 56, 349
Duhl, F. J., 334, 335, 336, 337, 338, 353
Dunham, H. W., 186, 187, 349, 350
Dunham, W. H., 186, 192, 349
Dunlap, K., 131, 349
Dupertius, C. W., 56, 349
Durkheim, E., 167, 168, 182, 184, 186, 187, 188, 195, 313, 349

E

Eaton, J. W., 175, 349
Edelson, M., 107, 164, 250, 251, 349
Edgerton, R. B., 173, 176, 177, 187, 349, 364
Elenmeyer-Kimling, L., 81, 349
Ellenberger, H. F., 28, 259, 263, 266, 274, 349, 360
Ellis, A., 149, 150, 151, 349, 350
Endicott, J. D., 38, 64, 350, 369
Engel, G. L., 337, 350
Engels, F., 251, 360
Epictetus, 149
Erikson, E., 123, 124, 350
Esterson, A., 235, 236, 237, 287, 311, 358
Everitt, B., 66, 350
Ey, H., 124, 125, 127, 180, 350
Eysenck, H. J., 38, 138, 142, 143, 144, 350

F

Fairbairn, W. R. D., 111, 211, 212, 229, 350
Farina, A., 230, 350
Faris, R. E. L., 186, 187, 350
Fawcett, J. A., 63, 359
Fechner, G. T., 49
Federn, P., 218, 350
Feighner, J. P., 39, 350

Fenichel, O., 112, 350
Ferster, C. B., 140, 350
Festinger, L., 147, 350
Feyerabend, P., 293, 350
Field, C. M. B., 76, 347
Fischer, A. K., 176, 369
Fish, F. J., 61, 351
Fish, R., 234, 242, 372
Flaubert, G., 272
Fleck, S., 230, 231, 359
Fleiss, J. L., 38, 66, 350, 351
Flentge, F., 79, 364
Flor-Henry, P., 80, 351
Fodor, J. A., 145, 351
Foerster, H., 244, 355
Fogarty, T., 223, 351
Fothergill, L. A., 72, 355
Foucault, M., 184, 351
Foulkes, S. H., 215, 351
Frankl, V. E., 154, 276, 277, 292, 351
Franks, C. M., 139, 351
Freedman, 164
Freize, J., 154, 372
French, T., 300, 351
Freud, A., 112, 351
Freud, S., 3, 7, 13, 14, 18, 28, 34, 97, 98, 105, 106, 107, 108, 109, 110, 111, 113, 114, 120, 126, 151, 167, 168, 211, 251, 253, 254, 255, 258, 273, 274, 294, 315, 346, 351, 352
Friedhoff, A. J., 76, 351
Friedricks, R. W., 205, 352
Fromm, E., 18, 31, 168, 194, 195, 196, 198, 199, 283, 292, 352
Frumkin, R. M., 289, 352

G

Galinsky, M. D., 213, 214, 218, 220, 367
Garfinkel, H., 172, 352
Garrett, M. F., 145, 351
Garside, R. F., 62, 357
Gaylin, W., 151, 352
Gedo, J. E., 107, 112, 352
Geer, B., 19, 345
Gendlin, E. T., 297, 352
Gerard, D. L., 191, 352
Gill, M. M., 108, 353, 365
Gjessing, R., 69, 352

Glasser, W., 12, 316, 317, 318, 353
Glazer, H. I., 155, 372
Glazer, N., 197, 365
Goethe, J. W., 248
Goffman, E., 173, 174, 202, 220, 353
Goldberg, A., 107, 112, 352
Goldfried, M. R., 161, 353
Goldiamond, I., 140, 355
Goldstein, K., 120, 250, 284, 353
Goodman, P., 120, 364
Goodwin, F. K., 71, 347
Gottesman, I. I., 88, 353
Gough, H. G., 208, 353
Gould, M. S., 38, 176, 349
Gray, W., 334, 335, 336, 337, 338, 353
Green, D. S., 166, 361
Greif, A. C., 231, 365
Griesinger, W., 57
Grinker, R., Sr., 31, 336, 353
Gross, M. L., 175, 353
Grühle, H. W., 86
Guerney, B., 241, 362
Gurland, B. J., 39, 348
Guthrie, E. R., 96, 353
Guttman, L., 227, 353
Guze, S. B., 39, 350

H

Habermas, J., 8, 168, 195, 339, 340, 353
Hafner, H., 272
Haley, J., 232, 234, 237, 238, 239, 240, 242, 344, 353, 359
Halmos, P., 353
Halonen, P., 69, 365
Handel, G., 222, 225, 354
Hansen, S., 76, 364
Hare, A. P., 208, 353
Hare, E. H., 186, 191, 353
Harley-Mason, J., 76, 353
Harper, P., 76, 346
Harré, R., 167, 195, 196, 289, 353
Hartmann, H., 31, 110, 115, 118, 162, 290, 354
Hayek, F. A., 310
Heath, R. G., 69, 354
Hebb, D. O., 142, 354
Hefferline, R. E., 120, 364
Hegel, G. W. F., 146, 251, 252, 253, 354

Heidegger, M., 270, 272, 273, 274, 354
Heider, F., 153, 354
Heinroth, A., 312
Hempel, G. C., 41, 354
Henry, J., 221, 354
Heraclitus, 33
Hesnard, A. L., 272, 354
Hess, R. D., 222, 225, 354
Hill, R., 224, 227, 354
Hippocrates, 89
Hirsch, J., 175, 362
Hirsch, S., 225, 373
Hobbes, T., 167, 168, 282
Hobbs, G. E., 191, 346
Hoffer, A., 76, 354
Hollingshead, A. B., 41, 173, 176, 189, 204, 354
Hollister, L. E., 76, 351
Holmberg, A. R., 170, 354
Holroyd, K. A., 55, 354
Holzman, M., 354
Homans, G. C., 166, 167, 218, 354
Homme, L. E., 158, 354
Horney, K., 115, 116, 117, 118, 194, 354
Hornykewicz, O., 70, 354
Horton, J., 195, 205, 354
Hoult, T. F., 166, 355
Houston, L. G., 191, 352
Howe, R., 244, 355
Hudson, W. S., 297, 313
Hughes, E. C., 19, 345
Hughes, J., 72, 355
Hull, C. L., 34, 128, 130, 157, 355
Hume, D., 14, 27, 94, 355
Husserl, E., 99, 258, 260, 261, 355
Huxley, A., 355

I

Ihde, D., 251, 355
Isaacs, W., 140, 355
Isham, H., 294, 355
Ittelson, W. H., 268, 355

J

Jackson, D., 232, 234, 237, 242, 344, 355, 372
Jackson, H. J., 124, 300, 355

Name Index

Jacob, T., 231, 355
Jacobson, E., 139, 151, 355
Jahoda, M., 31, 355
James, W., 49, 105, 355
Janet, P., 104, 105, 124, 355
Janowsky, D. S., 71, 347
Jaspers, K., 86, 248, 263, 269, 270, 272, 275, 304, 356
Jefferson, T., 309
Jilek, W. G., 177, 356
Jilek-Aall, L., 177, 356
Joan of Arc, Saint, 169
John of the Cross, Saint, 304
Johnson, J. M., 166, 349
Jones, M., 138, 220, 356
Jourard, S., 170, 183, 197, 356
Jouvet, M., 71, 356
Joyce, J., 259
Jung, C. G., 105, 253, 283, 294, 299, 307, 356

K

Kafka, F., 278, 302, 356
Kallmann, F. J., 80, 83, 356
Kanfer, F. H., 140, 356
Kant, I., 27, 101, 146, 147, 258, 259, 282, 315, 356
Kantor, D., 222, 223, 224, 356
Kantor, R. E., 62, 356
Kaplan, A., 6, 356
Kardiner, A., 32, 356
Kaufmann, W., 194, 356
Kasanin, J., 300, 351
Kazdin, A. E., 161, 357
Keeney, B. F., 240, 242, 243, 244, 357
Kelly, G. A., 148, 149, 357
Kelly, H. H., 153, 357
Kendall, P. L., 19, 168, 182, 188, 361
Kendell, R. E., 39, 62, 63, 348, 357
Kessler, S., 5, 10, 357
Kety, S. S., 76, 364
Khayyam, O., 268
Kierkegaard, S., 268, 269, 281, 302, 357
Kiev, A., 178, 357
Kiloh, L. G., 62, 357
Kisker, K. P., 272
Klein, M., 111, 211, 212, 229, 357
Kleinberg, O., 27, 357

Kleist, K., 61
Koch, R., 51
Kohn, M. L., 176, 357
Kohut, H., 110, 111, 357
Kora, T., 153, 357
Korf, J., 79, 364
Korzybski, A., 258, 357
Kosterlitz, H. W., 72, 355
Kotarbinski, T., 7, 357
Kraepelin, E., 10, 40, 49, 50, 57, 58, 59, 63, 64, 65, 69, 177, 357
Krasner, L., 127, 132, 133, 134, 137, 141, 357, 371
Kretschmer, E., 83, 84, 85, 248, 357
Kris, E., 121, 299, 357
Krueger, D. B., 363
Kubie, L. S., 31, 357
Kuhn, M., 207, 358
Kuhn, R., 272, 275, 358
Kuhn, T. S., 145, 293, 336, 358
Kukla, A., 154, 372
Kulpe, O., 86
Kutash, S. B., 268, 355

L

Lacan, J., 107, 253, 254, 255, 256, 257, 258, 358
Lagache, D., 272, 358
Laing, R. D., 235, 236, 237, 278, 279, 300, 303, 306, 311, 328, 358
Laird, A., 76, 353
Lakatos, I., 145, 358
Langer, S., 250, 358
Langner, T. S., 175, 289, 369
La Piere, R., 314, 358
Laplin, I. P., 78, 358
Laqueur, H. P., 237, 358
Lasswell, H. D., 310
Lautrec, T., 302
Le Bon, 167
Ledwidge, B., 138, 358
Leff, J. P., 191, 371
Lehmann, H. E., 63, 358
Lehr, W., 222, 223, 224, 356
Leibnitz, G. W., 101
Leighton, A., 175, 176, 177, 189, 358
Lemert, E. L., 171, 184, 199, 358
Lemkau, P. W., 363

Lentz, R. J., 140, 364
Leonhard, K., 63, 358
Leslie, S. A., 76, 346
Levine, S., 62, 364
Levis, D. J., 139, 369
Levi-Strauss, C., 101, 102, 182, 241, 254, 256, 359
Levitt, E. B., 140, 350
Lewin, K., 120, 206, 208, 209, 215, 223, 239, 359
Lewinsohn, P. M., 137, 359
Lewis, A. J., 62, 359
Lewis, N. D. A., 69, 359
Lidz, T., 230, 231, 359
Liebel-Weckowicz, H., 128, 372
Lieberman, M. A., 215, 372
Lindmann, E., 300, 359
Link, B., 38, 176, 349
Linsky, A. F., 205, 359
Linton, R., 32, 168, 179, 359
Lippit, R., 223, 359
Locke, E. A., 127, 137, 359
Locke, J., 282, 309
Lunberg, G. A., 359
Lundberg, G. A., 166, 359
Luria, A., 161, 359
Lynn, S. J., 319, 365

M

Maas, J. W., 348, 359
MacBeth, 315
McGaugh, J. L., 12, 346
McGuire, W. J., 147, 360
Macintyre, L., 76, 364
McIsaac, W. M., 77, 360
MacIver, R. M., 166, 359
McKay, H. D., 186, 368
McLellan, B., 69, 343
Madaness, C., 237, 238, 239, 240, 359
Maddi, S. R., 292, 359
Magret, A., 208
Mahoney, M. J., 146, 147, 154, 157, 158, 159, 161, 359, 370
Maier, S. F., 155, 367
Malinowski, B., 169, 182, 359, 360
Mann, H., 237, 303, 307, 368
Mannheim K., 203, 360
Marcel, G., 271, 360

Marcuse, H., 168, 195, 360
Margaret, A., 347
Margolis, J., 16, 291, 360
Marie, A., 68, 360
Maruyama, M., 209, 360
Marx, K., 193, 194, 185, 251, 272, 273, 282, 310, 360
Maslow, A., 31, 110, 118, 243, 283, 285, 286, 287, 290, 291, 292, 293, 294, 360
Masters, J. C., 140, 365
Matson, F. W., 293, 360
Mauriello, V., 254, 360
Mauss, M., 254, 360
May, R., 118, 259, 263, 266, 274, 281, 283, 360
Mayer-Gross, W. A., 86, 264, 360
Mead, G. H., 118, 199, 207, 225, 360
Mechanic, D., 170, 360
Mednick, S. A., 130, 131, 360
Meehl, P. E., 42, 88, 360, 361
Meichenbaum, D., 157, 161, 361
Meier, D. L., 189, 361
Melzack, R., 72, 361
Mendels, J., 62, 361
Menninger, K., 38, 52, 65, 68, 127, 337, 361
Merleau-Ponty, M., 99, 253, 261, 262, 271, 272, 278, 279, 360
Merton, R. K., 19, 168, 182, 188, 361
Meyer, A., 89, 361
Meyer, J. E., 267, 361
Meynert, T., 61
Michael, J., 140, 344
Michael, S. T., 175, 189, 369
Michaels, J. W., 166, 361
Milgram, N. A., 208, 361
Mill, J. S., 28, 134, 167, 282, 310, 361
Miller, J. G., 335, 361
Miller, N. E., 34, 128, 130, 137, 161, 349, 361, 362
Miller, W. R., 155, 362
Milner, P., 78, 363
Minkowski, E., 261, 265, 266, 362
Minuchin, S., 226, 241, 254, 362
Mishler, E. G., 230, 362
Montalvo, B., 241, 242, 362
Moreau de Tours, J. J., 69, 362
Morel, B. A., 69, 362
Moreno, J. L., 217, 362
Morgan, B. A., 72, 355

Name Index

Morris, C. W., 249, 362
Morris, H. R., 72, 355
Moustakas, B. M., 283
Mowrer, O. H., 12, 130, 312, 313, 314, 315, 316, 318, 362
Munoz, R., 39, 350
Murphy, D. L., 70, 71, 347
Murphy, J. M., 173, 174, 362
Murphy, R. J., 190, 362
Murray, H. G., 175, 362
Myers, J. K., 190, 362
Myerson, A., 191, 362

N

Nagel, E., 166, 362
Naroll, R., 188, 362
Needleman, J., 272, 362
Neill, D. W., 76, 347
Neisser, U., 163, 363
Nettler, G., 189, 194, 363
Neugebauer, R., 38, 176, 349
Neurath, O., 334
Nielsen, M., 71, 346
Nietzsche, F., 251, 268, 273, 294, 363
Nixon, J., 66, 373
Nugent, J., 231, 365
Nunnally, J. C., 173, 363
Nurnberger, J. I., 140, 350
Nystrom, B., 70, 363

O

Offer, D., 22, 363
Olds, J., 78, 363
Olson, D. H., 225, 227, 228, 240, 363
Olson, L., 70, 363
Opler, M., 177, 178, 363
Opler, M. K., 175, 178, 189, 363, 369
Ornstein, R. E., 303, 363
Osgood, C. E., 157, 363
Osmond, H., 59, 69, 76, 89, 90, 236, 237, 303, 305, 307, 311, 319, 321, 324, 330, 354, 363, 368
Oxenkrug, G. F., 73, 358

P

Panza, Sancho, 83

Paradowski, W., 81, 349
Park, R. E., 186, 363
Parmenides, 33
Parsons, T., 27, 89, 169, 170, 182, 188, 221, 230, 363
Pasamanick, B., 38, 363
Pascal, B., 268, 363
Paterson, M. R., 69
Paterson, T. T., 90
Paul, G. L., 140, 364
Paul, N., 241, 364
Pavlov, I. P., 128, 364
Perls, F. G., 120, 217, 364
Perris, C., 63, 364
Perry, J. R., 300, 364
Perry, T. L., 76, 364
Peters, R. S., 93, 94, 95, 98
Peters, R. W., 13, 308, 364
Peterson, M. R., 371
Phares, E. J., 154, 364
Philips, L., 43
Phillips, J. S., 140, 356
Piaget, J., 101, 102, 119, 122, 123, 364
Pilowsky, I., 62, 66, 364
Pinel, P., 4, 296
Plato, 134, 146, 310
Plessner, H., 273
Plog, S. C., 176, 177, 187, 364
Pohorecky, L. A., 155, 372
Pollin, W., 76, 364
Pollitt, J., 62, 364
Polyani, M., 293, 364
Popper, K. R., 93, 294, 310, 364
Post, F., 62, 364
Powell, E. H., 189, 364
Premack, D., 135, 365
Price, R. H., 319, 324, 336, 365
Prince, M., 104, 105, 365
Protagoras, 282
Proust, M., 302
Psathas, G., 166, 365

Q

Quetelet, A., 23, 24, 25, 365
Quixote, Don, 83

R

Radcliffe-Brown, A. R., 365
Radnitzky, G., 321, 322, 328, 339, 340, 341, 365
Rank, O., 283, 294, 295, 298, 299, 305, 365
Rapaport, D., 108, 365
Rappaport, R., 224, 365
Raush, H. L., 231, 365
Rayner, R., 371
Reader, G. G., 19, 168, 182, 188, 361
Redlich, F. C., 41, 173, 176, 189, 204, 354
Reed, L., 154, 372
Reich, W., 216, 365
Reiss, D., 226
Rennie, R. A. C., 175, 189, 369
Rest, S., 154, 372
Reusch, J., 233, 337, 365
Reyner, R., 138
Richardson, F., 161, 369
Rickert, H., 247, 365
Ricks, D., 231, 371
Ricoeur, P., 251, 252, 253, 257, 258, 262, 365
Ridges, A. P., 76, 346
Rieff, P., 290, 365
Riesman, D., 197, 365
Rimm, D. C., 140, 365
Rimon, R., 69, 365
Rizzo, N. D., 33, 335, 336, 337, 338, 353
Roberts, B. H., 190, 362
Roberts, D. W., 363
Robins, E., 39, 350
Rogers, C. R., 33, 110, 118, 149, 281, 283, 287, 290, 296, 297, 298, 313, 366
Roheim, G., 168, 366
Rosen, A., 42, 361
Rosenbaum, R. M., 154, 372
Rosenhan, D. L., 39, 42, 366
Rosenow, E. C., 68, 366
Rosenthal, D., 80, 81, 133, 366
Rostan, 83
Roszak, T., 303, 366
Roth, R. H., 74, 75, 348
Rotter, J. B., 153, 366
Rousseau, J. J., 282
Rümke, H. C., 262, 264, 366
Rushing, W. A., 205, 366
Russell, B., 232, 372

Russell, C. S., 225, 227, 228, 240, 363
Ryckoff, I., 225, 373
Ryle, G., 92, 99, 100, 308, 366
Ryle, J. A., 25, 366

S

Sabshin, M., 22, 363
Saint-Simon, Comte de, 310
Samsa, Gregor, 278
Sanchez, J., 73, 348
Sanua, V., 230, 366
Sarbin, T. S., 174, 366
Sartre, J. P., 32, 105, 236, 271, 272, 278, 280, 366, 367
Satir, V., 232, 237, 239, 355, 366
Saussure, F. de, 253, 254, 255, 367
Schacht, R., 194, 269, 367
Schachter, S., 150, 153, 367
Schafer, R., 107, 250, 251, 367
Schank, R. C., 145, 367
Scheff, T. J., 45, 46, 172, 173, 200, 201, 202, 203, 204, 311, 321, 367
Scheler, M., 262, 264, 273, 367
Schelling F., 249
Schilder, P., 262
Schildkraut, J. J., 367
Schildkrout, J. J., 78
Schleiermacher, F., 247
Schneider, K., 62, 82, 86, 87, 88, 261, 262, 264, 367
Schopenhauer, A., 294
Schuetz, A., 262, 278, 367
Schut, T., 79, 364
Schutz, W. C., 216, 367
Schwartz, G. E., 337, 367
Schwartz, M. S., 220, 369
Secord, P. F., 167, 195, 196, 289, 353
Sedgwick, P. R. D., 278, 367
Seeman, M., 189, 194, 367
Seiger, A., 70, 363
Seligman, M. E. P., 155, 156, 343, 362, 367
Selye, H., 51, 55, 367, 368
Shaffer, J. B., 213, 214, 218, 220, 367
Shakespeare, W., 248
Sharpe, L., 39, 348
Shaver, K. G., 96, 153, 368
Shaw, C. W., 186, 368
Shaw, D. M., 79, 368

Name Index

Sheldon, W. H., 84, 85, 368
Sheppard, P. M., 76, 346
Shields, J., 88, 353
Shils, E., 182, 363
Shoben, E. J., 130, 368
Shure, M. B., 369
Siegel, F. L., 37, 373
Siegler, M., 59, 89, 90, 237, 303, 307, 311, 319, 321, 324, 330, 368
Sigerist, H., 29, 368
Simmel, G., 193, 368
Simon, F. J., 39, 348
Singer, J. E., 150, 153, 367
Singer, J. L., 178, 363
Singer, M., 225, 373
Skinner, B. F., 11, 17, 100, 131, 134, 136, 159, 283, 310, 368
Skynner, A. C. R., 211, 229, 368
Smith, A., 167
Smith, J. A., 164, 370
Smith, T. W., 72, 355
Smythies, J., 69, 76, 305, 354, 363
Smythies, J. R., 76, 353
Socrates, 276, 282, 290
Solomon, G. F., 69, 343
Sorokin, P. A., 293, 368
Speck, R. V., 237, 368
Speer, D., 224, 368
Spence, D. P., 164, 368
Spence, K. W., 128, 130, 368
Spencer, H., 167
Spiegelberg, H., 258, 260, 261, 262, 272, 281, 369
Spinoza, B., 13, 135, 150
Spitzer, R. L., 38, 64, 350, 369
Spitzer, R. S., 39, 369
Spivack, G., 369
Spranger, E., 248, 369
Sprenkle, D. H., 225, 227, 228, 240, 363
Spring, B., 88
Srole, L., 38, 175, 176, 189, 369
Stampfl, T. C., 139, 369
Stanton, A. H., 220, 369
Stein, L., 77, 78, 369
Steingert, 164
Stekel, W., 106, 314, 369
Stevenson, C., 27, 45, 369
Stierlin, H., 226
Stoll, W. A., 70, 369

Stonequist, E., 185, 369
Stoyva, J. M., 140, 346
Straus, E., 261, 266, 369
Strauss, A. L., 19, 345
Suinn, R. M., 161, 369
Sullivan, H. S., 103, 118, 119, 120, 122, 210, 211, 212, 370
Susser, M., 51, 370
Swanson, D. W., 164, 370
Swets, J. A., 44, 370
Szasz, T. S., 12, 16, 18, 45, 236, 308, 309, 310, 311, 312, 321, 328, 329, 333, 370

T

Tannenbaum, F., 199, 370
Tanner, W. P., Jr., 44, 370
Taylor, C., 13, 370
Taylor, J. A., 128, 130, 368
Teasdale, J. D., 155, 156, 343
Tellenbach, H., 272
Thersa of Avila, Saint, 304
Thomas, J., 140, 355
Thoresen, C. M., 157, 158, 161, 370
Tienari, P., 80, 370
Tillich, P., 271, 370
Tinbergen, N., 102, 370
Tolstoy, L., 271, 370
Tomkins, S. S., 163, 370
Tooth, G., 175, 177, 370
Toporkoff, N., 68, 360
Torrey, E. F., 69, 318, 333, 370, 371
Trilling, L., 278, 371
Turner, J. H., 218, 371
Tversky, A., 44, 45, 348

U

Ullmann, L. P., 127, 132, 133, 134, 137, 371
Usdin, E., 70, 344

V

Vaihinger, H., 115, 371
Valius, S., 154, 348
Van Belle, H. A., 296, 313, 345
Van den Berg, J. H., 264, 371
Van der Berg, J., 261

Van Dusen, H. P., 315, 349
Van Gogh, V., 302
van Kaam, A., 281, 297, 338, 356
van Praag, H. M., 63, 79, 364
Varela, F., 338, 371
Vaughn, C. E., 191, 371
Vergote, A., 272, 371
Viola, 83
Vogel, E. F., 230, 371
von Bayer, W., 272
von Bertalanffy, L., 18, 35, 103, 135, 209, 288, 334, 335, 336, 371
von Gebsattel, V. E., 262, 266, 273, 352
von Humboldt, W., 249, 256
von Mises, R., 310
von Wagner-Jauregg, J., 68
von Wright, G. H., 28, 371
Vygotsky, L. S., 161, 371

W

Wallner, J. M., 62, 356
Walters, R. H., 140, 159, 344
Wanklin, J. M., 191, 346
Waring, M., 231, 371
Watson, J. B., 101, 127, 138, 157, 371
Watzlawick, P., 232, 234, 242, 372
Waxler, N. E., 230, 362
Weakland, J., 232, 234, 344, 372
Weber, M., 167, 172, 247, 372
Weckowicz, T. E., 128, 268, 372
Weil, R. C., 175, 349
Weiner, B., 96, 154, 372
Weisenbeck, H., 69, 373
Weiss, J. M., 155, 372
Weiss, P., 335, 372
Werner, H., 122, 126, 372
Wernicke, C., 61
Wertheim, E., 224, 372

Westall, R. G., 76, 347
Westphal, C., 61
Whitaker, C., 241, 372
Whitaker, D. S., 215, 372
White, R. K., 223, 359
Whitehead, A. N., 232, 242, 372
Wild, C., 299, 373
Wilden, A., 242, 250, 253, 373
Williams, R. J., 26, 37, 373
Wilson, T., 242, 373
Winch, P., 167, 373
Windelband, W., 247, 373
Winder, C. L., 62, 356
Winett, R. A., 154, 373
Wing, J., 66, 373
Winokur, G., 39, 350
Wise, C. D., 77, 369
Wittgenstein, L., 167, 172, 309, 373
Witz, J. P., 69, 373
Wolf, H. G., 51, 55, 373
Wolpe, J., 129, 131, 138, 139, 141, 142, 158, 373
Woodruff, R. A., 39, 350
Wundt, W., 49, 58
Wunsch-Hitzig, R., 38, 176, 349
Wynne, L., 225, 230, 235, 243, 373
Wyrsch, J., 264, 373

Y

Yap, P. M., 178, 179, 180, 184, 373
Yates, A. J., 131, 140, 373
Young, R. D., 132, 346

Z

Zigler, E., 43
Zubin, J., 23, 66, 88, 351

SUBJECT INDEX

A

Adlerian psychotherapy
    description of, 115
Adrenochrome theory
    schizophrenia and, 76
Alienation
    anomie versus, 194-196
Alienation model
    description of, 196-199
Amok, 179
Angst, 271
Anlage, 82, 102
Anomia scale, 189
Anomie
    alienation versus, 194-196
    definition of, 185-196, 189
Antidepressants
    mania and, 78
Antireductionism, 287-288
Anxiety
    gamma-amino-butyric acid and, 71
Assertive training, 139
Athletic physical type
    description of, 83
Attribution theory, 96, 153-155
Authoritarianism
    clinical psychology and, 20
    psychiatric social work and, 20
    psychiatry and, 19
Autonomy, individual
    societal conformity versus, 9, 17-18
Aversive therapy, 139

B

Bayes theorem, 42-43
    equation for, 42

Becoming, 285
Behaviour, human
    causal explanations and, 93, 94, 95
    determinism versus indeterminism, 9, 12-14
    end-state explanations and, 93, 94-95
    end-state versus his reason, 95
    explanations of
        types of, 93
    "his reason" explanations and, 93, 95
    hybrid explanations and, 97
    libertarian model and, 308
    removable structure, 99
    structures of, 99
    symbolic form, 99
    syncratic structure, 99
Behaviourism (*see also* Behaviouristic model)
    humanism versus, 287-289, 293
    logical, 93-94
Behaviouristic model (*see also* Behaviourism; Behaviour therapy)
    characteristics of, 128
    description of, 127-128
    Hans Eysenck and, 142-145
    history of, 127
    Hullian, 130-131
    Pavlovian, 128-129
    Skinnerian, 131-137
Behaviour therapy (*see also* Behaviourism; Behaviouristic model)
    cognitive models and, 157-161
    criticisms of, 12
    description of, 96-97, 98-99, 100, 137-142
    group, 217-218
    history of, 138-139
    peripheralism versus centralism in, 99-100
Being and Nothingness, 217

Being and Time, 270
Being Mentally Ill, 200
Beyond Freedom and Dignity, 134, 135
Biofeedback, 140
Biogenic amines (*see specific chemicals*)
Biological ideal, 30-31
Bipartite (combined disease-constitutional) model
   description of, 86-88
Body-mind dualism
   history of, 48-49
Body-mind relationships, 9, 10-12, 124-125
Bouféé délirante aiguë, 179
Brain lesions
   dementias and, 80
   organic
      psychosis and, 80

C

Circumplex model of family systems, 227, 228
Civilization and its Discontents, 18
Class, social
   mental illness and, 174, 176, 189-191, 204-205
   psychoneurosis and, 41
   schizophrenia and, 41
Clinical psychology
   authoritarianism and, 20
   current changes in, 8
   current problems in, 3, 4
   training and, 20
Cluster analysis
   disease model and, 66
Co-consciousness
   definition of, 104-105
Cognitive development
   Harry Stack Sullivan and, 118-120
   Jean Piget and, 122-123
   stages of, 119
Cognitive models
   Aaron Beck and, 151-153
   Albert Ellis and, 149-151
   attribution theory and, 153-155
   behaviour therapy influencing, 157-161
   current trends in, 145-146, 147-148
   description of, 146-148
   George Kelly and, 148-149
   Martin Seligman and, 155-156
   psychoanalysis and, 161-165
Cognitive psychology
   computers and, 100-101
   current interest in, 100
Communication
   schizophrenia and, 231-234
Computers
   languages used with, 100
   psychoanalysis influenced by, 162-164
The Concept of Motivation, 93
The Concept of the Mind, 92
Concrete operational stage of development, 122
Conditioning, classical, 129, 135
Conditioning, operant, 131-137
Conflict model (*see also* Alienation model; Labelling model)
   alienation and, 194
   description of, 193
   Erich Fromm and, 196-199
   Karl Marx and, 193-194
   structural-functionalist model versus, 205-206
Conformity, societal
   individual autonomy versus, 9, 17-18
Constitution
   definition of, 56
   physique versus, 56-57
Constitutional-behaviouristic model, 142-145
Constitutional model
   body physique and, 82-86
   description of, 56-57, 82-83
   heredity and, 82
   psychiatry and, 82-86
Convention
   psychiatric diagnosis and, 39
Critique of the Dialectical Reason, 236
Croonian Lectures, 124
Cultural lag
   definition of, 185
Cultural relativism
   humanistic psychology and, 298
   mental illness and, 169-170, 173, 203-204
   normality and, 32-33
   social science and, 168-169
Culture
   language and, 255-256

Culture-bound reactive syndromes
    description of, 178-180
Current Concepts of Positive Mental Health,
    31
Cyclothymic character
    description of, 84

D

Dasein, 270
Das man, 271
The Death of Ivan Ilyich, 271
The Death of Psychiatry, 333
Decision making
    models of, 42-45
    psychiatric diagnosis and, 41-45
Dementia
    causes of, 125
    diffuse organic brain lesions and, 80
Dementia praecox, 40, 58, 59 (see also
        Schizophrenia)
    etiology of, 59, 69
*Dementia Praecox or the Group of
        Schizophrenias*, 59
Depression (see also Manic-depressive
        psychosis)
    bipolar versus unipolar, 63
    definition of
        difficulties in, 61-62
    dopamine and, 71, 78
    electrolyte imbalance and, 79
    endogenous versus exogenous, 63
    etiology of, 62, 69, 137, 151, 156
    involutional melancholia versus manic-
        depressive psychosis and, 63
    noradrenaline and, 71, 78
    "one disease" theory of, 62
    reactive versus endogenous, 62
    reserpine and, 79
    serotonin and, 71, 78
Depression, bipolar
    definition of, 63
    unipolar depression versus, 63
Depression, unipolar
    bipolar depression versus, 63
    definition of, 63
Depressive developmental stage, 211
Descriptive phenomenology, 263-265
Desensitization, systematic, 139

Determinism
    definition of, 12
    Freud and, 13, 14
Developmental models
    causes of psychopathology and, 121
    description of, 109-110
    Erik Erikson and, 123-134
    Heinz Werner and, 126
    Henri Ey and, 124-125
    Jean Piaget and, 122-123
    Karl Menninger and, 127
    similarities between, 126-127
    stages of, 110
Developmental psychology
    nativism versus empiricism and, 101
Deviancy, social
    mental illness and, 17-18, 171
    primary versus secondary, 199-200
    residual, 201
Diacritical theory of meaning, 255
Diagnosis, idiographic
    definition of, 47
Diagnosis, nomothetic
    definition of, 47
Diagnosis, psychiatric
    Bayes theorem and, 42-43
    conventions and, 39
    decision making and, 41-45
    disease and, 41
    labelling and, 45-47
    nomothetic versus idiographic, 47
    prognosis and, 40-41
    reliability of, 39
    signal detection model and, 44-45
    social class and, 41
    syndromes and, 40
Diagnostic Statistical Manual of Mental
        Disorders (DSM-III), 39, 64
    disease categories and, 64-65
    purpose of, 64
Diathesis-stress model
    definition of, 54-55
    description of, 88-89
Dimensions of Family Therapy, 237
Dimethoxyphenylethylamine (DMPE)
    schizophrenia and, 76
Disease
    definition of, 40, 50-51
    etiology of, 51-52

Subject Index

logotherapy and, 276-278
   phenomenological anthropology and, 273-278
Experimental psychology
   description of, 96, 97
Extraversion-introversion, 142-143

F

Factor analysis
   disease model and, 65-66
Family(ies) (*see also* Family therapy)
   adaptability and, 224-225
   cohesion and, 225-226
   longitudinal development of, 227-229
   social functions of, 222
   systems theory and, 222-223
   triadic interactions and, 223-224
Family Therapy, 212
Family therapy (*see also* Families)
   communication-structural school, 241-244
   current interest in, 220, 237
   description of, 221-222
   dimensions of, 237-238
   extended family systems school, 240-241
   schizophrenic patients and, 229-237
   schools of, 238-239, 240
Formal operational stage of development, 122
Freedom, individual
   libertarian model and, 309-311
Freud, Sigmund
   determinism and, 13, 14
   views of society, 114-115
Freud and Philosophy, 251
Freudian psychoanalysis
   criticisms of, 106-107
   description of, 3, 97-98, 108-115
   hermeneutics and, 251-253
   humanism versus, 287-289
   moral transgression model versus, 314-315
   psychodynamic models and, 104
   structuralism and, 101
   structural-linguistic model and, 253-258

G

Gamma-amino-butyric acid (GABA)
   anxiety and, 71

Gene(s), recessive
   disease and, 54
Gene penetrance
   definition of, 54
General adaptation syndrome (GAS), 55
A General Introduction to Psychoanalysis, 107
General paralysis of the insane (GPI)
   etiology of, 68
General Psychopathology, 86, 248
General systems theory, 334-338
Genetic-structural and categorical phenomenology, 265-267
Gestalt therapy, 120-121, 217
   structuralism and, 101
Group dynamics theory, 208, 215-216
Group psychology, 210-213
Group Psychology and the Analysis of the Ego, 211
Group psychotherapy (*see also* specific types of group therapy)
   categories of, 214
   goals of, 214
   history of, 213

H

Hallucinations
   noradrenaline and, 71
   schizophrenia and, 42-43, 69-70
Hallucinogens, 305-306
Health
   definition of, 23
Heidelberg school of psychiatrists, 86-88
Heredity, genetic
   constitutional model and, 82
   dominant versus recessive genes and, 54
   environment and, 55
   gene penetrance and, 54
   language and, 101
   manic-depressive psychosis and, 80-81
   schizophrenia and, 80-81, 88
   single versus multiple genes, 52-53, 54
Hermeneutic-linguistic models, 246-258
   Paul Ricoeur and, 251-253
Hermeneutic method, 246-247
Hermeneutics
   definition of, 246

Historical relativism
  social science and, 168-169
Homeostasis
  definition of, 34
  psychology and, 34-35
Humanism (see also Humanistic psychology)
  behaviourism and Freudian theory versus, 287-289, 293
  definition of, 31
  description of, 282-283
  happiness and, 291-292
  history of, 282, 283
  mental health and, 31-32
  science and, 292-293
  social science and, 166-167
Humanistic models, 282-307
  humanistic psychology and, 283-299
  supersanity models and, 299-307
Humanistic psychology (see also Humanism)
  Carl Rogers and, 296-297
  C. G. Jung and, 294
  cultural relativism and, 298
  description of, 284-294, 297-299
  Gordon Allport and, 296
  Otto Rank and, 294-295
  Sidney Jourard and, 297
  the Third Force and, 295-297
Huntington's chorea
  etiology of, 71
Hysteria, anxiety, 112
Hysteria, conversion, 112

I

Idealistic positivism
  description of, 115-116
The Idea of Social Science, 167
Idiographic method, 247
Iich aa, 179
I-it relationships, 269
Imu, 178
Insight psychotherapy
  description of, 106, 107
Interactional theory, 234-235
Interpersonal-developmental model
  Harry Stack Sullivan and, 118-120
Interpersonal-situational model
  Gestalt therapy and, 120-121

Intrapersonal-developmental model
  Adlerian theory and, 115-116
  Freudian psychoanalysis and, 108-115
  Karen Horney and, 115, 116-118
Introversion-extraversion, 142-143
Involutional melancholia
  manic-depressive psychosis versus, 63
I-Thou relationships, 269

J

Jemeinigkeit, 270

K

Karyotype
  definition of, 57
Koro, 179

L

Labelling
  psychiatric diagnosis and, 45-47
Labelling model
  description of, 199-200, 201-202
  history of, 200
  Thomas Scheff and, 200-204
Language
  cultural structure and, 255-256
  genetic heredity and, 101
  libertarian model and, 309
Languages, computer
  description of, 100
Latah, 178
Learned helplessness, 155-156
Lectures on Clinical Psychiatry, 50
Leptosomic physical type
  description of, 83
Libertarian model
  human behaviour and, 308
  individual freedom and, 309-311
  language and, 309
  psychiatrist role and, 312
Lived Time, 265
Logotherapy, 276-278

M

Macrosocial model (see also Conflict model; Structural-functionalist model)

Macrosocial model (*Continued*)
    definition of, 181
Man
    Adlerian view of, 115-116
    alienation view of, 196
    anomie view of, 195
    Aristotelian view of, 286
    cognitive view of, 146-147
    Hobbesian view of, 289
    humanistic view of, 167
    Leibnitzian view of, 288-289
    Lockean view of, 288
    moral transgression view of, 313
    positivistic view of, 167
    Rousseau's view of, 289
    society and, 167-168
    stoic view of, 150
Mania, 114 (*see also* Manic-depressive psychosis)
    antidepressants and, 78
Manic-depressive psychosis, 58 (*see also* Depression; Mania)
    body physique and, 85
    etiology of, 68, 73, 75-76, 77, 78-79, 80-81, 125
    heredity and, 80-81
    involutional melancholia versus, 63
    regression and, 111
Maslow's hierarchy of needs, 291-292
Mean, statistical
    normality and, 23-24
Medical model(s), 3-5, 6-7
    advantages of, 4
    criticisms of, 5-12, 245, 311
    mental health fields and, 3-5
    psychological models versus, 103-104
Medicine
    current changes in, 8
Melancholia, 113-114
Melatonin
    schizophrenia and, 77
Mental health
    morality and, 9, 16-17
    psychiatric definition of, 23
Mental health field
    body-mind relationships and, 9, 10-12
    current changes in, 8-9
    current problems in, 3, 4, 8
    goals of, 7

    models and, 6-7
    philosophical issues of, 9-18
    professional conflicts in, 19-21
    science versus, 7-8
Mental illness
    ascription and, 172-173
    biological versus social factors, 174-175, 180
    brain diseases and, 57-58
    causes of, 10-12
    criteria for determining, 171-172
    cultural relativism and, 169-170, 173, 203-204
    definition of, 246, 258
    difficulties in studying, 175-176
    disease versus social deviancy and, 170-172
    humanistic view of, 298
    intraindividual versus interactionist, 181
    Jacksonian theory of, 124-125
    language and, 249-250 (*see also* Hermeneutic-linguistic model; Structural-linguistic model)
    libertarian model and, 308, 309, 311
    models of
        medical versus nonmedical, 48-49
    moral-legal models and, 307-308
    moral transgression model and, 312, 313-314
    "one disease" theory and, 65
    science and, 245
    social class and, 174, 176, 189-191, 204-205
    social deviancy versus, 17-18
    societal definition of, 170-174
    stereotypes and, 173-174, 202
    studies investigating, 175-178
    supersanity model and, 299-300
Mesomorphy
    description of, 85
The Metamorphosis, 278
Methionine
    schizophrenia and, 76
Microsocial models
    artificial groups and, 213-220
    definition of, 181
    Kurt Lewin's group dynamics theory, 208
    natural groups and, 220-244

Microsocial models (*Continued*)
   psychoanalytic theory of group psychology, 210-213
   symbolic interactionism, 206-208
   systems theory, 209-210
   theoretical framework, 206-213
Mind, human
   computer models of, 100-101
   concept of, 92
   energy system model of, 102
   functionalist model of, 102
   information processing system model of, 102
   interactionist model of, 103
   structuralist model of, 102-103
Mitwelt, 216, 274
Model(s) (*see also specific types*)
   classification of, 319-321
   comparisons of, 312-330
      philosophical-moral models, 328-330, 331-332
      scientific models, 324-328
   definition of, 5-7
Models of Group Therapy and Sensitivity Training, 213
Models of Madness and Models of Medicine, 89, 330
Morality
   mental health and, 9, 16-17
   psychotherapy and, 291
Moral-legal models, 307-318
   description of, 307-308, 318
   libertarian model and, 308-312
   moral transgression model and, 312-316
   social irresponsibility model and, 316-318
Moral transgression model, 312-316
   Freudian psychoanalysis versus, 314-315
Mourning and Melancholia, 113, 151
Mysticism
   hallucinogens and, 305-306
   history of, 304
   schizophrenia and, 303-304, 305-306
   uses of, 304-305
The Myth of Mental Illness, 308

N

Narcissism
   description of, 110-111

Negative practice, 140
Neurosis
   causes of, 111, 117, 119, 125
   social class and, 41
Neuroticism, 143
The New Organon, 294
New Heidelberg School of Psychiatry, 272-273
Nichomachean Ethics, 34, 286
Nomothetic method, 247
Noögenic neurosis, 277
Noradrenaline
   biochemical functioning of, 72
   depression and, 71, 78
   hallucinations and, 71
   metabolic formation of, 72, 73, 74
   metabolic pathways of, 71
   schizophrenia and, 71
Normality
   absence of illness and, 36-38
   biological ideal and, 30-31
   concept of ideal and, 27-36
      static versus dynamic, 33-36
   continuity versus discontinuity, 38
   cultural ideals and, 32-33
   difficulties in defining, 22
   dynamic, 35-36
   existentialism and, 32
   humanism and, 31-32
   individuals and, 33
   mental health ideal and, 31-32
   objectification of, 22-23
   relativistic approach and, 25
   social norm concept of, 26-27
   standard deviation and, 24-25
   static, 34-35
   statistical concept of, 23-26
      problems with, 25-26
   statistical mean and, 23-24
   values and, 27-29

O

Object relationship, 211-212
Obsessive-compulsive neurosis, 112-113
On Liberty, 134
Organic psychiatry, 49-50, 67
Orthogenesis
   description of, 126

Subject Index

P

Paranoia, 113
  etiology of, 257
Paranoid schizoid developmental stage, 211
Parataxic stage of development, 119
Personality
  layers of, 120
Personality integration
  levels of, 301-302
Personality types
  body physique and, 83-86
Perspectivism, 338-341
Phenomenological anthropology, 273-278
  Ludwig Binswanger and, 273-275
  Medard Boss and, 275
  Roland Kuhn and, 275
  Victor Frankl and, 276-278
Phenomenological-existentialist models, 258-281
Phenomenological philosophy
  description of, 260-261
Phenomenological psychology
  criticisms of, 99
  description of, 98, 99, 263, 267-268
  descriptive, 263-265
  genetic-structural and categorical, 265-267
Phenomenology
  definition of, 259-260
  existentialism and, 258-259
  Husserl and, 260-261
  Jaspers and, 263-265
  Merleau-Ponty and, 261-262
  Scheler and, 262
  Schuetz and, 262
  social science and, 166-167
The Phenomenology of the Mind, 251
Phenotype
  definition of, 31, 56
Phenylketonuria (PKU)
  description of, 53-54
Philosophical anthropology, 273
Philosophical-moral models
  description of, 245-246
Philosophy in a New Key, 250
Phobia, 112
Physique, body
  constitutional model and, 82-86
  constitution versus, 56-57

personality types and, 83-86
types of, 83, 84
Pibloktoq, 178
Positive disintegration model, 300-303
Positivism
  social science and, 166
Pragmatism
  cognitive models and, 148-149
Preconscious
  definition of, 105
Preoperational stage of development, 122
Principles of Preventive Psychiatry, 193
Prognosis
  psychiatric diagnosis and, 40-41
Propetology
  definition of, 37
Protaxic stage of development, 119
Protestant ethics
  behaviour therapists and, 133
Psychedelic model, 303-307
Psychiatry (*see also* specific types)
  authoritarianism and, 19
  body-mind dualism and, 19
  current changes in, 8
  current problems in, 3, 4
  definition of, 118
  heredity versus environment and, 82
  history of, 19
  medical model of, 3-5
    advantages of, 4
    criticisms of, 5
  medical training and, 19-20
Psychoanalysis
  cognitive models and, 161-165
  Colby's computer model of, 162-164
  psycholinguistics and, 164-165
Psychoanalytical therapy groups, 214-215
Psychodrama therapy, 217
Psychodynamic models (*see also*
    Interpersonal-developmental model;
    Interpersonal-situational model;
    Intrapersonal-developmental model)
  concept of unconscious and, 104-106
  description of, 104
  history of, 104
  types of, 107-108
Psycholinguistics
  psychoanalysis influenced by, 164-165

Psychological models
  medical models versus, 103-104
  types of, 104
Psychology (see specific types)
Psychoneurosis Is Not an Illness, 302
Psychopath(s), 113
Psychopathology (see Mental illness)
Psychopathology of Everyday Life, 97
Psychosis
  causes of, 119
  localized organic brain lesions and, 80
  regression and, 111
Psychosis, functional
  definition of, 67
  organic psychosis versus, 66
Psychosis, organic
  functional psychosis versus, 66
Psychosomatic disorders, 113
Psychotherapists
  role of, 107, 290, 312
Psychotherapy (see also specific types)
  morality and, 291
Psychoticism, 143-144
Pyknic physical type
  description of, 83

R

Rational-emotive therapy (RET), 149-151
Rationalism
  cognitive models and, 149-151
Reality therapy (see Social irresponsibility model)
Reductionism, 333-334
Regression, 111, 112
  developmental model and, 121
Reinforcement
  types of, 136
The Republic, 134
Research Diagnostic Criteria (RDC), 39
Reserpine
  depression and, 79
Role Construct Repertory Test, 148

S

The Sane Society, 196
Schism family, 231

Schizoid character
  description of, 84
Schizophrenia (see also Dementia praecox)
  adrenochrome theory of, 76
  body physique and, 85
  communication and, 231-234
  criteria for diagnosis of, 60-61
  definition of, 60
  DMPE and, 76
  dopamine and, 71, 77-78
  double bind theory, 233-234
  etiology of, 60, 61, 68-70, 73, 75-78,
      80-81, 119-120, 125, 129,
      130-131, 235-236, 257, 306-307
  family structure and, 225
  family therapy and, 229-237
  Freudian psychoanalysis and, 114
  hallucinations and, 42-43
  hallucinogens and, 305-306
  heredity and, 80-81, 88
  interactional theory, 234-235
  melatonin and, 77
  methionine and, 76
  mysticism and, 303-304, 305-306
  noradrenaline and, 71
  reactive versus process, 62
  regression and, 111
  social class and, 41
  symptoms of, 60
  types of, 60, 61
Schizophrenia, catatonic, 60
Schizophrenia, hebephrenic, 60
Schizophrenia, paranoid, 60
Schizotaxia
  definition of, 88
Schizotypy
  definition of, 88
Science
  humanism and, 292-293
  mental health field versus, 7-8
Scientific models
  roles of, 6
  description of, 95-96
  models of mind and, 103
Self
  aspects of, 117
  Horney's concept of, 117
  Perls's concept of, 120
  Sullivan's concept of, 118

Subject Index

Self-actualization, 286-287, 290
Self-conception(s), 207-208
Semiotics
  definition of, 249
Sensory-motor stage of development, 122
Sertonin
  biochemical functioning of, 72
  depression and, 71, 78
  metabolic formation of, 73, 75
Sexual perversion, 113
Sign
  definition of, 40
Signal detection model, 44-45
Significates
  definition of, 159
Significants
  definition of, 159
Skewed family, 231
Social disorganization-anomie model
  adaptation to social stress and, 188-189
  Chicago School of Sociology in America and, 186-187
  criticisms of, 187, 191-192
  description of, 184-185
  Emile Durkheim and, 187
  history of, 186-187
  Talcott Parsons and, 188-189
Social irresponsibility model, 316-318
Social science(s)
  cultural and historical relativism and, 168-169
  existentialist view of, 166-167
  humanistic view of, 166-167
  individual psychology and, 167
  idiographic and nomothetic methods and, 247-248
  nature of man and, 167-168
  phenomenological view of, 166-167
  positivistic view of, 166
  value-free, 9, 14-16
Social Structure and Anomie, 168
Social work, psychiatric
  authoritarianism and, 20
  therapy groups, 214
  training and, 20

Society
  behaviour therapy and, 134-135
  Freudian view of, 114-115
Sorge, 270
Standard deviation
  normality and, 24-25
Stereotypes
  mental illness and, 173-174, 202
Stress
  disease and, 55-56
Stress and Disease, 55
Structural-functionalist model
  conflict model versus, 205-206
  description of, 182, 192-193
  social disorganization-anomie model and, 184-193
  Talcott Parsons and, 182-183
Structuralism
  description of, 101-102, 254
  epigenetic, 103
  history of, 253-254
  preformist, 103
Structural-linguistic model, 253-258
Suicide, 187
Suicide
  types of, 187
Suicide, altruistic
  definition of, 187
Suicide, anomic
  definition of, 187
Suicide, egoistic
  definition of, 187
Suicide, fatalistic, 187-188
Suk yeong, 179
Supersanity models
  description of, 299-300
  positive disintegration model and, 300-303
  psychedelic model and, 303-307
Susto, 178
Symbolic behaviour
  description of, 207
Symptom
  definition of, 40
Syndrome
  definition of, 40
  psychiatric diagnosis and, 40
Syntaxic stage of development, 119

Systems theory, 209-210
   families and, 222-223

T

Tabula rasa
   definition of, 101
Thanatomania, 178-179
Theatre of Spontaneity, 217
Therapeutic community therapy, 220
Therapist
   role of, 141
Third Force, 283
   description of, 295-297
Thought stopping, 139-140
Token economy, 140
Totem and Taboo, 254
Towards a Psychology of Being, 285
Transactional psychotherapy, 218-220
Treatise of Human Nature, 14
Type 1 statistical error
   definition of, 46
Type 2 statistical error
   definition of, 46

U

Ulysses, 259
Umwelt, 274
Utox, 178

V

Value(s)
   definition of, 27
   moral versus instrumental, 28-29
Variability, biological, 23-24
Verstehen
   definition of, 86
   model, 248-249
The Vital Balance, 65

W

Walden Two, 134
Weltanschauung
   definition of, 8
Windigo, 179

DATE DUE

MAR 06 '91			
APR 02 '91			

DEMCO 38-297